1963

This book may be kept

HITLER'S CONSERVATIVE OPPONENTS
IN BAVARIA
1930-1945

HITLER'S CONSERVATIVE OPPONENTS IN BAVARIA 1930—1945

a study of
Catholic, monarchist, and separatist
anti-Nazi activities

BY

JAMES DONOHOE

Assistant Professor of History
The University of Arizona, Tucson

LEIDEN

E. J. BRILL

1961

PRINTED IN THE NETHERLANDS

To my Mother

TABLE OF CONTENTS

FOREWORD

I wish gratefully to acknowledge my debt to several people without whose help I could not have completed this work. In the first instance I should like to thank the following who provided me with documentary and other materials which are the basis for this study: to Curt Rosenow who opened all doors to me at the Berlin Document Center and who made it possible for me to have over two-thousand pages of documents microfilmed; to Canon Alois Nattarer who allowed me free access to his files of the Bavarian *Klerusverband,* and who helped me to find documents of the *Rhätia* fraternity; to the Very Reverend Dr. Johann Neuhäusler, Auxiliary Bishop of Munich, for his patient answers to all my questions; to Father Anton Maier for helping me to find the material for Chapter III; to Franz X. Fackler for giving me a copy of the *Gestapo* report of monarchist activities; to Father Karl Schuster for his *Memoir* of the events of August, 1939; to Therese Freifrau zu Guttenberg for her most gracious hospitality at her home, and for presenting me with a complete file of the *Weisse Blätter,* as well as the several documents of Karl Ludwig Freiherr zu Guttenberg; to Elizabeth Freifrau von Guttenberg for generous and considerate help during my stay in Munich; to Gabrielle Freifrau von Harnier for the several documents relating to Adolf Freiherr von Harnier; to Karin Klublatt, Angelika Probst and Dieter Sasse for the letters and *Memoirs* of Christoph Probst, as well as for the pleasant hours spent at Tegernsee; to Clara Huber for all of her generous help and assistance in gathering together the documents relating to Professor Kurt Huber; to Birgit Huber, Professor Huber's daughter, for typing out copies of those documents, work which

caused many an interruption of her music lessons; to Professor
Karl d'Ester of the University of Munich for a *Memoir* reprinted
in Chapter IV, and also for the many hours of instructive conversation; to Regierungsdirektor Braun for material relating to
Freiheits-Aktion Bayern; to the late Hilda R. Boeninger of the
Hoover Library for two documents relating to Chapter V; to
P. Max Pribilla, S.J. for his profound insights, his delightful
sense of humor, and for his book, *Deutsche Schicksalsfragen,* a
fundamental work for anyone re-thinking recent German history;
also to P. Otto Pies, S.J., and, indeed, to all the members of the
Jesuit community in Munich, to Professor Heinrich Hermelink,
Dr. William Hoegner, Dr. Waldemar von Knoeringen, Dr.
Joseph Müller, Bishop Hans D. Meiser, Dr. Fabian von Schlab-
brendorf, and Professor Franz Schnabel—all of whom aided me
generously in many different ways.

I should like to thank some of my friends here at home,
among them my colleagues at the University of Arizona, most
especially, Professor Russel C. Ewing and Professor Hermann
Bateman, both of whom read the manuscript and were generous
in covering its faults; and to Dr. Francis Roy, Dean of the
College of Arts and Sciences, who very kindly arranged my
hours of teaching last spring so as to enable me to work on this
book. I wish also to express my gratitude to friends in Cam-
bridge, Massachusetts: to Dean Reginald Phelps of the Graduate
School of Arts and Sciences, Harvard University, for valuable
bibliographical suggestions; to Mrs. Mary T. Henderson for her
careful critical ability, and for her gracious hospitality; to Dr.
Mary Catherine Davis for making sense in English of some remarkable German prose; to Dr. Charlotte Teuber-Weckersdorf
for lending her practiced eye to the tiresome business of proof-
reading. And I should be very remiss if I did not mention my
debt to my former teacher and friend, Professor H. Stuart
Hughes, Harvard University, who has always given me advice

and encouragement, and to whom I owe whatever critical sense
I have of German history. Finally, I owe a very special acknow-
ledgement to Mr. Richard C. Webb not only for his painstaking
preparation of the corrected proofs, but most of all for his
thoughtful criticism and constant encouragement.

Tucson, 1960.   J. D.

"The people generally ill-treated, and contrary to right, will be ready upon any occasion to ease themselves of a burden that sits heavy upon them. They will wish, and seek for the opportunity which in the change, weakness, and accidents of human affairs, seldom delays long to offer itself. He must have lived but a little while in the world, who has not seen examples of this in his time; and he must have read very little, who cannot produce examples of it in all sorts of governments in the world."

JOHN LOCKE

"Habet mundus iste noctes suas et non paucas."

St. Bernard of Clairvaux

CHAPTER I

INTRODUCTION TO THE PROBLEM

In the course of any discussion, however casual, of the opposition to Hitler that existed in Germany before and during the Second World War, those Germans who sought to diminish or destroy the influence of National Socialism are likely to be referred to as "the good Germans." This is particularly true in England and the United States. Happily, the phrase is at once generous and justified, yet there are those among us who are irritated by it.

Mr. A. J. P. Taylor, for instance, in his volume entitled *The Course of German History*, characterizes "those good Germans" as people who obtrude "into every discussion of the German question, their 'goodness' being synonymous with ineffectiveness. The historian," he goes on to admonish us, "cannot deal with the politically impotent except in so far as their dead weight is thrown into the scale by more agile and positive forces." [1]

Were the present study an arena for polemics, one might ask those who share Mr. Taylor's view whether they regard history solely as the record of those who achieve their goals and whether they consider success the measure of the heroic in the lives of men and women. But the mood of this discussion is not polemical: its aim is to cite some of the movements and incidents which reveal the courage and the high purposes as well as the weaknesses of those "good Germans" of whom Mr. Taylor writes so disparagingly. The reader may then be in a position to discern the nature of the obstacles which stood in the way of their prac-

---

[1] A. J. P. Taylor, *The Course of German History*, (New York, 1946), 8.

tical success, and to determine for himself the degree and the extent of their "goodness."

It might be well to remind the reader that Englishmen and Americans are in general inclined to measure the political goodness of other peoples in terms of their similarity to Anglo-American political thinking and behaviour. From this our sense of disillusionment (obviously not always warranted) is wont to arise. From this, and from our failure to take into account the difference in the means and methods to which resistance to authority may resort, come grave misapprehensions.

Those who during the war too readily discounted the opposition to Hitler which existed in Germany, saying that everyone who opposed the government was either dead or in concentration camps, and that for all significant purposes opposition had ceased, were unaware of the fact that men and women and even mere boys and girls were being crowded almost daily into the prisons and concentration camps of the Third Reich because of their opposition to the government.

It should not have been forgotten, moreover, that whatever the extent and durability of the opposition to Hitler, he came to power with only forty-four per cent of the electorate voting for his party. Neither should it have been forgotten that it was only with the cooperation of the Nationalist Party that the Nazis gained a simple majority; and that it was only with the complete collapse of the center parties' opposition in 1933 that Hitler achieved the two-thirds majority necessary to permit the passage of the Enabling Act.

Thereafter opposition might well have seemed futile, yet it did not cease.

Foreigners traveling in Germany in the 1930's often remarked that although ninety-eight per cent of the population voted in favor of the National Socialists, one seemed invariably to encounter the remaining two per cent. But, often as not, this "two per cent" expressed its opposition to the Nazi regime by nagging complaints, by repeating scurrilous rumors or nasty anecdotes about the leaders of the Third Reich, or, at best, by voicing a very deep conviction that the "new Germany" had departed from values and traditions of which Germans had once been so proud. A vast accumulation of such "opposition" can be found in the records of the lower courts of Nazi Germany, records which promise to be at once rewarding and disconcerting to the historian.

For example, in 1943, Hedwig Buchberger received a sentence of six weeks in prison because she was quoted as saying that everyone knew that Hitler was suffering from a nervous breakdown. [2] (Had the United States a system of justice comparable to Nazi Germany, one wonders how many loyal Americans might have suffered accordingly in 1943 for similar remarks about their Chief of State.) Fräulein Buchberger's treatment, however, was mild compared to some others. On April 19, 1943, Michael Blum was sentenced to two years in prison for having said in public:

Rise up, brave Hindenburg and help to make us stronger;
There's a Corporal in the east who can't hold out much longer. [3]

On May 21, 1943, a priest, Father Richard Hessler, was sentenced to four years in the penitentiary for listening to non-German radio broadcasts. [4] About that same time Ignatz Arnold, a peasant from Loderbach bei Millenburg, went to a local tavern

---

[2] Material relating to Hedwig Buchberger to be found in the records of *Das Sondergericht für den Oberlandesgerichtsbezirk Bamberg, bei den Landesgerichten Würzburg.* These records are now located in the Berlin Document Center.

[3] *Ibid.* "Du tapfrer Hindenburg stehe auf und kämpfe weiter,
   Im Osten steht ein Gefreiter und der kann nicht mehr weiter."

[4] *Ibid.*

and shouted in a loud voice: *"Der Adolf Hitler kann mich am A ... lecken!"* For this greeting he received nine months in prison. [5] Again there was the incident in January, 1945, which earned Magdalena Nöth a ten-months prison sentence. She told the following story: Hitler was driving around Munich with the famous comedian Weiss-Ferdl. Hitler wondered why the population received him so coldly; why they looked so glum. Weiss-Ferdl offered to remedy the situation. He stopped the car and attached a sign to the rear. Suddenly the entire city burst into cheers and shouted *"Heil Hitler!"* Enormously pleased Hitler asked Weiss-Ferdl what he had written which had made the people's response so different. Weiss-Ferdl replied: "I wrote, we are leaving you; we are leaving the country." [6]

Fate was kinder to Fräulein Nöth that it was to the Nazis, whose power was gone before a little more than three months of Fräulein Nöth's sentence had expired. Yet there were Germans who, because of an outburst hardly more serious than Fräulein Nöth's anecdote, learned what has aptly been described as the "theory and practice of hell." [7]

In May, 1935, Emil Stohrer was lying ill in the hospital at Ochsenfurt. [8] On either side of him the beds were occupied by Karl Helfinger and Willy Mohr. At that time Hitler was about to make an address and Helfinger went to the nearest tavern to hear it. Returning to the hospital, he brought the greetings of the *Führer* to those who had not had the same pleasure as Helfinger. Stohrer, in disgust, uttered a most common Bavarian response: *„Der Hitler kann mich am A ... lecken, kannst es ihm sagen!"* Helfinger, horrified, denounced Stohrer at once.

---

[5] *Ibid.*

[6] *Ibid.* "Wir verlassen Euch. Wir fahren ins Ausland."

[7] Eugen Kogon, *The Theory and Practice of Hell* (New York, n.d.), Engl. Trans. *Der S.S. Staat* (Munich, 1946).

[8] Emil Stohrer, born November 16, 1899. Information taken from dossier in the Würzburg Gestapo files, now located in the Berlin Document Center.

After six weeks in protective custody in Ochsenfurt, he was sent to Dachau concentration camp. Two years later he was still there. Report came back to Würzburg that he was "most uncooperative" and that he had, in general, a "bad attitude" toward the regime. Beyond that single denunciation of Hitler, a phrase, by the way, one may notice repeated over and over again in the correspondence dealing with Stohrer, there is no further evidence of opposition; nor is any explanation of the source of this opposition offered.

There were other instances where the opposition was somewhat more fully articulated. For example, in 1944 Max Zimmermann, a farmer near Würzburg, wrote a letter to a friend then serving on the eastern front, which was intercepted by the censors. He wrote openly describing the situation in which Germans found themselves as one of "total slavery" and then went on to say: "I think often of the unfortunate Russian prisoners of war and of the Polish laborers and of all those unhappy creatures who are victims of this horrid period; driven around like animals, pressed together, down and back; without rights; without defense. May the devil take this wretched regime." [9] Max Zimmermann was sentenced to prison for two years and a half.

It is worthwhile to recall also an interesting episode which involved a man of rather distinguished position in society. Sometime during the summer of 1939, Albert Emil Ernst von Manstein, the fifth son of Otto Sigismund von Manstein, and the heir of a long tradition of loyalty to the Prussian state, notified the mayor of Würzburg that he was changing his religion. From then on he wished to be registered as a Jew. [10] We can well

---

[9] *Das Sondergericht für den Oberlandesgerichtsbezirk Bamberg, bei den Landesgerichten Würzburg.* See above 3, footnote 2.

[10] Dossier in Würzburg Gestapo files. Letters from Gestapo Headquarters in Würzburg and Berlin dated July 13, 1939 and July 19, 1939. These records are now located in the Berlin Document Center. For information on the von

imagine the consternation in the minds of officials in a country where for several years severe anti-Semitic laws had become generally accepted, and where since November, 1938, a regular pogrom had existed aimed at the destruction of people who were Jewish in origin.

Needless to say, the mayor reported the affair to the Gestapo who in turn were utterly perplexed as to what should or could be done. The local authorities were most particularly outraged when, after announcing that he was Jewish, he continued to greet officials as well as passers-by on the street with *"Heil Hitler."* So, in that land of judicial chaos, the Gestapo arrested him and his wife, Fanny Bezold von Manstein. The Würzburg authorities wrote to Berlin for instructions as to how they should proceed. The reply, sent by a Dr. Zimmermann, advised the people in Würzburg that, according to current laws, von Manstein, being of German blood (*"deutschblutig"*), was still an Aryan; that, given his advanced years (he was seventy at the time) he was not likely to have much influence; and that, given the absurdity of his proposal, a proposal which Dr. Zimmermann felt the Jews would most certainly not accept, he might just as well be left free. However, the Berlin authorities warned that neither von Manstein nor his wife should be allowed to use the greeting *"Heil Hitler,"* nor should they be allowed to display the flag. If these injunctions were violated, he was to be arrested at once. [11]

One other example will serve to illustrate, finally, something about this kind of oppositon, opposition which might otherwise appear relatively insignificant. Between May, 1944 and April, 1945, a simple nun succeeded in smuggling packages to the in-

---

Manstein family, see *Gothaisches Genealogisches Taschenbuch der Adeligen Häuser, Teil A, 1935* (Gotha, 1934), 300.

[11] Dr. Zimmermann, Letter from Gestapo Headquarters, Berlin, (B.N. II B 4 791/39 J) now in Berlin Document Center.

mates of the concentration camp at Dachau. Her name was Sister Josefa. [12] Many of her packages contained those material necessities, food and clothing, which the prisoners prized highly. However, it is not for those things that she is significant. It was she who brought by bicycle from Munich to the Jesuits and other priests imprisoned at Dachau the sacramental bread and wine which enabled them to cary on their religious life. In view of direct orders from the Commandant of the concentration camp forbidding the practice of religious rites, there is clearly only one important reason why Sister Josefa did what she did. It is a reason which one finds echoing throughout Bavaria in the years 1933 and 1945. Quite simply, it was her loyalty to the Church. In other words, it was not simply a case of venting one's spleen, a thing which may well explain why a peasant could shout out in public vulgarisms about the Chief of State; nor was it comparable to the priest who desired an honest appraisal of current events and therefore listened to a Swiss or an Allied news broadcast. The actions of Sister Josefa, however isolated she may have felt at the time, were connected to a greater whole, something which had the character of a movement in opposition to those currently in power. When she rode out on her bicycle from Munich to Dachau, she was conscious of the risk she was taking. By her very actions she was expressing her conviction that there was such a thing as loyalty to an institution higher than the state. For her that loyalty was to the Church, the center and core of

---

[12] Otto Pies, S.J., *Stephanus Heute* (Keuclaer, 1950), 157-166. (Her full name was Sister Josefa Irma Mack.) (This remarkable book is one further study of life in a Nazi concentration camp. The major concern of the book is with the life of Karl Leisner, a Catholic student from Baden who had been studying for the priesthood. He was denounced by a Nazi fanatic and sent to Dachau. He continued his studies there under the direction of several Jesuits. Late in 1944 he was ordained a priest by a French Archbishop, also an inmate of Dachau. Just before the American army reached Dachau, all the priests were discharged. Too weak to proceed on his journey home, Karl Leisner died in May, 1945.)

all the opposition to National Socialism which will be considered in this study.

Recalling these examples—only a few out of many hundreds—
helps us to understand why such an accumulation in the records
of the lower courts of Nazi Germany should prove to be both
promising and disconcerting. For one thing, it bears witness that
decency could survive even when conditions for its survival
seemed most impossible. Yet at the same time we are presented
with the fact that the Nazis had, apparently, no consistent concept of equity. The same civil offence which in 1935 sent a man
to Dachau for an indefinite period, in 1943 was punished with
a prison sentence of but nine months. Nor must we suppose that
as the war progressed the Nazis became more tolerant of civil
disobedience; the contrary is far more likely. This chaos of justice was shown in one episode which involved the leaders of a
Bavarian monarchist group. In the course of their trial, they
were separated from one another because, quite by chance, the
chief witness against one of them was unable to be present on the
day scheduled for the trial. The first trial ended with one leader
being given a penitentiary sentence of seven years. The second
trial ended with his accomplice being hanged. The evidence in
both trials was the same. [13]

To be sure, the Nazis did their share in diminishing the
world's appreciation of those who opposed them. To the outside
world they gave astonishingly high figures of German approval
of all they did. To the German people at home, the Nazis pointed with pride to international recognition and approval of their
achievements. Unfortunately, since the collapse of the Nazi dictatorship, critical scholarship on the opposition to National Socialism has been relatively meagre. [14]

---

[13] Baron von Harnier and Joseph Zott are discussed more fully in Chapter
III of this study.

[14] It is not intended by the phrase "relatively meagre" to impugn in any

Years have passed since the Allies invaded a defeated Germany. At that time one heard on every hand rarely the hoped-for *mea culpa,* but nearly everywhere the insistent chant that these people had always, from beginning to end, been opposed to Hitler. Hardly a decade later from this same defeated people comes that remarkable phrase — *"Aber wir waren immer dagegen"* — twisted into the bold accusation: *But you also were one of us.* [15]

That popular opinion in Germany should fluctuate with the fortunes of that nation should not make one too apprehensive or even disillusioned. It is to the great advantage of the phrase, *vox populi, vox Dei,* that the voice remains, as a rule, unrecorded. What people say is not nearly so important as what they write; and what has been written on the opposition to Hitler is of the greatest importance to the present study.

Most of the standard treatments of opposition to Hitler, especially those written fairly soon after Germany's defeat, were written either as apologies or as memoirs, a fact which by no means impugns their validity. A good many such accounts tend to explain the problem in terms of Hitler's success, trying to answer the question why it was that the German people supported the Nazi government so enthusiastically. That is quite another problem from the one which is discussed in this study. However fascinating the greater problem in German history of Hitler's success may be, the immediate task here is to arrive at

---

way the work of Professor Gerhard Ritter whose *Carl Goerdeler und die deutsche Widerstandsbewegung,* (Stuttgart, 1954), is as monumental as it is exceptional. Nor are the efforts of Professor Hans Rothfels and all the scholars associated with the Institut für Zeitgeschichte in any way questioned. The *Vierteljahreshefte für Zeitgeschichte* necessarily has had to devote greater attention to a clarification of events more directly related to leading National Socialists rather than to an examination of the activities of the opposition groups.

[15] Peter Kleist, *Auch Du Warst Dabei,* as discussed by Hans Buchheim in *Vierteljahreshefte für Zeitgeschichte,* (April, 1954), 177-192.

a fuller appreciation of those few Germans who sought to limit if not end the Nazi supremacy. The publication of such documents as will aid the historian in his effort to obtain a clearer understanding of that opposition is, therefore, particularly welcome.

One such collection of documentary evidence, first assembled by Ricarda Huch, has now been published as *The Silent Revolt: A Report of the Resistance Movement of the German People, 1933-1945.* [16] The work is edited and contains an introduction by Günther Weisenborn. In spite of this work's auspicious origins, its total effect does much to obscure the scholarly world's understanding and appreciation of the "Resistance Movement" in Germany.

It is not solely because of Herr Weisenborn's insistence that the Allies deliberately destroyed evidence of opposition to Hitler, as such evidence might embarrass the occupation forces, that one takes exception to this book. [17] Indeed, in the face of the publishing of the Nürnberg trials and the existence of the Berlin and Darmstadt Document Centers, one would hardly suppose a refutation necessary. It is rather the series of implications with which he confuses and confounds his readers. Above all, Herr Weisenborn seems to insist that anti-Nazis were all united in their political beliefs; that anti-Nazis were the source whence German democracy would come; and that anti-Nazis shared the world-view of the Allies. [18] In these things his opinions are much more nearly wrong than right.

---

[16] Günther Weisenborn, *Der Lautlose Aufstand; Bericht über die Widerstandsbewegung des Deutschen Volkes, 1933-1945* (Hamburg, 1953). For a critique of this work see Ernst von Salomon, "The Silent Revolt," *Confluence*, III, No. 3 295 ff. Also, see Gerhard Ritter, *Carl Goerdeler und die Deutsche Widerstandsbewegung* (Stuttgart, 1954), 459.

[17] "Die Sieger hatten wenig Interesse an der Veröffentlichung ... Sie beschlagnahmten fast alle Unterlagen und liessen sie in ihren Archiven verschwinden." *Ibid.* 14. See also, *Ibid.* 17.

[18] "Aber es war deutsches und mutiges Blut, das freiwillig vergossen wurde,

It is particularly from his last generalization—that members of the opposition held the same world-view as the Allies—that the most serious confusion comes. It is this very difference in political behaviour between, for example, the English and the Germans, which has stimulated Germany's critics to make their eloquent denunciations. Those Englishmen, for instance, who point out Germany's long tradition of paternalism and militarism which have in part been favorable to the growth of totalitarianism, are quite justified in that assumption; yet, however strong these forces may have been in molding the German character, it is patently absurd to infer that Germans are incapable of desiring or striving for the good life, even if that good life does not express itself inside the framework of liberal democracy. From this point of view, the foreign critics and those German apologists who insist that "the good Germans" are really democrats have both missed the mark.

As a matter of fact, most of those who were actively opposed to Hitler in the years after 1933 were equally opposed to the to the old-fashioned nineteenth century liberalism. It would be hard to find a record of opposition to National Socialism which was based on the fundamental tenets of either economic or political liberalism. This would be particularly true of those Germans whose politics tended to be right of center, the part of the parliamentary spectrum with which we are chiefly concerned here. Any number of important personalities ultimately associated with the great effort to rid Germany of Hitler were themselves at first willing to give the National Socialists an opportunity to establish a new political and economic order, one which was expected would transcend the limitations of parliamentary democracy. One could cite such names as Dr. Carl

---

um die Abschlachtung Millionen anderer zu verhindern, um den Krieg zu beenden. Es war das Blut, aus dem eine starke Demokratie hätte geboren werden können." *Ibid.*, 16. See also *ibid.*, 14,'38.

Goerdeler and Ulrich von Hassell, amongst many others, men who patiently endured that Nazi tyranny until, in some cases, as late as 1938 when they were forced to admit that such hopes as they might have held in 1934 were vain. Precisely because of facts such as these, the historian will find it difficult to pin-down exactly what is meant by the phrase "the German resistance movement."

This difficulty might be obviated altogether if one were willing to follow the simple course offered by Hans Bernard Gisevius in his book *To the Bitter End*. He tells us there that any effort to "classify the German opposition must necessarily fail." And he suggests why.

> Basically, there were only oppositionists. Each of these more or less strong personalities had a group of friends who agreed with him. Each of them sought to extend his influence and therefore tried to establish contact with other groups and circles. This resulted in those many interesting and tangential lines which so confused the picture. None of these men could possibly appeal directly to the masses. Never were they able to issue common slogans. [19]

But if one were to accept this statement as a satisfactory description of the opposition to Hitler which existed in Germany from 1933 to 1945, we would be no further along in our study than the chronicle of woe evidenced in the archives of the *Sondergerichtshof*. We would have to accept the resistance movement in Germany as a series of isolated and apparently unconnected events. All the same, this analysis, coming as it does from one who was privy to the preparations for the heroic event associated with the Twentieth of July, may serve the historian as a warning against making a too hasty generalization about motives of the various groups which sought to rid Germany of the Nazis. The thing one must be very careful to avoid is to sug-

---

[19] Hans Bernard Gisevius, *To the Bitter End*, 418-419.

gest by the phrase "the German resistance movement" that there
was one national effort which had the single aim of ridding
Germany of the National Socialist scourge, an aim which might
appear comparable to the national resistance movements which
existed in all the other European nations.

The resistance movement in Germany may not then have been
as unified as some have suggested; but its several manifestations
do not seem so "tangential" as Herr Gisevius would lead us to
believe. Those men who opposed Hitler can be said to have belonged to different resistance movements in so far as they were
moved to act by different ideas. Those conservative opponents
of Hitler who discovered, in some cases at an embarrassingly
late hour that Germany under the Nazis was being transformed
into something hardly to be distinguished from Soviet Russia,
such men could hardly be said to have based their opposition on
principles or ideas which were the same as Hitler's Communist
opponents. At the same time, the Communists were among the
most active in the resistance movement in Germany; indeed the
Nazis, to be sure for their own special purposes, rarely tired of
declaring the Communists to be their most formidable oppo-
ments, a fact for which there is abundant evidence in the *Gestapo*
and *Volksgerichtshof* archives. [20]

[20] A sampling of records in the Würzburg Gestapo archives now located
in the Berlin Document Center revealed that of one hundred and twenty persons about whom there were short notices—apparently suspected of anti-Nazi
activities for the year 1938-1939—seventy of that number were said to have
been Communists. The others included twenty-three Catholic priests, thirteen
Social Democrats, four Lutheran pastors, three Bavarian monarchists and separatists, two members of the Bavarian People's Party, one member of Otto
Strasser's Black Front, and five cases which were not easily classified. The
author.

For further discussion of the Communist opposition to Hitler, cf. Walter A.
Schmidt, *Damit Deutschland Lebe; ein Quellenbericht über den deutschen
antifaschistischen Widerstandskampf, 1933-1945,* (Berlin, 1958). (It should
be pointed out here that although this study purports to be a study of the
entire anti-Fascist struggle in Germany, the tendency of Herr Schmidt and his

Again, the socialist tradition in Germany was not wiped out overnight on May 2, 1933. Leading personalities of the Social Democratic Party whether they were in exile or in prison camps in Germany furthered an information service by means of an underground which kept alive hopes for a reestablishment of a democratic socialist state. [21] But these hopes of socialists for the future as well as the plans which were suggested for ridding Germany of Hitler, reveal not only the unique characteristics of a resistance movement, but also these facts reveal some of the difficulties which await the historian who undertakes to write a critical account of this movement in opposition to National Socialism. [22] Which is not to say that a history of rightist opposition, even when that history is limited to Bavaria, does not run the risk of certain dangerous misconceptions and confusions.

One of the frequent misconceptions about those conservatives who opposed Hitler is that, as reactionaries, they were really not very different from the National Socialists. Although this is patently absurd, it is worthwhile to phrase it in this stark form if only to clarify the issue once and for all.

It is possible that the root of this problem lies in a paradoxical phrase which Hugo von Hofmannsthal is supposed to have invented in 1927 while addressing the students at Munich. The unfortunate phrase is, "The Conservative Revolution." [23] This is one of those examples of a paradox, a confusion of opposites out of which it is hoped truth will emerge. The only ones who ever profited by such a synthesis were, apparently, the National Socialists. They profited because some conservatives delivered themselves and the whole country into the hands of a revolutionary group "whose creed was action for action's sake and whose tactics were the destruction and undermining of all that is of value in the existing order." [24] This sorry mistake was realized, needless to say, only when it was too late. There never was any lasting bond, however, between "conservatives" and "conservative revolutionaries." This fact will be seen more clearly if one looks, not at the history of National Socialism proper, but at some of those organizations which parallel the aims and practices of the Nazis. Two such groups, groups often labeled as part of the radical right, were Otto Strasser's "Black Front," and Ernst Niekisch's "Resistance Movement."

The Black Front was plainly a National Socialist heresy. [25] Its founder, Otto Strasser, was the brother of Gregor Strasser who was among the victims of the Nazi purge in June 1934. [26]

---

that militarism was committing suicide in Germany." *Trial of the Major War Criminals*, XII, 226-227 (Nürnberg, 1948).

[23] Klemens von Klemperer, "The Conservative Revolution in Germany, 1913 through the Early Years of the Republic. The History of an Idea." (Unpublished Ph. D. dissertation, Harvard University, 1949). An excellent bibliographical analysis of this problem may be found in Armin Mohler, *Die Konservative Revolution in Deutschland* (Stuttgart, 1950). The several books of Hermann Rauschning are, in general, elaborations on the theme of the Conservative Revolution. The best of these is, undoubtedly, *Germany's Revolution of Destruction* (London, 1939).

[24] Rauschning, *op cit.*, 12-13.

[25] Otto Strasser called his organization *Kampfgemeinschaft Revolutionärer Nationalsozialisten.* For his own account of these events, see his *Germany Tomorrow* (London, 1940), *Hitler and I* (London, 1940). See also Douglas Reed, *Nemesis? The Story of Otto Strasser and the Black Front* (Boston, 1940).

[26] Strasser, *Die Deutsche Bartholomäusnacht* (7th. ed., Prague, 1938).

Before Hitler's final victory, both Strassers were out of the Party because they felt the Party had deviated from its radicalism. Otto Strasser had to flee to Vienna early in 1933 and moved soon after to Prague where he organized his oppositional activities: radio broadcasts, broadsheets, pamphlets, books, etc. The general line taken by the Black Front was that Hitler was not living up to his promises of rooting out the real enemies of Germany, enemies which might be more generally described as clericalists and western liberals.

A good example of his thinking can be found in a pamphlet written in 1934, called *Socialist Revolution or Fascist War*. [27] There he denounced Hitler's real supporters: capitalists, fascists, imperialists, and clericalists. He made it plain that a continuation of the Hitler regime would mean a continuation of the "liberal-November-government," the Versailles Treaty, Roman law, concordats with the Vatican, a federalist structure in German government and, worst of all, a continuation of that Weimar "dummy," the constitution. [28] It is quite clear that his sole objection was based on the conviction that Hitler was not enough of a Nazi.

Inside Germany the "Black Front" had some followers, chiefly among Captain Röhm's Storm Troopers. [29] In the first year of Nazi supremacy, it was they who felt somehow left out of the real victory celebration; they were not able to be as ruthless in effecting their revolution as they had once hoped they would. This feeling of neglect prompted a response to the Black Front appeals which were couched in a jargon revolutionary radicals were not likely to misunderstand. [30]

---

[27] Strasser, *Sozialistische Revolution oder Faschistischer Krieg?* (Prague, n.d.).
[28] *Ibid.*, 2, 4-7, 10.
[29] Strasser, *Germany Tomorrow*, 40, 241. See also *Bayerische Politische Polizei*, Memorandum, Nr. 468/36, II IC/HU, April 2, 1936, now located in Ritter von Epp file in Berlin Document Center.
[30] Strasser, *Germany Tomorrow*, 40. The letters sent by Strasser to the

This is not the place to examine in any detail the history of Otto Strasser's activities in opposition to Hitler, but there is one aspect of all of Strasser's opposition which is of vital concern to anyone interested in the main problem of this study. [31] Sometime in the late thirties, possibly about the time of the Munich Pact, the Black Front had more or less disintegrated. [32] Otto Strasser left Prague at the opening of the Second World War and made his headquarters for a time in Paris. After the fall of France, he escaped to Spain where he hid from Gestapo agents in a Benedictine monastery. From there, October 1940, he sailed

---

S.A. were called *Huttenbriefe*. A good example of one of these letters is the following: "On June 30, 1934, was murdered by Goering's order . . . . the man who, in conjunction with Moeller van den Bruck, may be regarded as the chief herald and pioneer of German socialism — Gregor Strasser."

"Through him alone it was that millions of Germans of both sexes made acquaintance with the new idea of national socialism . . . . For in spite of, nay, because of Hitler's monstrous treason to the German people, it is needful, instructive, and comforting to keep our eyes fixed upon the lofty aim that was once put forward as that of the National Socialist Party, that National Socialist Party which in practice the Hitler system has so shamelessly betrayed, so basely desecrated . . . . In very truth it was for this German socialism that the fighters in the troubles of the post-war period went to their tombs . . . ." *Ibid.*, 240-242.

[31] There are a number of trials of members of the black Front in the archives of the *Volksgerichtshof* now located in the Berlin Document Center. The trial of Marianne von Gustedt (Nr. 8J GO/38-2H 73/78) reveals how minimal the activity of the Black Front was. At her trial one witness insisted that von Gustedt was "deep-down a real National Socialist" but that she felt the Third Reich should have a Socialism which was "more Prussian" in character. *Ibid.*, 18, 20, 23. See also Günther Weisenborn, *op. cit.*, 109, for discussion of the *Stein Kreis* to which von Gustedt belonged. Another trial of Kark Schaffer of Vienna, (*Volksgerichtshof*, 8 J 368/38 -1 H 4/39) gives some material on the operations of the Black Front in Austria prior to the *Anschluss*.

[32] One of O. Strasser's most trusted companions and wealthiest supporters, Friedrich Beer-Grunow (Heinrich Grunow) who published in Prague much of the Black Front literature, circulated among leading members of the Black Front a private letter (*Denkschrift*) dated Paris, February 1938, copy No. 41

for England. [33] Whether or not his general progress westward
and the more specific event of his sojourn in a Benedictine
monastery have any direct bearing on his rejection of some of
the important tenets of the Black Front would be difficult to
show; but there is no denying its metaphorical significance. For
when he got to England he began to see man's problems in another light. He felt that they could never be solved in any lasting way unless there were a revival of religious life. In one of
his books he said quit simply: "We are Christians; without Christianity Europe is lost." [34] When he said that, if he meant it, he
abandoned one of his most important revolutionary doctrines:
that nothing must stand in the way of achieving the radical reorganization of European society. In England he could see more
clearly than ever before what the conservative revolutionaries
really stood for. He saw that "revolution of nihilism" and lost
heart.

Inside Germany there were other groups whose aims parallel-
ed the Nazi's and the Black Front's, and none was more thoroughly nihilistic than the "Resistance Movement" founded by
Ernst Niekisch. [35] Other than Nazi sources it would be hard to

---

of which is found in the files of the Gestapo Headquarters, Berlin now
located in the Berlin Document Center. Grunow accused Strasser of un-called
for bravura, and declared Strasser would do more harm than good if he ever
got control of Germany. See *Denkschrift,* 2, 9, 11.

[33] Douglas Reed, *The Prisoner of Ottawa: Otto Strasser* (London, 1953),
193-197.

[34] Strasser, *Hitler and I,* 104. See also *Germany Tomorrow,* 72.

[35] The history of the *Widerstandsbewegung* is fully covered, however from
a Nazi point of view, in the trial of Ernst Niekisch before the *Volksgerichtshof,* Berlin, January 1939 (Nr. 8 J 214/37 - 1 H 31/38). There are other
discussions of National Bolshevism, such as Klemens von Klemperer's article
in the *Review of Politics,* XIII, April 1951. An earlier account is Erich
Müller, "Zur Geschichte des National-Bolschevismus," *Deutsches Volkstum,*
October 1932. Ernst Niekisch has summed up his current opinion in *Ost-West;
Unsystematische Betrachtungen,* (Berlin, 1947), and also in *Das Reich der
niederen Dämonen,* (Hamburg, 1953.) Cf. also Hans Buchheim, "Ernst Nie-

find a better example of Rauschning's "voice of destruction" than in the writings of Ernst Niekisch. He openly advocated the complete undermining and destruction of all that is generally regarded as important in western civilization. He was convinced that before any real advance would be possible for humanity, the west, with all its "works and pomps," must be annihilated. [36] Further, he accepted the inevitability of a new civilization which would come from the east and promise relief to men now suffering because of the tensions in western countries. It was this last feature of his argument which gave it such a pro-Russian if not pro-Communist bias.

In the early days of the Nazi supremacy, the "Resistance Movement," however curtailed by limitation of publishing materials, was not suppressed. Too many of those who formed the basic cadres in the National Socialist movement thought along lines similar to Ernst Niekisch. This was especially true of ex-Free Corpsmen, men who after the First World War had fought in the Baltic countries to suppress Communist governments and had found themselves very much in a love-hate relationship with the new Russian experiment. From that very area, the Baltic countries, Niekisch foretold that the conqueror would sweep down and subdue the west. He called his conqueror the "Barbarian," the third figure to emerge and dominate the stage of world history. The other two are analyzed in one of Niekisch's most important works: *The Third Imperial Figure,* a book which the Nazis allowed to circulate for a year after its publication in 1935. [37]

In that work he sums up his philosophy of history—a philosophy remarkably like Alfred Rosenberg's, especially in its em-

kisch's Ideologie des Widerstands," in *Vierteljahreshefte für Zeitgeschichte,* 1957, 334-361.

[36] Ernst Niekisch, *Politik Deutschen Widerstands* (Berlin, 1934), 7.

[37] Ernst Niekisch, *Die Dritte Imperiale Figur* (Berlin, 1935).

phases upon physical and racial types. Niekisch spends a good deal of time explaining the chief characteristics of western civilization wherein, he insists, two figures have contended for mastery. [38] One of these figures he calls "the Roman." To him Niekisch applies all that seems somehow remotely Mediterranean. With consummate lack of regard for historical relationships, he pours into one stew the Ceasars, the Popes, classical art, the Middle Ages and in the end he comes out with the Roman's alter ego, the Jesuit. He is equally chaotic in his treatment of the other imperial figure, "the Jew." To him Niekisch credits Protestantism, Masonry, liberalism, the Revolution, humanitarianism, and from him has come an alter ego, namely, the Yankee. The only significant thing about Niekisch's summary of these unhappy characteristics of western civilization, all summed up in the Roman and the Jew or the Jesuit and the Yankee, is the prophecy that very shortly all of that will be annihilated by the Barbarian's alter ego, namely the Tartar Warrior. [39].

Although this is not the place to discuss in detail Niekisch's further activities in opposition to Hitler, there is at least one important observation which must be made if there is to be a clear understanding of the relationship between the conservatives and these radical rightists. In 1936 an article "Fascism and National Bolshevism" appeared in the *Schweizer Monatshefte*. [40] The Nazis claimed that the author, Friedrich Baumann, was in reality Ernst Niekisch, a fact which has now been confirmed by the editors of that journal. [41] The article adequately expressed

---

[38] *Ibid., passim*, 38, 39 44, 56, 102.

[39] *Ibid.*, 26.

[40] Friedrich Baumann, "Faschismus und Nationalbolschevismus," in *Schweizer Monatshefte*, XVI (July-August 1936), 196-204.

[41] Trial of Ernst Niekisch before the People's Court, January, 1939, 85. See also, Dr. F. Rieter, Präsident des Vorstandes der *Schweizer Monatshefte*, letter to the author, November 10, 1954.

the feelings of many National Bolshevists who knew by that
time that the radical right in Germany was completely dominated
by the National Socialists. What these National Bolshevists, like
the Black Front people and Captain Röhm's Storm Troopers,
objected to most in National Socialism was, in their eyes, its
defection to the west. As 'Baumann' said:

> The National Bolshevists wanted to mobilize that antibourgeois
> feudal remnant in Prussia, and, under the symbol of Potsdam,
> bring about a Prussian Bolshevism.... But the tragedy has been
> that Fascism, coming from the south, has conquered that area
> which by right ought to be Bolshevist: the northern, Prussian,
> Protestant part of Germany. Once the Fascists acquired that, they
> could easily present themselves as the synthesis of Rome and
> Potsdam, of southern Germany with its Catholic urbanity and
> northern Germany with its Protestant barbarism.... [The Nazis
> could present themselves as] Rhenish Jesuits living an east Elbian
> barracks life. [42]

That is further testimony of the success of the National Socialists, that they could have presented themselves as all things
to all people. But what is particularly of concern here is the clear
understanding of how much those who were part of the radical
right had in common with the Nazis, and how little they had
in common with those Germans who thought of themselves as
conservatives in the traditional meaning of that word. [43]

Conservatism, as it is understood in most western countries,
is still that conservatism which has found its finest expression
in the writings of Edmund Burke. It was he who championed
the oppostion to the Revolution of his own day, a revolution
which found its fullest realization in Jacobinism. His chief

---

[42] Baumann, *op. cit.,* 201-203.

[43] There was a popular joke in the Third Reich which illustrates how the
Germans thought of the radical rightists in the Nazi party. "Welche Ähnlich-
keit besteht zwischen einem SA-Mann und einen Beefsteak? Beide sind aussen
braun und innen rot." Richard Hermes, *Witz Contra Hitler* (Hamburg, 1946),
137.

weapon in fighting Jacobinism was the Christian religion. That, along with the monarchy, the family, and the idea of private property, was the foundation for the society he wished might live and be passed on to future generations. In those years when Germany appeared to be undergoing its own Jacobin terror, the opposition to National Socialism which came from Bavarian conservatives was the kind of opposition which one finds implicit in the writings on the French Revolution by Edmund Burke.

In so far as the Bavarian conservatives who will be discussed in the following pages belonged to any sort of resistance movement, that movement was Christianity. [44] It was that which gave lasting form and true dimension to their opposition to National Socialism. There is no doubt but that in Bavaria the leadership in that movement came from the Catholic Church. Precisely because of this, conservative opposition to Hitler had all the strength and all the weaknesses which are bound up with the Christian tradition. For example, Catholic layman were required to respect the special oaths of allegiance which bound the Roman Catholic hierarchy to the German state. The Nazis hamstrung the Christians with one of their own most sacred weapons, an oath before God and men.

Yet the Nazis were by no means free from blunderings. By a policy which inevitably promised a de-Christianized Germany, Catholics were aroused to action. In the course of defending the liberty of the Church, they found themselves pushed into ad-

---

[44] These remarks should not be taken in such a way as to suggest that this movement was limited to Bavarian territory; far from that. This movement was just as evident amongst Prussians and, indeed, north Germans generally. The words of Count Helmuth von Moltke, leader of the Kreisau circle,—"I stood before Freisler not as a land-owner, not as a member of the nobility, not as a Prussian, not even as a German; I stood before him as a Christian and nothing other than that."—can be taken as typical and representative of this movement altogether. (The quotation is from one of von Moltke's last letters and is taken from Karl Ströllin, *Verräter oder Patrioten*, (Stuttgart, 1952, 45).

vocating political opposition to the Nazi regime. Franz von
Papen, the man most immediately responsible for Hitler's accession as chancellor, and a Roman Catholic, warned the Nazi
leaders on June 17, 1934 that by their blunderings in confusing
religion and politics they could expect only to be defeated; for
where a religious tradition is strong, it becomes stronger under
attack. [45] The following chapters will show the force and extent
of that opposition which came from Bavarian conservatives who
listened to the words of the Psalmist and "trusted in God more
than in princes."

---

[45] "Es ist zuzugeben, dass in dem Widerstand Christlicher Kreise gegen
staatliche oder parteiliche Eingriffe in die Kirche ein politisches Moment liegt.
Aber nur deshalb, weil politische Eingriffe in den religiösen Bezirk die Betroffenen zwingen, aus religiösen Gründen den auf diesem Gebiet widernatür-
lichen Totalitätsanspruch abzulehnen. Auch als Katholik habe ich Verständnis
dafür, dass eine auf Gewissensfreiheit aufgebaute religiöse Überzeugung es
ablehnt, sich von der Politik her im Ureigensten kommandieren zu lassen."
Reprinted in *Trial of Major War Criminals before the International Military
Tribunal* (Nürnberg, 1948), XL, 552. The speech was written by Edgar F.
Jung, von Papen's secretary and friend, who also wrote *Die Herrschaft der
Minderwertigen* (Berlin, 1930). Jung was murdered by the Nazis on June 30,
1934.

CHAPTER II

THE CHRISTIAN REALISTS

a) INTRODUCTION

Nothing would seem to violate both the spirit and the letter of the New Testament more than opposition or resistance to authority; indeed, there is abundant evidence both in the words of Christ and the apostles enjoining the opposite. [1] We need hardly recall those incidents prior to His crucifixion when Christ was "obedient even unto death"; when He set aside the sword as a means of opposition. [2] Nor can we forget that brief utterance with regard to the coin of tribute, ("Render unto Caesar the things which are Caesar's, and unto God the things which are God's"), which is at once the corner-stone of Christian political philosophy and the source of all political-religious anxiety. [3]

In this same connection, however, the teaching of the apostles leaves little room for doubt.

> Let every soul be subject unto the higher powers. For there is no power but of God; the powers that be are ordained of God. Whosoever therefore resisteth the power, resisteth the ordinance of God: and they that resist shall receive to themselves damnation. [4]

---

[1] The best contemporary treatment of this problem can be found in Max Pribilla's *Deutsche Schicksalsfragen* (Frankfurt, 1950). See especially the chapter "Vom Widerstandsrecht des Volkes." See also a dissertation by Mother Mary Alice Gallin, "Ethical and Religious Factors in the German Resistance to Hitler," (Washington, 1955).

[2] Matt. xxvi: 53. For a Roman Catholic interpretation of this and the other texts which follow, cf., Dom Bernard Orchard, *et. al.*, *A Catholic Commentary on Holy Scripture* (London, 1953).

[3] Matt. xxii. 21.

[4] Rom. xiii. 1.

The text is the celebrated thirteenth chapter of St. Paul's Epistle to the Romans. But is was no more explicit than the words of St. Peter who enjoined the faithful to obey not only good and temperate rulers, but to bear reverence to those who are ill disposed. "It is the patience of the innocent sufferer," he wrote, "that wins credit in God's sight." [5] Again, the early Christians took to heart the words of St. John, ("Do not be surprised that the world should hate you,") [6] and endured persecution even unto death, because that they took to be the essence of the Christian way to life.

Happily, or, perhaps, unhappily depending upon one's conception of that way of life, about the 4th century of our era, it became a much more involved and complicated affair than these simple texts would lead one to believe. The reader hardly need be reminded of the consequences for Christianity of the Edict of Milan and the events which followed from that edict. It was after that that the Church—and here and throughout this chapter, unless otherwise designated, we mean the Roman Catholic Church—ceased to be a sect whose mission was to the faithful, to the believers; soon enough it became the official religion of the Empire, whose priests performed the public rites and sacrifices in the name of all, and whose bishops became the guardians of public morality. This can rightly be taken as a happy event by all those who regard the impact of Christianity on the making of the West as something positive, inestimably good. At the same time, however generous one's attitude toward the history of the Church may be, one need never be blind to the highly ambiguous role of the Church in society, one which is characterized by her own children as "in the world, but not of it." As things turned out, in the centuries, say, between Charlemagne and Napoleon, the Church worked valiantly to perfect a Christ-

---

[5] 1 Peter ii. 20.
[6] 1 John iii. 14.

ian society; but, unfortunately, in the course of this effort in the world, she became increasingly worldly. [7]

The Middle Ages represent the first great flowering of a Christianized world. Then the Church effectively fulfilled all of her offices, not least of which she considered to be the guardianship of public morality. And in a society characterized by an emerging national monarchy there was no aspect of public morality more in need of clarification than the relationship of the Church and the community of believers to authority perverted by tyranny.

As in so many other cases this became subject to the keenest minds of that age, none of whom has left quite so brilliant a synthesis as St. Thomas Aquinas. He left little doubt that the Church had the power to abrogate any rights or dominion over the faithful by infidels "in virtue of her Divine authority." He goes on to say: "For infidels on account of their unbelief, deserve to lose their power over the faithful who are become the sons of God." [8] Although the reader need not be reminded that the word "infidel" referred to the non-Christianized world and that it has a rather specialized meaning in a religious society, yet no one can fail to observe the extent to which the power of the Church had grown since the days before the Edict of Milan; what is more, how different since that period the whole attitude of the Church toward the civil authority had become. Nowhere is this more forcibly illustrated than where St. Thomas writes on the subject of the Christian's attitude toward tyranny.

> Tyrannical government is unjust government because it is directed not to the common welfare but to the private benefit of the ruler. This is clear from what the Philosopher says in *Politics,*

---

[7] For a very suggestive study of this problem, see H. Richard Niebuhr, *Christ and Culture* (New York, 1951).

[8] Saint Thomas Aquinas, *Summa Theologica, Secunda secundae partis,* Q. X, Art. 10, as quoted in A. P. d'Entreves, *Aquinas' Selected Political Writings* (Oxford, 1948), 153.

Bk. III, and in the *Ethics*, Bk. VIII. Consequently the overthrowing of such government is not strictly sedition;

Again, the reader having reached this point cannot but be amazed at the transformation in Christian thinking. Yet St. Thomas was a realist in more than the purely philosophical meaning of that word; for he adds this notable caution:

> ... the overthrowing of such government is not strictly sedition; except perhaps in case that it is accompanied by such disorder that the community suffers greater harm from the consequent disturbances than it would from the former ruler. 9

This *caveat* has long impressed Catholical political thinkers, and, on the whole, has put the Church almost invariably on the side of the established civil authority.

In spite of all Suarez and Bellarmine may have tried to do in pointing out the dangers of the growth of absolutist states; in spite of Mariana's justification of tyrannicide; in the period between the Reformation and the French Revolution the main body of Catholic thinkers followed Bossuet and St. Alphonsus Ligouri: divine right monarchy was the keystone of Christian society; rebellion, violence, and sedition were all clearly anathematized. 10 And with such thinking as this, the Church entered the unhappy decades of the French Revolution, the event in modern times which has done most to fix the enmity between Church and state. One may say from 1789 until our own day no completely satisfactory solution has been found to this grave issue. This is not to say there have not been attempts; the nineteenth century was full of such attempts.

With the exception of socialism and communism which re-

---

9 *Ibid.,* Q. XLII, Art. 2, quoted in A. P. d'Entreves, *op. cit.,* 161.

10 For a general history of the attitude of the Catholic Church to the problem of tyrannnicide, see A. Bride, "Tyrannicide," in *Dictionaire de Theologie Catholique,* (Paris, 1950), col. 1988-2016. For a discussion of St. Alphonsus Ligouri, see Max Pribilla, *op. cit.*; see also Mother Mary Alice Gallin, *op. cit.,* "Resistance to Tyranny," 26-39.

legate the realities of religion to something quite secondary, there have been since the French Revolution three major solutions offered to the problem of the relationship of Church and state. First of all, there was the "restoration of throne and altar." From the standpoint of the Church, however, the "altar" was never fully restored, especially not restored to all of her former material possessions. [11] Nevertheless, what in the nineteenth century was generally labeled "reactionary," may be regarded as part of the thinking which found its best expression in the writings of Prince Metternich and its fullest articulation in the papal *Syllabus of Errors*. To a very large extent, particularly among French and Italian Catholics, "the restoration" was as far as most Catholic thinking in the nineteenth century ventured. On the other hand, in England and the United States there were liberal-democratic societies, tolerant and pluralist, which gave the Church considerable freedom and toward which the Church in turn formed a kind of loyal opposition. [12] Germans offered the third solution to the problem.

In an effort to find an answer to the socialists as well as relief from the excesses of liberalism, certain German Catholics began a long flirtation with corporatist ideas, a flirtation which had not entirely ended when the Nazis seized power in 1933. Chief among the leaders of the Church who gave his support to this movement was William Emmanuel Baron von Ketteler, the Bishop of Mainz. Society, he felt, ought to be reorganized on a Christian basis and, most particularly, the worker in the Trade Union ought to be made to feel his significance as a part of a greater whole. As he said in his writing on the labor question,

---

[11] For repercussions of this fact in the twentieth century, see Cardinal Michael von Faulhaber, *"Das Reichskonkordat — Ja oder Nein?"* (Munich, 1937), 12.

[12] An interesting discussion of this problem can be found in Emmet John Hughes, *The Church and the Liberal Society* (Princeton, 1944).

The old Christian corporations have been dissolved, and men are still zealously at work trying to remove the last remnants, the last stone, of this splendid edifice. A new building is being erected to replace it. But the latter is only a wretched hut built on foundations of sand. Christianity must raise a new structure on the old fundations and thus give back to the workingman's associations their real significance and their real usefulness. [13]

Bishop von Ketteler was seeking to Christianize the new industrial order, and in this he had some followers. The most notable one was Father Franz Hitze who wrote a monumental treatise on *Capital and Labor and the Reorganization of Society* in which there was a subtle argument in favor of a kind of neomediaevalism. [14]

Although these advocates of social reform in Germany went unheard, there were echoes of their sentiments in the writings of Pope Leo XIII. However, after the *Kulturkampf* Catholics in Germany subsided into a unique position of holding the balance between the socialists and the nationalist parties, a position they continued to hold during the lifetime of the German Republic. And although the leadership of the Center Party tended to ignore corporatist theory, the same cannot be said for all Catholics. [15] When the liberal democratic experiment of Weimar appeared to be failing, certain Catholics were abe to find justification for the radical organization of society under a regime of National Socialism. [16] They must have accepted only those parts

---

[13] William Emmanuel Baron von Ketteler, *Die Arbeiter Frage,* as quoted in Ralph Bowen, *German Theories of the Corporative State* (New York, 1947), 86.

[14] Franz Hitze, *Kapital und Arbeit und die Reorganisation der Gesellschaft* (Paderborn, 1880), a full analysis of which can be found in Ralph Bowen, *op. cit.,* 96-106.

[15] Cf., Edgar F. Jung, *Die Herrschaft der Minderwertigen, (Ihr Zerfall und ihre Ablösung durch ein neues Reich)* (Berlin, 1930). For a general discussion of Edgar Jung, see Rudolf Pechel, *Deutscher Widerstand* (Zürich, 1947), 76-77.

[16] For a discussion of some Catholics who were at first favorably impressed

of National Socialism which appeared to be somehow vaguely corporatist. [17] To this extent they may be regarded as blind, shallow, naïve and ignorant. How culpable that ignorance was is not a problem which can be analyzed here. The result of that ignorance is now a matter of history, and it played its part in making possible the so-called bloodless revolution of March, 1933. It is also interesting to observe the extent to which sincere anti-Nazis in the period, say, around 1940 still found in these corporatist schemes a promise of relief from the excesses of either liberalism or socialism. Thus where they presented a positive plan for the reorganization of society, likely as not it would have a corporatist ring to it. But such speculation, however agreeable it might have been to certain members of the German hierarchy and clergy, was never put forth as an official position of the Catholic Church. On the contrary, the basis for the opposition of the Church to National Socialism was quite simply that her rights, guaranteed by positive law, were inviolable. The results of the fifteen year struggle may have encouraged an entire re-evaluation of political thought by Catholics in Germany, but that does not concern us here. The pages which follow tell again the story of what the Church in Bavaria did to oppose Hitler.

b) VORMÄRZ, 1931-1933

The National Socialists unwittingly, it may be assumed at first, involved themselves in a struggle with the Church largely because of the twenty-fourth point of the Nazi program.

---

with National Socialism, see, Alois Natterer, *Der Bayerische Klerus in der Zeit dreier Revolutionen: 1918, 1933, 1945.* (Munich, 1946), 240 ff.

[17] The most famous Catholic apologia for National Socialism was written by an Austrian bishop resident in Rome. See, Alois Hudal, *Die Grundlagen des Nationalsozialismus; eine ideengeschichtliche Untersuchung* (Leipzig, 1937).

The National Socialist German Workers Party is in favor of all religious beliefs within the state to the extent that they do not constitute a danger to the existence of the state and in so far as they do not conflict with the moral feeling of the German race. [18]

Such an absurd phrase as "the moral feeling of the German race" could easily have been altered or expunged, and the whole tenor of the article changed by some such sentence as: "We believe in the freedom of Germans to practice the Christian religion," implying neither acceptance nor rejection of the established Churches, while at the same time leaving themselves free rein to eliminate, if necessary, the fringe sects and, of course, the non-Christian religions. Such an approach one might have expected from so Machiavellian and opportunistic a movement as National Socialism. Unfortunately for the Churches, the Nazis preferred to lure the industrial proletariat, Socialists and Communists, by appealing to their latent anti-clericalism. Fortunately for the Churches this policy was observed in good season and the Catholic Church responded forcefully.

In the fall of 1930, to borrow a celebrated phrase from Robert D'Harcourt, the parish priest of Kirschhausen in Hesse brought himself and "his hamlet into history." [19] As far as we know he was the first to lay down the law on the Nazis. He said, in effect, that no Catholic could belong to the Party; that Nazis could not attend church in a uniformed body; and that no member of the Party might receive the sacraments. The reader need hardly be reminded that this was tantamount to excommunication. What is more the parish priest was supported by the hierarchy.

On February 12, 1931, the Bishops of Bavaria issued the following warning to the clergy:

---

[18] As translated in Robert D'Harcourt, *German Catholics* (London, 1939), 5-6.
[19] *Ibid.*

1. National Socialism contains in its cultural-political program grave errors, because contained therein are numerous ideas which Catholic belief abjures or looks askance at. The leaders of this Party would set these ideas up in opposition to Christian belief. We do not wish to concern ourselves here with state-political matters; we only ask ourselves what sort of an attitude this group takes toward Catholic Christianity.

Leading proponents of National Socialism put race on a higher level than religion. They abjure the revelation of the Old Testament and even set aside the Mosaic law of the Ten Commandments. Because he is in a non-German country, they deny the primacy of the Pope in Rome and play with the idea of establishing a dogma-free German national church. In paragraph twenty-four of the program they assert that the everlasting moral law of Christianity must be tested by the moral feeling of the German race. Conceptions of the right of revolutions which are accompanied by success, and also the superiority of power over justice—these stand in contradiction to Christian social teaching. From pronouncements either by the leader of the Party or by other Party chiefs we know that what National Socialism calls Christianity is not the Christianity of Christ. The Bishops, therefore, as guardians of the Faith and of Christian moral teaching must warn against National Socialism's cultural policies which are at odds with Catholic doctrine.

2. It is forbidden for a Catholic priest to have any part in the National Socialist movement. Surely a Catholic priest who because of his theological training is able to distinguish Dogma from error can see how inimical this Party is to the Church and religion; surely he can recognize in the fact that it abjures all concordats, demands a school system without religious training, and encourages a radical nationalism. For a priest there can be no question in this matter of a guiltless, erring conscience. For the same reason the clergy have the duty to instruct the faithful in a calm and factual manner that although National Socialism had at its inception a violent anti-Marxist tone, it has more and more come in its cultural policies in open war against the Church and her Bishops. Over and over again the press of this movement has criticized Catholic pronouncements and has even found it possible to put into the Holy Fathers' appeal for defense against Bolshevism ideas which were in no sense contained in the original.

3. The participation of National Socialism in Church functions in a uniformed body is and remains forbidden, lest the people gain the impression that the conflict between National Socialism and the Church has been healed. However, if an individual National Socialist comes into church wearing the badge of his Party it can be permitted but only if there is no disturbance of the ceremonies of the church.

4. As to the question whether a National Socialist may receive the Sacraments of Penance and Holy Eucharist, that must be determined in each case separately; it must be decided whether the individual is only a fellow-traveler who is not clear about the religious and cultural policies of the Party; or whether he is a representative or a journalist or an agent for the entire aims of the Party which is to say for all the ideas which stand in opposition to Christianity. Amongst the masses who voted National Socialist in the last election there were many who were so inclined for purely patriotic reasons—hoping for a revision of the Versailles Treaty, hoping for a cure of economic ills, hoping for a reduction of unemployment. Many of those who voted for the National Socialists did not concern themselves with questions involving the Church and religion, or they did not choose so to involve themselves, thus trying to live in good faith. In such case the confessor must decide whether or not membership in the National Socialist Party means a near occasion of sin. The question of how much knowledge the priest must have in this matter is to be tested by the usual rules regarding the care of souls.

5. The pastoral principles concerning National Socialism remain the same as those concerning the old liberalism and socialism. Even amongst adherents of these errors there were and are persons who have never abjured their confirmation oath and have been steadfast in their loyalty to the Church. As to the question arising when an individual National Socialist should die suddenly without receiving the last sacraments whether or not he should be permitted Christian burial, such questions must be decided on the basis of the individual's participation in the life of the Church— whether he fulfilled his Easter duty and in general whether he died at peace with the Church.

6. Should National Socialism develop into a thing comparable in its aims and attitudes to Bolshevism—a thing we hope will not occur—then we will not be able to recognize a *bona fides* in in-

dividuals. For the rest, the position taken at the Bishops' conference at Fulda and at Freising against anti-Christian organizations
are still valid.

(signed) The Archbishops and Bishops
in Bavaria [20]

Ten years later all the worst predications and fears implicit
in this pastoral warning had been fulfilled. But from the beginning there were Catholics in Bavaria who took these words to
heart. Among them were members of a fraternity, *Rhaetia,* whose
motto might as well have been "Bavaria for the Bavarians," and
who held strongly to the Church and monarchy. In a letter issued
with the caption "Secret, under the fraternal oath," the officers
of *Rhätia* stated their position as follows:

> As a Catholic organization we naturally accept the direction
> which our Bishops give us in fundamental questions which con-
> cern our way of life.
> Several Bavarian Bishops in agreement with other German as
> well as the majority of the non-German episcopate have publicly
> declared that the National Socialist conception of life (*Weltan-
> chauung*) as gleaned from their program as well as from state-
> ments from their leaders contradicts in many important questions
> the teaching of the Catholic Church. Our first principles demand
> that we give our unfeigned loyalty to the Catholic way of life
> which includes obedience to the directions of our Bishops.
> Our second principle requires an especial devotion to our Bava-
> rian homeland and our people. Not the most generous critic of
> the National Socialist movement could possibly maintain that there
> is not in that movement a minimizing of Bavarian interests. But he
> who has given his oath to a Bavarian organization and either
> inside or outside that organization works in opposition to Bava-
> rian ideals, violates his oath. Fully conscious of their duty, the
> leaders of the Fraternity seek to maintain the aims and practices
> of our Fraternity. We are of the conviction that the National
> Socialist conception of life contradicts our two first principles and

---

[20] "Nationalsozialismus und Seelsorge," *Eichstätter Pastoralblatt,* III (February, 1931), 11 ff.

therefore a good *Rhaete* cannot at the same time be a National Socialist. [21]

The conflict between the Christian way of life and the Nation Socialists was published more widely by two champions of Catholic morality, Fritz Gerlich and Father Ingebert Naab, O.F.M. They were co-editors of a Catholic weekly published in Munich called *Der Gerade Weg*. [22] Their criticisms were centered on the pagan and heathen aspects of the Nazi movement, particularly on Rosenberg's blood and race theories. With resolute courage they trumpeted their warnings to all Germans, but especially to Catholics.

> We know not the future of our beloved country [they wrote in 1931]; but one thing we do know: should this hideous [National Socialist] catastrophe befall us, then we shall have to admit that the intellectuals bear a large share of the guilt. It can happen only if we are short-sighted and sloppy in our reasoning, or because we lack character and posses only a Christian façade. [23]

Such blows were aimed directly. By July, 1932 Dr. Gerlich's criticism became so sharp and forceful, not to say effective, that the Nazis succeeded in convincing the Munich police that *Der Gerade Weg* had violated the statute on the freedom of the press and ought to be banned for six weeks. The editorial which brought on the action was entitled, "National Socialism is a Plague."

> After war in mediaeval times, the plague came as an additional scourge to mankind. After the last war with its unfortunate consequences of revolution, inflation, economic crisis and unemployment, there has followed a spiritual plague: National Socialism.

---

[21] From a printed broadsheet to members of *Rhaetia* entitled *Erklärung* and marked with the phrase *"Vertraulich unter Burschenwort!,"* signed by L. Bruner, *Oberstudiendirektor, Phil. Senior*; n.d. Full text in Appendix C.

[22] *Der Gerade Weg,* (Munich, 1929-1933). All quotations presented here are from *Prophetien Wider das III. Reich,* edited by Johann Steiner, (Munich, 1946).

[23] *Ibid.,* 73, *Der Gerade Weg* (February, 1931).

The misery under which mankind suffers can be righted only by agreements, reconciliation, disarmament, and peace.

National Socialism means enmity with our neighbors, tyranny, civil war, world war.

National Socialism's real colors are deceit, hate, fratricide, boundless anxiety.

Adolf Hitler has sanctioned the right to lie in the first eleven editions of his book; on page 202 of *Mein Kampf* we read: "The German has no idea how one must swindle people if one is to have a following with the masses." You, you who are about to be victims of this tyranny, awake! This concerns Germany, her future, and the fate of your children.

Do not listen to the generals and Hitler, their drummer boy, when they try to tell you that the German people were responsible for Germany's defeat in the last war; it was the Imperial government with Hindenburg and Ludendorff who lost the war.

Do not listen to Hitler when he puts the blame for Versailles and reparations on the political parties; rather you should blame all those who sought to continue the war and who refused to accept the peace proposal of 1917. These are the same people who want to put Hitler in power and bring about a new war.

Hitler, the militarists and the industrialists may revile the political parties; but it is the political parties who have rescued the German people when they stood at the edge of an abyss. That is the true picture.

We are fighting for a new State; we are fighting for the rights of nations, for social justice, the freedom of the German people, for reconciliation and agreement with France, the only thing which promises us all a decent future. We are fighting for peace, employment, social welfare, for a Christian social order.

We who write these lines are not desirous of power; we serve no particular party; we serve no one but our consciences. But we say to you: whoever fails to vote, sins before God and sins in the name of his children's children.

To you do we say: Catholics are bound in conscience to vote for the party which has the interests and defense of the Church in view—the Center or the Bavarian People's Party.

Anyone, even though he be not a Catholic, can give his vote to these parties; for they represent the interests of justice against tyranny. However, if you cannot cast your vote for either of these, vote Social Democratic, or the German State Party or for the Christian Social *Volksdienst*.

Next Sunday is the day for our crusade. Be active until the last voter has left the polling place. The halt, the lame, and the blind must all be gotten out to vote. To be lukewarm at such a time is a sin. Every Catholic must bring another person with him to the polling place. We must bring victory to our cause. To the front! [24]

In spite of such exhortations Hitler's Party in July, 1932 increased its strength. In November of that year, however, it began to lose ground. Some people thought hopefully that this was a sign of a greater defeat to come. But the events of the winter of 1933 shattered their hopes. Hitler was by that time the Chancellor, and preparations were being made for the election of March 5. It was at this time that Father Naab wrote his final appeal in *Der Gerade Weg,* urging the people to support those parties who were dedicated to preserving the Constitution of Weimar.

We vote because we are Christians (the editorial began).

If one were to read and believe the Nazi press, one would suppose that they are the only protectors of Christianity; that Hitler, in fact, is a second Redeemer.

We differentiate sharply between Mr. Adolf Hitler and the Chancellor. The Chancellor exercises authority, and all authority comes from God—even the present Chancellor's. According to Christian principles there is no power except it be from God. We will never hesitate in our loyalty to the state. We Christians are not revolutionaries; we do not wish to set aside with force of weapons any legitimate authority. We are willing to acknowledge all that is good in a government, and help it to achieve worthy ends.

But we cannot say that all that the person now in power does is done by God's grace. It may be done by the Devil; it may be so perverse that no rational being can possibly approve of it. We stand for Christian freedom . . . . God has not given you the right to sanction injustice.

---

[24] *Ibid.,* 437-438.

When we vote on March 5th, it must be with this Christian concept of the state in mind . . . . We alone are fighting for positive Christianity, which is to say for the belief in Christian teaching and for the practices of Christian morality. National Socialism talks a lot about protection of Christian teaching and morality. To this we reply:

So long as the *Führer* permits Rosenberg to continue as the editor of the *Völkische Beobachter*—this man who abjures our God as a Jewish machination—we cannot believe that in his speeches the Chancellor is really asking for God Almighty's blessing. Otherwise he would denounce this Rosenberg. And if Hitler claims to be the protector of Christian morality, he ought to remove himself from such a one as Röhm—and all the others! He knows them better than we do. Clean off your own doorstep and then start praying again.

We know how many National Socialists have remained loyal Catholics. We do not criticize the National Socialist movement because it brings together Protestants and Catholics. We could not expect Hitler to demand of these Protestants that they rid themselves of all anti-Roman feeling as long as it is born of inner conviction. But we are able to see through that maneuver to win Catholic friends to the Party. All sorts of techniques are used to pretend that the Nazis are the protectors of Christianity. Now, we are a good-spirited group, but not stupid. We do not say there will absolutely be a *Kulturkampf*. Unfortunately we cannot see into the future . . . . But we do know that there are those in the Party who would wish for such a fight, and they are people not without influence . . . .

We know when we vote that our ultimate power does not lie in parliaments; a Catholic's power lies elsewhere. The faith of our fathers does not depend upon Catholic parliamentarians; the faith is not made manifest by politicians.

The Church can wait. Her great strength lies in this waiting, in her ability to suffer, and in gaining new strength from the grace which proceeds from her Head to the members. That power rests in our tabernacles. The votive lamps which burn before those tabernacles are the lamps which light our path; we see them again in the teachings of our popes and bishops. Things can be wretched for years—wretched by human standards—when we cannot smile or find happiness in anything. But all of that is insignificant; the hour of the Lord will come.

But we go to the polls to vote for the parties which promise a Christian social order: the Bavarian People's Party or the Center. We know all too well that many of the representatives may not be real adherents of the above doctrine; but we will mend that amongst ourselves; we will rebuild and try to live according to Christian principles. The real issues remain:

Our loyalty to what is really German.
Our adherence to God's commandments.
Our belief in the freedom of the Christian religion.
Our adherence to the idea of divine providence. [25]

Fritz Gerlich and Ingebert Naab both met ignominious ends. In the spring of 1933 Dr. Gerlich was imprisoned at Dachau. According to Otto Strasser, Hitler regarded Gerlich as one of his most deadly opponents and he was, accordingly, put to death on June 30, 1934. [26] A similar if less cruel end awaited Father Naab, who after hiding in a Franciscan convent for a year, managed to escape to Strasbourg where he died full of sorrow at the turn of events in his native land. On his tombstone were part of those eloquent words of Pope Saint Gregory VII, *Dilexi iustitiam et odi iniquitam,* avoiding at the same time the obvious conclusion: *proptera morior in exilio.* [27] All his and Dr. Ger-

---

[25] *Ibid.,* 568-574. *Der Gerade Weg,* March 5, 1933.

[26] "In the course of my investigation (of the murders committed on June 30, 1934) I came across the name of a well-known journalist, Gehrlick (sic.), whose murder at first seemed quite incomprehensible. Why was this poor man, who had been in prison since Hitler's accession to power, shot now?

The explanation of the mystery was bound up with a still more atrocious crime, the details of which I did not learn until two years later.". . . . (Strasser then tells of Hitler's murder of Gely Roubal, his niece) . . . . "An inquest was opened in Munich . . . but Fürtner, the Bavarian Minister of Justice, stopped the case. It was announced that Gely had committed suicide . . . Gehrlick (sic.), the editor of the *Right Way* . . . made a private investigation at the same time as the police, and collected overwhelming evidence against Hitler." Otto Strasser, *Hitler and I* (Boston, 1940), 201-203

[27] *Prophetien wider das III. Reich,* 10.

lich's energy seemed spent in vain—yet what they had said was
already an echo in the words of the Bavarian bishops, words
which resound like an apocalyptic warning throughout the entire
period we are about to examine. Cardinal Faulhaber, Bishop von
Galen, and the Munich Students all borrowed unhesitatingly
from their writings. They were, as their post-war friends have
aptly named them: prophets crying out in the Weimar desert
against the fate which ultimately was Germany's under the
Third Reich.

c) THE CONCORDAT VIOLATED

In the early spring of 1933 Franz von Papen, then Vice-
Chancellor of Germany, accepted the assignment to work out a
modus vivendi for Catholics in Germany which would satisfy
both the Vatican and Berlin. [28] There is little reason to doubt
the sincerity of all those who were immediately involved in these
negotiations; certainly Cardinal Pacelli, Monsignor Kaas and
Franz von Papen worked to end the conflict between Church
and state. [29] One question will always remain: what did the top-
level Nazis think of this agreement when it was signed? Unfortunately it is not a question which can be investigated here.
Suffice it to say, we do know that every major article in the
Concordat was ultimately violated by the government of Germany, and that, by the opening of the Second World War, plans
were already in effect which forbade the use of some Catholic

---

[28] Some mention should be made here of the withdrawal of the prohibition
of membership in the National Socialist Party by the Catholic bishops of
Germany. The decree read in part: "ohne die in unseren früheren Massnahmen
liegende Verurteilung bestimmter religiössittlicher Irrtümer aufzuheben, glaubt
daher das Episkopat das Vertrauen hegen zu können, dass die vorbezeichneten
allgemeinen Verbote und Warnungen nicht mehr als notwendig betrachtet
zu werden brauchen." Quoted from the *Archiv für Katholisches Kirchenrecht*,
(Mainz, 1933), in Max Pribilla, *op. cit.*, 61.

[29] Franz von Papen said after the Concordat was signed: ". . . at this historic
hour in German destiny German Catholicism must step boldy out of the

churches for services. [30] In the period 1933-1939 each violation of the Concordat met official opposition from the bishops of Germany. Pastoral letters, pastoral warnings, sermons—these comprised the record of how the Church opposed Hitler. They were published by the Church and offered for sale in religious bookshops; later on, when the Nazi pressure against their opponents was greatest, the sermons and letters were often as not circulated privately and they took on the character of documents of the "underground." [31] But for the most part the Church refused to relinquish her position as the guardian of public morality and for that very reason, no matter how few of her children may have lived up to her high ideals, she was able to leave behind a not inconsiderable record of public opposition to the established civil authority.

One of the indefatigable champions of this opposition was Michael von Faulhaber, Archbishop of Munich. He was born in Klosterheidenfeld in Lower Franconia, March 5, 1869. Ordained a priest in 1892, in 1903 he became a professor of Old Testament exegesis at Strasbourg. In 1911 he was consecrated Bishop of Speyer; in 1917 he was made head of the Archdiocese of

---

sphere of negation, out of the Ghetto." Quoted in Robert D'Harcourt, op. cit., 134. For von Papen's own account of the Concordat see his Der Wahrheit eine Gasse (Munich, 1952), 313-318. For a general critique of Von Papen, see Robert D'Harcourt, op. cit., 127-136.

[30] Alois Natterer, op. cit., 389. On the general subject of the Nazi persecution of the Catholic Church in Germany, see the fundamental work by Johann Neuhäusler, Kreuz und Hakenkreuz, Bk. I. Der Kampf des Nationalsozialismus gegen die Katholische Kirche (Munich, 1946). An English translation of nearly all of Bishop Neuhäusler's documents has existed since 1940, The Persecution of the Catholic Church in the Third Reich, facts and documents translated from the German, (London, 1940). See also, The Nazi War Against the Catholic Church, published by the United States National Catholic Welfare Conference, (Washington, 1944); Martin Borman, Le National-Socialisme et le Christianisme, published by the Free French Delegation in the U.S.A. and used by the French Resistance during the German occupation.

[31] Inge Scholl, Die Weisse Rose (Frankfurt am Main, 1952), 23.

Munich-Freising; in 1921 he became a Cardinal of the Roman Church. He died in the late spring of 1952. Although this chronology is meagre, it is none the less suggestive. Cardinal Faulhaber lived through the birth and death of the modern German state; the heights and depths which Germany experienced during his lifetime must have served as eloquent testimony to the vanity of the things of this world, especially things of the material order. But such an insight one might expect from a man whose office was the one which Cardinal Faulhaber held.

From the very start he was a cautious and realistic shepherd, even when dealing with the Nazi "wolves." Lacking the zeal and, perhaps, the enthusiasm of Bishop von Galen, the most undaunted of all the German bishops in the fight with the Nazis, Cardinal Faulhaber seems to have taken a middle course between Bishop von Galen and Bishop von Preysing of Berlin on the one hand, and those other bishops, such as Archbishop Bertram of Breslau and Archbishop Groeber of Freiburg, men whose courage seems to have failed at an hour when it was needed most. The case of Archbishop Groeber is perhaps the most unfortunate example of the illusion that the Church could get along with the Nazis. [32] During the early years of the Nazi regime he was popularly hailed as the "brown Bishop." No such epithet was ever applied to the Archbishop of Munich. In fact he was generally regarded as the official opponent of National Socialism, a position he earned because of his famous sermons given in Advent, 1933 on the general theme of the Old Testament.

Essentially, they are a reply to a resolution passed by the German Christians—a sect which sought to retain a certain Christian façade for their essentially pagan cult—on November 13, 1935 in the Berlin sports palace.

---

[32] A good impression of Archbishop Groeber can be gained from reading through his *Handbuch der religiösen Gegenwartsfragen* (Freiburg im Breisgau, 1937).

Donahoe, James

Hitler's __Conservative Opponents in Bavaria__

(place ? pub., Publisher, and date ? pub.?)

9434

D686

We expect [the resolution reads] our national churches to shake themselves free of all that is un-German, in particular the Old Testament and its Jewish morality of rewards. [33]

Cardinal Faulhaber attacked this resolution in his sermon given in St. Michael's Church on that first Sunday in Advent. Almost at once he was involved with the Jewish question. He was careful to point out, however, that he was speaking only of "pre-Christian Judaism;" and yet even in doing so he paid reverent tribute to the heritage of Israel: "You have excelled them all by the sublimity of your religion," he said; "among all the nations of antiquity you have exhibited the noblest religious values." Nor was he afraid to quote Cardinal Manning's famous words to the Jews: "I should not understand my own religion, had I no reverence for yours." [34] Such words cannot have fallen agreeably on ears which had become used to Hitlerian diatribes against the Jews.

Repeatedly, Cardinal Faulhaber stressed the religious, ethical and social values of the Old Testament, indicating how each of them finds fulfilment in Christianity. On the last night of 1933, he chose to make a frontal assault on racism. The great Jesuit church was overcrowded and many others heard the sermon broadcast into neighbouring churches and chapels. He posed the question:

What is the relation of Christianity to the German race? From the Church's point of view there is no objection whatever to racial research and race culture. Nor is there any objection to the endeavor to keep the national characteristics of a people as far as possible pure and unadulterated, and to foster their national spirit by emphasis upon the common ties of blood which unite them. From the Church's point of view we must make only three conditions: First, love of one's own race must not lead to the hatred of other nations. Secondly, the individual must never consider

[33] Michael Cardinal von Faulhaber, *Judaism, Christianity and Germany,* English translation (New York, 1934), 35.
[34] *Ibid.,* 5, 8.

himself freed from the obligation of nourishing his own soul by
the persevering use of the means of grace which the Church
provides. The young man who is always hearing about the blessedness of his own race is apt too easily to conceive that he is no
longer bound by duties to God and his Church, duties of humility
and of chastity. Thirdly, race culture must not assume an attitude
of hostility to Christianity. What are we to say of the monstrous
contention that Christianity has corrupted the German race, that
Christianity—especially because it is burdened with Old Testament
ideas—is not adapted to the genius of the nation, and that therefore it is an obstacle in the way of national consciousness?

What is the relationship of Christianity to the German race?
Race and Christianity are not mutually opposed; they belong to
different orders. Race is of the natural order; Christianity is a
revealed religion and therefore of the supernatural order. Race
means union with the nation; Christianity means primarily union
with God. Race is nationally inclusive and exclusive; Christianity
is a world-wide message of salvation for all nations. The concepts
of revelation and redemption, of supernature and grace must not
be watered down. The fourth gospel makes a distinction between
those who are born of blood and those who are born of God—
(John, I, 13). Christ also clearly distinguished between what flesh
and blood had revealed and what was revealed by the Father in
Heaven—(Matt. XVI, 17, foll.). We are Christians not because
we are born of Christian parents; we are Christians because after
our birth we were reborn and made a new creature by baptism in
Christ (2 Cor. XV, 17).

No nation has ever insisted more on race and ties of blood than
did the Israelites of the Old Testament. But in the fulness of time
the dogma of race was eclipsed by the dogma of faith. Around
the cradle of Bethlehem there were Jews and pagans, shepherds
from the land of Judah and wise men from the East. In the kingdom of this Child, according to the words of his Apostle, "there
is no distinction of the Jew and the Greek, for the same is Lord
over all." (Rom. X, 12).

What is the relation of Christianity to the German race? The
Christian, so long as he observes these conditions, is not forbidden
to stand up for his race and for its rights. It is possible, therefore,
without divided allegiance, to be an upright German and at the
same time an upright Christian. Hence there is no need to turn

our backs upon Christianity and to set up a Nordic or Germanic religion, in order to profess our nationaliy. We must never forget that we are not redeemed with German blood. We are redeemed with the precious Blood of our crucified Lord. (I Peter, I, 9). There is no other name and no other blood under Heaven, in which we can be saved, but the name and the blood of Christ. [35]

Cardinal Faulhaber tried to give a temperate appreciation of the problem of national loyalty. In doing so he restated the classic Christian doctrine that one must render to Caesar the things which are Caesar's, but at the same time he asserted the primacy of the things which are God's. If excessive interest in one's own race leads to hatred of others, it is anathema. If racism leads one way from reliance on the need of grace for salvation, it is anathema. If racism sets blood as a condition for membership in the Church, it is anathema.

In all this the Archbishop of Munich left little doubt. The only difficulty was the ever increasing monopoly of the word "German" by the Nazis. And however much the Cardinal along with other conservative Germans might deplore the transformation of their Germany, it was becoming increasingly difficult for an upright Christian to maintain that he was, at least in the Nazi sense, an upright German. The fight to retain one's sense of uprightness in both areas was one of the most impossible tasks required of any man. It is only to be marvelled at that people like Cardinal Faulhaber were able to maintain as even a sense of balance as they did. To a very large extent they were as public in their fight against the Nazis as they were only because they had a public document, namely the Concordat, to hold on to. The history of the violations of that agreement remain the focal point of the Church's opposition to the Nazis.

Looking back now to the years 1933-1939 it is clear that it

---

[35] *Ibid.*, 107-110. A few minor changes have been made in this translation based on a reading of the original text, "Christentum und Germanentum," (Munich, n.d.), 16-18.

was a vain hope that the Nazi government would adhere to a contract within the tradition of diplomatic exchange. But this was not a matter of simple perfidy; it was a master stroke of *Realpolitik*. For in the sixteenth article of the Concordat, the National Socialists had hamstrung the Catholic hierarchy, and with them the whole body of Catholic believers. By that article all the German bishops were required to take the following oath.

Before God and the Holy Gospel I swear and promise allegiance to the German Reich and to the province of (e.g. *Land Bayern*). . . , as becomes a bishop. I swear and promise to hold the constitutional government in esteem and to prevail upon my clergy to do the same. I recognize it as my duty to work in the exercise of my office for the public weal and the interest of the German State and ever to strive to ward off any harm that may threaten it. [36]

This oath, an act of grave significance for a Christian, was compensated for by the Nazis: immunity from harm and protection of existing institutions within the Church was guaranteed. By 1937, nonetheless, it was abundantly clear that the Nazis had no intention of keeping their agreement. Perhaps the agreement ought to have been abrogated publicly. [37] Cardinal Faulhaber evaluated that possibility and his words bear re-reading. In a sermon given on Papal Sunday (mid-February, 1937) he said in part:

How unfortunate it is that there even exists a positive and a

---

[36] Article XVI of the Concordat as translated in F. F. Schrader, *Church and State in Germany* (New York, 1933), 12.

[37] It should be noted, however, that this oath by the Bishops was an allegiance to the Reich, Province, and an oath to uphold the constitutional government. The Churchmen can hardly claim to have been placed in the extraordinary position in which the German officers and men of the Army found themselves after August 2, 1934. From that day on their oath read: "Ich schwöre bei Gott diesen heiligen Eid, dass ich dem Führer des deutschen Reiches und Volkes, Adolf Hitler, dem Oberbefehlshaber der Wehrmacht, unbedingten Gehorsam leisten und als tapferer Soldat bereit sein will, jederzeit mein Leben für diesen Eid einzusetzen." As quoted in Karl Ströllin, *Verräter oder Patrioten*, (Stuttgart, 1952), 21.

negative approach to the Concordat. Today the negative is much more evident. [38]

After a few remarks on how difficult the government was making the simple ministry of the Church—for example the Pastoral Letter of December, 1936 had been banned by the police—the Cardinal went on about the Concordat:

> I know that there will always be a great variety of opinions in this country—no one could ever say that the Germans are but a collection of tin soldiers. I know that there have always been points of tension. In the days of Joseph II of Austria, the state went so far as to decree the number of candles which might burn at any one time on the altar, and that one must have the state's approval before entering a religious order. I am quite aware that there are always difficulties in getting a concordat to work; indeed, all is not ideal even in Italy. And yet here in Germany we notice that there seems to exist only a negative approach to the Concordat. There are, in fact, even among the Church's friends those who add to this negative attitude. One can hear from the laity and perhaps even more often from members of the clergy: 'The Concordat will not be kept; it will continue to be broken; nothing is gained by our adhering to it. What cannot be adhered to is better set aside. We shall all be hanged with the Concordat; without the Concordat we will all be condemned to death as were the English Martyrs, and then hanged, drawn and quartered.' To these people we answer: As long as both parties do not agree to abolish the Concordat; as long as the German bishops continue to employ all means, both by letters and personal intervention to try and get matters straightened out, the clergy and the laity must suspend judgment in this matter. According to the Syllabus of Pius IX, a concordat between Church and state is much to be preferred to a separation of Church and state.... The Concordat is the only legal means we have today to deal with the government on Church affairs. You cannot expect the other side to keep faith if we sew mistrust. [39]

---

[38] *Papstpredigt*, February 14, 1937 (Munich, n.d.), 8.
[39] *Ibid.*, 8-12.

For our purpose here there are several things significant about this sermon. For one thing all of this was said at a time when the struggle between Church and state had long since started; nevertheless Cardinal Faulhaber kept his forces from becoming hysterical. He along with the other bishops took the grave responsibility for negotiation with the government; the lower clergy and the laity were enjoined to keep silence. It should be noticed also that the Cardinal recognized the doubts and hesitations about continuing the Concordat which existed among the clergy and the laity. They said, in effect: "Since we are going to be martyrs in any event, why not be called so?" Comparisons were made with the sufferings of the Church in England during the sixteenth century, reference being made, doubtless, to the fate of such heroes as Thomas More and John Fisher. Some of the lower clergy must have urged the leaders of the Church in Germany to follow that path. Cardinal Faulhaber did not choose to follow that path, but not from fear of martyrdom. Rather, one can say, that because he was convinced that legality and justice lay on the side of the Church, the Nazis sooner or later would come to their senses and right the wrongs already committed. In the course of the Church's struggle with the Nazis Cardinal Faulhaber's opposition to the National Socialist state was not less real because his actions were tempered by a combination of worldly wisdom with the virtue of prudence.

In the period from 1936 until the beginning of the war, the Church vigorously campaigned against the state's destruction of Catholic educational institutions. Although the sermons and pastoral letters were heard and read by millions of Catholics in Bavaria, the Nazis were none the less successful in their effort to remove Christian influence from the public school system. All this was done in open violation of the following articles of the Concordat:

Art. 21: Instruction in the Catholic religion at elementary, middle and higher schools is obligatory for Catholic pupils and will be given in accordance with the principles of the Church. Religion must be taught definitely in the spirit of Christian doctrine and moral law so as to develop a sense of patriotic, civic and social duty, as is the practice in the other branches of learning. The subject matter and text books for religious instruction will be selected in agreement with the Church authorities. To these authorities opportunities will be given by the school boards to ascertain whether pupils receive their religious instruction in accordance with the demands of the Church.

Art. 22: When Catholic teachers are to be employed for teaching religion, an understanding between bishop and the state government must precede. Teachers, who because of their doctrinal or moral conduct have been declared by the bishop to be unfit, shall not continue to be employed as teachers of religion as long as that obstacle remains.

Art. 23: Private Catholic schools are guaranteed their continuance and new schools of the same kind may be established. In all communities where parents demand it, Catholic public schools will be opened whenever the number of pupils warrant it.

Art. 24: In all Catholic elementary schools only teachers belonging to the Church and approved by the Catholic Church are to be employed.

Art. 25: Religious orders and congregations are entitled within the law to establish and carry on private schools. Such schools, in so far as they follow the curricula of the state schools, are to be accredited like them to the universities. For the employment of religious orders as teachers in elementary, middle and higher schools the same conditions apply as to other state teachers. [40]

In Bavaria, as in certain other areas of western civilization, Catholic sisters had been employed as teachers in state schools, especially in areas where the population was over ninety per cent Roman Catholic. To a Bavarian there was nothing unusual about this: Church and school had long since been identified in their efforts to civilize man in this world and prepare his soul for the next. In 1936, however, six hundred such nuns so employed

---

[40] F. F. Schrader, *op. cit.*, 13-14.

were dismissed; the remaining number of sisters would be replaced gradually during a three year period. [41] A pastoral letter was appointed to be read in all the churches of Bavaria on December 13, 1936. It sums up rather better than any other words can the attitude of the Church toward the state at that time. It follows in its entirety:

> To their beloved Clergy and Faithful the assembled Bishops of Bavaria send greetings and blessings. Dearly beloved. We wish to send out a common pastoral letter in order that we may strengthen you in your faith and in your loyalty to the holy Church.
>
> After the wretched fight against Christianity and the Church which was carried on by Marxists, Communists, Free Thinkers and Free Masons, we greeted with thanks the confession of National Socialism to positive Christianity. We are convinced that many hundreds of thousands still are loyal to this confession of faith and, indeed, observe with sorrow how others tend to remove themselves from the Christian belief and from the program of the *Führer*, and by this means put the Third Reich on a new basis, a *Weltanschauung* which stands in open contradiction to the commandments of Christianity. This constructing of National Socialism into a *Weltanschauung* which cuts it away from any foundation in religion, is developing more and more into a full scale attack on the Christian faith and the Catholic Church. All of this bodes ill for the future of our people and fatherland.
>
> Our *Führer* and Chancellor in a most impressive demonstration acknowledged the importance of the two Christian confessions for the state and to society, and he promised to the two confessions his protection. Unfortunately men with considerable influence and power are operating in direct opposition to these promises and both the confessions are being systematically attacked. Certain of those who lead the attack on the churches wish to promote a united church in which the confession of faith will become meaningless. Most especially they seek to rid Germany of the Catholic Church which they find to be a foreign body in the country and amongst the people. These people lack all real understanding of our holy faith and of the Christian religion in any form.

---

[41] Johann Neuhäusler, *op. cit.,* II, *Der Kirchliche Widerstand.* (Munich, 1946), 102.

In 1933 a Concordat was signed between the Holy Father and the German Reich. As it says in the preamble, this was done from a 'common desire to consolidate and enhance the friendly relations existing between the Holy See and the German state.' But instead of the much wished for friendship, there has developed an ever-growing struggle against the papacy, a struggle carried out in writings and speeches, in books and study courses, in organizations, schools and camps. A hate for 'Rome' has been engendered even in the ears of children. The attempt has been made to sever the bonds between the laity and the hierarchy in an effort to establish a free-from-Rome Church. To be a Catholic for these enemies of the Church means to be un-German. Loyal Catholics are under pressure from these people all the time now, treated as if they were foreigners in their own home, set aside as if they were diseased. But he who breaks with the Church, such a one is regarded by these men as trustworthy. Of late there has been an increase of those who declare themselves no longer members of the Church, especially members of the Party organizations, but also in the youth groups.

Catholic organizations and societies were promised the protection for continued existence under the Concordat. But instead of continued protection, the exact reverse has taken place until by gradual means the continuation of these organizations has been made impossible. As the north German bishops said in their Pastoral letter on November 15th: 'An unheard of conflict in conscience' has been forced on members of Catholic organizations together with economic pressure to force them to renounce membership. These pressures extend to members of purely Church organizations with religious purposes, and thus the attack is extended to within the Church itself, a new more hideous development. According to the Bavarian Concordat 'there were to be no special requirements of religious instructors in schools which would not apply equally to lay-instructors.' In spite of this contractual agreement, the nuns have been removed from the elementary schools. In spite of all our words and the wish of ninety per cent of the parents that the nuns be allowed to continue teaching, no attention was paid to us. On November 16th, the parents' wishes in this matter was no longer of any significance; the law was changed. Just before Christmas, in the middle of the school year, more than one-hundred nuns have had to give up their teaching activity without one word of explanation; they have been guilty of nothing. Now many of these nuns have neither roof nor bread. Amongst these are sisters who have served the community for twenty, thirty, some even more years. Working in those years for little pay, only what was necessary for their simple life, they are now charges of mercy and charity. Because the mother-house can take care of so few, they must find temporary asylum in the world. Anyone who will aid in this work receives our undying gratitude, just as we owe so much thanks to these dear sisters who have given their lives to this work, in charity and loyalty. We thank these sisters for their loyalty to their Order, in spite of offers from the authorities to leave religious life and live again in the world.

According to the Concordat, insults to the clergy were to be punished. But where is the *protection* against such insults which come in speeches, writings, broadsheets and pictures? Where is the state protection for the honor of clergy when it comes to cartoons and billboards which are set before the eyes of children even in the remotest villages? It is reported to us that an anti-clerical cartoon was exhibited in a class-room; when the parish priest urged the teacher to remove it, he refused.

When were pastoral letters mocked in journals as they are today? One blushes for shame to read pastoral letters described as 'scraps of filthy paper,' as 'frivolity' as 'meanness.' These can be found in the magazine of the *Hitler Jugend* for August 1936. In spite of the promise of protection under the Concordat, the bishops are openly ridiculed in these magazines.

According to the Bavarian Concordat, 'those who teach in Catholic elementary schools must be prepared and equipped to teach accurately the Catholic religion and to educate the children in the spirit of the Catholic faith.' Many Catholic teachers are doing this today and to them we send our warmest thanks for continuing in their duty to the Church. But there are those who instruct in an un-Christian spirit, who are giving the class in Bible history. The children are receiving false instruction. This anti-Church position is accentuated by means of pictures and cartoons in an attempt to destroy the foundations of the Christian religion. This is having untold effect on the children. They hear anecdotes, tales and short-stories all aimed at destroying the Bible. In one periodical it says: 'All observation, no matter how insignificant, concerning Catholic action, must be reported to the Youth

Leader at once.' Does this not mean a breaking down of all authority? Does this not mean that children are being educated in the spirit of faithlessness and characterlessness? Does this not mean division in the family? Whilst the *Führer* with this view toward world problems has called up all forces to fight political and economic Bolshevism, there are forces at work right here at home on the lowest level, which because of their religious fervour might be considered the best defense against Bolshevism; but instead the youth are being driven directly into the religion of Bolshevism. The north German bishops complain in their pastoral letter, that parents have come to them in sorrow 'describing in heart-rending phrases how the belief of the parents is mocked, and how the children are turned from Jesus Christ and His church; and how by this means relations between home and Church are cut off.' Can this destructive work continue without the most deplorable and frightful results?

It is often pointed out that Catholic Spain fell victim to Bolshevism in spite of the faith. But something is overlooked: for twenty-five years there was no religious instruction in the schools, and thus more than two-thirds of the Spanish youth grew up without religious instructions. Thus were they made ripe for Bolshevism.

It is said that all over the world the Church is losing its power over souls. To this we answer with the words of Our Holy Father when he addressed some Spanish refugees on September 14th. 'What shall the Catholic Church do if her charitable influence on family, youth, and society is fought at every turn? What can the Catholic Church do when at every turn her press is hindered or destroyed, and in these same lands all freedom is allowed to the anti-Christian press which furthers new religions? What can the Church do when at every turn her influence on the youth is prevented and the religious duties are not fulfilled?'

Nothing could be further from our intentions than to present an inimical attitude toward, or a renunciation of the present form which our government has taken. For us the respect for authority, the love of Fatherland, the fulfilling of our duty to the state are matters not only of conscience but of divine ordinance. To this command we will always require our faithful to follow. But we will never regard it as a refraction of this duty when we are defending God's laws, His Church, or when we defend ourselves against attacks on the Faith and the Church. The *Führer* can be certain that we Bishops are prepared to give all moral support to his historic struggle against Bolshevism. We will not criticize things which are purely political. What we do ask is that our holy Church be permitted to enjoy her God-given rights and her freedom.

Dearly beloved, Christmas is once more upon us. We encourage you as follows: celebrate this holy feast as a feast worthy of our faith, love and peace. Celebrate it as a feast of faith in the sense of the fundamental truths and mysteries of Christianity, the incarnation of the Son of God, our Redeemer, Jesus Christ. More and more do we confess after two thousand years: 'I believe in Jesus Christ, the only begotten Son of God, Our Lord, conceived by the Holy Ghost, born of the Virgin Mary.' We wish to celebrate Christmas as a festival of Love in the spirit of those words of the Apostles: 'God so loved the world that He gave His only begotten Son; that all who would believe in Him, would have life everlasting.' (John 3, 16). And think also of the command of Our Lord: 'A new commandment have I given unto you, that you will love others as I have loved you.' (John 13, 34).

We want to celebrate Christmas as a festival of Peace, singing with the angels: 'Glory to God in the highest; Peace on earth to men of good-will.' We long for peace for ourselves, for our families, for our people and Fatherland. 'If it be possible, as much as lieth in you, live peaceably with all men.' (Rom: 12, 18). We must never set aside the ideal of peace. We wish all our brothers and sisters, our enemies, the hand of peace. We close with the wish of the Apostle: "the God of peace be with you all, Amen.' (Rom: 15, 33). [42]

No reader of this document can fail to sense the impact of the sentence: "Nothing could be further from our intentions than to present an inimical attitude toward or a renunciation of the present form which our government has taken." It is perhaps not too much to say, as one critic of the Church's attitude toward National Socialism suggests, that partly because the Church failed

---

[42] *Hirtenwort der bayerischen Bischöfe vom 1. Adventsonntag, 1936.* reprinted in Konrad Hofmann, *Zeugnis und Kampf des Deutschen Episkopats* (Freiburg im Breisgau, 1946), 52-57.

to appreciate fully the totalitarian form of government she lost nearly all her struggles with the state. [43]

If the Bishops of Bavaria found the removal of nuns from the public schools a bold act, what must they have thought two years later when they were ordered to close all Catholic schools? In Bavaria in 1938 there were eighty-two schools owned and operated by societies within the Church. Their enrollment was something above fifteen thousand students. The Nazis ordered forty-one of the schools to close down completely by the end of the term in 1938; the other forty-one were permitted to continue functioning until all the students were graduated out, but they could admit no new students. If ever the Church had an opportunity to rouse up the faithful it ought to have been on such an issue as the forced closing of Catholic schools. In accordance with the general policy as outlined by Cardinal Faulhaber when he spoke on his attitude toward the Concordat, he took it upon himself to write the single protest to the Bavarian Minister of Education. The letter did not suggest that the order would not be carried out; instead the Archbishop compared the situation to one experienced in countries controlled by Bolshevists, Marxists and Freemasons. [44] He also warned the Minister that "this action will be regarded both by the conscience of today and the future as nothing but a flagrant example of your fight against the Church and as a document of unmitigated dictatorship." [45]

The reader may well wonder if there were any manifestations of such sentiments as Cardinal Faulhaber described in the Bavaria of the late thirties. When the sisters were forced out of the public

---

[43] Mother Mary Alice Gallin, *op. cit.*, 200.

[44] A letter signed by Cardinal Faulhaber from the Bavarian Bishops Conference to the Bavarian State Ministry of Education and Religion, dated January 25, 1938, now located in Father Natterer's files of the *Klerusverband* in Starnberg, Bavaria, (15 pp. typescript), 12.

[45] *Ibid.*, 13.

schools two years earlier, the *Stützpunktleiter* of Schwanenkirchen sent the following report to the *Kreisleiter* of Deggendorf.

The pastoral letter of June 28, 1936 was read on that Sunday in the local parish church. The order of the government in connection with the removal of monastic teachers has been regarded by nearly all the population as unjust and, indeed, as a direct attack on religion; it has caused no end of disturbance even amongst Party members. This order has caused special hardship in this area because there is a monastic school here which has existed from time immemorial and whose teachers have always been diligent and effective with youngsters. The nuns have done much extra-curricular work with the children, teaching them to work with their hands, etc. No other girl's school in the area can boast of such success. The population feels that if lay-teachers were to come in, they would not take the time and interest which the sisters have taken with the children. The population cannot understand the necessity of this new order, especially when the monastic school has been of such value to all classes and elements of society. Then there is the problem: where will the nuns go when they are dismissed. The population is enraged by all of this and not a little is aimed at the Party. Even some Party-members have indicated to me their attitude quite openly. I must report that this proclamation is not at all appreciated by the population here; they are nearly one hundred percent against it; and, further the Party has lost stature by putting it into force.

As head of the *Stützpunkt* of the National Socialist Party I have been asked to bring this matter to the attention of the *Kreisleiter* by both Party members and non-Party people alike, that you might indicate how the population here has reacted to this new proclamation relating to the removal of the religious from the schools. Also no end of difficulties will arise for the construction of new buildings in communities where up till now only the monastic school has existed. [46]

It is very difficult to say what might have been the results had the Church urged the faithful to defend the Catholic school system more actively. But it is not beyond our capacity to appre-

---

[46] Johann Neuhäusler, *op. cit.*, 102.

ciate the struggle in conscience which must have gone on in the minds of loyal Bavarian Catholics, particularly those who also had Party membership. As far as the public record in defense of Catholic education in Bavaria went it is quite lamentable. In 1933, eighty-nine per cent of the population voted for the continuance of the Catholic school system; in 1935 the number fell to sixty-six per cent; in 1936 there were thirty-five per cent who still favored it; by 1937 there were only four per cent, that is, four per cent in a Nazi plebiscite. [47] It is useless to try to get any reliable interpretation of the state of mind of German Catholics from such figures; yet they appear to be devastatingly eloquent, demonstrating the incredible success of National Socialism.

So ended the Church's fight to maintain its own school system. And at the very same time that the struggle over education was in progress, a systematic campaign was undertaken by the government to destroy all youth organizations other than the *Hitler Jugend*.

It need hardly be said that the Concordat had guaranteed immunity to all Catholic organizations dedicated to religious, cultural and charitable ends. Article thirty-one of the Concordat goes on to say:

> Those dedicated also to kindred aims, social or professional, or pertaining in part to some organization of the state, shall enjoy the same protection, providing always that they pursue their aims outside of any political party. The German episcopate together with the government of the Reich will decide which organizations and associations belong to this category. When the Reich or State take direct concern in activities of sport or youth organizations, care will be taken that their members can attend divine service on Sundays and holy days and that they are not obliged to do things which are not in line with their religious convictions and duties. [48]

That this article was violated over and over again by the Nazi

---

[47] Figures quoted in Robert D'Harcourt, *op. cit.*, 242.
[48] Frederick Franklin Schrader, *op. cit.*, 15.

government we know from the standard works on the persecution of the Church in Germany in this period. [49] For our
purpose let it suffice to mention that on January 20, 1938, the
Catholic Young Men's Association, the Catholic Young Ladies'
Association, and the Fraternity called *Neudeutschland* were dissolved by governmental fiat. [50] Again the Bavarian bishops met
and issued the following pastoral letter. It was read in all the
churches of Bavaria on February 6, 1938, and is reproduced
here in its entirety.

> Dearly Beloved: The Catholic Young Men's Association and all
> of its affiliated societies, the Young Ladies' Sodality and the
> fraternity, *Neudeutschland,* have been dissolved by order of the
> Secret Police as of January 20, 1938; any further activity on their
> part is forbidden; their property has been confiscated. Many of
> you are witnesses in your own parishes as to the manner in which
> all of this has been done. Here and there they have actually taken
> away the blessed troop banners which happened by chance not to
> be in the church. They did not respect even missals and hymnals,
> religious pictures—all of which were confiscated. Sorrow and
> sadness mingled with righteous indignation has filled the com-
> munity which regards the Church and the state as equally important
> for the common welfare.
>
> We Bishops have registered our complaint against the action of
> the *Gestapo* to the responsible authority; we have asked that the
> order of dissolution be rescinded. Now, publicly we make solemn
> protest against this action by the police which has so deeply
> wronged the Church in her rights and duties.
>
> The *Gestapo* justifies its action on the basis of the President's
> order of February 28, 1933, the introduction to which reads as
> follows: 'For the defense against Communists and other bodies
> dangerous to the state.' We take exception to those who would try
> to link our activity with that of the Communists; we are not Com-
> munists, but Christians; we do not harm the state but support it;
> we are not seeking a forceful overthrow of the government, but

---

[49] *Persecution of the Catholic Church in Germany,* 82-108; Johann Neuhäusler, *op. cit.,* I, 165-168.
[50] Robert D'Harcourt, *op. cit.,* 164.

rather do we acknowledge the existing authority. Thousands of you, beloved young people, know from your own experience how before the Third Reich came into existence, you used to battle with the Communists intellectually in offices and in your workplaces, and how you were strengthened in your struggle by coming together at your meetings always in the forefront battling Communist propaganda. Thus we Bishops find the dissolution on this basis as bitterly unjust. We Bishops have never at any time noticed the slightest trace of Communist influence on our youth.

Whoever would seek to defend society against Communist influence must not destroy the Catholic youth organizations; they must rather seek their perpetuation and do everything to protect them. This was recognized by the state authority when only a few months after the above mentioned order of the President a Concordat was signed with the Holy See, guaranteeing the protection of Catholic youth organizations. Thus we take exception of their dissolution because it violates the Concordat.

Our Catholic Young Men's Organization and the Young Ladies' sodality have been true to their principles and sought to labor for the well-being of the country; just as many of you will remember who took part in those celebrations on May 1, 1933. Soon, however, the fight against the Church and her asociations commenced. First, double-membership was prohibited. Then came the decree concerning the secularization of public life; and after that the restriction of the Catholic associations to the church and places immediately adjacent to the church, as well as the prohibition of any but purely religious activity. Because all of this was not enough to destroy the Association, the police order has been invoked.

The accusations which have been used to justify this act you have read in the newspapers. We have made public to the proper authorities our objections.

Article 31 of the Concordat acknowledges that Church associations are subordinate only to ecclesiastical authority. Therefore, by virtue of our full spiritual authority and by virtue of the rights acknowledged in the Concordat, we Bishops declare: The Young Ladies' Sodality as far as church functions are concerned is neither dissolved nor forbidden. Ecclesiastically they continue in their full existence with all ecclesiastical rights, and with the favors and indulgences granted to them by Holy Church—a thing which no power on earth can take away.

Catholic Youth! In spite of all your sorrow, one thing you may be proud of: you have been true in your holy fight unto the end; you have weakened only before force.

Looking back you may thank God for the good religious habits formed in those days when you were together; for the building of good character; for the leadership in the fight for your belief; for all of your comradeship; those are spiritual rewards which will endure. You must keep them alive. Your thanks to God ought to be evidenced in your continued loyalty to Christ and in your religious convictions. We thank God with you for your Christian fortitude which comes with His grace. We thank you for all your suffering and endurance of disabilities which you have borne because of your membership in these organizations. We thank in particular those who have served in leading capacities.

That which was such a treasure and so highly prized—your flags and banners—has been taken from you by a greater force. But that which is more holy and more precious, Christ and His Church, no force can take from you. So long as the order of dissolution is not rescinded, remain true to your principles and set aside any thought of underground activity. We know that you have learned discipline. No matter how painful all of this must seem, we are fighting a battle for Christ and the Church; we use only spiritual weapons.

Therefore do we enjoin upon you: be disposed as is becoming to a Christian. Pray, attend Mass and receive the holy sacraments often. Attend the liturgy as before in your parish. Give good example to all. Strengthen your belief by active participation in days of meditation, spiritual exercises and common youth festivals. You will still receive various youth periodicals through the mails or from your parish.

We Bishops assure you that your sorrow is our sorrow. You have by baptism and confirmation become a part of the Church—bound to Christ; you will not break your confirmation oath.

With special apostolic love do we bless you all and your parents in the Name of the Father, and of the Son, and of the Holy Ghost.

(Signed) The Bishops of the Bavarian Dioceses
The Archbishop of Munich-Freising,
Michael Cardinal Faulhaber [51]

---

[51] *Hirtenbrief,* Michael Cardinal Faulhaber responsible for publication

Clearly the bishops accepted defeat. What is more they enjoined the youth to "set aside any thought of underground activity . . . ." to "be disposed as is becoming to a Christian." Yet we may wonder why the bishops should insist that although the Young Men's Association was dissolved until the order was rescinded, the Young Ladies' Sodality continued to function. Undoubtedly the Young Ladies met only for church services and their presence at Mass in a body could hardly be challenged; whereas the Young Men met socially and in quarters separate from the church proper. Still the whole affair is an unfortunate example of a far too indulgent reception of state interference in her life by the Church.

In connection with these failures of the Church in her fight to maintain her organizations intact in a totalitarian society, it is interesting to see what someone like Cardinal Faulhaber had to say on "euthanasia," a practice the Nazis accelerated during the war. Fulfilling his office as guardian of public morality he wrote the following letter to the German Minister of Justice.

Munich, November 6, 1940

To the German Minister of Justice, Dr. Guertner.

In spite of all efforts to keep the public in the dark with regard to the condition of patients in the so-called sanatoriums; in spite of all refusals to relatives for permission to visit their sick; in spite of the vagueness of the reports dealing with these sick persons, the general public is now well aware that patients are transported in groups by omnibus to larger centers at Grafeneck in Württemberg, or Hartheim near Linz, or to Sonnenstein in Thuringia. After about eight days at one of these places the relatives

---

Signed by Michael Cardinal-Archbishop of Munich; Jacobus, Archbishop of Bamberg; Ludwig, Bishop of Speyer; Matthias, Bishop of Würzburg; Michael, Bishop of Regensburg; Josef, Bishop of Augsburg; Michael, Bishop of Eichstätt; Simon, Bishop of Passau. December 13, 1938. Copy in Father Natterer's file of the *Klerusverband,* Starnberg, Bavaria.

are suddenly informed that the patient is dead. At the same time they are informed that 'because of police regulations,' or 'because of sanitary regulations' the body was cremated. In their sorrow these poor souls turn to the Church asking what can be done about Christian burial. Naturally, the German Bishops, in spite of Church regulations, permit Christian burial because this action has been taken without the permission of those concerned. Our people urge us to do what we can to change this unfortunate development of official removal of the sick members of society.

In Article 16 of the Concordat the German Bishops promise to do what they can to protect the moral interests of the German people and to prevent injury to the governmental structure. The Archbishop of Munich reacts to all of this not only as a violation of the Concordat, not only as a violation of divine law, no only because the people demand ever more loudly that something be done about this; but also because he expects that the Justice Department ought to do something to halt this practice of euthanasia which is going on in public clinics.

You are well acquainted with the viewpoint of the Catholic Church in this matter of euthanasia; the German bishops sent you a letter in 1934 setting forth our views on a new scheme to remove the useless from this life. Euthanasia was declared incompatible with Christian moral teaching. As we wrote then: 'The same holds true for the killing of those who are mentally incurable.' We enlarged the point in the same year, 1934, in a paper sent on to the criminal law commission. In 1936 the second edition of your own *Das kommende Strafrecht* appeared (*Verlag* Franz Vahlen, Berlin) and on page 375 you quoted the following from Dr. Graf von Gleispuck:

'Permission to destroy the so-called useless members of society is not tolerated. The chief issue concerns the mentally ill or the idiotic. The National Socialist state seeks by means of strict regulation to limit and curtail the possibility of producing more of these unfortunate persons in society. But the force of the moral law not to kill cannot be weakened here simply to attain the immediate goal of removing persons who are bound to the body social by their past or outward offences only.'

Accordingly the German episcopate hoped that a binding legal principle would forbid any further destruction of these unfortunates. All these hopes have been dashed in the last four months.

The presiding Bishop of the Fulda Conference, His Eminence Cardinal Bertram of Breslau, has been forced to lift his voice in disapproval and in warning to Dr. Lammers in a letter dated August 11, 1940. I take it that the substance of that letter is known to the Minister of Justice.

The natural law—Thou shalt not kill—has been taken over into Christian moral teaching. Only God determines the hour of man's end. Suicide and willful murder are both criminal in the sight of God.

Natural and Christian moral teaching give the state the right to defend itself with arms. The state also has the right to take life when crime is involved, that is when gravity warrants it. But Christian teaching forbids any such ideas as euthanasia for economic purposes. Even should such a law as euthanasia be enacted by the state, it would still contradict Christian moral teaching and would therefore be invalid.

According to the Christian view of life, the sick and the suffering have a place in this world along with the military and the materially productive. One must rely upon divine providence in all these things. The sick must not be judged simply according to their economic usefulness. Any number of examples can be suggested of most useful members of society who daily stand in danger of a nervous breakdown because of the intensity of their mental efforts.

The civilized state—even if it is not a welfare state—has its origins in Christianity and thus will aid the sick in a generous manner. This very tradition has educated doctors, built hospitals, and encouraged the care of the sick. It would be a serious contradiction to our past should we permit the state today to do away with the mentally ill only because of the number of nurses it takes to care for these people or because hospital space is needed for others. We cannot believe that men of the medical profession whose sole purpose it is to cure and save lives could so pervert their aims so as to permit the destruction of the sick. Nor can we believe that those whose business it is to see that justice is administered would permit such action and call it just.

The victims of euthanasia are not criminals; they are the sick. Mental illnesses can come from excesses in alcohol or from sexual aberrations. But in most cases the rule is that neither he nor his parents have sinned. Nor is he always a complete idiot. Sometimes,

as in the case of epileptics, work can be found in the garden or
in the fields or at the work-bench. Nor is it just a matter of those
persons in public institutions. Gradually persons who are patients
in purely charitable institutions are forced to be turned over to
the state and are sent on then to death.

My dear Minister of Justice! I am not going to roll out the old
question of whether the state is the only source of justice; nor am
I going to debate the question of whether 'right is what is useful
to society.' I feel myself bound to say that it is not going to be
useful to our society if people are not going to be able to trust the
words of the officials. This opinion is spreading today because
of the very problem we have treated here. No person is going to
believe that the corpse had to be cremated for sanitary reasons or
out of fear of infection. This will never stand the test of proof,
the thing we expect in a lawful society.

It will not be of use to our people when they learn how little
individual life is valued, when the very right to live has been so
shaken to its roots. There will always be false individuals who
speak of an 'alleviation' of all pain for the incurably sick. But such
people are reduced to silence at once if you remind them that in a
moment they too might come into a similar circumstance, even
though they appear to be in the best of health. One has only to
recall the name of Nietzsche, that man who wished to remove all
pity and love for the sick, to remember that he himself was the
beneficiary of such tender care in the last days of his mental
illness. The same Nietzsche it was who made such slurring remarks
about the Germans ought never to be a guide to us today. What
will happen to the morals amongst the people if the one person
whose task is the care of the sick is so to be degraded? Or what
will happen if such crass materialism is allowed to triumph which
would permit nurses to declare one person ready for destruction
in order to make room for the next?

It will not be to the advantage of our people if they lose all
trust in their doctors or in hospitals because of this prevalent attitude toward the so-called incurables. Patients are delivered to the
respective institutions in good faith; the state or charitable institutions take these patients in good faith. Yet no one can deny
that unrest is prevalent in our country because of the mass-deaths
of the mentally ill. Rumors spread telling the number, the manner
of death, etc. The whole business of secrecy attached to these ope-

rations—the patients are taken away at night in buses with closed curtains and are not permitted visitors—all of this, does not encourage keeping rumors down. Panic is already observable in old people's homes and sanatoriums for the tubercular.

I need hardly assure you, Dr. Guertner, that what I have written above has not been done in a spirit of contrariness. I have raised my voice in this moral and non-political question because as a Catholic Bishop I cannot permit myself to remain silent in a matter which concerns public morality. I have done so because I am bound by my oath in Article 16 of the Concordat to protect our nation from any sinking of its standards of culture. We appreciate that in wartime extraordinary measures must be taken to protect our country and to insure the proper freedom of our nation. We instruct our people that in wartime great sacrifices must be made in true Christian spirit and we note with respect those who can be seen on our streets wearing the black veil of mourning. Yet the unchangeable principles of the moral order and the principle of justice cannot be set aside in wartime.

I ask that the Minister of Justice reply to the above remarks, if he has not already answered the letter of the Bishops' conference sent earlier.

Cardinal Faulhaber
Archbishop of Munich. [52]

The letter stands as eloquent testimony of Cardinal Faulhaber's opposition to one of the accepted policies of the Nazi regime. [53] For better or worse his appeal is clearly that of a reasonable man presenting his arguments to one whom he considers as rational and as objective as he was himself. Only by inference does the

[52] Cardinal Faulhaber, letter, November 6, 1940, to *Reichsjustizminister,* Dr. Guertner. A copy exists in Father Natterer's files at the *Klerusverband,* Starnberg, Bavaria.

[53] This is not the only expression of the Church's opposition to this Nazi policy of euthanasia. Cardinal Faulhaber discussed the problem openly in one of his Pastoral Letters in 1934. The careful student of Catholic opposition to National Socialism may find it instructive to compare the writings of different German bishops on this subject thereby gaining a greater insight into the quality of opposition as it manifested itself in the different dioceses of Germany. Cf. Neuhäusler, op. cit., I, 363-365.

Archbishop question the omnipotence of the state. The letter remained unanswered, needless to say.

Such was the quality, in general, of the Church's opposition to the National Socialists, particularly evident in those instances where the Church suffered defeat in its struggle with the Nazis: the schools, the youth associations and the moral question of euthanasia. Had the Church required all Catholics to abjure in their loyalty to the civil authority we cannot say what the outcome may have been. It is interesting, nonetheless, that such a mediaeval tactic does not seem to have appealed to the Church in the twentieth century. Perhaps there existed reasons which explain this, reasons which sprang from the unfortunate condition of nationalism.

The Catholic Church in the modern national state is in a most ambiguous, not to say precarious position. Almost all the European nations have tried to dominate her and have very often succeeded in doing so. In Germany the ending of the *Kulturkampf* meant, ostensibly, that a good Catholic could be a good Prussian; and the Catholics, in general, fell in with this, believing that the German state was what it claimed to be: a *Rechtsstaat*. Cardinal Faulhaber went right on believing this theory to the very end of the Nazi regime. What seems hardest of all to understand about the position of the bishops in Bavaria was their apparent refusal to denounce Nazi tyranny as a contradiction of the concept of the *Rechtsstaat*. Again, one must never underestimate the intensity of German nationalism, particularly under the Nazis who played upon every natural and unnatural slight which Germany had ever experienced. For whatever it was worth to them, Catholics valiantly maintained their loyalty to their fatherland; and they did so in the face of such ignominious treatment. How patient and long-suffering must the Cardinal Archbishop of Munich have been when, for example, carrying the Sacred Host in procession through the streets of Munich a voice cried out from a balcony: *"Landesverräter."* [54] (Traitor.)

But there were two areas of conflict between the Church and the Nazis in which the Church won more than partial victories: the scandals of the morality trials and the attempt of the Nazis to undermine the loyalty of the lower clergy to the hierarchy.

d) THE CLERGY DEFENDED

In the summer of 1935 in the Nazi press and over the radio, the German people were acquainted with information which purported to expose scandals in Catholic religious communities. The Nazis claimed that these institutions were breeding-grounds for gross and unnatural vice. In December, 1936 the Bavarian Miniser of Education withdrew the teaching licenses from the Marist Brothers, the Brothers of the Christian Schools and the Augustinian Fathers. The involved and complicated history of these charges does not concern us here. Those tendentious reports are clarified in detail in the standard works on the persecution of the Church in Germany. [55] What does concern us, however, is what the Church did to inform Germans about the fallacious character of these reports. How did the Church answer these savage attacks?

The world had news of these events through *Osservatore Romano,* which, on June 9, 1937 published some statistics relating to these trials. Of the twenty-one thousand four-hundred and sixty-nine diocesan priests, forty-nine had been involved in litigation, of which number twenty-nine had been convicted. Of the four-thousand one hundred and seventy-four members of religious orders, (Jesuits, Benedictines, Franciscans) nine had been tried and only one had been convicted. [56] In all Bavaria

[54] Neuhäusler, *op. cit.,* I, 306.
[55] *Ibid., 122* ff.
[56] *Persecution of the Catholic Church in Germany,* 306.

there were three convictions of thirteen priests involved in these charges. [57]

Yet the Church suffered merely by the accusations. Given the nature of the offense and the tendency to depend upon gossip for evidence, the good name of the Church was inevitably dragged into the mud. And to such accusations there is rarely an adequate defense, the charge having such monstrous proportions.

But there soon appeared one who was ready to stand up and defend the Church. In a celebrated broadsheet which gained circulation far beyond the Bavarian borders, Father Joseph Lechner, a professor at the diocesan seminary at Eichstätt answered those charges. The broadsheet took its name from Joseph Goebbels, the *Goebbelsbrief,* because it was an answer to a public attack on the Church which he made on May 28, 1937. [58] It follows here in its entirety:

> In a meeting at Chicago of five hundred members of the clergy, His Eminence George Cardinal Mundelein, that well-known benefactor of Germany during the time of her post-war troubles, spoke out about German justice in the morality trials. In the Cardinal's words you were able to find your long-awaited opportunity to give your own evaluation of these mock trials, a thing you were able to do before a well-picked audience of Party-people on May 28, 1937 at the *Deutschlandhalle.* It might be added here that these trials although held in German courts followed the Russian model of justice.
>
> Indeed, you did not once muster courage honestly and truthfully to tell your uncritical public then any more than you did your equally uncritical German press what Cardinal Mundelein really said. Nevertheless you need not worry that anyone in Germany could possibly embarrass you with questions concerning the content of his speech. You possess the power. To be sure the possession of power did not save your regime from the incredible rebuff which it received when it tried to protest to the Holy See.

---

[57] Johann Neuhäusler, *op. cit.,* II, 116.
[58] Alois Natterer, *op. cit.,* 260.

If your assertions are true — and we will assume for the moment, at least, that they are—Cardinal Mundelein made the accusation that in Germany law and justice are used for selfish ends. You imagine that you have refuted this accusation by your speech. A close examination of your very speech shows to any thinking person that the accusation brought against the 'brown regime' is in every way justified.

It is the custom in a *Rechtsstaat* for crimes to be punished as soon as they are discovered. In Germany, just as in Russia, by the the way, it is not so; the criminal is left alone or kept in private custody. In other words, real or supposed crimes are 'put on ice' in order to be able, on a suitable occasion, to 'take them off,' arrange them in groups, and make them useful to the ends of propaganda for the Party.

What better timing for a criminal suit against Catholic priests and religious than the publication of the Papal Encyclical of March 21, 1937? Or do you really think that you can convince the world that it was only a coincidence that the publication of the trials began immediately after the reading of the Papal Encyclical? No, Mr. Goebbels! We Germans may be possessed just as Mr. Hitler said of 'rock-bound stupidity' (A. Hitler, *"Mein Kampf"*, *Volksausgabe,* S. 412); but in spite of our willingness to give him 'four years,' we are not so stultified as not to notice that legal proceedings are being used for state propaganda. Fortunately the execution of such trials are left to officials of justice.

2. According to your own unfortunate statement, the material for these trials is gone over professionally in the Propaganda Ministry. Is it not a scandal that the line between the Propaganda Ministry and the administration of justice should be eradicated? In other words in Germany the Ministry of Justice worked on foreign territory. Then you dare to assert that it is slander when you are reproached with the fact that in Germany justice and law are misused for selfish, which is to say Party purposes. But you have done something even more incredible. You have threatened that if any more doubts are raised about the validity of these charges you will put persons of high position among the clergy under oath and make them answer questions concerning these charges in court. Mr. Goebbels; do you not see what your statement does for German justice? The situation is now such that the Minister of Propaganda

can at his own will commence legal proceedings within a legal apparatus made subservient to him.

3. You mentioned (to shed light on another remark) something about 'official documents.' What did you really mean by that? The prosecution documents, perhaps, which, as everyone in Germany knows, with the help of the Party and its minions were 'handed over' to the courts for this pupose? If so, then we will remind you what the court officials of the Supreme Court at Leipzig said on the occasion of those treason trials which were never completed back in 1933. It was announced somewhat hastily, we fear, in your own press that 'the material which was given to us by Party sources was either worthless or falsified.'

Or did you mean, perhaps, material of the sort with which you 'proved' that 'sadistic sex-murder at the monastery in Mange' in Belgium? However much they are like you, not even the Communist press presumed to attach the crime of a half-wit to the door of Belgian monks. Besides you have already had to retract this matter once, Mr. Goebbels. Of course, you have accomplished this task in a really characteristic fashion and warmed up some cold hash in addition.

Mr. Goebbels, on the one hand you have made the assertion that 'in Germany any number of religious have acted contrary to law and that untold numbers of these priests and monks are active in the confessional, where, with their pathological bent they ruin healthy people.' On the other hand, in the very same speech you discussed the 'innumerable letters' you have received, 'which give testimony of the regard for the sad condition of the Church.'

Mr. Goebbels: Which of your statements is fabrication: the first or the second? We will tell you: both! Neither have untold numbers of secular or regular clergy failed in their duties, nor have you received innumerable letters from thousands of clergymen. If you must lie, at least try to tell your lies within the realm of calculable probability.

Yet you don't stop at this. You dare to assert that the 'countless priests and monks' who have failed; that 'the thousands upon thousands of cases which have been brought to justice, represent but a fragment of the picture of almost total degradation.'

Mr. Goebbels, one scarcely knows whether to be more astonished at the gross clumsiness or the abysmal shamelessness with which you set up your degrading, slanderous assertions without a trace of proof. What is left of your thousands of decent religious? We challenge you: out with your documentary material. Set it before the world in huge folio volumes! The Propaganda Ministry has plenty of money from the pennies of the radio partisans who enjoy your speeches and radio bulletins every day.

You asserted — and this was your second point — that the bishops covered up for regular criminals. You know very well this is untrue. The bishops have only interfered to the extent that they have been involved with canon law: that's the point. They may have become aware of things by means of the Sacrament of Penance. That they may have allowed 'justice to be tempered by mercy' (*cum misericordia judicium* — C.I.C. 2214) which is in accordance with ecclesiastical tradition. The showy display on the part of your prosecuting attorneys was therefore rather uncalled for.

You recommended to the bishops that they emulate the edifying example of the Party in treating criminals in its own backyard. As you said 'the Party has set a plain and simple example. In 1934 over sixty persons who tried to breed this vice within the Party were unceremoniously shot. The Party enlightened the nation concerning this event with the full story.'

Mr. Goebbels: Few assertions in your speech will have caused more attention than this incautious reminder of the thirtieth of June, 1934. You are very much mistaken if you think that the 'justice' you practiced in 1934 and are, in fact, still practicing that that is regarded by anyone else as real justice. The regime continues to show its weakness. It does not have the courage to allow the accused to speak for themselves. With unauthorized shootings, justice is never served; only Party stench gets hushed up.

Further, may we jog your memory a bit? According to the speech which Mr. Hitler made in the *Reichstag* on July 13, 1934, two weeks after the purge, it was not sixty but rather seventy-one. Three of the sacrifices ended in 'suicide.' Among those are not included all the others, such as Beck, Edgar Jung, Dr. Gerlich, Dr. Klausener, Dr. von Kahr, Willi Schmid, etc. whom Goering had murdered.

And then you say you enlightened the people concerning the thirtieth of June? You are not so naïve as to think that Hitler's yarns are believed by anyone. You confirm now by your most recent statements that Röhm and his cohorts were not executed for high treason, but you do not prove that they were executed for homosexuality. Homosexuality only became a crime when Röhm and his cohorts became politically uncomfortable; people had to be filled with disgust for these criminals.

Listen to Mr. Hitler on Röhm: ' . . . I covered this man for years with my unswerving loyalty.' On New Year's, 1934, Mr. Hitler sent his intimate friend a handwritten letter. The simple truth is: Mr. Hitler, and with him the whole Party has been well aware of the obscenities of Röhm along with many other S.A. and S.S. leaders, and they have kept these facts secret for years.

There are other trivialities which you have kept secret: The *Vehmgericht* murder of Edmund Heines and the bestial murder of Party opponents, e.g. Potempa. We might add: The Party covers up completely all dirt in its ranks, as long as no unpleasantness comes of it.

You have had your own system of Party liability in force ever since December 1, 1933 and you take care of your own criminals at Party tribunals. You have the infamous expedient of getting rid of all your opponents in the interest of the safety of the state, all done quietly and without legal fuss.

Do you think that it has escaped the eyes of the sharpsighted that at the suggestion of Dr. Guertner the Federal Government has thrown out a 'law concerning the arrest of leaders of the National Socialist Party and its branches.' In this law it is decreed that sub-leaders of the Party and its affiliates need permission to become witnesses in circumstances where it might appear to be their duty to remain silent. The law goes on to explain that when the safety of the state is at stake, the permission must be withheld. And since the Party and the state are one, the safety of the Party is to be considered the safety of the state. What is that but incredible corruption of justice in favor of the Party?

Yes, Mr. Goebbels, it would not be to the Party's benefit if the people should ever gain an insight into all the Party dirt: the extortion of funds by Party members in Düsseldorf; the giant embezzlements in the winter-relief collections; the sexual excesses in country homes and *Hitler Jugend* camps; the bad camp morals; the B.D.M. girls made 'young mothers'; the luxury in villas, houses, autos, yachts of the leaders of the so-called 'workers' Party. Yes, Mr. Goebbels, to circulate such things among the people would scarcely benefit the Party. Thank God you are in the happy position of being able to hush these things up legally.

How much better, Mr. Goebbels, had you continued in that 'sphere of silence' which you praised in your speech.

Don't worry about the Church! The Catholic Church knows how to take care of any unworthy elements in her ranks; she will reform what wants reform. Worry about your Party! The corruption rules—as is apparent from your own remarks: corruption in principle; German justice is serving this corruption!

That is what has resulted from your speech. That is what all true Germans and true friends of Germany abroad are shocked at. Cardinal Mundelein of Chicago can be satisfied with you: you have given by your speech conclusive proof that the chief part of his complaint was justifed.

Michael Germanicus. [59]

The coupling "Michael Germanicus" was obviously a play on the patron saint of Germany: St. Michael. Those who read this long expose—according to one source thousands of copies were circulated throughout Bavaria and other parts of Germany— could not fail to grasp Father Lechner's very important statement that the Church would know what to do with any of her "unworthy elements." [60] Right in Father Lechner's own diocese, in the very year that the "Goebbels letter" was written, there was a very interesting example of exactly how successful the Church could be when she wished to discipline "unworthy elements" in her ranks.

Late in 1936, the parish priest of Hitzhofen, Father Anton Heuberger, wrote an open letter to the local *Kreisleiter*. It was published in Weimar under the title: "Open Letter of a Catholic Priest": "Can one be a good priest and at the same time a good National Socialist?" [61] The letter began with a description of sunset in a cemetery in Yugoslavia where Father Heuberger had gone to pray at the grave of his brother who was killed in action

---

[59] Johann Neuhäusler, *op. cit.,* II, 283-287.

[60] Alois Natterer, *op. cit.,* 260.

[61] Anton Heuberger, *Guter Priester und bzw. oder Guter Nationalsozialist* (Weimar, 1936).

there in the First World War. The letter was in the form of a
dialogue between the priest and his dead brother, to whom the
first sentences were directed.

> Dear brother, can I really be wrong in trying so hard all these
> years to be a good National Socialist and a good priest at the same
> time?... It is said that religion, Christianity itself, is in danger
> in our country today; that National Socialism is but a new pagan-
> ism, its gods, blood and earth; its idols, *Führer* and folk. The
> leaders of the new society are said to be anti-Christian, haters of
> the Church, and desirous of forming a church free from the direc-
> tion of Rome. You know all this from the letters of our Bishop.

Then Father Heuberger said that his brother, who stood before
him, began to smile gently and he replied:

> What is all this talk of religion in danger! It is always being in
> danger—ever since Christianity started; but now, alas, more from
> inside than from without. Is not the love of one's country and one's
> fellow countrymen a great part of religion and Christianity? ....
> Besides, no one is prevented from going to the sacrements ....
> No one is denied entrance to the church .... I need hardly say,
> dear brother, that a great deal of the ill-feeling need never have
> occurred had the leaders of the Church backed the [National
> Socialist] movement from the beginning .... By the words 'posi-
> tive Christianity' I mean more religion and less creed, more uniting
> and less dividing.

Troubled by the materialistic overtones of the doctrine of
Blut und Boden, Father Heuberger had his brother dismiss these
scruples with remarkable casuistry:

> Brother, you are a Catholic priest. Surely you realize better than
> some that God put no higher price on anything than that the
> blood of Christ, His Son, should be shed. Daily He reminds us
> of the secrets of the earth from whence we have sprung and to
> which we shall return.

The dialogue continued:

> But brother, we cannot go along with those who insult the
> Pope, attack priestly celibacy as immoral and seek to establish a
> national church free from Rome.

Why not? Didn't we front soldiers all fight together? Did we form a special regiment for theologians? Did we not all contribute to one another for the good of all?

Yes, dear brother, but that was war. In peace it is different.

Why so? You should take a command of Christ to go into the world and preach the Gospel to all men—not to rule them—but to teach them, and especially by your example. . . . The whole question of celibacy is raised not out of spite, but rather out of concern for the health of the nation. Not Christ but the Pope decreed that men should make this heroic effort of life-long celibacy; and only God knows, in the end, whether it will have been worth it all.

But what do you say to these attacks on our dear nuns who teach, and also the attempts to destroy our religious schools?

Yes, these dear souls do rend my heart. But do you think these attacks are really born of anti-Church sentiments? I think it has all come about by those who have forced a struggle in conscience on simple souls. . . . Is it really so bad when Catholics and Protestants go to the same school? Have they not the same blood, language, the same Father in Heaven, the same history on earth. . . . Listen to these last words of one who died fighting for his country, and I speak especially to the priests: Leave your martyr complexes behind—leave your desire for separate organizations—leave the Ghetto; join the popular front; join our new society, blessed by God, in true, honest, serving piety; believe unfeignedly in our divinely blessed *Führer* and in his movement. Then and only then will the doubters, the embittered, the erring return and find peace and be able to believe in you and in your message. [62]

What followed the publication of Father Heuberger's broadsheet is an excellent example of clerical discipline. But more important for our purposes, it gave the Bishop of Eichstätt, Michael Rackl, an opportunity to answer in full the statements and implications of Father Heuberger's broadsheet. In the *Pastoral Bulletin* for the diocese of Eichstätt the following letter appeared on February 9, 1937. It was the complete transcription of a letter from Bishop Rackl to Father Heuberger.

---

[62] *Ibid.*

It is with a heavy heart that I write to a priest of my own diocese, one who has been educated in our own house, ordained by ourself, and to whom this same priest has promised respect and obedience and who now has turned in open opposition to his Bishop, the entire episcopacy of Germany and against the Pope himself. How I should have loved to let the entire incident pass in silence! But you have not retracted your open letter of November 17, 1936 and have not hindered its further distribution, even though your Bishop has on two occasions publicly denounced the letter. Unrest amongst Catholics has grown because of this letter and others have fastened on to it as 'an official expression of a Catholic priest.' I have heard that in Beilngries, it has been spread from door to door. The Bishop is bound, therefore, to pronounce clearly and definitely in this matter. The laity has waited long enough. But as I have already said in another place, I did not wish to let this be done in the heat of the moment; rather due consideration should be taken and an objective presentation made.

In the first instance your publication is an act of disobedience against the authority of the Church. It is a matter for discipline. According to Can. 1386 of the *Codex Juris Canonici* you are not permitted to publish *sine consensu ordinarii,* a point to which you are bound, not only by your vows at ordination, but by the positive law of the Church, Can. 127 *speciali obligatione.* But especially in such an important instance, something which is today of the greatest moment, under no circumstances should you have set yourself up in opposition to the view of the pastoral letters of the German bishops. Where would we be if everyone did what he wanted? What do you suppose would happen to a local leader of the National Socialist Party if he set himself up in opposition to the Party in a manner comparable to your action? It is in such manner that schismatics have behaved and by such action they have rent Church unity and have brought about cleavage in discipline and belief.

Your open letter betrays most evidently an inner severance with the authority of Rome and the Holy Father. A newspaper which carries a line similar to the one you seem to hold—I refer to the *Romfreie Katholik,* periodical for the Catholic National Church Movement, E.V.—published in its issue of January 16, 1937 an article which begins as follows: 'Someone must finally speak out. A Roman Catholic priest discusses Christianity and National Socialism and tries to free himself, step by step, from simple matters of creed. Anton Heuberger is not afraid to go along with those who see the Pope for what he is; with those who question the morality of celibacy; with those who strive for a *Romfreie* National Church. To be sure it seems to him that a *Romfreie* National Church is not quite possible just now; he nonetheless recognizes the inevitability of this feeling amongst the people. And Father Heuberger sees that enforced celibacy does harm to the community and its development. He sees little to be gained "in enforced confessional schools." Indeed many roads lead to Rome; but just as many lead away! One must speak out at long last, says Father Heuberger. Well, what next?'

So much for quotes from the *Romfreier Katholik*. And now I ask myself also: What next? Do you not admit by your sentence: 'Someone must finally speak out!' you were bringing yourself into open conflict with the hierarchy? I can only say that a person who writes as you have written is no longer a Catholic in his heart. Now, can a priest who is no longer a Catholic in his heart, be permitted the cure of souls?

I should like to draw attention, now, to those passages in your letter which contradict the doctrine and teaching of the Church.

'More religion and less creed'—so begins one of the sentences which dominate your letter. By this we are given to understand that all which is specifically Catholic is a matter of secondary importance. Further, we might say, all that which is Christian is of secondary importance: the belief in the Holy Trinity, Father, Son, and Holy Ghost; the belief in Jesus Christ, the incarnate Son of the Father, our crucified Redeemer—is all of this merely peripheral? And what of the sign of the cross? What of the Holy Eucharist, the sacrifice of the Mass, confession, the intercession of the saints, Mariology, indulgences, and the like; can one simply set these aside? Can you not see that this will lead to an indifferentism of the worst sort? About all we could say is: 'Whether Jew, Christian or hottentot; we all believe in one God!' What think you of the absolute character of Christianity, and of the necessity of the Church for salvation? When, as you would have it, the state would decide who the better citizen is: he who is a believer in the Church or he who does not believe? And how can a Catholic priest advocate a school system which would remove the influence of religion in the interest of a unified society? Does this priest not know that a firm social foundation can only be found through the *una sancta catholica et apostolica ecclesia*. Recently it has come to my attention that in the new school system only a neutral prayer is possible, folding of hands having been done away with, as well as the sign of the cross which is now regarded as unworthy, apparently, of German youth! Now can a Catholic priest really believe that such a system will make for the *una Ecclesia*? Christianity must be set aside in such an arrangement. That the laity might be confused and perplexed by all of this we can understand; but that a member of the clergy who must teach and instruct his parish in matters which are the subject of bitter controversy and with which the Pastoral letters of last year have concerned themselves; that a priest could add to this confusion is most undesirable. I must say that I was really shocked by your letter of December 30th in which you said that if anything were not clear in your open letter, you would be glad to talk to me about it. You added then, 'in such delicate matters as these, in spite of my very best intentions, such difficulties might come up—especially in a letter written by a non-specialist [*Nichtfachmann*].' If you felt yourself not to be a specialist, why on earth did you feel called upon to write an open letter in the name of German Catholicism in direct opposition to the 'specialists?' Why didn't you go to see a 'specialist?' Why did you contact your Bishop only after your letter had already been published? Why did you publish another explanation on January 6th without your Bishop's permission? Why didn't you examine the problem a bit more carefully before presenting yourself as *Praeceptor Germaniae*? It occurs to me how little you understand Catholic theology, especially of the modern period. You deprecate theologians without knowing their work. Had you read, for example, my article in *Divus Thomas* on 'Märtyrdom' you would not have had occasion to put those words into your brother's mouth: 'Look, brother, how they speak of "martyrdom" and never recognize as martyrs those who offered their lives on the battlefield for the new Germany.' If only you would have studied the enormous literature on Dogma and practical life— again I have an article called 'Powers of Life in Dogma'—you would not have attacked the theologians with your remark: 'Don't be just a protector of dogma; be rather a living holder of dogma.' Had you but a superficial acquaintance with the problem of nature and grace you could not have said that the theologians are more

concerned with their personal creation rather than evidence which
God gives to us in his work in nature. And when you speak of
the fabrication of books, have you in mind, perhaps, Holy Scripture?

[The Bishop goes on to admonish the priest for his stand on
nature, informing him that the Church does take cognizance of
the beauty in nature. He then proceeds to the question of love of
fatherland, answering Heuberger's question: "Is the love of
fatherland and fellow countrymen not a large portion of religion?" The Bishop replied:]

Today that is hardly the question. We bishops have always
taught that; the question today is whether love of fatherland is to
be the sum and substance of religion not just a part, but the whole
of religion. Then again the question of the 'common good' as
opposed to the 'individual good.' The mediaeval theologians treated
that question quite adequately, speaking of *bonum commune*. Any
student of systematic-theology reading your open letter will ever
be reminded of the old adage: 'What is true is not new; and
what is new is not true.'

Amongst the laity your attitude toward celibacy of the clergy
has caused untold anxiety; it is thoroughly un-Catholic. You say:
'God did not choose, nor did His Son, but rather His Vicar on
earth, the Pope, decided that weak men should be shackled with
such a life-long prohibition. Only God knows whether over the
centuries this struggle against nature has brought more good than
otherwise.' . . . . No Catholic is duty-bound to take the vow of celibacy; no one is duty-bound to enter religious life. More often are
those who enter upon this life reminded that they are free to leave
before they take orders; indeed, they must all sign a statement
that no pressure has been exerted on them to enter this life.

One who accepts such life must vow himself to celibacy.

[There follow thirty lines of scriptural defense of the idea of
celibacy.]

Finally I must say something about the form of your letter, the
manner of its presentation, that is to say, that you should put
such words into the mouth of your dear, honorable brother—words

he never would have spoken, most certainly not from beyond the grave. I knew your brother well here in the seminary; I was his prefect. I can say with all sincerity that you have given a most unfortunate picture of your brother to the uninformed public. Worse, there are those who look upon this whole episode as a revelation from beyond by which means your words are sanctified and transcend human significance. It is this which makes the situation so dangerous.

My dear Father Heuberger! It is with a heavy heart that these words are written; and even heavier heart must now suggest the consequences. I do not damn you, nor am I permitted to. *Est qui judicat Dominus*! I will fulfill my office on the basis of the principle: *De internis non judicat praetor*. Therefore I limit myself to your open letter. I regret that our talk on the second of January could not take place; I was ill. However, your talk with the Vicar General and your own letter of January 6th convince me well enough. The whole case rests on your own statements in which you encourage the publication of your broadsheet in its entirety as a manifestation of your 'most sacred convictions.' The damage to the Church is great; the scandal is devastating. I should long since have invoked the punishment of suspension and removed you from office; but because of the nature of the times and of events I tried to be mild and long-suffering. I hope I shall be able to answer before God and my conscience when I temper justice with mercy and do not invoke the full statutory punishment. In order that you may depart from your parishoners without too much loss of honor, I extend to you the possibility of resigning your parish. If your resignation reaches me by this Saturday and you have departed from Hitzhofen by next week, I shall not demand further punishment in spite of the grave scandal which you have given. In the interest of the cure of souls and a peaceful relationship in Hitzhofen, I must ask you not to mention this subject again in any sermon in your parish. The entire incident, be advised, concerns itself with your open letter and not something which concerns your parishoners. The best arrangement in your parish from now on would be to give no more sermons. Whether and when you receive another parish depends on future developments. That you are bound in conscience *sub gravi* to make good the scandal you know from your catechism and moral theology. I hope you will send to me in the very near future a statement which I shall publish. As to an interview I am, as I am for any priest, even for you, always at your service.

Now I call to your memory the moment of your ordination when your Bishop asked: *'Promittis mihi et successoribus meis reverentiam et obaedientiam?'* You answered: *'Promitto!'* Set these words in action now that I may say to you: *Pax Domine sit semper tecum!* As I wrote in my statement of January 8th: 'All should know that the Bishop will ask according to the law in justice and righteousness, and also in a spirit of truth and charity.' I think I have kept my word. It is up to you to bow in humble obedience and as a priest to ask God's forgiveness. You wrote to me on December 30th that you wished to be a priest who was 'honest, open and upright as Christ had demanded of us.' What of humility and obedience; Christ spoke of these too? And it is written: 'He was obedient even unto death, unto death upon the cross.' 'Learn from me for I am meek and humble of heart.' *Humilis corde!*

Benedicat te omnipotens Deus, Pater et Filius et Spiritus Sanctus! Amen.

Michael, Bishop [63]

On January 31, 1937, the following letter was read publicly in all the churches of the diocese of Eichstätt:

By my open letter of November 17, 1936 I meant well both to my country and to my Church. It was my purpose to show that 'the best German was a church-going person and a believing Christian.'

However, after receiving his Excellency, the Bishop's letter, dated January 25, 1937, and after our three hour conversation, I have been convinced that my ways were wrong. There are in my letter many sentences which actually sound most un-Catholic and can be interpreted in a way which would contradict Catholic dogma and moral teaching. The objective meaning—*sensus objectivus*—bears witness against my orthodoxy. Therefore, I declare publicly, that I regret my publication and retract it. I withdraw my permission to circulate my letter of November 17, 1936. I wish to be completely with the Church and in agreement with her morals and

---

[63] *Pastoralblatt des Bistums Eichstätt*, 84 Jhg., Nr. 4, February 9, 1937, 26-32.

dogma; I accept, like a child, everything taught in the Apostles' Creed and whatever is given to us to believe by the Church, above all to the decisions and pronouncements of the Council of Trent, the Vatican Council, and of the *Codex Juris Canonici*. I regret deeply having caused any anxiety to Catholics. Whatever wrong I have done, I will try to make good. I give, therefore, his Excellency, the Bishop, permission to publish this letter. I myself will give it to the *Eichstätter Anzeiger* for publication. Most respectfully do I beg his Excellency, the Bishop, to permit me to remain in my parish, mainly because of my dear sister's poor health; a change at this time might endanger her life.

Written at Hitzhofen, January 31, 1937.

(signed) Heuberger, A., Parish Priest. [64]

It ought not to take much imagination to appreciate the impact of Father Heuberger's disciplining by the Bishop of Eichstätt: it was certainly a clear victory for the Church and her stand taken against certain Nazi ideas about religion. To be sure, Father Heuberger's attitude was scarcely typical of the clergy in Bavaria at the time. The vast majority of the clergy followed their bishops' advice and left to them the task of dealing with the civil authority whenever any problem arose. All the same there were priests who stood out from the others and championed the Church's part against the tyranny of Naziism. There were few who enjoyed greater renown for such behavior than the Jesuit priest, Father Rupert Mayer.

Father Mayer was born in Stuttgart on January 23, 1876, ordained a priest in 1899, and, in 1900, gained permission to enter the Jesuit order. During the First World War he served as an army chaplain on the eastern front where be suffered the loss of his left leg. After the war he became one of Munich's most celebrated street-preachers, most particularly famous for his battles with the Communists. In 1936 and 1937 he did not hesitate to attack in his sermons the National Socialists' policy toward

---

[64] *Ibid.*

Catholic schools, the so-called "morality trials," and their general attitude toward religion. [65] On March 29, 1937 in the convent church at Varsberg, he preached a sermon in which he admonished the faithful to adhere to the rightful authority. He phrased it quite bluntly when he said: "In all political, economic and social questions we will go along with our fellow citizens; but in religious matters we say to all others: keep your hands off!" [66] On may 2, 1937, speaking in St. Michael's Church in Munich on the topic of the "morality trials," he warned the Nazis that people who live in glass houses ought not to cast stones. Continuing he said:

> We are not revolutionaries, but if this continues, then will we—Catholic and Protestant clergymen alike—throw an enormous stink-bomb in their midst.... We will fight them tooth and nail. [67]

Neither was he afraid to say boldly as he did at Aichach on January 24, 1937, that from their writings, their radio broadcasts, their theatre, and their newspapers, in short from their every action one could see that the Nazis were making war on the Church. [68]

On May 28, 1937, realizing Father Mayer's powerful influence, and being incensed by his breezy attitude toward the state, and above all, fearing that his attitude might prevail amongst many more Germans, the Nazis deprived him of the right to preach. On June 5, 1937 be was arrested. On June 6 the following notice was read from all the pulpits of the Archdiocese of Munich:

> Because of the countless questions and rumors which have been

---

[65] See the records of this trial by the *Sondergerichtshof*, Munich, 1b KMS — So 32/37 (144) — 16 c Js So 548/39, p. 2. This trial, hereafter referred to as "Fr. Mayer Trial," is reprinted in Appendix B.

[66] *Ibid.*, 3.

[67] *Ibid.*, 8.

[68] *Ibid.*, 9.

set in motion concerning Father Mayer, the Chancery office feels called upon to make the following statement. First a word of comfort: Father Mayer's treatment and his physical and mental condition are all good. His only wish is that others of his Order will take care of his many tasks for the poor, the sick and the needy. Now a word of explanation: For a month and a half Father Mayer has been forbidden the right to preach outside of St. Michael's in Munich. But he went ahead and preached anyway, which is what led to his arrest on June 5th.

(signed) Buchwieser. [69]

Father Mayer was chaplain of the Men's Sodality which met each month at St. Michael's in Munich. We can imagine with what interest they awaited their next meeting which was held on July 4, 1937, and what their amazement was to find that they were being addressed by the Cardinal Archbishop of Munich. He spoke to them as follows:

Catholic Men! I have interrupted my confirmation journey, and, though somewhat exhausted by a five hour consecration ceremony of the church of the Holy Rosary in Rosenheim-Fürstadt, I have returned to Munich to be with you on this occasion of your meeting. Today is the first time that your director, Father Mayer, is not here in the pulpit. I am using this solemn occasion to declare publically the sentiments of indignation and surprise that were caused by Father Mayer's arrest on June 5th and also the tragic prolongation of his imprisonment. It is a time to speak.

Father Rupert Mayer, a priest of the Society of Jesus, went off to war a healthy man; as a chaplain he brought the comforts of religion to his brothers even in the combat zone, and because of his bravery returned to his home a man broken in physical health. And now he has the thanks of his Fatherland. Father Rupert Mayer, an apostle to the men of the Archdiocese, has held high the lamp of Christian doctrine, has shown the way to belief and from there to life in this belief. He has encouraged the men always to render to the state the things which belong to the state and to God the

---

[69] Mimeographed notice, to be found in Father Natterer's files of the *Klerusverband*, Starnberg, Bavaria.

things which are God's and of the Church. At the same time, as a true son of the people, he has exposed religious imposters and challenged Communism in meetings and speeches. He has convinced Communists by quiet personal talks of the blessings of a just political and social order. With the courage of St. John the Baptist, he had propounded the truth before the faces of the great ones of this world. Had he bound himself by his signature not to preach outside Munich he might have been freed long ago, but as an upright man, he scorned to repudiate the Catholic principle that 'the Word of God is not bound" (2 Tim. ii, 9) declaring that he would rather remain in prison than sign.

The Men's Sodality, though deeply affected by Father Mayer's arrest, has maintained discipline according to my request—and for this I thank you. Through diocesan channels, I have asked you, in spite of your reverence and enthusiasm for your director, and especially in view of your grief at his arrest; that in spite of all of this I asked you to refrain from any street demonstrations—. A street demonstration in the old sense would be today passé. No greater service could we do the *Gestapo* than to furnish them with means of bringing action with cudgels and arrests, with lockouts and dismissals against the odious Catholics, nowadays more hated and persecuted than the Bolsheviks. This is the way Father Mayer would have behaved, and he would have wished you to refrain from thoughtless words and deeds. There is also a time to keep silence.

My dear Catholic men, continue in this same discipline. Promise this to your Bishop, that you will not interrupt my words with calls or disturbing phrases, and that you will not give vent to your indignation. Rather, let us pray for your director in prison, and let us offer up this evening's devotions for his intention. It is before God that one can speak. Let us consider then three intentions: first, that Father Mayer may preserve the peace and composure of his soul. It is no easy thing to be sent into a lonely desert after an active life. Remember that he has preached every Sunday three or four times and that many a one has been broken by the silence of the grave-like prison. Secondly, that the time of affliction soon be at an end and that the gates of the prison be opened. Now do we understand why it is the Church prays on Good Friday: Lord, open the gates of prisons. Thirdly, do we pray that this evil may be turned into good.

Now as Bishop, I sent a protest to the *Reichsminister* for Ecclesiastical Affairs against curtailing his right to preach, which must have reached there on the 28th of May. This appeal was, needless to say, rejected and the prohibition of his preaching was not lifted. That is why I am turning today to you, the Catholic men of Munich. There is a time for silence and a time to speak.

On the 9th of June a few days after the arrest, the Vicar General of the Diocese sent a letter of protest to the following offices: Ministry of the Interior, the Foreign Office, Ministry of Ecclesiastical Affairs, the *Gestapo* in Munich, the *Reichsstatthalter* of Bavaria, and the Minister President of Bavaria. It ran as follows: 'Fr. Mayer has no need to prove his patriotism. His exemplary conduct, recognized on all sides both in the war and in the revolution of 1918, his grave wound, his numberless patriotic speeches at post-war military commemorations, his undaunted attacks on Communism and Marxism at hundreds of meetings, one of which, indeed, was with the *Führer* on the same platform, a fact which Hitler recognized in a letter to Father Mayer on the occasion of his 25th year jubilee as a priest. All of this speaks for his loyalty. Wherever he appeared, whether it was in the trenches, or in the military hospital, in the pulpit or on the platform, he proved his rare priestly character, that of a man's apostle of commanding and captivating qualities. He was a promotor of courage and conscientiousness, a champion of religion and morality, of authority and loyalty to the state, of order and public spirit.'

This true-born German who wears the Iron Cross, 1st Class, as does the *Führer,* and side by side with him has striven against the Communists of Munich and received from him an appreciative personal letter, is now consigned to prison. Fortunately, the sermon which Fr. Mayer preached before you, my dear sodalists, on May 23, has been preserved. You are witnesses to what he said at that time: 'We do not let ourselves be forced from our loyalty to the state. We set aside any self-defense of a revolutionary character.' And this is the same person who today is charged with enmity to the state.

It will be said that Father Mayer has brought politics into the pulpit. How often indeed has he had to denounce this slanderous slogan 'Political Catholicism.' The *Führer* has over and over again said in his book that he is not a religious reformer, and he continues in this belief today. But there are other powers at work

who would love to fashion a second reformation out of this political movement; persons who would like to root out all Christian
belief from German soil—against these Father Mayer has used his
spiritual sword—his sword of the spirit, as it is called in the
Epistle of the Ephesians. The *Führer* has said himself: 'Christianity
has been united with the German people for a thousand years.
This fact cannot be denied.' To this I add, that Christianity which
has been so closely interwoven for a thousand years with Germany
cannot be separated without inflicting deep wounds on both sides.
He, therefore, who defends Christian faith and morality in national
life serves the community and the state. In this respect the work
of Father Mayer takes on a national as well as religious-churchly
meaning.

Speaking as Bishop I pronounce this formal judgment on the
imprisonment of Father Mayer:

The state has no right to forbid a priest who complies with the
requirements of the Concordat and who has received jurisdiction
from his Bishop, or from his Religious superior, the right to
preach within the precinct of the church. Preaching is one of the
essential duties of the clergy and those duties are the Church's
concern only, for Art. 32 of the Concordat, while stating that
'clergymen are debarred from activity on behalf of any party,'
yet concedes that no infringement of the teaching and explanation
of the Church's doctrines, dogmatic or moral, incumbent on the
clergy is to be made. It is evident that the state has no right to
forbid authorized preaching of any priest, nor, on his refusal to
comply with their orders, to arrest him.

In the Acts of the Apostles, chs. 4 and 5, we read that, when the
Apostles were put into prison for the first time because they had
announced the Word of God, the High Council of the Jews gathered together, 'and sitting then in their midst, they asked: "By
what power have you done this, or by what name"?' The apostles
answered: 'If it be just in the sight of God to hear you rather
than God, judge ye.' When they had been set free, they went on
preaching, were again arrested, brought before the Council and
told: 'Commanding we commanded you that you should teach in
this name.' But Peter and the other Apostles answered: 'Man
must obey God rather than men.' With the arrest of Father Mayer,
my dear brethren, the record in the Acts of the Apostles of early
Christian times comes to life again. May God grant His grace to

the persecuted that the spirit of the holy confessors and martyrs of early Christian times may also revive.

On last Wednesday, the 30th of June, I visited Father Rupert Mayer in Stadelheim. Thanks to the officials of the court, and of course under the same conditions that anyone else may get in, I had ten minutes to visit, watched all the while by an official. (Would that all the visits in my house could be held under these well ordered arrangements.) I wanted to say in my visit to our dear director, that the Bishop and the Catholic men of Munich and the people in general have not forgotten him. It is, of course, a corporal work of mercy to visit the imprisoned. Father Mayer is in sound health of body and soul. A good conscience in prison is often as not a fine pillow for the head. He is in a cell by himself, a room, comparatively large and spacious, which ordinarily served as a room for the sick. It is lighted from above by two windows, simply furnished like a cell of one of the prophets. (4 Kings, 4, 10). Father Mayer is bearing his involuntary vacation with iron courage—much the same as when he fought in the war with the soldiers. He is bearing this time of silence with philosophical calm, that same spirit with which he went to the operating table on the eastern front when he lost his leg. He pointed out in his own humerous fashion, and laughed when he said it, that he had not had so much an opportunity for a good walk in the twenty-five years as he had here in the house of contemplatives; also that he had much time for study in the jail . . . . He passes his time not in grumbling about his lot, rather he prays, holds spiritual exercises and studies. I am saying this today in order that these silly rumors may disappear, for example that he has been sent off to Coblenz, these and others not set in circulation by the golden-hearted citizens of Munich, but by other vile tongues. After my visit in Stadelheim, I wrote to Father Mayer's eighty-three year old mother, telling her that her son is well, and is keeping himself with courage, and preserving that holy indifference which St. Ignatius emphasized so strongly in his Exercises.

Catholic Men! The arrest of Father Mayer has a significance which goes beyond mere persons. This arrest is but a sign that the *Kulturkampf* against the Catholic Church has entered a new phase. We are at the hour of decision. The son of man is about to separate the wheat and the chaff. The signal fires are ablaze! One of these is the arrest of the Munich men's apostle.

Recently in a speech at Fürstenfeldbruck, the arrest of Father
Mayer was joined with the whole Church politics of today. It was
said there: 'I regretfully tell you that there is one power, one authority which still disturbs national peace, namely the Church.'
Have we heard correctly? You say these disturbing forces do not
come from the Free Masons, nor from the Communists, nor the
Bolshevists? Is the last enemy of the state which must now be
slaughtered and beaten down, is this the Church? She is the 'only
one' who refuses to suit herself to the new order. Now we know
where we stand. It was not long ago that the Bolshevists were
labeled as Public Enemy Number 1. Don't we speak of this any-
more today? Well, at least the picture is clarified.

Without going into all the details of the Fürstenfeldbruck
speech, I should like to make a few points clear. Mention was made
of certain supplementary payments to the Church, and also the
subject of the bishop's salary. In the old Marxist days we used to
hear a good deal about this, and the Communist papers were full
of criticisms of this sort. What we miss here is, however, some
mention of the salaries of the Ministers of State. There is no
question that they would never allow this subject to be discussed
amongst the working class. Besides, nothing is said to the people
about where these funds which are paid to the Church and her
Bishops come from; these funds are but a small token payment
for what the Bavarian government took from the ecclesiastical
princes and monasteries. If the Bavarian State would return the
land and above all the tremendous forests which were robbed
from the Church at the time of the Secularization they could keep
all their payments and salaries.

Evoking a pious air, the speaker at Fürstenfeldbruck declared
all men to be equal before God and the law. Who can recognize
this equality in the public reports and the offences of clergymen
on the one hand and of Party members on the other? Or who can
consider the defense of the Christian denomination through press
and radio to be in any way equal to the attacks upon them?

My dear Catholic men! The signal fires are ablaze! Week after
week in German newspapers and periodicals, in articles and in
pictures the vilest slanders are hurled against Catholic bishops,
dogmas, the Church herself. All opportunity to answer these attacks by means of radio, correspondence bureaus or even in church
magazines is deprived us. Yet, we are bound in conscience to obey

constituted authority, and we must watch week in and week out
the authority of the Church brought down into the muck and mire
whilst the arm of the state does nothing. Some speeches and newspapers call for an open assault against the Roman 'rebels' and
'enemies of the state.' One newspaper boldly stated that all the
bishops were guilty of high treason. The Corpus Christi procession,
one of the most beautiful manifestations of faith, is labelled as a
treasonable activity. *Durchbruch* was allowed to publish slanderous
articles at the close of this year's Corpus Christi procession, producing as a proof of this year's procession two pictures of a previous procession.

Yesterday I received from Holland a letter in a disguised hand
purporting to reveal to the frontier and post-office police a plot
between Catholics and Jewish Bolshevism. 'We listened with great
interest' runs this libel 'to the oral report of Father Egidius . . . .
We shall inform you of the next steps in the Jewish German
union. We can easily obtain from India the necessary poison, a
small dose of which causes, at least, madness . . . . We are unani-
mous in dissuading you from this course . . . . We can get it in
Berlin . . . . Besides a young man who has no more interest in this
vale of tears has put himself at our disposal. Our common plan
will and must succeed.' The signature is a clumsily drawn Soviet
Star. This fraud can be recognized in every line, and yet we men
are suposed to believe that such madness is possible.

So I call the arrest of Father Mayer a signal blaze of our time.
When he received the order not to speak outside the church, he
obeyed this order. This is a fact; he did not speak in public
gatherings outside the church. When, however, he was forbidden
to speak even within the church, he could not in conscience hold
to this command. There is a time to keep silence and a time to
speak. One must obey God more than men.

In government circles people were upset because the news of
Father Mayer's arrest had been reported in the foreign press, and
in this connection mentioned my letter to the Minister of Church
Affairs. I myself never give information to the foreign press as a
matter of principle, and in the last few days have refused a telephone interview on this subject from someone in London. What
surprises me is all the hubbub about the fact that such information
gets into the foreign press, and not the fact of the arrest itself,—
by this they are not upset. The Gospel calls this a straining of

gnats and a swallowing of camels. It is quite obvious that the information concerning Father Mayer could not have been given out by any Diocesan authority because it contains, as is evidenced by the news broadcast of the Strasbourg radio, information that Father Mayer has been released, information which everyone in Munich knows to be false. The arrest on June 5 was discussed all around Munich. I had a letter sent out to all the parishes which was read from the pulpits that everything was being done to free Father Mayer, and that I had written a letter to the Minister for Church Affairs. We did this in order to prevent any demonstrations in the street by an embittered people, and to keep in check any thoughtless writings. A reporter of the foreign press in Munich would have to be deaf and blind not to have noticed all these goings-on. Besides enough evidence is printed right in the German press to convince any reader outside what the state of the Church in Germany is; no special reports are necessary.

Catholic men! In this hour of trial, we must learn the lesson of the Cross. This is the law and the secret of the Kingdom of God: the Church must always and forever bear the stigmata of her divine Master, for it is by this test that we recognize the Church of Christ. We will never go wrong if we are ready to take up with our holy mother, the Church, the purple cloak, the crown of thorns and the cross itself which was carried by the divine Founder; we too must offer ourselves, if necessary, to suffer for our faith.

> When the signal fires blaze
> Men will be needed at that hour
> Who have been reared upon the cross.

It is the hour of decision. Every individual will be asked the question: Are you simply a believer, or do you confess to Christ and his Church? To be a believer nowadays does not have the pressure of the first commandment given to us by Christ; to these people, a believer is no different from the Turks or the Hottentots: these believers have cut themselves off from Christ and his Church. They have betrayed Christ and have apostatised from his Church. The hour of decision has come. When one is asked: are you a believer, or what are you? Then it is the moment to speak and to confess without any buts or ifs, without hesitation or compromise. Then every Catholic must be with full courage, yea, even when it is demanded in writing, and answer: I am a Catholic. Not only do I believe in God, I believe in Christ and His Church. I am a Catholic. I am a Catholic. Yes and Amen. [70]

Father Mayer was released from prison on December 26, 1937 only to be arrested again on January 5, 1938. From that date until September 28, 1939 he was in and out of prison several times. On the occasion of his last arrest the charge was that he had lamented the arrest of one hundred and fifty monarchists in August of that year. [71] This time the diocesan authorities made no appeal or announcement directly to the faithful but sent the following notice to the clergy of the archdiocese:

> It is with exceedingly great sorrow that we inform the clergy of the Archdiocese that yesterday afternoon, November 3, 1939, the higher S.S. and police chief of Bavaria has demanded the arrest of Father Rupert Mayer, S.J., because of *Unbotmässigkeit* [insubordination]. This *Unbotmässigkeit* in the eyes of the *Gestapo* seems to be the mentioning of something which does not come under the heading of pastoral or clerical duties.
>
> Any spreading of this news or mentioning of this case in the church is not to be permitted.
>
> At all events, any further information or special action in the matter will be the concern of the diocesan authorities.
>
> (signed) Buchwieser
> Vicar General [72]

Late in December, 1939, Father Mayer was sent to Sachsen-

---

[70] Sermon, *Es ist eine Zeit zu schweigen und eine Zeit zu reden*, given by Cardinal Faulhaber in St. Michael's Church to the Marian Sodality, July 4, 1937, distributed by Archdiocesan authority for the personal information of the clergy of the Archdiocese, 10 p. This translation is based upon the one given in *The Persecution of the Catholic Church in the Third Reich*, 538-543. The phrase "the signal fires blaze" is one dear to Fritz Gerlich and Father Naab and also one found in the writings of the Munich Students, see *infra*, Ch. IV.

[71] Franziska Boesmiller, *P. Rupert Mayer* (Munich, 1946). See also *infra*, Ch. III.

[72] From the office of the Vicar General of the Archdiocese of Munich, Letter, No. 11949, November 9, 1939. A copy of this letter can be found in Father Natterer's files in the *Klerusverband*, Starnberg, Bavaria

hausen, a concentration camp in the north. After a year, he was back in Bavaria, this time under house-arrest in the Benedictine monastery in Ettal. He stayed there without any contact with his Munich friends until the war ended. He died on All Saints Day, 1945. [73]

There were many other cases in which the clergy came into open conflict with the National Socialists, cases which turned on the touchy question of authority. [74] And there was no group among the clergy who championed more fervently and consistently the cause of the Church than did members of the Jesuit Order. [75]

A good example was Father Alfred Delp, a sociologist who participated in the sessions at Kreisau, who wrote that he suffered death because he belonged to that celebrated community which was considered "*a priori* enemies and opponents of the [Third] Reich." [76] But perhaps no more pathetic example of the tragic results of this conflict of authority can be found than in the execution of Canon Dr. Johann Maier of Regensburg.

On April 23, 1945, when American tanks were within twenty miles of Regensburg, a delegation of townsfolk, including Canon Maier, went over to the Town Hall where many other men were already gathered to plead with the Nazi officials to surrender the city, and thus prevent further destruction. [77] While the meeting

---

[73] The life and death of Father Mayer are being investigated by the Sacred Congregation of Rites in Rome.

[74] For a partial list of the Bavarian clergy so involved, see Johann Neuhäusler, *op. cit.*, I, 333-350.

[75] For an interesting account of the Nazi attitude toward the success of the Jesuits in Munich in their fight to keep students within the Church, see a document from the Bavarian Ministry of the Interior reprinted in Appendix A.

[76] Alfred Delp, *Im Angesicht des Todes* (Frankfurt am Main, 1947), 181. The best description of the activity of the *Kreisauer Kreis* can be found in Theodor Stelzer, *Von Deutscher Politik, Dokumenten, Aufsätzen, und Vorträgen* (Frankfort am Main, 1949), 154-169.

[77] Infromation taken from a mimeographed report published by the Diocesan authorities in Regensburg, n.d., probably, May, 1945.

was in progress an air alarm was sounded. The people refused to disperse, even though the S.S. troops used water hoses. Canon Maier went up to the front door of the *Kreisleitung* and is reported to have said:

> We have not come here to make a disturbance; we Christians do not register any indignation against divinely ordained authority. We have come simply with a request: we ask that the city be surrendered for the following reasons: [78]

Then, with a suddenness unbelievable, he was struck and halted in his speech and taken away from the delegation by the S.S. A summary trial was held and before midnight he was declared guilty. In the early hours of April 24, 1945 he was stripped of his clerical garb, brought to the market place, and hanged from a gibbet. When the Americans entered the city on April 27th, his body was found still hanging with a sign reading: "Here died a saboteur." [79]

Two things might be noted about this episode: first, that Canon Maier felt compelled to join in urging action which he must have known the S.S. would never admit possible: surrender; and second, that he continued, one might almost say with a tragic insistence, to address the Nazis and the S.S. as "divinely ordained authority."

But turning from opposition which ended so tragically, no study of the period of Nazi tyranny would be complete without some mention of humour which served as a much needed escape mechanism. Cardinal Faulhaber was not above indulging in a certain lightness of touch, when he thought it might make a serious point more palatable. For example, he began one of his sermons in the cathedral with the words: "My dear friends and

---

[78] *Ibid.*

[79] A fuller account of these events as well as the trial of those former S.S. officers responsible for the killing of Canon Meier may be found in the *Mittelbayerische Zeitung*, 9. Jhg., January 27, Jan. 30, February 3, Feb. 6, Feb. 10, Feb. 17, Feb. 20, Feb. 27, 1948.

eaves-droppers." [80] Again in his celebrated sermon to the Men's Sodality on the occasion of Father Mayer's arrest, Cardinal Faulhaber found occasion to jest about the manner in which the interview with the Jesuit had taken place, wishing, the reader will recall, that audiences at the Cardinal's palace might be as "well-ordered." At another time, poking fun at those who might say that Catholics tried to heighten the differences between religious sects, he had occasion to tell this anecdote: It is said that the District President in the Rhineland wanted to find out if Protestants were still referred to as heretics (*Ketzer*) in the schools of Trier. He began his examination with questions on the Thirty Years War in which the Protestants were mentioned. He asked who they were. One student replied that they were Lutherans; another called them Evangelicals. The officer was not satisfied and finally broke down, asking outright: "Who then are the '*Ketzer*'?" There followed a long pause. Finally one boy answered: "*Der Kätzer ist das Männchen von der Katze.*" [81]

Nor was such lightness without its desired effect: the shepherds were thereby endeared to their flock and the laity counted slights against the clergy as ones against themselves. There is plenty of evidence for this, but let one example speak for many. A peasant farmer by the name of Franz Goetz of Birkenfeld in Lower Franconia, approached for an offering to the *Winterhilfe* —the national charity organization—replied to the fund-gatherer as follows:

> I am not giving any more money. We are not being treated as German citizens. I heard all about it in church today: we're just Roman Catholics. You people can collect all the money you like, but the Capuchin friars are not allowed to collect any more. [82]

---

[80] "*Meine lieben Zuhörer und Zuhorcher,*" from Cardinal Faulhaber's *Sylvesterpredigt,* December 31, 1937, (Munich, 1937), 2.

[81] Cardinal Faulhaber, *Papstfreierpredigt* (Munich, 1936), 8.

[82] Document in the *Gestapo* files of Würzburg, of a report from the *Gen-*

The police reported that Franz Goetz insisted that he was first and foremost a Roman Catholic; that loyalty to his religion preceded loyalty to his country. He remarked that he saw no reason to tolerate publications such as *Der Stürmer* which had caricatures of a priest appearing as a pig whilst hearing the confession of a young girl. The exchange ended with the money-collector saying: *"Heil Hitler,"* to which Goetz loudly replied: *"Grüss Gott!"* [83]

Such encounters with Nazi officials were met with all over Bavaria. In Neuhaus an der Pegnitz, for example, a certain S.S. official reported the following to Party headquarters:

> Here in this area [*Oberpfalz*] no one says '*Heil Hitler*'; they all say '*Grüss Gott*' or '*Guten Morgen.*' The population is completely dominated by the clericals [*schwarz*]. They stand united against us and embittered against the Party; but they never permit this sentiment to come out in a political dispute. I was actually stoned one evening recently by five youths. [84]

Never letting the sentiment come into open dispute was exactly the tactic encouraged by the Church. Nor has this whole dilemma ever received more thoughtful consideration than in Amy Butler's book written in England during the Second World War. In her generally favorable treatment of German opposition she puts these words into the mouth of a Catholic priest, a priest she met while visiting Bavaria:

> We don't know the answer, that is the heart of the tragedy. This enslavement is such that we have been taken unawares. And, whereas it often seems easy enough to judge, it is only with agony that one makes any decisions these days. You see, I cannot decide

---

darmerie-Station, Reuslingen, No. 1794, December 15, 1936, now located in the Berlin Document Center.

[83] *Ibid.* Because of Franz Goetz's advanced age the court gave him a money fine of sixty-five marks for this insubordination.

[84] Letter from Hans Schleicher in Neuhaus a.d. Pegnitz, dated June 22, 1935. (Sturm 2-/5, 21; now in Berlin Document Center).

whether to insist on entering my school and preaching, thus giving the Nazis the excuse to arrest me, which is exactly what they want. I would fight them if we had arms, for it would be a juster war than I've ever known, but we are totally unarmed.

If I accept their ban on teaching, other restrictions will follow, but so far I remain free to move among my people and visit them, and above all to give what help I can to the young who come for advice, as they in turn face questions, every day of the week, that are as difficult as my own. In our present circumstances to compromise at all is a dangerous path, and particularly so for the people to whom the young look for guidance. Should I withdraw? Nothing could suit the Nazis better than to lock up as many Catholic priests as possible.

Therefore, at present I have decided to remain free and to accept negative restrictions, but to refuse outright to take any part at all in Party ways, plans or greetings. Later I may decide I am wrong. I do not think we can be sure of the answer. I sometimes wonder what the martyrs of old would have done in these circumstances, for it does seem as though today individual martyrdom is not always the right way—and yet, how careful we need to be because we may be deceiving ourselves. [85]

In the following chapter it will be shown that there were many Christians who followed the pattern described by this priest, dissociating themselves from all that smacked of National Socialism, but yet who felt something more was necessary, some demonstration.

e) CONCLUSION

On Passion Sunday, 1942, that day on which the Church in solemn manner commences once again to reenact the drama of Christ's suffering and death; that day when the church's ornaments are veiled in purple, the liturgical color of penance and sorrow, Cardinal Faulhaber entered the pulpit of the *Liebfrauen* church in Munich to read a thunderous condemnation of the

---

[85] E. Amy Butler, *Darkness over Germany* (London, 1943), 17.

Kulturkampf which the state was then waging against the Church. He began as follows:

> Dearly beloved! For years now in our country there has been waged a battle against Christianity and the Church. Even in war, during which time we always expected to maintain a cessation of hostilities on the home-front (*Burgfriede*), the battle continues unabated; more than that, it has become bitterer and sharper and rests upon us all like a mountainous pressure, upon people who by the latest census adhere ninety-five per cent—here in Bavaria, ninety-eight per cent to Christianity. In continuation of my sermon to you all on last New Year's Eve, I should like to bring the following points to your attention. [86]

Cardinal Faulhaber then reviewed for his congregation once again—one hesitates to count the number of times since 1933— the violation of the Concordat, the destruction of Christian education, the maltreatment of the clergy and the members of religious orders. But, in the spring of 1942, when the armies of the Third Reich were advancing to their greatest extent, the Cardinal Archbishop of Munich rose to condemn violations of fundamental human liberties.

> A bishop, [he said] has as his duty not only to keep watch against violations of the rights and liberties of the Church, but also to defend the God-given rights of man (*gottverliehene Menschenrechte*). If there is no respect for the rights of man, the entire civilization will collapse.

---

[86] Johann Neuhäusler, *op. cit.*, II, 145. The reader may find it instructive to compare this sermon with one which Bishop von Galen gave in the Überwasserkirche in Munster, July 20, 1941. Amongst other things the Bishop said: "We have become now not the hammer but rather the anvil. We are being struck and beaten. The hammer forces our people, our youth, ourselves out of the ways of God. But learn this comfort from the smithy: what is forged takes its form not form the hammer alone but form the anvil also . . . . And yet, anvil though we must be, we cannot disregard the words of Holy Scripture, even when we are being most faithful to our people and our fatherland: 'Man must obey God more than men.'" *Bischof von Galen Spricht; ein apostolischer Kampf und sein Widerhall.* (Freiburg im Breisgau, 1946.)

1. Every man has the natural right of human freedom within the bounds of his duty to God, his respect for his fellow creatures his regard for the commonweal, and his respect for duly constituted authority. Your Archbishop raises objection to every disregard of personal freedom. We demand that all ordinances of punishment be re-examined. We demand that our fellow-citizens who are being held without proof of guilt be freed.

2. Every man has the natural right to live and the right to seek goods necessary in order to live. The living God, Creator of all life, is alone Lord over life and death.

The Cardinal again referred to the immorality of the policy according to which the mentally ill were put to death, ending his remarks with the words: "No one can be certain of his life if the Fifth Commandment is not observed: 'Thou shalt not kill.'" He continued his list of man's natural rights, saying:

3. Every man has a natural right to the possession and use of property justly acquired, and the right to protection of this by the state against willful attacks. And yet in the past few years Church possessions have been taken and put to other use—and not to serve war purposes either! Even churches have been dispossessed and profaned . . .

Developing this thought, the Archbishop referred to the robbing of religious orders of their properties and warned the faithful that what was today happening to the Church might tomorrow become general social practice.

4. Every man has a natural right to the protection of his honor against lies and slander. At the front and here at home, Christians are doing their duty to their country to the utmost. And yet Catholic priests are constantly watched, secretly suspected, and even openly designated as traitors of their follow-countrymen and enemies of the state. They are called such, however, only because they speak out for the liberty of the Church and for the truth of the Catholic faith . . .

Concluding his remarks he again reminded the faithful that there were at large in Germany people who sought nothing

less than the destruction of Christianity. But, he warned, these
people are at odds with the great and overwhelming majority
of Germans. He ended his remarks as follows:

> My dearly beloved! Today on this Passion Sunday I would
> have you all take part in this my heavy sorrow. Support all efforts
> toward religious peace and religious freedom by your prayers
> and by your unswerving loyalty, showing to all that you will
> defend your faith until the end. God bless our country and our
> holy Church. God give to the Church and to the country an
> honestly happy and lasting peace. [87]

As the war progressed and it became ever more clear that
Germany would have to follow the dolorous path to near anni-
hilation, Cardinal Faulhaber and the other members of the
hierarchy were not less vehement in their attacks on the state;
but they tempered this mood with greater emphasis on Christian
suffering. On May 19, 1944, after a great air-raid—the first in
a long series on the city of Munich—Cardinal Faulhaber took
occasion to preach on the general theme that God desired not
"the destruction of the sinner, but his conversion." [88] That the
Nazis would be converted had long been the wish of the Church,
and that wish seemed to have tempered the quality of the
Church's opposition to National Socialism. The Church in
Bavaria did not seek battle with the Nazis; the Church sought
peace—of that there can be no doubt. In general, the Church
based her action on the belief that things could hardly get worse,
only better, and in this she was hopelessly optimistic. Yet there
was, coupled with this curious optimism—one is almost inclined
to say tragic optimism—the very important doctrine of Christian
suffering which encourages man to imitate the life of Christ and
the early martyrs as a positive demonstration of the transitory
character of this world.

---

[87] *Ibid.,* 145-149.

[88] A mimeograph copy of this sermon of May 19, 1944 can be found in
Father Natterer's file at the *Klerusverband,* Starnberg, Bavaria.

Through it all the Church can be seen to have pursued what was considered then to have been a realistic policy. No more telling description of this realism can be found than in the words of one of the members of the Bavarian clergy, a certain Dr. Gmelch, who at a conference of Bavarian priests in June, 1935, said, amongst other things:

> Many are frightened as to what the future holds for them. But in my opinion, I say that we can look forward with great confidence. We wish but faithfully to fulfil our duty. Truth, clarity and cleverness (*Klugheit*) should be our motto. I mention the last of these with good reason; for certainly *Klugheit* will help us to prevent unnecessary conflicts and avoid sharpness of speech. It is always much easier to go past a bridge than to try to fix it up once it is broken. And there are many who overlook those who are very brave because they bravely endure suffering; they wait patiently whilst others battle. This is not to say that we will ever renounce one iota of our belief, nor will we be silent when it comes to a matter when we must do our duty by speaking out. But it is often as not possible to achive one's point by another means without much damage. Nor do I mean by this to encourage weakness of attitude. That never. On the contrary, I rejoice when a priest puts forth all his energy and strength for a just cause whenever it is necessary. But: *est modus in rebus. Fortiter in re, suaviter in modo,* must still hold true today. [89]

Thus, without for a moment minimizing the forceful opposition which the Catholic Church in Bavaria put up to National Socialism in all areas of conflict from that period when Gerlich and Naab predicted the inevitable loss of liberties which would come with a Nazi victory; through the controversy over education; the youth organizations; the removal of priests and nuns from public service, as well as all the attacks on the clergy; through all the years of agony and persecution which the Church patiently endured, it is possible to understand the quality of this opposition best in terms of the curious unity of optimism coupled

---

[89] *Bayer. Klerusblatt,* 19 VI 35, No. 25, 428.

with an acceptance of the inevitability of suffering. This is, in Christian terms, realism. Nor was there anything very new in this definition of realism. It embodied in part an optimism about wordly matters which is well expressed in the quotation from John Locke which can be found in the opening pages of this book. But it embodied also in a very significant way a peculiarly Christian dimension, a thing one misses in the heritage of the Enlightenment but which one finds again in the words of St. Bernard of Clairvaux: *Habet mundus iste noctes suas et non paucas.* [90] To this was added St. Thomas' *caveat,* that all means be exploited before encouraging revolt, and then, perhaps, avoiding the fateful step should there be danger of greater evils arising as a result of such action. It is under the aspect of reasoning such as this that the churchmen in Bavaria can justly be called Christian realists.

---

[90] These words of St. Bernard of Clairvaux are quoted by the great Dutch historian, Jan Huizinga, in his *In the Shadow of Tomorrow,* first published in Haarlem, 1935. To those who thought that his book had contributed too much to the gloom-and-doom spirit of the 1930's, Professor Huizinga had only this to say: "I am an optimist."

CHAPTER III

THE BAVARIAN LEGITIMISTS

a) INTRODUCTION

There is common impression of Bavaria, an impression which has gained considerable acceptance outside of Germany, as the land which gave life to German fascism. The usual inference is, of course, that Bavarians were to a very large extent responsible for the creation and, indeed, the success of National Socialism. [1] Such impressions and inferences are dangerously superficial and do violence to the realities as they are now known. This is not to say that Bavarians did not have a large share in undermining the success of the German experiment in democracy; they certainly did. They shared that negative approach to the Weimar Republic, however, with many of their fellow-Germans; yet, no one would be so naïve as to suggest that one could understand German fascism solely as the reaction to the failure of democracy

---

[1] The reader's attention is drawn to a fairly representative statement of this in a book by L. B. Namier, *Europe in Decay* (London, 1950), 234. He says, in part: "The makers of the Third Reich were Austrians, Bavarians and Rhinelanders, of the German *Stämme* which outside Germany have always been preferred to the Prussians; there was not one member of the old ruling class [Prussians] among them. But most of those who lost their lives in the unsuccessful attempt against Hitler in July, 1944, were North Germans and conservatives, Prussian *Junkers* or representatives of the old military and official class."

(A closer examination of those men involved in the July 20th plot will reveal that the participants came from all parts of Germany, with the south and the west well represented. Certainly Colonel von Stauffenberg was not a Prussian. Furthermore, the heir apparent to the Hohenzollern throne was a leading figure in the S.A., a function never performed by a Wittelsbach. The author).

in Germany. The fact is that during the twenties Bavarians expressed opposition to the German Republic in a variety of different ways and with different ends in view.

One such way was expressed by Bavaria's representatives in the *Reichsrat* where they were encouraged by their Minister-President to present an argument in favor of the reorganization of the Reich emphasizing its more federal aspects. [2] These Bavarians might be called "moderates," men who had less faith in *Deutschland* and more faith in the liberal-democratic process. Their goal was a loose federation of German states which was grounded in the principles of parliamentary democracy. This kind of opposition to the German Republic was hardly the same sort of thing one found amongst conservative-revolutionaries or Nazis. In fact, it was an opposition which was closer to a more traditionally conservative point of view, a point of view which can be labeled rather loosely as constitutional-monarchist. The difference, however, between the constitutional-monarchists and the moderates is not unimportant; for not only had the monarchists nothing but contempt for the German revolution of 1918, an event which the moderates had decided they would accept as unalterable, but also the monarchists were decisive in their refusal to accept any interference from Berlin in their Bavarian government. The monarchists tended to be separatists. [3]

---

[2] For the Bavarian proposals, see *Jahrbuch des Öffentlichen Rechts* (Tübingen, 1925), XIII, 100, N. 2; and XV, 10-11. For the wider significance of the Bavarian argument, see S. Magi, *The Problem of Federalism* (London, 1932), and William Robert Dittmar, *The Government of the Free State of Bavaria* (Williamsport, 1934).

[3] For a good example of Bavarian opposition to the Weimar constitution, see Erwein von Aretin, *Das Bayerische Problem* (Munich, 1924). An often quoted example of Bavarian contempt for the events of 1918-1919 is to be found in a statement which Cardinal Faulhaber is supposed to have made at the *Katholikentag* held in Munich in 1922. "Die Revolution von 1918 war Meineid und Hochverrat." Quoted in Kurt Sendtner, *Rupprecht von Wittelsbach, Kronprinz von Bayern.* (Munich, 1954) 513.

A closer analysis of the political life of Bavaria in the 1920's is not possible here. [4] Yet it does not take much scholarly endeavor to reach the conclusion that Bavarian attitudes toward other German states did not undergo serious revision in that first decade of German democracy. As the 1920's drew to a close the extent to which their entire heritage seemed in danger of extinction became increasingly clear to certain Bavarians. Those who felt this most keenly were monarchists and separatists (who were also, as a rule, Catholics). By 1933 they had already formed themselves as a force in their society, a force which during the next decade of Nazi leadership continued to live.

However much the monarchists theorized, planned and, in one case at least, plotted, it must be said at the outset that they had little mass appeal. Fortunately for historians, history is not solely the record of mass movements. What is more, history may be, often is, the record of a failure. Yet in spite of an almost unparalleled lack of success since the time when the French Revolution destroyed the principle of kingship, the Bavarian monarchists went on believing that their concept of the state was the only one likely to restore society to health and sanity. That belief was the essence of the monarchists' opposition to Hitler.

b) Vormärz, 1933

In the first years after the creation of the German Republic the monarchists had a difficult time. Even their political party, the *Königspartei*, founded in 1919, had folded up in 1921. [5] Its

---

[4] The reader is referred to the recent work by Karl Schwend, *Bayern zwischen Monarchie und Diktatur* (Munich, 1954).

[5] The *Bayerische Königspartei* was founded by Josef Mayer-Koy, November 30, 1919, and during the following year fell under the control of Karl Graf Bothmer. For a fuller discussion of the political fortunes of this group see Kurt Sendtner, *Rupprecht von Wittelsbach* (Munich, 1954), 502-504.

non-political functions had been taken over by a popular society called the *Bayerische Heimat- und Königsbund* whose chief function seems to have been to keep alive an interest in and a loyalty to the House of Wittelsbach. The leaders of the *Bund* tried to effect that idea by speech-making, usually on the occasion of some such memorable event in Bavarian history as the death of Ludwig II. [6] As an organization they did almost nothing actively to support a restoration of the kingship in Bavaria. Yet there were those who had membership in the *Heimat- und Königsbund* but took a more active part in agitating for a restoration. [7]

In 1929 a group of young conservatives began publishing a periodical which left few doubts in its title. It was called, simply, *Monarchie*. [8] In the years between 1929 and 1933 the content of the magazine emphasized in a more or less theoretical manner

---

[6] The *Bayerische Heimat- und Königsbund* was organized in 1921 under the leadership at first of Rudolf Kanzler, followed by General von Krafft, For a fuller discussion of the activities of this *Bund*, see K. Sendtner, *op. cit.*, 504-506.

[7] For a list of the leading personalities in the *Heimat- und Königsbund*, see Erwein von Aretin, Die Frühjahrstage, 1933 (Typescript, n.d., post-1945). Some of the more important people in the late twenties were: Enoch von Guttenberg, Karl Ludwig zu Guttenberg, Erwein von Aretin, Freiin von Stengel, Graf von Soden-Frauenhofen, Fürst Oettingen-Wallerstein, Professor Carl Nicholas Cossmann, Fritz Büchner, Fritz Schäffer, as well as members of the Bavarian ruling family, the Wittelsbachs.

[8] The official title of the organization was: *Arbeitsstelle für Konservatives Schrifttum.* They published *Monarchie,* a monthly journal with the sub-title, *Zeitschrift für Tradition.* Their offices were at Würzburg, Herrenstrasse 1. One of the financial backers of this organization and one of the early editors of the journal was Karl Ludwig Freiherr zu Guttenberg. Born in Würzburg in 1902, he came from an ancient Franconian family which has given much to the cause of opposition to Hitler. His brother, Enoch von Guttenberg, was active in the anti-Hitler circles before the outbreak of the Second World War; he lost his life in 1940 as the result of a bomb explosion on his ship. His sister was the Gräfin Schenck von Stauffenberg, and a cousin of Colonel Claus von Stauffenberg; she suffered in the general *Sippenhaft* after the failure of the July 20th plot. She died in 1946. Biographical details of this family can

the values and importance to all Germans of kingship. Late in 1932 with the ever increasing number of National Socialists and the eventuality of a fascist revolution, the editors of *Monarchie* asked Erwein Freiherr von Aretin to write a positive appeal to its readers to bring about a restoration. The appeal was to run for three issues: January, February and March, 1933. The last installment never appeared.

In those articles which were entitled *Konservative Gedanken,* von Aretin borrowed the criticism from the writings of Moeller van den Bruck who had said that conservatives were not seeking "yesterday" but seeking rather the "eternal." [9] And yet von Aretin does not leave the reader with anything so vague as a concept of timelessness. Although he colors his writings with appropriate quotations from Saint Augustine's *City of God,* one comes away from the two articles with a far livelier impression of nineteenth century Bavaria—of the Bavaria before the capitalists, the socialists and the Center Party. [10] After appropriate obeisances to the social teaching of Pope Leo XIII, von Aretin presents his readers with what he regards as the only possible solution: a restoration of the monarchy in Bavaria as well as her separation as an independent state outside the Reich. [11] Not unmindful of the effect such ideas might have on Prussians, von Aretin goes on to address the north Germans as follows:

> Should it ever come to pass that a quarrel would break out between the conservative South and the democratic-socialist North,

---

be found in a memoir by Therese Freifrau zu Guttenberg called "Lebenslauf, Freiherr Karl Ludwig von und zu Guttenberg," (Typescript, 2 pp., n.d.). Also see Elisabeth von Guttenberg, *Holding the Stirrup* (New York, 1952).

[9] *Monarchie* (1932-1933), "Klare Entscheidung," 17, and "Die Stunde Drängt," 36. Whether the third was suppressed by the editors or forbidden by the censors is not known.

[10] *Ibid.,* "Klare Entscheidung," 19, 20.

[11] *Ibid.,* 33.

the North should not fight against the South with a slogan that they are opposing 'separatism.' The sense of autonomy in Bavaria (*Selbstständigkeitssinn*) is nothing but another word for the same ideals which exist in the North. They too are oriented toward the crown. [12]

There were similar statements by other Bavarians published in the dark days of January, 1933. [13] However, the difficulty of finding men of courage who would act upon these principles remained.

If one were to accept the judgment of Erwein von Aretin that all Bavarians were monarchists *"bis in die Knochen,"* [14] one would be inclined to pass a hard judgment on the bungling of the plans for a Wittelsbach restoration which took place in February, 1933. And there were plenty of good omens for monarchy at that time. For example, on February 10, 1933 a performance of an operetta, *Der Vogelhändler,* was scheduled at the Bavarian National Theatre. Near the end of the second act of this operetta there is a grand *fête* in honor of a king. The monarchists resolved to turn this scene to their own uses through the use of white and blue flags, plus the very presence of Crown Prince Rupprecht. At the appropriate time a claque began shouting *"Hoch Rupprecht!"* whereupon the entire audience responded with unexpected generosity and enthusiasm. [15] Unfortunately for the monarchists the "omen" made but one appearance, for the operetta was not repeated. And apparently the monarchists needed many more assurances than just one demonstration. At the same time there was a curious naïvité amongst some of them

---

[12] *Ibid.,* 35.

[13] See also, Nicholas Cossmann, "Republik oder Monarchie," in *Süddeutsche Monatshefte,* XXX, (January, 1933), 14, and "Bayerns Stellung im Reich," *Monarchie,* (December, 1932), 90.

[14] Erwein von Aretin, *Wittelsbacher im K.Z.* (Munich, n.d.), 16.

[15] There are several accounts of this episode, all of which are in general agreement. See, *New York Times,* February 19, 1933, 14; Erwein von Aretin, "Die Frühjahrstage, 1933," (typescript, n.d.); Kurt Sendtner, *op. cit.,* 550.

that a restoration would come about without a *coup d'état*; that, as one of them put it to the *New York Times* reporter, "the simple assumption of regal rights—(would) determine itself." [16] Meanwhile there was some activity going on behind the scenes which took on the general character of a plot to restore the kingship in Bavaria.

Minister-President Held called an informal meeting at the Prinz Karl Palais in Munich for February 20; attending were Dr. Philipp Held, the Minister-President's son, and Freiherr von Stengel as a representative of the monarchist group. Dr. Held can be described as a realistic Bavarian patriot. He inquired seriously of the plans for a restoration, above all whether the monarchists had the necessary financial backing to carry the restoration beyond the initial step; whether they had army support; and whether they could rely on the civil service which included telephone, telegraph, post, finance and railroads, all of which were controlled from Berlin. [17] The monarchists felt that the answers to these questions depended entirely upon the success of the *coup*. [18] What was perhaps more devastating was their unwillingness to take the risk of provoking civil war in Germany, for they realized this would bring additional Prussian intruders in the form of an army defending the unity of the Reich. So it was that they hit upon what they thought must be a sounder and more legal device.

Crown Prince Rupprecht had moved from his country palace, Leutstetten, to the Leuchtenberg Palais in Munich attended by his son, Albrecht von Bayern, Freiherr von Stengel and his

---

[16] *New York Times*, February 11, 1933, 8. (Article signed by G. E. R. Gedye. The quote is from someone named "Enoch," very possibly Enoch Freiherr von Guttenberg).

[17] For a positive appreciation of Minister-President Held's attitude during the crisis, see an article written by his son, Dr. Josef Held, for the *Regensburger Tagesanzeiger*, No. 143 (November 24, 1950), 4.

[18] Erwein von Aretin, Die Frühjahrstage, 1933.

Kabinett-Chef, Graf von Soden-Frauenhofen. [19] This group was supported by another which was actively engaged in plotting at the Hotel Vierjahreszeiten under the aegis of Enoch von Guttenberg. [20] It was decided here and approved by the group in the Leuchtenberg Palais that a representative should go directly to Hindenburg, with the expectation that the President of the Republic would issue a *fiat* restoring the monarchy. Accordingly, Fürst Öttingen-Wallerstein accompanied by Alfons Freiherr von Redwitz drove to Berlin in the night of February 21/22. They went at once to Franz Speer, the Bavarian ambassador who was to have arranged the meeting. Although the audience took place, Hindenburg was physically and mentally beyond reach. Hitler had had him isolated and had been successful in convincing him that the leader of the National Socialists alone would bring back the monarchy—all in good time. [21] With this avenue blocked what was left open to the monarchists?

In Munich, meanwhile, Dr. Held might have sided openly with the monarchists had the Nazis forced his hand by more clearly defining what they meant by the centralization of the Reich. He insisted that at least Bavarian rights be maintained if not a Bavarian monarchy. Above all he preferred to have Bavaria out of the Reich than to have her ruled by a Hohenzollern monarch, a point made quite clear in an interview with the *New York Times*.

> In keeping with the letter of the Constitution, I shall defend Bavarian independence at all costs, even in the face of force, with

[19] Elisabeth von Guttenberg, *op. cit.*, 112.

[20] Erwein von Aretin, *op. cit.*, 10.

[21] Elisabeth von Guttenberg, *op. cit.*, 11. See also some very interesting insights by Father Max Pribilla, *Deutsche Schicksalsfragen* (Frankfurt, 1951), 14. He says, in part: "Hindenburg selbst scheint in dem Glauben gestorben zu sein, Hitler werde die Monarchie wieder herstellen. Das geht aus dem zweiten Teil seines Testaments hervor, das einen dahin gehenden Wunsch aussprach. Hitler had diesen zweiten Teil nach Hindenburgs Tod wohlweislich nicht veröffentlicht."

which we may be confronted. For this I am not only prepared but also determined, and it is to be hoped that the Bavarian people will be one with me in this resolve.

If it is proposed to rule alone by force and commit all authority into the hands of one party as a prelude to proclaiming a national regency to include Bavaria, I can only say that such a procedure is wholly unacceptable to us. We shall not consent to having a Prussian Prince foisted upon us as a German king. [22]

Clearly, Dr. Held was a proponent of the *status quo*. His greater loyalty was to Bavaria. Any further centralization of the Reich might find Bavaria outside the Reich. Dr. Held gave evidence of his unwillingness to listen to orders from the Nazi Minister of the Interior, Dr. Frick, by ignoring Dr. Frick's demand that the *Münchner Neueste Nachrichten* be suppressed for unfair treatment of National Socialism. [23]

Yet Dr. Held was vague in his attitude toward a Wittelsbach restoration in Bavaria. At one time he suggested that Crown Prince Rupprecht simply take over the job as Minister-President, and then make the next step somewhat as did Napoleon III. Monarchist circles found such a proposal beneath the proper dignity of a king. [24] Apparently this proposel was discussed by Dr. Held with Dr. William Högner, a leading Social Democrat, at a meeting held as late as February 26, 1933. At that time Dr. Högner pledged the support of the Social Democrats to the monarchy in preference to the inevitable dictatorship of the National Socialists. Republican though they were, they were not blind to the inevitable loss of basic freedoms under fascism; furthermore, a monarchy was, properly executed, a *Rechtsstaat*. However, even though a friendly agreement of cooperation was reached culminating in the possible combination of *Reichsban-*

22 *New York Times,* February 22, 1933, 10.
23 *Ibid.*
24 Erwein von Aretin, *Wittelsbacher im K.Z.,* 17.

ner and *Bayernwacht,* sub-organizations of the Social Democrats and Bavarian's People's Party, Dr. Held was incapable
of working out a solution to the legal problem of reconciling
the Bavarian Constitution and a monarchy. [25] That is why
Dr. Held continued to encourage the forces at the Vierjahreszeiten Hotel to delay. A sterner figure might have joined the
coup or might have arrested the plotters; another sort might
have resigned. This delay seems tragic now, considering the
apparent desire in the hearts of so many Bavarians to return the
Wittelsbach family to their honored place as head of the state.
Although Dr. Held's action was undoubtedly weak, it was much
less so than the action of those who wanted a restoration much
more than he and yet were guided by his warnings. Something
more was needed than plans to distribute a few flags and have
the Munich stations ready to play phonograph records of *God
Save the King* and the *Te Deum.* [26] In time many of those who
devoutly struggled to restore the Wittelsbachs lost their lives
because of the victory the Nazis were winning in those February
days of 1933.

The burning of the *Reichstag* was quickly followed by the
appointment of General von Epp as the *Reichsstatthalter* for
Bavaria. Bavaria was now more than ever a prisoner of the Reich.
Any alteration of Hitler's plan of a completely unified Germany
directed from Berlin was increasingly unlikely. And yet, those
writing in *Monarchie* continued to maintain the view that cultural and economic federalism must be emphasized if the "new"

---

[25] For a fuller discussion of this, see a letter written by Dr. William
Högner (dated October 19, 1948) to Dr. Josef Held, which appears in an
article by Held in the *Regensburger Tagesanzeiger,* (December 16, 1950; 4).
(Held's article is a reply to an article by E. von Aretin, "Königskrone oder
Hakenkreuz? — Dokumentarischer Tatsachenbericht," *Münchener Allgemeine
Zeitung,* number 7, 8; 1947-1948. Von Aretin's article views unfavorably the
role of Minister President Held in the events of February, 1933.)

[26] Elisabeth von Guttenberg, *op. cit.,* 114.

Germany was to go forward in health and happiness. [27] It is difficult to see how the Nazis could have followed this advice if one of their chief aims was permanently to unite the German people.

In the years which followed 1933 some Bavarians continued to maintain their opposition to centralism. We have the word of one cautious observer that by 1941 "an unprecedented hatred toward Prussia was rampant in Bavaria and Austria." [28] The National Socialists, having conquered Prussia and ruling through Prussia, were an obvious and easy target for these sentiments which south Germans had nurtured since 1871. [29] There were none who fed on these sentiments more consistently than did the publisher and writers connected with *Monarchie*. The editor responsible for the future of that journal as well as its successor, *Weisse Blätter*, was Karl Ludwig Freiherr zu Guttenberg, and it is his activities which must concern us now.

c) WEISSE BLÄTTER

In the first months of the National Socialist victory *Monarchie* gave little evidence of serious dissatisfaction. The editors still seemed to hope that their conception of the thousand year old Reich would at any moment come to life again, especially since as they phrased it "the alien contagion of non-Germanic theories had been so completely rejected." [30] The question still remained: who would wake the "sleeping giant at Kyffhäuser?" Could these monarchists have likened Hitler to Bismarck?

By January, 1934 *Monarchie* boldly announced that the exiled

---

[27] "Das Dritte Reich," *Monarchie*, (July, 1933), 108-09.

[28] Ulrich von Hassell, *Diaries* (Garden City, N.Y., 1947), 216 (October, 1941).

[29] For further discussion of the hopes of the monarchists in 1933, see Karl Schwend, *Bayern zwischen Monarchie und Diktatur* (Munich, 1954), 514-548.

[30] Arthur Hübscher, "Klare Entscheidung," *Monarchie* (1933), 5.

German Emperor would fill that gap in the hearts of an already awakened people. [31] The entire issue was dedicated to the celebration of William II's seventy-fifth birthday, full of adulation and apologies for this man's ability in all fields of human endeavor. At least for Prussians, here was serious competition for the new leader. Accordingly, in February, 1934, *Monarchie* was suspended by the Nazi government; the birthday greetings to an exiled sovereign were apparently too hearty. [32]

Undaunted by this, a new monthly was published at the same address beginning in May, 1934 under the rather more guarded title of *Weisse Blätter*. There was never any specific explanation for this title, nor, until the following year, did the periodical bear the subheading of a monthly devoted to "history, tradition and the state." [33] A careful reader of the journal in those years could easily perceive the very important place which religion enjoyed with reference to "history, tradition and the state!" In his introductory essay, the editor proclaimed his hostility to the nineteenth century with its liberal-democratic heritage. It was, in his view, to blame for the satisfaction which man seemed to feel with the superficial answers of the positivists and the pragmatists. Such satisfaction had been purchased at the price of what the

---

[31] *Ibid.,* (January, 1934), 1.

[32] Therese Freifrau zu Guttenberg, Lebenslauf, 1.

[33] *Weisse Blätter, Zeitschrift für Geschichte, Tradition und Staat,* (Würzburg, 1934, 1935-1942.) (The color white has had a variety of employments in European history. It is the color used on the highest festivals of the Church, with the exception of Pentecost. It is the Papal color, being used interchangeably with gold. It was the royal color of France, being long associated with the *Ancien Regime.* But is was also the color used by an anti-English agrarian society in Ireland during the 18th century. And, of course, it was used by the Munich Students as the title for their publications: *Blätter der Weissen Rose.* There are doubtless many other examples which one could find; but these few are mentioned only that the question be asked: why is a certain color selected as a symbol?)

Germans call, *die Tiefe.* [34] This depth, the editor made clear, was the proper religious approach to reality; all the big questions were in the last analysis religious questions. [35] He concluded his remarks with the conviction that when man realized the horror of the modern world, when he realized fully that the sanctuaries had been violated, the altars destroyed, then he would be provoked to return to a piety which would give him the strength to reach the "shore beyond." [36]

However much reduced here, this is the theme of the *Weisse Blätter* as a careful study of the volumes of the years which follow 1934 will indicate. The *Weisse Blätter* argued that western civilization—interestingly enough a phrase rarely encountered in this periodical—had reached a point of departure comparable to that at the end of the middle ages. Whether the chaos would take the form of "wars of religion" was not easily foretold; but piety would be gained only through suffering. Germany would need all the grace of the old order to suffer the birth of the new. What form the new order would take will be discussed in a moment. What of the end of the old?

One of the devices used by the editors to bring to the attention of other conservatives the extent to which "their" Germany was being transformed, was the publication each month of a chronicle. The publication of this sort of news was clearly intended not only to inform the readers of the *Weisse Blätter*, but also to alert them. It was this latter aspect which must be taken into account in reviewing the history of this journal as a part of the conservative opposition to National Socialism. [37] Although it would be impossible to reprint the

---

[34] "Zu Neuen Ufern," *Weisse Blätter* (May, 1934), 1.
[35] *Ibid.,* 2.
[36] *Ibid.*
[37] Rudolf Pechel writes similarly of his work in the *Deutsche Rundschau;* see his *Deutscher Widerstand* (Zürich, 1947), 286-291.

entire Chronicle in these pages, a sufficient sampling of the character of this effort must be recorded in order to indicate what a cleft existed inside Germany under the Nazis. At the same time one must realize how powerless the conservatives felt in the face of the radical changes going on in Germany; how inadequate were their facilities to put into effect the changes of which they approved and to resist those radical changes of which they so strongly disapproved. The chief areas which the chronicle touches on are matters of individual freedom, freedom of the press, religion, and, above all, the ever-growing octopus of the Party whose tentacles were reaching into every aspect of German life. The chronicle begins in January, 1935 reporting on events in the preceding month.

> *December 4.* Staatsrat Dr. Wilhelm Furtwängler has resigned his post as vice-president of the *Reichsmusikkammer,* director of the Berlin Philharmonic, and director of the state opera house, because of his insistence in maintaining a favorable attitude toward the composer Paul Hindemith, an attitude in opposition to one held by the National Socialist *Kulturgemeinde.*
>
> *December 22,* The *Deutsche Zeitung* and the *Ostpreussische Zeitung* will cease publication with the end of this year. [38]
>
> *January 15, 1935.* The *Führer* and Chancellor said in his speech on the Saar question that after its return 'the German Reich will make no further territorial demands on France.' [39]
>
> *February 3.* From this month on the *Danziger Tagesblatt* edited by Dr. Fritz Klein, the *Breslauer Zeitung,* and the *Rhein-Mainische Zeitung* will cease publication. [40]
>
> *March 14.* The Protestant Church of the old Prussian Union announced in a synod that there would be no abandoning of work amongst the youth.
>
> *March 18.* England formally protests compulsory military service in Germany.
>
> *March 28.* Reichsminister of the Interior, Dr. Frick, explained

---

[38] *Weisse Blätter, 1935,* 22.
[39] *Ibid.,* 50.
[40] *Ibid.,* 89.

at Nürnberg that the government would have to interfere in Church matters in order to establish what is right. [41]

April 2. A great festival in Berlin has celebrated the taking over the state courts by the central government.

April 3. The administration of discipline in the schools has now been centralized under one system.

April 13. A special court in Schwerin has sentenced Canon Leffers of Rostock to one and a half years in prison because of his remarks on Alfred Rosenberg's *Myth of the Twentieth Century.*

April 24. The state secretary in Saxony has announced that it has been necessary to arrest a number of Protestant ministers.

Dr. Frick, Minister of the Interior, announces that the swastika will now be displayed in the first position, before the black-white-red flag. [42]

May 3. Copies of a Catholic Church bulletin critical of the *Landjahr* have been confiscated.

May 27. The Munich police has issued a warning against anti-semitic terror groups. [43]

June 28. Dr. F. Mahling, the director of the Press and Cultural affairs in the *Reichsmusikkammer* has been dismissed from office because he is not reliable. [44]

July 1. *Baseler Nachrichten* forbidden in Germany.

July 7. *Reichsleiter* Rosenberg attacked the Bishop of Münster at a Party meeting in Westphalia because the Bishop tried to prevent the appearance of Rosenberg in Münster by a formal letter of protest to the government.

July 18. Minister Goering attacks political Catholicism.

July 23. None but National Socialists will be allowed to wear uniforms in the Reich. [45]

August 3. The Ministry of War orders all personnel in the army to salute leaders of the Party.

August 4. Dr. Goebbels condemns the Koelping Brothers for defamatory letters.

---

[41] *Ibid.,* 118.
[42] *Ibid.,* 142-143.
[43] *Ibid.,* 180-181.
[44] *Ibid.,* 212.
[45] *Ibid.,* 242-243.

August 15. Three Brothers of Mercy condemned to penitentiary for currency deviations.

August 18. Pommerschen Tagespost banned because its content not patterned after the spirit of National Socialism. [46]

September 11. A proclamation from the *Führer* read at the Nürnberg Party congress: 'We possess power and we intend to keep it; we will not tolerate any attempt to organize against this power; rather we will repress such attempts whenever they appear.' [47]

October 8. Professor Dr. C. Schmitt said: 'In our leader-state, the plan and the will of the *Führer* is law.'

October 13. [Winston] Churchill published an article in the *Strand Magazine* which is offensive to the Chancellor and *Führer* of the National Socialist Party. The German ambassador will protest. [48]

November 8. The NSDFB (Stahlhelm) is disbanded.

November 24. The Roman Catholic Bishop of Meissen, Peter Legge, was fined 100,000 R.M. because of currency deviations. [49]

December 11. The director of the Bureau of Information for diocesan authorities in Germany, Canon Dr. Banasch, has been arrested on suspicion of betraying state secrets. [50]

February 2. 1936. Baldur v. Schirach is quoted as saying: 'Some say the Hitler Youth is anti-religious, that they would tear down altars. I know and publicly confess in the name of all German youth: who loves Adolf Hitler loves Germany, and who loves Germany loves God.'

February 12. Adolf Hitler said at Schwerin: 'I must say here and now: on that route we have followed, we have neither met nor had to do away with one opponent; nor has there been any effort at a coup.' (*Attentat*)

February 19. The Evangelical Church—amongst others the Church in Bremen—has announced a number of re-entries to the Church membership list. [51]

---

46 *Ibid.*, 277-278.
47 *Ibid.*, 309.
48 *Ibid.*, 340.
49 *Ibid.*, 364-365.
50 *Ibid.*, 1936, 22.
51 *Ibid.*, 85-86.

April 22. The People's Court for trials of high treason has become a part of the ordinary tribunal system. [52]

May, 1936 is the last issue which carried the chronicle in this manner. From December of that year until the beginning of the war there was a substitute which went under the title *Mosaik der Zeit.* As before, inference, clear from the title, was everything. The reports, for example, for January, 1937 included among other things the portentous fact of the increase of Ludendorff's publications which were notoriously anti-Catholic. [53] In the same issue, one could read *Gauleiter* Simon's remarks at the opening of a new Teacher's College at Trier in which he praised it as a place free from all dogma. He pointed out that a true champion of freedom of the spirit was teaching there, Ferdinand von Spee, an ex-Jesuit. [54] The chronicle goes on in much this same way and must have caused considerable irritation to readers of the *Weisse Blätter.* The following are a few examples chosen from the years 1937-1939.

The *Landrat* of Tarnowitz has forbidden the Catholic Women's League to meet because they have not adhered to the rules governing associations. [55]

The Golden Party Badge will now be worn next to or above the Iron Cross, first-class. [56]

The Reich Minister of Interior forbids any publication—especially the reading of such names from the pulpit—of such individuals who withdraw from Church membership. Any deviation from this will be punished by prison or money fine. [57]

In place of the Nobel Prize—which has been rejected for all time—a yearly award will be made at the Nürnberg Party Congress. [58]

---

[52] *Ibid.,* 147.
[53] *Ibid.,* 1937, 17.
[54] *Ibid.,* 18.
[55] *Ibid.,* 1937, 47.
[56] *Ibid.,* 81.
[57] *Ibid.,* 114.
[58] *Ibid.,* 144.

The German ambassador at the Vatican has registered official complaint to the Cardinal Secretary of State in reference to the Papal encyclical of March 14th.

According to the Reich Minister of Education, Jews with German citizenship may not receive the doctorate at German universities, nor may any diplomas be renewed. This applies also to part-Jewish persons. [59]

The ambassador at the Vatican has been recalled because the Cardinal Secretary of State said that Cardinal Mundelein's speech in Chicago was exactly what the Germans deserved. A *Chargé d'Affaires* has taken over. Meanwhile, Minister Frick said in Bremen: 'We've had enough of those Pastoral Letters and don't want any more letters or encyclicals.' [60]

In a speech at Nürnberg, *Reichskulturminister* declared: 'The division of German schools according to religious points of view must cease as soon as possible.' The *Kulturminister* of Württemberg, Mergenthaler, declared: 'The education of German youth must be unified with the spirit of National Socialism. It must not happen that other influences are allowed a place which might then cause a rift in the minds of German youth. Religious instruction must aid in this work. Thus anything which might tend to offend the moral feeling of the German race must be removed. Certain portions of the Old Testament cannot possibly be taught; others must be kept in the background.' [61]

A decree of the Reich Ministry of Interior has declared that un-wed females may be called 'Frau' without official action Mothers of children born out of wedlock are to be called 'Frau' officially if they so register with the local police. They must, however, still register as 'single.' [62]

Gauleiter Burckl (Pfalz) issued the following statement: '... any attacks on the Party or the state coming from the pulpit or given in secret are to be reported at once. In all these cases the one involved will no longer be allowed to give religious instruction. The situation will be reported to the bishop; if nothing is

[59] *Ibid.*, 176.
[60] *Ibid.*, 206-07.
[61] *Ibid.*, 208.
[62] *Ibid.*, 232.

done by him, the Party authorities will handle it. Individuals should take no personal action.' [63]

In an important decision by the Dortmund *Landesarbeitsgericht*, if one leaves the NSDAP one is no longer bound by his oath to the *Führer*. [64]

At a convention of civil servants in Munich, Minister of Interior Frick declared: 'No official can really say: two souls live in my breast—one official, the other private. A person is either a National Socialist, or he is not. Half-way compromisings are not allowed. Every German official must be a National Socialist or he must struggle with all his power to become one.' [65]

The Bavarian Catholic Youth groups have been dissolved on the basis of the Law of February 28, 1933 (Law Protecting the State). These groups have been accused of editing illegal propaganda leaflets. [66]

The Thuringian *Landeskirche* announces that Jews are no longer members of the Church; clergy are not required to assist in the cure of their souls. Taxes will not be collected from them. A similar statement was issued by the Saxonian *Landeskirche*. [67]

At the exposition hall in Reichenberg, Rosenberg spoke out against three fronts: Jewry, reaction, and political Catholicism. He also said that there can be no distinction between the state and the *Weltanschauung*. [68]

At the Eucharistic Congress in Algiers the Papal Legate was greeted by the leaders of the Mohammedan and Hebrew faiths. The latter spokesman said: 'We greet you as the representative of one who is not afraid to speak out with the power of his authority against hate and persecution of religion. [69]

Jews in the Protectorate of Bohemia have been ordered to register all their valuables at the National Bank; gold, silver, platinum and jewels.

The Protestant theological faculty at the University of Münster

---

[63] *Ibid.*, 277.
[64] *Ibid.*, 336.
[65] *Ibid.*, 364.
[66] *Ibid.*, 1938, 54.
[67] *Ibid.*, 1939, 116.
[68] *Ibid.*, 157.
[69] *Ibid.*, 154.

has taken back Karl Barth's honorary degree which was given to him in 1922, 'because he has shown by his actions that he is unworthy to hold a German academic honor.' [70]

To be sure, this is but a part of the chronicle which covered those years; it does not seem, however, that reprinting more items here can serve to clarify the point. It must be apparent why a periodical like the *Weisse Blätter* should print such a chronicle of unflattering ill-tidings. Plainly it was an effort to inform like-minded Germans of the transformation and total eclipse of their traditions. The reader will have noted the warnings—in some cases in the words of Hitler or Goebbels—against any revolt or serious effort to set aside the Nazis.

Apparently the most important task which the editors of the *Weisse Blätter* saw for themselves was the making of a clear statement of what was at stake in contemporary Germany. They placed greatest emphasis on the importance of a steadfast loyalty to Christianity, if the Germany they knew was to survive at all. Commenting on what seemed an inevitable conflict in German history, they argued that politics could never be allowed to overshadow religion; if this happened, the very principles upon which the Reich was founded would be contradicted. [71] These principles go back to the medieval conception of the crown as the symbol of authority, and this crown had religious and sacramental meaning also. There were a number of articles in the *Weisse Blätter* which kept this way of thinking alive, but none were more consistent nor more frequent than the articles by Reinhold Schneider. [72] An article which clearly suggested the

---

[70] *Ibid.*, 231.

[71] "Von den Werten und der Bewahrung," *Ibid.*, 1935, 1.

[72] See Reinhold Schneider, "Der Geistige in der Geschichte," *Ibid.*, 1934, 97; "Die Burg Hohenzollern," *ibid.*, 3; "Dom und Dichter," *ibid.*, 178; "Religion und Revolution," *ibid.*, 35; "Speyer und Potsdam," *ibid.*, 65; "Die Wirklichkeit des Glaubens," *ibid.*, 1935, 289; "Kreuz und Geschichte," *ibid.*, 289; "Wesen und Wandel des Papsttums," *ibid.*, 265; "Christ und Anti-

misfortune which would befall a nation when the people sub-
stituted a dictator for the traditional form of government was
one entitled "Cromwell and the Crown." [73] In the course of his
discussion Schneider quoted a conversation which must have
seemed very familiar to a contemporary German. A citizen was
complaining to Cromwell that, had the English still their king,
a certain event could not have taken place. Cromwell is said to
have replied:

> Ah yes, but I am not a king; I am not bound to behave like a
> king. I am the Lord Protector. Show me the law which binds the
> Lord Protector to act in a certain manner. [74].

If the article had any meaning, other than purely historical,
it could only be taken as a warning by example. There were
many such efforts to warn Germans by the examples of the past.

For example, English history of the Reformation years provided fruitful comparisons, a good example being found in the
life of Thomas More who suffered death for his loyalty to an
ancien regime. [75] However, no other historical problem seemed
so exact a parallel to the German situation as was the life and
death of Sparta. In an unsigned article in the *Weisse Blätter,*
Sparta was clearly rejected and placed in the dust-bin of world
history. And however superficial this judgment of the Spartan
ideal may appear to the student of Greek civilization, one can
easily perceive what it was that conservatives were objecting to
in the history of Sparta. Quite simply it was a society which was
fed on fear and sought to assuage its anxieties by militarism. The
judgment of the author of the article in the *Weisse Blätter* was

---

Christ," *ibid.,* 1936, 289; "Staat und Bischof," *ibid.,* 161; "Englands Krone,"
1937, 4; "Jeanne d'Arc." *ibid.,* 1939, 213; "Das Unbezwingliche im Menschen," *ibid.,* 1940, 62; "Der Sinn aller Zeit," *ibid.,* 3; "Die Stefanskrone,"
1942, 4; "Kyffersberg," *ibid.,* 188—to give only a few of his titles.
[73] "Cromwell und die Krone," *ibid.,* 1936, 227-233.
[74] *Ibid.,* 231.
[75] J. F. Leistner, "Thomas Morus," *ibid.,* 1934, 71.

a very apt warning to Germans: *Sparta musste untergehen.* The clear inference was that any nation which pursued policies of force, militarism, suppression and fear was bound to enjoy Sparta's fate, that of being but a fragmentary aspect of world history. [76] What might these conservatives have done to rescue their Germany from such a fate?

Interestingly enough, the quality of the opposition to Hitler from these conservatives was not unlike that official position taken by the Catholic hierarchy in Bavaria, especially as represented by Cardinal Faulhaber: a curious combination of prudence and suffering. Yet these monarchists were not without plans for that which would replace the National Socialist experiment. In fact, there is, by inference, the suggestion that the National Socialist revolution might very well be manipulated to ends more in keeping with conservative ideals. That may well explain why Reinhold Schneider chose to quote Charles I's interesting remark just prior to his execution: "For I have observed, that the Devil of rebellion doth commonly turn himself into an angel of reformation." [77] Remarks of this sort were intended to be taken as a commentary on recent developments in Germany. That political enthusiasm of Germans for the corporative state might conceivably have been the means of turning Hitler into an "angel of reformation."

Perhaps the most straight-forward communication in this matter was an article by Ulrich von Hassell which was highly regarded in conservative-monarchist circles. [78] The article was on the surface an account of Freiherr von Stein's conception of the organic state; actually this served as but a point of departure to discuss Germany's past and present. The first thing von Hassell

---

[76] "Sparta musste untergehen," *ibid.*, 1934, 89-91.

[77] R. Schneider, "Cromwell und die Krone," *ibid.*, 228.

[78] U. v. Hassell, "Der Organische Staatsgedanke des Freiherr von Stein." *ibid.*, 1939, 249; see also Elisabeth von Guttenberg, *op. cit.*, 136.

made clear to his reader was that Germany must not be confused with the democratic west; the real Germany had never been
associated with the liberal-democratic way of life, which, according to him, was essentially mechanistic. Unfortunately, Germany
had picked up some democratic notions and in consequence had
experienced class warfare. The real Germany would accept only
an organic state, the kind von Stein would have set up after
Prussia had dethroned "the son of chaos." [79] Alas for this
effort! Yet, Germany was offered a second chance to enter upon
a life which promised rich rewards for all at a time when the
future never seemed blacker. Von Hassell proceeds then to quote
from an article he wrote in 1918 discussing what Germans might
have done in their darkest hour. He said, in part:

> We Germans stand in a ruined field. Ought we simply to
> gather together the fragments and try to reconstruct the old house?
> Certainly not! After such a dark night one does not simply start
> working where one left off the day before. The political earth-
> quake has so completely transformed the earth that it would be
> impossible to rebuild on the old plans. But neither do we feel
> that the temporary structures which are now being built on these
> ruins ought to be regarded as the prototype of what we really
> want for a new state. We do not want any class rule, even if this
> class be the masses. Nor do we want a *Volksstaat* in name only.
> And we do not want any old-fashioned ideas in modern dress. We
> want a *Volksstaat* in which the people themselves—agricultural,
> industrial, university, workers, employers—will determine the
> course of political action. Nor do we want to leave the thing to
> the professional tribunes who with their ability in oratory will
> agitate for class interests. [80]

But, in 1939, when von Hassell was writing, he found this
warning had gone unheeded; the Weimar Republic fulfilled
the worst of von Hassell's fears in 1918. He did not, however,
openly disavow the National Socialists at this point—but rather

---

[79] *Weisse Blätter. ibid.,* 249.
[80] *Ibid.,* 253.

ended with the remark: "Then came National Socialism and with one blow put an end to the whole parliamentary-democratic chaos." [81] Although von Hassell's bitterness against National Socialism is known from other sources, his real hopes for Germany were that this episode would pass, especially since the democratic poison had been pumped out. He sought a new, hitherto untried experiment, namely, corporative. [82]

This was the most consistent of the biases which the *Weisse Blätter* encouraged: a plea for an organic state based upon corporations. It is the apparent explanation for the several articles on Stein, von Ketteler as well as repeated quotations from the writings of Goerres and Moeller van den Bruck which bear directly upon this problem. [83] It is interesting to see how close these conservatives were to the thinking of van den Bruck. In his writings they found a creed for conservatives which was reprinted in the *Weisse Blätter*. The chief articles of that creed were stated simply:

a) national security
b) the preservation of the family
c) the preservation of the monarchy
d) a life governed by discipline
e) a life protected by the principle of authority
f) a society based upon self-governing, corporative units [84]

Those were the ideals which the conservative monarchists kept before them during the years of their opposition to Hitler. They fully realized that they were living during a period of transition; they confidently expected that the National Socialist revolution would pass and that, on the "other shore," they would find that

---

[81] *Ibid.*
[82] *Ibid.*, 251.
[83] *Ibid.*, 252. See also A. Ritthaler, "Bischof Ketteler's Nationalpolitische Bedeutung." *ibid.*, 1940, 6-11; on Görres, see *ibid.*, 1934, 132; Moeller van den Bruck, "Conservativ-Reaktionär," *ibid.*, 1934, 13.
[84] Moeller van den Bruck, *loc. cit.*, 13.

society which they thought best for Germany; a society which had the characteristics described by Moeller van den Bruck.

One thing they must have felt, however, as each month of their chronicle unfolded some additional deprivation of traditional rights: it was unlikely that they would ever find peace with the Nazis. The warfare against traditional Christianity, for example, was not something calculated to win conservative-monarchist support. In fact, Karl Ludwig zu Guttenberg said as much to the *Kreisleiter* of Neustadt a. d. Saale who had invited him to become a member of the Nazi Party. In his reply he said in part:

> These remarks are necessary because I regret that I cannot accept your honorable invitation to join the Party. Every decision which I make after due consideration, must be one which is acceptable in all its parts. The manner with which religious and ecclesiastical matters are being handled by the Party at the present time, are so contrary to my position and my feelings that I could not possibly join the Party. These questions and their solution are of such grave importance for the whole people as well as for individuals that they can never be overlooked in any fundamental decision one might make. [85]

Two years after this letter was written, Germany had involved the world in another war. It was one thing to refuse a political alliance; quite another to refuse the call to "defend one's home." The depth of this tragic situation has been preserved in a letter written by Karl Ludwig's brother, Enoch von Guttenberg, to his wife:

> I cannot tell you what a state of mind I'm in. I can hardly face it; the most terrible crime since history began has been committed by loosing this war on Europe. It has been committed by Germany, my dear, and the boys and I must fight on the wrong side in this hideous battle. [86]

---

[85] Karl Ludwig Freiherr zu Guttenberg, letter, Septemebr 5, 1937, to Kreisleiter A. Ingebrand. Complete text, Appendix E.

[86] Elisabeth von Guttenberg, *op. cit.,* 147.

It was much the same with Karl Ludwig. He continued his work as editor of the *Weisse Blätter* even after his call to service, while he was on the staff of the *Abwehr* under Colonel Oster. [87] Here he was not only in a position to see a variety of opinions on the military and political situation, but through conversations and introductions he met many distinguished people who were actively engaged in the various plots to do away with Hitler. Sometime after July 20, 1944, he was arrested by the Gestapo. Part of a statement which he made while in prison has survived and in it, among other things, he explains in a fairly reasonable way the genesis of his opposition to National Socialism. His own words follow here:

> About that time—I asume it was the end of 1941—I got to know Dr. Goerdeler; we met, one day, at the Anhalt station. It was my intention then, as it had been for some time previous, to get him to do a piece for the *Weisse Blätter*. On this occasion we fell into a discussion of the current situation—there was plenty of material which I had at my command in my work at the office. Basing his judgment on economic factors, Goerdeler was extremely pessimistic. In fact, I believe he envisaged a catastrophe in at most three months, and also maintained the view that the generals would have to do something in order to assure a change of government. According to his view the Allies were fighting National Socialism, and, if there were a change of government, they would be prepared to give easier peace terms. The exact details of Dr. Goerdeler's remarks I no longer remember; nor can I remember how we took our leave.
>
> For my own part, I did not share his point of view that a change of government would guarantee better peace terms. I was convinced that the Allies were in a position to beat down any [German] government and to shackle it with such restrictions as would leave Versailles far in the shade. Yet it seemed to me necessary that people in appropriate positions who felt deeply concerned or critical, ought to be able to do something (or say something) to their opposite numbers—for example, the generals ought

---

87 Therese Freifrau zu Guttenberg, Lebenslauf, 2.

to be able to present their case to the leaders in the government.
However, this is based on the judgment that the future of the war
is predictable. Yet the more I looked at my materials, the more
skeptical I became of the possibility of relying on a fixed conclusion to the whole situation. More and more I took quite a
different view from that which Dr. Goerdeler expressed: I came
to believe that in spite of all the serious catastrophes, etc., it would
be utterly impossible to predict either the manner or the form of
the end of the war; at any moment the wholly unexpected might
happen. Every prediction of future developments even though
based on the most accurate information appeared dubious to me.
That is why I came to the conviction that no single action, however unified on the part of the generals, could really be expected
to accomplish much because the available materials did not warrant
assuming so much . . . .

Should it come to pass that the war be lost, then certainly I
would regard it as possible that men such as Goerdeler and Beck
would have to take charge in order not to let the country fall into
the hands of the Communists. For certainly I had little doubt that
if the war were lost, there would be a change of government. [88]

Although it must always be kept in mind that the statements
were made under impossible conditions before an S.S. officer,
they are not so far removed from what we know to be the real
sentiments of Karl Ludwig zu Guttenberg. He had cooperated
with his brother in an effort to restore the Wittelsbach monarchy in February, 1933; and this had come to naught. He had
found himself on the list of those to be executed in the "night
of the long knives" of June, 1934; and this he had managed to
escape. [89] He had consistently held the conservative line in his
periodical, urging, above all else, a loyalty to Germany's traditional religious form as the only safe guide through troubled
times. It was this attitude which kept him from joining the Na-

---

[88] Karl Ludwig Freiherr zu Guttenberg, "Zusamenfassung meiner Angaben
vor Standartenführer Huppenkothen, am 9. Nov. 1944," copy, annotated by
Therese Freifrau zu Guttenberg, 4-5. Complete text in Appendix F.
[89] See Elisabeth von Guttenberg, op. cit., 125.

tional Socialist Party. Finally, he had cooperated with those who sought a way out of Germany's impossible war by overthrowing Hitler; and, for this, he paid the supreme price. In the early hours of April 24, 1945, he was taken from his cell in Berlin and, along with Graf Bernstorff and the former Minister Schneppenhorst, he was shot by S.S. guards. [90]

d) THE VON HARNIER KREIS

There were other Bavarians, some of whom had been influenced by the ideals of the *Weisse Blätter,* who came to manifest their opposition to National Socialism in a quite public manner. In August and September, 1939, when Western attention was focused on the invasion of Poland and the beginning of the Second World War, a *Gestapo* action in Bavaria imprisoned one hundred and twenty-five enemies of the Third Reich, individuals accused of actively plotting to restore the Wittelsbach family to rule in Bavaria. [91] Of this rather large number, nine were ultimately brought to justice, but only after a prolonged investigation which kept some of the original one hundred and twenty-five still in prison as late as 1941. [92] Of the final nine, one met death

---

[90] Therese Freifrau zu Guttenberg, Lebenslauf, 2.

[91] Weintz, Die Illegale Monarchistische Bewegung in Bayern, typescript, 250 pp. (Munich, 1939). This is an account of the activities of the von Harnier circle which was prepared for the Munich *Gestapo* and dated October, 1939. The informant for the *Gestapo* was Michael Fischer. A copy of this *Gestapo* report was sent to the German consulate in Zürich where, after the war, it was recovered by Father Siegfried Huber, one of the monarchists who had escaped to Switzerland just prior to the arrest of August, 1939. In 1945 he returned to Bavaria bringing also this document. It is now located in Prien am Chiemsee with the Huber family. Hereafter the document will be referred to as *Weintz.*

[92] The evidence which corroborates this is rather interesting. A letter sent out by the Munich *Gestapo* to Stadelheim prison, inquiring about Christoph Fischer of Landshut, can be found in the Berlin Document Center in the file of the Munich *Gestapo*. The letter is dated March, 29, 1941; the signature is illegible. Fischer's name appears on the list of arrests in *Weintz,* 205. There

by hanging in Berlin, January 1945; the other eight received various prison or penitentiary sentences. [93]

The first thing one notices about the nine brought to justice was their almost total lack of homogeneity—a lawyer, a gardener, a mechanic, a tailor, a truckdriver, a business man, a sculptress, a contractor, and a priest. Each was different in social background, education, occupation, and yet all were firmly united in their opposition to National Socialism and agreed that Germany's future must be linked with the established principle of monarchy. The history of their meetings goes back to the period just after Hitler came to power, after the effort in February, 1933 to restore the Wittelsbachs had failed. The group was first organized by Margarete Elizabeth Freiin von Stengel.

Margarete von Stengel was a sculptress who had been born in Munich and lived most of her life there. [94] Active in her support of the *Heimat- und Königsbund,* she continued to hold meetings for like-minded members even after the Nazis had banned the association. And for this she had gotten into trouble with the *Gestapo* in 1935. She was arrested, having been denounced by a certain Bernhard Egger as an enemy of the state, but she was later released because of insufficient evidence. [95] That she would have been so lightly treated by the *Gestapo* is not surprising; for her activities and associations were such as might be regarded by the Nazis as not too significant—in the way of opposition. In this she was much like her friends of that time, Heinrich Weiss and

---

is also a reference in B. Gisevius, *To the Bitter End,* 406, to forty Bavarian legitimists whom Himmler offered to implicate in the "attempt" on Hitler's life which took place in the Bürgerbräukeller, November, 1939.

[93] Franz Fackler, "Der Ruf des Gewissens," in *Film und Leben* (Munich, 1950), 45. See also the trial of the monarchists: *Volksgerichtshof, 6H 92/94, 75, 32/44,* 6 *Senat,* June 28, 1944. 2 pp. The full text is reprinted in Appendix I.

[94] M. von Stengel, born Munich, February 10, 1898.

[95] *Weintz,* 1.

Wilhelm Seutter von Lötzen. Heinrich Weiss was the head gardener at Schleissheim, a state monument once owned by the Wittelsbach family. [96] His chief enthusiasm was the past, which accounted for his belief that the present could be vastly improved by a return of the monarchy. He was, apparently, without an integrated plan as to how this should be achieved, and equally unaware of the serious consequences which awaited one who advocated such a reactionary notion in the Third Reich. [97] The main thing in his life was loyalty to the Wittelsbachs and for this he was willing to take whatever consequence awaited him. Later he was to learn from others that opposition to Hitler could not be simply bravura.

Seutter von Lötzen, though a younger man, had much in common with Weiss. [98] He had a similar propensity for heedless action. After the dissolution of the *Heimat- und Königsbund* he joined *Stahlhelm* only to find this organization in the process of disbanding on order from the rulers of the Third Reich. Meanwhile he eked out an existence as a truck-driver for a Catholic printing house in Donauwörth. By this means he came into contact with fairly conservative people, and found his way to the gatherings at the von Stengel home. An enthusiastic monarchist, he gave glowing reports of his contacts throughout southern Bavaria with legitimists, reporting the number of those who would support a restoration to be in the thousands. [99]

There were others who found their way into the von Stengel circle. A certain Dr. Sturmann was responsible for interesting a man who turned out to be one of the most significant figures

---

[96] Heirich Weiss, b. July 4, 1887, Laufen a.d. Saale.
[97] *Weintz*, 21.
[98] von Lötzen, b. December 31, 1901, in Lindau am Bodensee.
[99] Johann Mertel, Die Bayerische Widerstandsbewegung und das Haus Wittelsbach, typescript, 3 p.p.

in this monarchist group, Joseph Zott. [100] During the day Zott
worked as a city-contractor. Evenings, he and Sturmann had
already associated themselves with a group of opponents of the
Third Reich who gathered at a tavern called the "Steinecke."
Among these were Berthold Feuchtdanger, Dr. Dietrich von Hildebrand and a Johann Beimler. This group presented a curious
mixture of conservative and radical opinions with the common
purpose of reaching an understanding of Germany's plight. Von
Hildebrand and Sturmann were Catholics, conservative and monarchist. By gradual degrees they won Zott to their point of view.
They did this, however, only by making constant reference to
Catholic opinion on social questions as formulated by Pope Leo
XIII. Zott described himself as a Christian socialist who was
prepared to agree to a limited monarchy pledged to social reform. [101]

The admission of Zott to the group at von Stengel's was the
first event to give serious dimension to the group. From his
appearance he was very much a type of hard-headed peasant, an
effect he strengthened by allowing his beard to grow out fully.
The first thing he did when he entered the group of monarchists was to read to them his broadsheet attacking the Nazis.
He felt that this familiar technique would be the best to follow.
He called this broadsheet, "The First Thousand Days of the
Third Reich." It follows here as he wrote it:

> We have kept silence for a thousand days. We have given the
> government a thousand days to fulfil the promises of twelve
> years. For a thousand days we have given to the Reich the un-
> questioned moral right to achieve the wishes of the people. But
> the thousand days of unquestioned power are now over; the time
> of reckoning has come. For after a thousand weeks there will be

---

[100] Because of a fluke at one of the investigations held by the *Gestapo*
after his arrest, Joseph Zott became separated from the others; he was tried
in Berlin and later executed. Joseph Zott, born March 16, 1901 in Munich.
[101] *Weintz*, 10, 11, 12, 21; Fackler, *op. cit.*, 43.

no more German Reich; and who is there who will wait a thousand years?—that could only be demanded of lunatics! During these thousand days the Hitler government has brought the German people to the standard of beggary; the treasury is empty, full of debts and worthless paper money.

German workers, employees, and officials: wake up! You are being cheated out of your sickness-insurance money as well as the money you pay for old-age pensions; there are only piles of debts left. German workers: you have never known before the misery which will be yours now. Wake up! The thousand days of patience are over! Now is the time for action. Look to it, German workers, and salvage what you can from the ruins.

German men of commerce and industry: all of you have hoped and longed for the rebirth of the German economy. To you, most particularly, they have made endless promises now for twelve years. These thousand days must show you how impossible it is for Hitler to fulfill his promises. Whatever has been given to you is all sham. The German worker stands at the edge of a void. When you think that you must reckon with the loss of all your material possessions, that must give you pause. Consider how all of this has gone to build up fortunes in foreign countries for prominent members of the government. You must act; tear down these props and let us all build a Reich based upon peace and honesty.

German peasants: you too are being ruined by all of this. What today seems to be yours, can in a moment become the possession of someone else. Therefore, awake German peasants, awake! This is a matter which concerns German land!

German soldiers and German officers! You are the pride and support of the people. The people still have faith in you. Show them that you are worthy of this trust; show the people that it is their common good that you seek; show them that you are not in league with those who are about to bring about the economic ruin of the German people.

German judges: we make you responsible for every political judgment which falls after the thousandth day. It is up to you to administer German justice and not Party justice. Remember that you are paid in money soaked in the blood of the workers and the peasants and not the Party.

And to you members of the NSDAP—you props of the government! Your days are over. For twelve years the prominent members of your Party have expanded its membership, but only through lies, swindlings and false promises. We assume that you did these things for the benefit of the German people. But surely you now must see the basis upon which your government is founded and how this will lead shortly to the collapse of the German Reich. Although we will not hold you responsible up to the thousandth day of rule, yet from that day on, you who continue your membership in the Party will be held responsible. There will be plenty of photographs of uniforms and Party badges upon which to base the knowledge of who is responsible.

We are fighting for the future of the German people and for the unity of the Reich. We are German workers, employees, peasants, men in business and industry.

We are the awakened German people. [102]

It is difficult to categorize such an effort, except to notice that it in no way reflects the idea that a restoration will solve any of these problems. Its appeal is to the socially-minded German who thinks in terms of groups, classes and material needs. The broadsheet was given to Johann Beimler, one of Zott's associates at Steinecke's, who had it circulated with a few deletions. [103] This occurred in January, 1936. By the fall of that year, the meetings at the von Stengel home had undergone an important change; for there was now a man who had come into the circle who could provide the much desired leadership, Adolf Freiherr von Harnier. [104]

Since its inception, Baron von Harnier had been active in the *Heimat- und Königsbund* and would have been more active in Bavarian politics had this avenue not been closed by the success of the Nazis. In the early years of the Third Reich he spent most

102 *Weintz*, 5-7.
103 In the revised edition, the appeal to the German officers was omitted. At the end of the broadsheet the following was added: "Wir sind die erwachte, nicht parteigebundene, anti-Faschistische deutsche Einheitsfront. Süddeutschland, Januar, 1936." *Weintz*, 16.
104 Born, Munich, April 14, 1903; d., Straubing, May 12, 1945.

of his time at the family home in Regensdorf. However, in 1936 he moved to Munich where he took up the practice of law, much of which seemed to involve defending those who were suffering porperty losses by forced emigration. [105] Still not satisfied with this obvious expression of opposition to the laws and practices of the National Socialists, he sought out friends in whom he might put his trust and with whom he might engage in some productive criticism of the Nazi regime. He found Freiin von Stengel and her group already formed. [106] The great contribution of Freiherr von Harnier was a very obvious one: it was he who gave to the group form and dignity, both of which were born of his excellent mind, his sensitive character and his commanding personality.

With such a diverse group there were difficulties almost at once. If this was to be formed into a significant movement, von Harnier felt that leadership would be essential. As the acknowledged leader of the group, his first task was to establish discipline. Baron von Harnier was a convert to Roman Catholicism, and, as is so often the case in conversion, he held very strictly to Catholic moral teachings, particularly on matters about which in traditionally Catholic countries there appears to be sometimes an accepted laxity. Heinrich Weiss was the subject of his wrath because of a number of improprieties and Weiss was ultimately separated from close contact with those who worked in this group. [107] The dislike may also have arisen from the fact that Weiss had been within the circle before von Harnier, and this may have been the source of some jealousy. But this was not the only difficulty this monarchist group had, nor was it the easiest to solve.

---

105 Ludwig Kastl, "Eidesstattliche Erklärung," Photostat-copy, Munich (date unclear, post-war).

106 *Weintz*, 25.

107 *Weintz*, 91-92.

Clearly Joseph Zott and Adolf von Harnier were the two most powerful and active minds in organizing this opposition to Hitler; yet because they were so very different it would have been surprising had they not also disagreed. The points which Zott emphasized in his hopes for a post-Hitlerian Germany were almost entirely social and economic issues; he felt that these were of such importance that before he would support a restoration, Rupprecht should be required to make a statement favoring a greater share for the workers in management. [108] Zott's general line of argument followed the thinking of many social reformers since the industrial revolution: the right to work; maximum wage increases; minimum hours—thirty-six a week; an improvement of social insurance legislation; greater care for rural and farm workers; and, a strong adherence to Christian morality. [109] It was this last which proved to be the needed opening for von Harnier, a cue he may well have taken from reading the *Weisse Blätter*. [110]

Baron von Harnier felt that Germany's problem was essentially the problem of two distinct societies trying to get along, but succeeding only by the use of force. He felt Germany was not meant to be a united country; that the arrangement of 1871 was disastrous; that it was unsuitable that the "Catholic-conservative line running from Cologne to Munich" and the "liberal anti-church line running from Berlin to Nürnberg." should be united as one country. The Germans would have to begin anew, re-building western Germany on the basis of Catholic-Christian social teachings. Baden and Württemberg would follow Bavaria's lead and restore their royal houses. Then Austria and Bohemia could join this league of states within a "Catholic orbit." The

---

[108] *Ibid.*

[109] *Ibid.*, 74.

[110] Adolf Freiherr von Harnier, Reply to the Prosecution Brief at his trial before the People's Court, March 13, 1944, 2. Full text in Appendix H.

states themselves would have room for all of Zott's social reform; they would achieve these and other reforms as a *"Stände-
staat."* [111]

During this period the group put out several broadsheets,
some of which were intended to arouse Bavarian feelings about
their national colors. [112] However, more stridently oppositional
is this one which was written on January 22, 1937 by von Harnier,
and intended to be sent as a newsletter to like-minded friends.

How long?

The state is headed by a lunatic!
This lunatic is in the hands of criminals!
The state is being plundered whilst the interests of the whole
nation are betrayed. People are being done away with. The rights
of the people are being everywhere violated.
Arise comrades!   Assist us!
The state is in danger.

Some side-lights on foreign affairs

The Prince of Wales has 'studied' Germany. And he has been
cut off by the British Ambassador in Berlin. Meanwhile, Ribbentrop, Hitler's Ambassador in London, has come home to be present
at this reception. This 'study-unit' is the last ray of a sinking sun
over what will soon be the battlefield of England and Hitler
Germany. There are few Englishmen who still hold fovorable
notions of Fascist dictatorships. And just as Duke Edward's fate is
sealed, so is that of Ribbentrop. In a short time he will depart from
London and seek employment elsewhere. His efforts to get a satisfactory successor for State-secretary Meissner as leader of the pre-
sidential (which is to say the *Führer's*) cabinet has met with as
little success as have his efforts in behalf of that Bavarian Judas,
Epp. (In our oppinion, the ambassador ought to go back to selling
wine; perhaps he understands something of this. Hitler might
send Weber Christian as ambassador to the Court of St. James,
because in that land of horses and beautiful women he would have

---

[111] *Ibid.,* 39-40.
[112] *Ibid.,* 67-68.

such succes. His world famous ability in conversation will put him in good stead).

The international-national-socialism has found support in Hungary in the person of Admiral Horthy and Minister Gombos. Both men's attitudes contradict their duty. Their oath of loyalty to their Apostolic King has fallen victim to their vanity. And yet far above such insignificant figures sways the crown of St. Stephen.

In connection with the fifteenth anniversary of the establishment of Mussolini's government, a grand festival was held in Rome, to which Hess, Frank, Wagner, Streicher, *et. al.*, were invited. This is especially interesting since as recently as three years ago Mussolini quoted from Horace and Ovid selections which showed that he had nothing but supreme disgust for the people north of the Alps, finding them to be of little cultural significance when compared with the heirs of Rome. It was especially odd that Hess should have been there, for not too long ago he (Mussolini) called him (Hess) an *"unreifen Lausbub"* with whom one could hardly be expected to talk politics.

Think! What were Hitler, Hess, Himmler; what were Goering, Ribbentrop, the Bavarian Minister Wagner, Schmid, Baldur von Schirach, Fischer, Weber Christian, etc., etc. [before the seizure of power?]

But who of these does not now own a villa, an estate, an automobile, etc., etc.?

Where oh where has this trash gotten the money for such luxuries?

Answer these questions ......

Schmied von Kochel [113]

There was no special plea in this newsletter, nor was there any apparent ideological basis. Perhaps von Harnier feared indicating too clearly by means of a broadsheet what he would advocate after the Nazis would be overthrown. In any case, aside from having mentioned the legendary Bavarian figure, the Schmied von Kochel, and an outspoken epithet applied to Epp,

---

[113] *Weintz,* 69-71. Cf. Baron von Harnier's comments on this newsletter in his Reply to the Prosecution, Appendix H.

there seemed nothing very Bavarian about the piece. The fact was, von Harnier did not approve of this method of communication with his friends and, accordingly, he decided to stop the printing of broadsheets sometime in 1938. [114] His greater aim was to keep alive the idea of monarchy amongst ordinary men who could be relied upon, when the time came, to effectively support a restoration. Von Harnier and Zott were assisted in this work by three loyal comrades who were closely associated in all their endeavors; Gebhard Fahrner, a tailor; [115] Franz X. Fackler, a business man; [116] and Heinrich Pfluger, a mechanic. [117] These men came together often in the period from January, 1938 until August, 1939—in fact the *Gestapo* recorded sixty meeting. [118]. Usually they would gather at Pfluger's or Zott's home, or perhaps at the *Drei Rosen,* a favorite drinking place for the group. They never allowed more than seven to gather at one time, thus allaying serious suspicion. In their discussions they attacked the rule of the Nazi Party, while at the same time endeavoring to gain some clearer understanding of the political scene. Yet they were not without hopes for furthering their contacts not only in Bavaria, but also in western Germany and Austria.

Contacts with Austria had been pursued since 1935 but without significant success. Von Harnier went to Vienna in August, 1937 with plans to contact Fr. Muckermann or Dr. von Hildebrand, both of whom might have aided either with advice and information or by providing a closer alliance with Austrian legitimists. However, nothing came of the trip. [119] The same might be said of Zott's interest in activities in Cologne, whither he

---

[114] *Weintz,* 142.
[115] Born of Frommenhausen, June 21, 1896.
[116] Born in Munich, October 28, 1895.
[117] Born in Munich, June 4, 1908.
[118] For a list of the meetings and the attendance, see *Weintz,* 111-115.
[119] *Weintz, passim.,* 77-79.

had been invited by a Rhenish priest who assured him that the anti-Nazi feeling was growing and being encouraged by friends in Holland and Belgium. [120] It must have been made increasingly clear, however, that any success these monarchists could hope to achieve must be first well-grounded in Bavaria. And this they decided ultimately must be their major endeavor.

One of the tasks discussed at the meetings of this monarchist group was a system of organization. The most obvious method of attaining any sort of large membership roll was to have each member encourage three or four like-minded persons who whould in turn do the same; there could soon be literally "thousands" on the list. [121] To this end Seutter von Lötzen used his automobile to travel through the rural areas of *Oberbayern,* while Franz Fackler journeyed to Augsburg to enlist friends who had formerly been members of the Christian Trade Unions. [122] To be sure, it was a simple answer which these men offered; yet one cannot decry the response which seems to have been immediate.

By August 1939 there was in existence a complete list of functionaries, not only for Munich proper, but for rural areas as well. [123] The general leadership was in the hands of Adolf von Harnier, assisted by Zott, Fackler and Seutter von Lötzen. There

---

[120] *Weintz,* 80-81.

[121] *Weintz,* 47.

[122] *Weintz,* 49.

[123] In his reply to the Prosecution's Brief, Baron von Harnier wrote in 1944 that he had warned Zott and Weiss not to draw up any list of functionaries or of members. Undoubtedly Zott, Weiss, or one of the others was induced by the *Gestapo* agent to draw up such a list which gave to the group an organized quality which, in fact, must be taken as exaggerated. Naturally enough, Baron von Harnier on trial before a National Socialist judge, would tend to minimize the notion that he was in any real sense "the leader of a monarchist movement." He did not, however, at any time deny that he was part of such a movement in Germany; indeed, he admitted to believing that ultimately Germany would return to a monarchical form of government sometime in the future. Cf. his statements which are reprinted in full in the Appendix H.

were also leaders in Lower Bavaria (Erich Chrambach) and in Swabia (Albert Kaifer). The city of Munich was divided into five districts, each having a director and an assistant. [124] The chief aim of these people seemed to be little else than keeping alive the idea that a monarchy was the answer for Bavaria's wants after Hitler was defeated. However, they did have certain financial obligations and these they discharged in a curious fashion.

In order to give the cause both form and content, Baron von Harnier hit upon the idea of having Franz Grainer, long-time photographer to the Wittelsbachs in Munich, make a number of postcards with pictures of the Crown Prince and Crown Princess Antonia. He printed five hundred such cards at a modest rate, and von Harnier offered them for sale at one mark each. Accordingly each of the leading members were responsible for the distribution of a given number of cards. Later on, another photographer, Joseph Fink, was engaged to put out a series of monuments significant in Bavarian history. The first of these was the thoroughly monstrous statue of "Bavaria" on the Theresienwiese in Munich; later, the cards included works of greater artistic merit. [125] The *Gestapo* estimated that by mid-summer 1939 the monarchists had collected a sum of probably 15,000 marks. [126] The cards themselves cost four, six and ten *Pfennige* for the three different sizes. Fink claimed that over a period of eighteen months he received only about sixty marks. However, if all cards fabricated were actually sold, an arithmetical mind might easily figure out the number of cards printed. But that hardly seems so important here. What is important is that they got money enough to supply a car with gasoline and so kept up their contacts with monarchists throughout southern Bavaria.

Yet monarchists were not their only contacts. During the

---

[124] For a complete list of "Functionaries," see Appendix G.
[125] *Weintz*, 131.
[126] *Ibid.*, 134.

summer of 1939, a certain "Dr. Lederer" suddenly appeared in
Munich seeking out these monarchists. His real name was Dr.
Alfred Loritz—later in post-war Bavaria to achieve a certain
notoriety. [127] Loritz had gained contact with them through two
priests: Father Siegfried Huber, who fled to Switzerland just
previous to his arrest, and Father Karl Schuster. It was through
Father Schuster that Loritz came to Heinrich Pfluger's home,
offering money for anti-Nazi activity as well as opinion and
advice. He was not at all impressed with their notion of restoration, nor did he have flattering things to say about the higher
clergy, views which were not calculated to appeal to the Bavarian
monarchists. In general, however, the group was interested in
opponents of National Socialism, although they felt that to have
form, this opposition must look to something which would replace the fascist dictatorship, and, for them that form was
monarchy. [128]

The question which must long have been in the reader's mind
is: what contact did these people have with the Wittelsbachs?
And what did the Wittelsbachs think of this activity in their
behalf? However ardently the Bavarian royal house may have
desired a restoration, both Crown Prince Rupprecht and his
son, Prince Albrecht, knew that the times were, to say the least,
not propitious. Prince Albrecht, who was regarded generally in
Bavaria as more ambitious than his father, had discouraged this

---

[127] Alfred Loritz, born, Munich, April, 24, 1902.

[128] *Weintz*, 166, 172, *passim*. The *Gestapo* file from Würzburg has a
circular seeking information on Alfred Loritz, dated October 11, 1939. Father
Huber fled to Switzerland when the general arrests were being made; it was
through him, however, that the Weintz document was found in Zürich
and returned after the war to Father Huber's family at Chiemsee in Bavaria.
This is also the only contact of the monarchists with Father Karl Schuster. At
the trial Freiherr von Harnier admitted to not knowing him previous to their
imprisonment. See, Adolf Freiherr von Harnier, Reply to the Prosecution's
Brief, March 13, 1944, 7.

group when they came to see him as early as 1935. [129] Again, on July 24, 1938 Baron von Harnier, Zott, Fackler and Pfluger were received by the Crown Prince but again discouraged. [130] Zott was, in fact, so dejected by the experience that he thought the group ought to try a younger figure; but the only plausible candidate was Prince Albrecht. In May 1939 the Prince received them with harsh words, telling them not to be engaging in "*Dummheiten*." [131]

Indeed, events in the summer of 1939 proved how impossible the Wittelsbachs thought restoration. Rupprecht took an extended trip to visit his brother in Hungary, the consequence of which was that he was not allowed to return to Germany. [132] It is perhaps worth noting that both Himmler and Heydrich were convinced that the Wittelsbachs were the center of opposition activities in southern Germany, and they tried, therefore, in every way to besmirch that family. The actions of Freiherr von Harnier and the others were used as material to support the argument that leading Catholics, members of the aristocracy, as well as former officers in the Bavarian Army, all looked to Rupprecht as a possible counter-weight to National Socialism. Himmler and Heydrich were successful in getting citizenship rights withdrawn from the Wittelsbachs who were forced to remain in Florence throughout the war. Near the end of 1944, the Crown Princess was arrested and subjected to vile treatment at the hands of Nazi torturers, because it was thought she had known or might know particulars in the plot of the twentieth of July. [133]

---

[129] *Weintz*, 3.

[130] *Weintz*, 156.

[131] *Weintz*, 160.

[132] Letter from Freiherr von Redwitz to Kreisleiter Buchner, Starnberg, September 16, 1939. Berlin Document Center.

[133] On the citizenship problem, see letter from Heydrich, August 30, 1940, in Appendix J. Several other letters on this same subject from Reichsminister

To be sure, the Wittelsbachs, unlike the Hohenzollern family, profited not at all from the National Socialist government; indeed, like so many others who were loyal to ideals different from the Nazis, they suffered accordingly, both in life and property. [134] Yet, neither Crown Prince Rupprecht nor Prince Albrecht felt that the action of Baron von Harnier and his friends could lead to anything but further bloodshed. This was one of those unfortunate traps in which people of firm convictions found themselves during the Nazi regime. Unwilling to see blood flow by their own hands, they passively witnessed a national, indeed an international, blood-letting at the hands of the National Socialists.

So it was that in the first days of August, 1939 nearly all the principal members of the group were arrested. But the *Gestapo* did not stop at that. By the end of October, there were one hundred and twenty-five being held in Stadelheim prison. Although some of these were later released, one year later there were still eighty under arrest. [135] In June, 1944 a trial was finally arranged in the People's Court. [136] By some curious workings of chance, the chief witness against Josef Zott could not appear at the trial in June, so his name was separated from the others. His trial was held in Berlin under much harsher circumstances, and on October 26, 1944 he was condemned to death for plotting to change the government. He was hanged in Berlin on

---

of Interior, Bavarian Minister of Interior, General von Epp, Heinrich Himmler, Gauleiter Wagner, Freiherr von Redwitz, can be found in the Berlin Document Center. On the indignities suffered by the Wittelsbach family, see Erwein von Aretin, *Wittelsbacher im K.Z.* (Munich, 1947).

[134] Crown Prince Rupprecht received Ritter von Epp soon after his appointment as *Reichsstatthalter* for Bavaria and greeted him with one word: "Traitor!" See, Konrad Heiden, *A History of National Socialism* (New, York, 1935), 279.

[135] Letter from *Reichssicherheitshauptamt*, August 30, 1940, to *Reichsminister des Innern*, signed Heydrich, now in Berlin Document Center.

[136] *Volksgerichtshof*, 6H, 92/94, 75, 32/44, 6 Senat., June 28,, 1944.

January 16, 1945. [137] His death was unhappy testimony of the chaos of justice under the Nazis. The others were given varying sentences in penal institutions for the same deeds for which Zott paid with his life. [138]

Freiherr von Harnier, however, was also a victim of Nazi prisons; for, having succumbed to a typhus infection, he died on the day of his liberation.

These two who suffered death and the hundreds who suffered imprisonment, suffered directly because they opposed Nazi Germany. The records of their triumphs may be regarded as slim: the broadsheets, the propaganda spread by word of mouth, the gatherings in homes or taverns in Munich, the visit to the Crown Prince, the gift of roses on his birthday, [139]—these seem petty when viewed at a distance.

To keep such events in focus one must try to remember that such apparently trifling things as have been mentioned above were the way some men chose to express their adherence to ideas and values which were clearly at odds with National Socialism. And one must never forget the great price which some men paid for that adherence.

---

[137] *Bayerische Landeszeitung*, February 11, 1949, 11.
[138] *Volksgerichtshof, 6 H 92/94, 75, 32/44, 6 Senat., June 28, 1944.*
[139] *Weintz*, 136.

CHAPTER IV

THE CHRISTIAN IDEALISTS

a) ORIGINS

Opposition to a political order can seldom have found expression in more selfless devotion to ideals than it found in the events which have come to be known as the Munich Students Revolt. What follows is an attempt to re-examine this movement, to seek out its motivation in the lives of those who participated in it, and to suggest some of its consequences. [1] February 18, 1943, is usually cited as the date of the revolt, yet on that day the students did only what they had done on at least five other occasions. [2]

On that bright and sunny Thursday morning Hans Scholl with his sister Sophie, although fully aware that the *Gestapo* was closing in upon them, took a small case to the University filled with mimeographed leaflets. [3] Most of these they quickly distributed in the hall-ways and lecture rooms. Then, finding that some remained, they hurried to the top floor, opened a window and threw those that were left into the courtyard below. The porter, Schmid, saw the leaflets, and discovering what they were, ordered all doors of the building locked. He caught the Scholls in the corridor and brought them at once to the main office. From there they were brought to the *Universitäts-Syndikus* where

---

[1] Cf., the author's article, "The Munich Student Revolt," *The Pacific Spectator*, (Stanford University Press), Winter, 1950.

[2] K.Z., "Der 18. Februar," *Gegenwart*, (Freiburg im Breisgau, 1946), 20, 21.

[3] Inge Scholl, *Die Weisse Rose* (Frankfurt am Main, 1952), 59, 61. Dieter Sasse, Bericht über die Münchener Studenten, Typescript, 3.

a report was made. They were then handed over to the *Gestapo*. [4] On the way to *Gestapo* headquarters, Hans Scholl tried to destroy a draft for a broadsheet prepared by Christoph Probst; but he was not successful and on Saturday Probst was arrested in Innsbruck. [5]

Hans Scholl, Sophie Scholl, and Christoph Probst were the first to pay the penalty of death for their part in the Munich Student Revolt. Three other students and one professor met a similar fate. Many others were arrested and sentenced in the penal institutions of the Third Reich. Naturally, one is anxious to know more about such people who risked their lives in opposition to National Socialism. Who were these young people? How did they come together? What did they talk of? Was there any special or principal motivating force for their actions? What did they advocate? A brief chronicle of the students' lives may be a beginning in answering such questions.

The two Scholls were born in Württemberg: Hans Fritz on September 22, 1918 at Ingerstein an der Jagst; Sophie Magdalene on May 9, 1921 in the village of Forchtenberg. [6] During their infancy their father was the mayor in various villages, changing from place to place. Possibly because his advanced social views clashed with those of the local intelligentsia, he gave up that kind of work and, taking his family to Ulm, he became

---

[4] *Mitteilungsblatt des Bayerischen Staatsministeriums für Sonderaufgaben*, 3. Jhg., Nr. 18, Munich, October 30, 1948, 71-72. The trial of Schmid, the porter who found the Scholls in the University building, before the court of denazification.

[5] Christoph Probst, Letter to his mother, February 22, 1943, reprinted below, 239.

[6] Richarda Huch, "Die Aktion der Münchener Studenten gegen Hitler," *Neue Schweizer Rundschau*, XVI, 1948, 284; *Volksgerichtshof*, 85/35/83 — 114/47/43, the trial of Hans and Sophie Scholl and Christoph Probst, February 22, 1943, now to be found in the Berlin Document Center. Hereafter referred to as Trial of the Munich Students, I. (Note: Hans Scholl's birthplace erroneously given as "Ingersheim.")

an economic adviser. [7] The children were reared as Protestants, but in a rather indifferent fashion; the values the children were taught tended to be their father's notions of cosmopolitanism and pacifism. [8] Here perhaps is the root, the beginning of what took shape and flowered in Hans' efforts in 1942 and 1943 when he and his friends wrote and distributed the leaflets. Indeed, in the summer of 1942, Herr Scholl was denounced, tried and sentenced to four months in prison for calling Hitler "God's scourge on humanity." [9] That was the culmination of years of silent opposition to the Nazi system. Originally the Scholl children, like many other youths in Germany, were not willing to learn by the example of their parents. It was hard for them to see why their father did not greet with greater enthusiasm the advent of the Nazis to power. Hans had to discover for himself the terrible consequences of the Nazi regime with its insistence upon uniformity, regimentation and intolerance. And that was not long in coming.

At first Hans was an enthusiastic *Hitler Jugend* leader. [10] He participated in all the youth activities and was privileged to go to Nürnberg to one of the Party meetings, where he carried the flag for his group. His sister has described his return to Ulm as follows:

> When he came back we could scarcely believe our eyes. He looked tired and the expression on his face betrayed disillusionment . . . . Little by little we discovered that the youth he met [in Nürnberg] who were supposed to be such ideal types were, in fact, anything but ideal types . . . . [11]

---

[7] R. Huch, *op. cit.*, 284.
[8] Inge Scholl, Letter to author, 3; R. Huch, *op. cit.*, 285.
[9] Inge Scholl, *Die Weisse Rose*, 31-32.
[10] *Ibid.*, 13; Franz Joseph Schöningh, Sonderdruck aus der *Süddeutschen Zeitung*, Nr. 88, November 1, 1946.
[11] Inge Scholl, *Die Weisse Rose*, 13.

There were other things about the Nazis which disillusioned him. He discovered that he could not read whatever he wished; that he could not sing certain songs. He found that Stefan Zweig, his favorite author, had been placed on a list of forbidden authors. Thus it was that he began to shun Nazi meetings and to seek friends in other less rigidly organized groups. Until 1938 he could still find such organizations. He joined what was called the *Jungenschaft,* a branch of the *Bündische Jugend.* However, in 1938 he was among those of its members who were arrested in the general wave which swept across Germany bringing their activities to a close. [12] What had they done?

Most members of the *Bündische Jugend* and the *Jungenschaft* had done little except to stand in the way of complete mastery by the *Hitler Jugend* of all German youth movements. They wore special shoes, dark shorts, bright colored shirts; made camps of a tent called the *"Kothe"*—a style used by the Laplanders—; they interested themselves in the culture of all nations, particularly in their folkmusic. The Nazis maintained, however, that the general policy of these groups was not only to look with far too much enthusiasm on things Russian, but also to organize an active opposition to the National Socialist state. They claimed that these groups were supplied with literature from abroad which stimulated their opposition to the regime in power and encouraged revolutionary action. [13]

---

[12] *Ibid.,* 18, 28.

[13] The Nazis were never ones to stint themselves when it came to accusing their opponents of treason. The evidence here presented is based on two trials of members of the *Bündische Jugend,* from the *Volksgerichtshof* archives, Nr. 8J, 162/40, 2H/77/41, September, 1941, and, Nr. 8J, 232/40, 2H, 76/41, August, 1941. These records are now located in the Berlin Document Center. The *Jungenschaft* was founded by Eberhard Köbel on November 1, 1929. However, he entered the Communist Party in 1932 and the leadership passed to Karl Paetel. In 1935 Paetel emigrated to Paris where he edited a periodical for these groups and was active in keeping contact with friends inside Germany. One of his friends, Helmut Giesen, admitted at his trial that Paetel had en-

Whether the group to which Scholl belonged had contact
with other groups; whether his cell was so advanced in its thinking as to suggest the possibility of "revolution," we shall never
know. Certain it is that in his attitude he was more carefree when
he was twenty than he was four years later. His sister has re-
captured some of that life which her brother enjoyed with his
friends and assessed it in the following way:

> For such youth life was a great and marvellous adventure, an
> expedition into an unknown and yet enticing world. They would
> go on week-end trips and try even in the bitterest weather to live
> in their "Kothe" .... They sat about the fire, reading or singing
> to the accompaniment of the Klampfe, banjo or balalaika. They
> collected songs of all nations and composed words to their own
> marvellous melodies and delightful popular tunes. They painted
> and philosophised, they wrote verse and prose .... climbed moun-
> tains .... laughed and joked .... went to museums .... con-
> certs 14

One is tempted to add that they did all those things which
the youth of all nations love to do. The one thing they refused
to do was to dress their activities in the garb of National Socialism. And for that they were arrested.

That brush with the Nazis which involved Hans Scholl in a
mild reprimand, must have shown him better than anything else
how clearly he stood in opposition to the regime in power. Yet
his opposition was not clarified fully; it wanted orientation;
it wanted an ideological basis. After the French campaign of
1940, he began his medical studies at Göttingen. Still in the
Army, he was transferred to a Medical Student Company at the
University of Munich where he found that orientation which he
had been seeking.

In the winter of 1941-1942 he met two Catholics of consider-

---

couraged them to organize cells of opposition which would aid in the overthrow of the Nazi regime. Criminal Case 8J, 162/40; 2H, 77/41, 10, 33.

14 Inge Scholl, Die Weisse Rose, 18.

able fame: Karl Muth, the editor of *Hochland*, and Theodor Haecker, gifted essayist, philosopher and critic. These two men were probably the most important single cause, one is tempted to say the real catalyst in the minds of the students which brought on their public action. We know little, very little of their meetings. We do know, however, that Karl Muth (1867-1947) engaged Hans Scholl to put his library in order, a task he was daily occupied with when the first *Leaflet of the White Rose* was issued. [15] We may well imagine conversations between this great Catholic thinker and Hans Scholl. Fortunately for us Theodor Haecker (1879-1945) has left a collection of his thoughts and deepest convictions, most of which were aimed at exposing the horrors of the Nazi system. It is not unlikely that what now is called *The Journal in the Night* may be considered typical of what Haecker contributed to the Munich students. It is indeed a poignant example of writing in a period otherwise barren of evidence of this kind. [16]

No attempt can be made here to analyse all the thoughts which appear in this diary; that would be a separate work in itself. But because of the close connection with the students, it might not be outside of the scope of this chapter to indicate where Haecker seems to display a marked influence on what the students wrote. [17] Apparently Haecker was called in by the *Gestapo* to give an account of a conversation he had had with Hans Scholl in which it was recorded that he had said that "above all things

---

[15] Franz Joseph Schönigh, *op. cit.,* Georg Smolka, Letter to the author, Wessling, Bavaria, November 2, 1948.

[16] Theodor Haecker, *Journal in the Night,* (Trans. from the German *Tagund Nachtbücher,* by Alexander Dow) (New York, 1950.) Haecker's works are discussed (pp. xxii-xlvi) adequately. Dow shows Haecker's relationship to Newman, Kirkegaard, and Péguy. Haecker became a Roman Catholic in 1920. He was employed by Heinrich Schreiber, a Munich printing house.

[17] Oddly enough there is only one entry in which Scholl is mentioned by name and that in a most enigmatic fashion. It is dated June 9, 1944.

the Germans lacked humility." To this charge he simply stated
that he meant that quite literally. He was dismissed then with
the following comment: *"Also, das ist in Ordnung."* [18]
But had the *Gestapo* official had the patience to listen to
Haecker as he spelled out the meaning of that phrase, he would
hardly have found that such thinking fitted in with the new
order. Haecker shows himself in his *Journal* to be in complete
opposition to the Nazis. What is most significant, his basic objection was religious; the German people were fighting a war
in the cause of the anti-Christ. Consider these telling passages:

> Whitsunday. 12th May, 1940. The fate, and thus the task of
> the German Christian is without an example which he might fol-
> low. It is even without the remotest analogy which, on a different
> level indeed, might serve as a guiding thread. He is alone! Every-
> thing that he feels, thinks and does has a question mark to it,
> questioning whether it is right. The leadership of Germany today,
> and of this there is not the slightest doubt, and it cannot be evaded,
> is consciously anti-Christian—it hates Christ whom it does not
> name. We are making war against peoples and states which al-
> though often only euphemistically Christian could not in any single
> instance be called definitely anti-Christian. And one cannot there-
> fore avoid recognizing the fact, that over and above being a war of
> power—it is a war of religion. And we Germans are fighting this
> war on the wrong side! . . . . From the very beginning, the repeated-
> ly successful trick of these inhuman beings, sent to plague Europe,

---

"Friday morning towards ten o'clock. In the cellar. High explosive bombs.
The house and my flat destroyed. Unbelievable destruction. Some good people,
helpers, who console me by being what they are and by helping! Scholl. And
also some *crapule*. Upright souls. And miserable souls. God is merciful! God
is great! God is precise, but magnanimous. What has happened to me is no
injustice." *Ibid.,* 218.

It is not possible to know why, at that particular juncture, Haecker should
have chosen to mention Scholl; nor does it seem profitable to speculate. It is
significant, however, that the name should appear at all; for any comments,
certainly favorable comments on the Scholls discovered by the Nazis would
have meant imprisonment, if not death.

[18] *Ibid.,* XV.

has been to combine, more or less, the special interests of their basely impulsive, greedy natures, intellectually speaking, soulless and half-educated, with the true and genuine wishes and claims of the German people, combining them by an unprecedented skill in the art of lying.... The German people will be beaten, but not struck down and wiped out. The one ray of light in my mind is this: it is better for a people to be defeated and to suffer, than to win and apostatise. But if it were to be victorious, I should not then give up my faith. I can always pray: Lord, help thou my unbelief. [19]

We as a nation, apostatised on the 30th of January, 1933. Since then, as a nation, we have been on the wrong road, on the wrong side. Yet even now there are few among us who suspect what it means: to be on the wrong road and on the wrong side. [20]

That, more than likely, was the manner in which Haecker talked with the students who visited him. He insisted that National Socialism was a religion in opposition to Christianity and therefore the enemy of every Christian. Interestingly enough, he saw in Prussia, the Prussia of the Hohenzollerns and the Prussia of the Nazis, the positive manifestation of Germany's evil. Consider these passages:

The Germans too want to be a nation 'like others.' But without success. They can only be much worse than others. They are the abhorrence of the whole world. The Prussian leaven has soured the whole nation and falsified its mission. [21]

In that part of the history of Christian Europe which is the history of Germany, this war might, and I hope will be the end of the hegemony of Prussia, which had in fact reached its height at the beginning of the war. [22]

Under the hegemony of Prussia, today at its peak, the Germans have always been driven back more and more, whether they wished it or not, upon the motto: *Oderint dum metuant.* (Let them hate

---

[19] Theodor Haecker, *Tag- und Nachtbücher* (Munich, 1947), 85. Translation based on Dow's, only slightly altered.
[20] *Ibid.*, 142, (Entry 486, 1941), (Dow's translation).
[21] *Ibid.*, 11, (Entry No. 49, 1938).
[22] *Ibid.*, 18, (Entry No. 74, 1940).

as long as they fear!) That leads to a bitter ending, for the fear will disappear, and the hate will remain. [23]
German idealism, in Kant and Fichte, is a Prussian affair. Schelling belongs elsewhere; he was a spontaneously speculative mind and agnostic. Hegel too was originally a great speculative mind, but as happened again and again with so many South German minds, he became infected with Prussianism and was corrupted. Prussian idealism took the heart of flesh and blood from the German and in its place gave him one of iron and paper. The German heart is now a material all of its own, of paper and iron, claptrap and act. That is really the 'inhuman' quality of the German as a Prussian product. [24]

Although he lived in Munich, he was not a Bavarian, nor, in fact, were most of those connected with the Munich Students. They were mostly Württembergers. Nearly all of them, however, were anti-Prussian, a fact which is not surprising. [25] They belonged to that segment of the German population which had always resented the Prussian solution to the problem of German unification, largely because that solution excluded Catholic Austria and gave the preponderance in Germany to Protestant Prussia. [26]

---

[23] *Ibid.*, 42, (Entry No. 173, 1940).

[24] *Ibid.*, 72, (Entry 275, 1940).

[25] It may be worthwhile to clarify this point which might otherwise lead to some confusion. Anti-Prussianism does not necessarily imply Bavarian separatism. Inge Scholl stressed this in a letter to the author, October 26, 1948, and I had occasion to use that opinion in my article in the *Pacific Spectator,* *op. cit.,* Winter 1950, 50. The students equated the worst features of Prussianism and National Socialism, especially the idealization of the uniformed man, the regimental life, and military discipline. However, as I shall presently show, Professor Huber, the author of the "Manifesto of the Munich Students," was not in agreement here with the students' opinion. In his defense speech at his trial he insisted that the achievements of Prussia were among the most significant in German history. He admitted, also, that his point of view clashed with that of the students, and that this led to open argument with Hans Scholl. See Kurt Huber, Defense speech, Appendix K. Cf., *White Rose Leaflet,* No. IV, *infra.*

[26] In this connection, the reader's attention is drawn to Meinrad Hagmann,

As we shall see, the Munich students were feverishly opposed to a continuance of this Prussian hegemony in Germany, for which attitude, along with their Christian philosophy of life, they were not a little indebted to Theodor Haecker. But before considering the actual content of the Munich students' opposition, let us look at the others who made up this group.

When Scholl went off to France in the campaign of 1940, he was already acquainted with two students who shared his disgust with National Socialism. [27] One of these was Alexander Schmorell, born in Orenburg in the Ural Mountains, September 17, 1917. His father was a German doctor; his mother was the daughter of a Russian priest. He was very proud of his heritage, called himself a Russian monarchist, and continued to attend the Orthodox church services even after he and his father had returned to Germany in 1921. [28] Dr. Schmorell remarried in 1926 into a family rather closely bound up with National Socialism. As a result, "Schurik," as Alexander liked to be called, joined the *Hitler Jugend,* and became a leader. Soon, however, he, like Scholl, descovered that no deviation or adverse criticism would be tolerated. It was only through the efforts of his step-uncles that he was not more seriously punished after he had a quarrel with his Nazi superiors. We know from the record of his trial that in the period after his work service, when he was about to enter the army, he asked to be relieved of his duty because he doubted his ability to render full service to the *Führer.* This was public

---

Der Weg ins Verhängnis, (Munich, 1946), a compilation of the voting records of the various German states, 1919-1933. Although such figures may be misleading, it is curious that the Nazis had considerably greater success in elections held in preponderantly Protestant and Prussian territories than in other parts of Germany.

[27] R. Huch, *op. cit.,* 287.

[28] *Volksgerichtshof,* Criminal case 6J 24/43, 1H, 101/43, Trial of Alexander Schmorell, Kurt Huber, Willi Graf, etc., April 19, 1943, 6. Hereafter referred to as Munich Students Trial, II.

admission of his opposition. [29] However, this met with no success. It was not long before he found himself a medical technician in France, and later, in the fall of 1940, on inactive duty as a student of medicine at the University of Munich. [30] Had Schmorell had his own choice he would have been a sculptor. [31] Yet he was not concerned exclusively with reproducing nature, he was anxious to be as close to it as possible—to be what the Germans call *naturverbunden*. It was not unusual for him to spend an entire day riding his horse down the Isar valley to the accompaniment of Russian songs, pausing some place for a glass of wine. Ironically enough, when the Germans invaded Russia, Alexander Schmorell could not have been happier. No matter how curious other Germans were to see the Russian people, we can be certain that his joy was peculiar to himself: he felt that he was returning home. [32]

For Christoph Hermann Probst, the other member of this triumvirate, Bavaria could provide quite an adequate diet of scenery and natural beauty as, indeed, it had for his ancestors since the sixteenth century. "Christel," as he was always called, perhaps the real favorite of the group, was born in Murnau, November 6, 1919. [33] Both of his parents felt the strain of an overexacting religious upbringing, and were determined to allow the choice in these matters to the children themselves. Thus neither Christoph nor his sister, Angelika, was baptized. From early youth on he appears to have developed an uncommon sensitivity towards nature and the beautiful, a thing one notices

---

[29] Munich Student Trial, II, 6.
[30] *Ibid.,* 6.
[31] Dieter Sasse, Die Münchner Studenten, Typescript, n.d., 2.
[32] Inge Scholl, Das Andere Deutschland, Typescript, 10; R. Huch, *Neue Schweizer Rundschau, op. cit.,* 359.
[33] Trial of Munich Students, I, 1; other biographical details found in Karen Klublatt (Christoph Probst's Mother), memoir typescript, 3 pp.

in reading his letters written during the war. But he was not simply a nature worshipper. It is clearly evident that talks with Muth and Häcker were giving form as well as content to the thinking of young Christel. The following excerpts from letters written to his brother give some evidence of the extent to which his life mirrored the Christian virtues:

My dear good Dieter!

At your birthday this year our wishes for you are the warmest ever because now you are far from us, alone with yourself. May the coming year be rich in blessings and fruitful for you. May it deepen your appreciation of life, increase your desire to live, and ripen your spirit. Live during this coming year with full realization that everything has meaning and nothing in this world happens by chance; that all things are related to the struggle for good, even though we are unable to see it so clearly as we might like to. Even in what appears to be chaos, there is meaning: it leads the individual to his goal, leads him to his salvation—a thing which is not manifested externally but only something which is an inner completion of his being. Life, you know, does not simply begin with birth and end with death. Life is the great truth set before man; the great task of becoming; a preparation for an existence in another form. All things large and small serve to further this end. To be sure, we cannot see it all so clearly now, we cannot see all the connections; but we know it must be meaningful. Later on we will see clearly, our lives will be illuminated. For the present we accept our lack of perfect knowledge and seek out the path which leads upward, the path which leads to happiness—real happiness, happiness which no one will ever be able to take from us [34]

Try to endure all your suffering; take it without anxiety; say to yourself over and over: it is not in vain that I suffer; this is sent from God just as is happiness; that this is not only a preparation for further trials in this world, but, indeed, a preparation for life after death. [35]

---

[34] Christoph Probst, Letter to Dieter Sasse, Munich, July 27, 1942. (Christoph Probst's Brother.

[35] Christoph Probst, Letter to Dieter Sasse, Munich, December 13, 1942.

Christmas is upon us .... You must pass these otherwise beautiful days alone, while the flood of memories will doubtless cast your spirits low, making you morose. But there is an exterior and an interior Christmas. This feast expresses itself only very modestly in the enjoyment of material happiness—the getting and giving of gifts. After all, that is only an external reminder of an inner experience, a yearly reminder to Christians everywhere of the birth of the Christ child, their true Redeemer. It is hard, especially so when one is young, to set aside the joys of this beautiful feast. But the important thing is to experience and to celebrate the inner meaning of this day. It is a day when one ought to thank his Creator for all His goodness; that He has sent Christ unto us through whom we know that our suffering, our very lives have been made meaningful; Christ who suffered for us, who made suffering understandable, who sanctified it; Christ who preached love and the true brotherhood of all men; Christ who brought to us the Bread of Life; Christ, whom none can doubt. Every individual's life is important. We are all dear to God and He will have it that we all should love Him. For love is the power of the world: it engenders all life; it protects us; it leads us to blessedness; it is the power which has created the world. By contrast see how far hate is bringing us and has brought us: destruction, blood and death, and out of which there is nothing either lasting or good. And what has love engendered? Upon love cultures have been built: cathedrals have risen up. Love is the bond between all men. Love makes all happiness possible—for what would man be alone? Love was there from the begining of the world; for God made the world. You must think about love, Dieter, about the brotherhood of man, about peace.... My dearest, my thoughts are often with you. My hopes for you are the highest, and I do not exaggerate when I say, your sufferings are also mine.... [36]

Is it not easy to understand why such a person would not find himself the opponent of a system which not only mocked but, indeed, which sought the destruction of such values as he expressed in this letter? Christoph Probst's opposition, like that of others, was motivated primarily by his conversion to Christ-

_____

[36] *Ibid.*

ianity. Immediately before his execution, in *articulo mortis*, he was received into the Catholic Church, an action for which he had been preparing for two years. [37]

These three were the original "Munich Students." We may assume that they were really close friends by some time in 1941. For one thing this meant that they drank together, something which they could do to their heart's content at a delightful Italian restaurant called the *Lombardi*. [38] But there was more to their friendship than drinking wine and singing songs: there were serious discussions about their Germany. They discussed the problems of their country under the aspect of its apostasy from Christianity. They digested and made part of themselves the thoughts of Muth and Haecker. Finally, they sought to bring their convictions and beliefs to a wider circle by writing articles which they labeled: *Leaflets of the White Rose*. Alexander Schmorell and Hans Scholl pooled their finances in order to buy a typewriter and a mimeograph machine. [39] In April or May of 1942 they wrote the first leaflet of which they printed one hundred copies. [40] It follows, now, in its entirety:

> Nothing could be worse than that a civilized nation, without any show of opposition, be 'governed' by an irresponsible clique given over completely to their own lusts for power. Is it not so that today every honest German is ashamed of his government? And who amongst us has any idea of the extent of the outrages which we and our children must one day bear witness to when finally the shades are lifted from our eyes and we will behold in broad daylight all the hideous and monstrous crimes? But if the German people have become so corrupted and rotten at the very core that they can idly stand by without so much as raising a finger to stop the process by which they may well lose their most precious gift, that part of man which distinguishes him from all

---

[37] Dieter Sasse, *op. cit.*, 3.
[38] Inge Scholl, *Die Weisse Rose*, 29.
[39] Trial of the Munich Students, II, 7.
[40] *Ibid.*, 7.

other creatures, namely, his free will; if the German people are
unwilling to enter decisively into the business of history and order
it to their best purposes; if the Germans so divest themselves of
individuality; if the Germans develop into an unthingking and
cowardly mass—then, oh then, do they deserve complete oblite-
ration.

Goethe once spoke of the Germans as a tragic people, comparing
them to the Jews and the Greeks. Today they might better be
described as a sickly and aimless herd rushing madly to its own
disaster. Thus does it appear—but this is only appearance. For the
whole thing has been planned in such a gradual, systematic and
deceptive fashion, that one finds himself locked a prisoner of his
own mind; only when he is thus bound is he aware of his fate.
There have been a few who recognized this threatening disorder;
but their heroic warnings have cost them their lives. The final
evaluation of these men is by no means fixed.

But if everyone waits until his neighbor does something even
while the vengeful Nemesis moves ever closer upon us, we shall
find that the last victim will already have been tossed into the
jaws of the insatiable demons. That is why every individual who
is aware of his responsibility as a member of Christian and western
civilization must arm himself in this final hour and work against
the scourge of humanity, work against Fascism and every sinister
aspect of the absolute state. Try some form of passive resistance—resistance—wherever you may be; stop this atheistic war
machine before it is too late, before all our cities are like Cologne
—rubble heaps; stop this war before all our youth's blood has
been spilled because of a criminal's hybris. Never forget that a
people gets the kind of government it deserves! From Friedrich
Schiller's *The Legislation of Lycurgus and Solon*: '. . . . Considered
with reference to his own end, the legistation of Lycurgus is a
masterpiece of political science, and knowledge of human nature.
He wanted to establish a powerful, self-sustaining, indestructible
republic; political strength and durability were his aim, which he
accomplished as far as possible with the means at his command.
But if the aim of Lycurgus is contrasted with the great aims of
humanity, an emphatic condemnation must take the place of the
admiration which a first hasty glance had extorted from us. Everything may be sacrificed to the highest interests of the state except

the end for which the state itself is designed. The state itself is not the end; it is important only as a means to the realization of this end, which is none other than the progressive development of all the powers of man. If a constitution impedes this development, it is unworthy of our approbation, were it otherwise ever so ingenious and complete within itself. In such a case its durability becomes a reproach rather than a distinction—it is only the prolongation of an evil; the longer it continues, the more obnoxious it becomes.

The political character was formed at the expense of morality. Sparta knew nothing of conjugal love, maternal affection, filial piety, friendship; it knew citizens and civil virtues only.

Inhumanity against their slaves was enjoined by law; in the Spartan code, the dangerous rule was laid down to consider men as means, not as the end, a perversion that led to a legal demolition of the foundations of natural right and morality. Morality was sacrificed in order to obtain an end which can only be valuable as a means toward the establishment of this morality.

Now a much finer example is afforded by the rude warrior Caius Marcius in his camp before Rome, who sacrifices vengeance and victory, because be cannot bear to see his mother's tears flow.

The republic of Lycurgus could not enjoy perpetuity unless the minds of the people stood still; hence it could only secure its existence by overlooking the highest and only object of political government.'

From Goethe's *Des Epimenides Erwachen*, Act II, Sc. 4:

Geniuses: Whatever has risen up from the abyss, 'though its conquest be one-half the world, its fate is sealed. Behold already the signs of anxiety; what folly to resist! Yet all who stand by him are bound inexorably; with him they will perish.

Hope: Now do I begin to see my comrades who have gathered in the night to be silent but not to sleep; and that beautiful word freedom is spoken softly and with hesitation, until at last one day, gathered on the steps of our temple with full conviction we will all cry out with one voice: Freedom! Freedom [41]

---

[41] All the extant *Blätter der Weissen Rose* have been published in Inge

Here is plainly enough an intellectual's appeal to German reason. It does not spell out in detail how the German is to resist; it only indicates that if he does *not,* then all will be in jeopardy, even his "free will." Interestingly enough there is great reliance on individual responsibility and an encouragement not to wait for one's neighbour to act—a point they will emphasize over and over in the leaflets. The only positive course is "passive resistance," a phrase not clearly delineated. The addition of the masterpieces by Schiller and Goethe, especially the symbolism which must have been intended, must have been aimed at the German intelligentsia.

b) THE CIRCLE WIDENS: MAY-AUGUST, 1942

Some time after the first leaflets appeared, Hans Scholl's sister, Sophie, arrived in Munich to study philosophy and natural sciences. [42] It was, indeed, a joyous occasion and Hans and his friends made the most of that warm night in May, 1942, eating home-baked cakes, drinking wine, singing and wandering through the *Englische Garten.* [43] Sophie was quiet, refined, and possessed a depth of character not often found amongst students of either sex. In her diary she wrote as she felt: as a believing Christian.

Many people think of our time as the period before the end of the world. And, indeed, all the enormities of our time would lead one to concur. But is this belief not of secondary importance? For must we all not be ready—no matter when we live—at all

---

Scholl's *Weisse Rose,* 85-110. The versions presented here are translations of those. In this first *Leaflet of the White Rose,* the reader's attention is drawn to the suggested comparison between Nazi Germany and Sparta, something which had previously been suggested in the *Weisse Blätter.* See *supra,* Ch. III,
[42] Inge Scholl, Das Andere Deutschland, Typescript, 5.
[43] Inge Scholl, *Die Weisse Rose,* 35-36.

times to appear before God, to give an account of our lives? Can
I know whether tomorrow morning I shall be alive? A bomb could
destroy us all tonight and then my guilt would not be one whit
less than if I were to cease to exist with the stars and the earth.
— I cannot understand how it is that 'pious' people can fear the
existence of God whilst men go about trying to eradicate every
trace of Him with swords and foul deeds. It is as if God did not
have the power (I feel as if really all things rest in His hands).
The only thing one needs to fear is the threat against the existence of mankind. They have turned away from Him who is their
life. 44

Here again is a near classic statement of one of the Munich
students: Germany's troubles began with the apostasy from
Christianity. One finds this great faith in God in all the bits and
pieces which are left as fragments of such noble lives. It is easy
to see how these young people would admire Theodore Haecker.
Consider this passage from his journal as a parallel of the above:

A short dialogue:
I do not wish to be on the losing side. I want to belong to the
victorious party.
That is a very human desire, but there are times when it is more
honorable, and therefore more human, to be on the losing side.
You misunderstand me. I mean that I want to be on the side
that wins in the end, to belong to the party that is ultimately
victorious.
Why do you suppose that I misunderstand you? My query is still
the same: May it not be more honorable, perhaps, to be on the
losing side?
That is a question arising from the despair of unbelief. For in
the end, Christ is victorious. And where is there greater honor than
in Christ. 45

Hans Scholl caught that spirit completely when he wrote in
his diary words which may be taken to apply specifically to his

---

44 *Ibid.,* 57.
45 Theodor Haecker, *op cit.,* 182, (Entry No. 603, 1942).

own opposition to National Socialism, or more generally to his fight against worldliness.

Had Christ not lived and had He not died, would there be any meaning to all of this? In senseless tears and in self-destruction ... such would be the end. [46]

In some cases, as expressed in the letters of Christoph Probst and in Sophie Scholl's *Diary,* the situation could only "be seen as in a glass, darkly"; a man's fate was in God's hands. And yet, curiously enough, although the life of Christ was a life of suffering, a life which, as Probst said, had "sanctified suffering," [47] nonetheless man is expected to do what is right, to do the "will of God," to be, perhaps, victorious in Christ by being on the "losing side" even in a war. Thus might the Munich students have articulated their ideals and realized the necessity for fighting against National Socialism. But in this fight they needed help. They needed to widen their circle. In a university town like Munich that was not too difficult. In May, June and July, 1942, the students came together in small groups often. Sophie Scholl had been listening to lectures given by Professor Kurt Huber; she detected a sympathetic mind. And so one evening in June he was invited to the home of Frau Dr. Mertens to meet the students. [48]

Kurt Huber was born of German parents in the town of Chur, Graubünden, in Switzerland on October 24, 1893. [49] His family, however, moved to Stuttgart where he was reared in an academic environment which prepared him well to take his doctorate at the University of Munich in 1917. [50] He was exempt from military service because of a partial paralysis which left him with a minor

---

[46] Inge Scholl, Das Andere Deutschland, Typescript, 9.
[47] See pages 158-159, Letter from Christoph Probst.
[48] Kurt Huber, Defense speech, *loc. cit.,* 1.
[49] Clara Huber, *Kurt Huber, zum Gedächtnis* (Regensburg, 1948), 17.
[50] *Ibid.,* 13.

speech defect and caused a slight limp in his walking. [51] Despite his affliction, he set out on a brilliant academic career in which his research and teaching embraced the disciplines of psychology, philosophy and music. He taught at the University of Munich until 1937, when, because of his distinguished work on European folk music, he was called to Berlin to work in the National Archive of Folk Songs. [52] This appointment was short-lived because of a disagreement which he had with Fritz Metzlar. (He quarreled with Metzlar's argument that the major was the only scale natural to Teutonic peoples. [53])

For a short time, actually for only two years, he had belonged to the Bavarian People's Party. He gave up his membership because he found the alliance of religion and politics too close. [54] In 1940, largely under pressure from society and to gain greater security for his family, he joined the National Socialist Party. [55]

---

[51] Walter Rubsamen, "Kurt Huber of Munich," *Musical Quarterly*, XXX (1944), 227.

[52] *Ibid.*, 231.

[53] *Ibid.*, 231. In the Trial of the Munich Students II, 7, reference is made to his position as *Abteilungsleiter in dem Staatlichen Institut für Musikforschung in Berlin*. It goes on to say that he had to give that up, "da er die Genehmigung seiner vorgesetzten Dienststelle nicht erhielt." Returning to Munich he became an *ausserplanmässiger Professor* — "mit einem Lehrauftrag für experimentelle Psychologie, Ton- und Musikpsychologie."

[54] Trial of Munich Students, II, 8.

[55] According to the NSDAP records now in the Berlin Document Center. Kurt Huber joined the Party on April 1, 1940, receiving the number: 8-282-981. Included in the file is a letter from NSDAP headquarters, Munich, dated May 21, 1938, which evaluates Prof. Huber's political attitude. It reads in part: "... Dr. Huber [hat] starke Bindung zum Katholizismus ... [die] eine ausgesprochene parteifeindliche Stellung einnimmt. Insbesondere scheint er es für seine Aufgabe zu halten, jeden Einfluss von Parteikreisen auf die Volksliederarbeit unmöglich zu machen. Während einer erst vor kurzem abgeschlossenen Expedition nach Jugoslawien an der Huber teilnahm, warnte er die an dem sehr darüber erstaunten Teilnehmer vor der Einflussnahme des Rosenbergkreises." In the Trial of the Munich Students, II, 8, we read that although he entered the NSDAP he was, nonetheless, "in gewissen Punkten mit der national-sozialistischen Kulturpolitik nicht einverstanden."

And this action can now be understood for what it actually signified. [56] Temperamentally he was a solid middle-class German who rarely, if ever, took the name of Deutschland in vain. To him Germany's great days were the era of Stein and Hardenberg; of the liberation from Napoleon. His heroes were Schiller's "Tell" and the celebrated Andreas Hofer. [57] To his very last days in prison, Professor Huber never forgot to call the blessing of God upon his fatherland, giving to Germany, his wife and his children equal places in his loyalty. [58] Such loyalty was heightened by the behavior of the Nazis, super-patriots and chauvinists of the worst sort who were ruining the good name of Germany. That is why patriotic duty became such an important element in Professor Huber's thinking. Irritated and outraged by the abandonment of what was for him "traditional" in Germany, he was prepared to talk to young people with ideas, particularly, ideas which would counter the existing situation. We do know that he was irritated mostly by what he called the "bolshevization" of Germany through certain elements in the National Socialist

---

[56] Dr. August Deppisch, Prof. Huber's lawyer at the trial, has written a memoir, dated Munich, August 27, 1945. He says there: "Er [Prof. Huber] sei an und für sich kein Feind des Nationalsozialismus. Es habe ihn vielmehr sympathisch berührt, dass der Nationalsozialismus die deutschen Wissenschaften (Volkskunde, deutsche Sprachenforschung und Volkslieder), sowie das völkische und rassische Moment betone. Er begrüsse auch den Grundsatz des nationalen Selbstbestimmungsrechtes der einzelnen Völker, des weiteren den Kampf gegen den Überkapitalismus. Ferner billige er eine verständnisvolle Sozialisierung der Wirtschaft. Schliesslich freue er sich über die tatkräftige Unterstützung der Leibesübung durch die massgeblichen staatlichen und Parteidienststellen. Dagegen lehne er den Kampf gegen das Christentum, dem wir doch unsere abendländische Kultur zu verdanken hätten und das auch heute noch mit seiner Sittenlehre die Grundlage einer geordneten Staatsführung bilden müsse, unter allen Umständen ab.", 8-9.
[57] Kurt Huber, Defense speech, 1; Clara Huber, op. cit., 12.
[58] Clara Huber, op. cit., 37.

Party. [59] In this he had not a little in common with members of the Catholic hierarchy in Bavaria who, as often as not, felt that National Socialism and Roman Catholicism need not necessarily clash; they would clash only because of certain "bolshevist," "anti-Catholic" elements in the Party. But in that, as has been demonstrated, both he and the hierarchy were lifted up by vain hopes.

The first gathering of student oppositionists he attended was in June, 1942 at the home of Frau Dr. Mertens. The group organization might be said to have been patterned after the seminar system of our universities. Frau Dr. Mertens read a short paper on the meaning and importance of a religious revival. Apparently this caused some unfavorable criticism on the part of certain medical students present. As the discussion developed, Hans Scholl fell into rather heated debate with a Dr. Ellerman. The discussion moved more and more toward broad cultural differences and finally settled on that favorite theme: northern Germany at odds with the south. Hans Scholl was vehement in his attacks on Prussia. [60]

Towards the end of that June another meeting composed of the same group took place this time at the Schmorell's home in Harlaching, a residential area in Munich. Hans Scholl, accompanied by Traute Lafrenz, met Professor Huber at the *Heiliger Geist* tram stop; the three went on to the Schmorell's. While walking from the streetcar to the house Hans brought up the subject of the *White Rose Leaflets*. Traute Lafrenz asked Professor Huber if he had received any. He admitted that he had, and, in fact that he had occasion to discuss them with Prof. Dr. A. Karl von Müller, one of his close friends. At that time he was unaware that the students were the authors of the leaflets. [61]

---

[59] Kurt Huber, Defense speech, 10.
[60] *Ibid.*, 1.
[61] *Ibid.*, 1; see also August Deppisch, *loc. cit.*, 2.

When the group was gathered, the same theme, the basic differences between north and south, was renewed. This time, according to Huber's own words, he took the side of Dr. Ellerman, praising the contribution of Prussia in the making of Germany, most particularly in the period of 1813. From there the discussion turned on the unfortunate influence of the Nazi Party on Germany. [62]

The next time the students came together in a large group—although Professor Huber admitted having seen Scholl often after lectures—was the last in this period of their activity. This time they all met at the work-shop of an architect named Eickemayer. The occasion was the last farewell before the members of the Medical Student Company reported for a tour of duty to the eastern front. [63] We may assume, then, that Hans Scholl, Alexander Schmorell, Christoph Probst, Sophie Scholl, Professor Huber and, their host, Eickemayer, were certainly there; and, possibly, Gisela Schertling, Katharina Schüddekopf, and Traute Lafrenz, all of whom had knowledge of these meetings and were sentenced accordingly by the People's Court. One young friend of Scholl, Hans Hirzel, came all the way from Ulm to be present at this final gathering. [64]

The general mood of the group was that the defeat of Germany was at hand. [65] The question before them was: what is the attitude of other students here and in other universities? How could they get together in order effectively to do something about ridding Germany of Hitlerism. [66] They were particularly vehement in their attacks on the Party and its behavior in occupied territories; they attacked the S.S. for their mass-murders;

---

[62] Kurt Huber, Defense speech, 1-2.
[63] *Ibid.*, 2.
[64] Trial of Munich Students, II, 12.
[65] *Ibid.*, 12.
[66] Kurt Huber, Defense speech, 2.

they strongly protested their loss of intellectual and religious freedom. [67] Before Prof. Huber left the gathering, he encouraged the students to write to him and tell him of their experiences in Russia. He departed at about ten-thirty. But the students stayed on and talked of their own activities of which Professor Huber was still unaware. The possibility of erecting anti-Nazi placards was also discussed. [68]

That evening in late July, 1942, was more than a point of physical departure, for it was then that they determined to increase their activities and attempt an even closer contact with their fellow-Germans. Until then the students had been content to write exhortations, appeals aimed more particularly at their colleagues in the university. Fortunately all of these leaflets have survived; we lack only the exact dates of their writing and printing. We do know that the leaflets of the White Rose stopped appearing in July, 1942; when they next appeared they bore another title: Leaflets of the Resistance Movement in Germany. [69] These leaflets of the White Rose are tangible evidence of real opposition by the Munich students; they are unequalled in their selflessness and their idealism. The second, third and fourth follow here in their entirety:

White Rose Leaflet Nr. II

It is utterly impossible to discuss National Socialism rationally because it is not a rational system. It is absolutely false to speak of the National Socialist *Weltanschauung*; for, if there were such a thing, we would have to use ideas to prove or disprove it. The facts are quite the reverse. At its embryonic stage this movement was built upon the idea of deceiving humanity; because humanity was already so disintegrated they could only hope to save it by lies. Hitler himself wrote in an earlier edition of 'his' book (a book, by the way, which is written in the most wretched German I have ever

[67] *Ibid.*, 2.
[68] Trial of Munich Students, II, 12.
[69] Inge Scholl, *Weisse Rose*, 105.

read—a book which a nation of poets and thinkers in expected to accept as the Bible.) : 'One does not realize to what extent one must deceive a nation in order to govern it.' That this cancerous growth could not be observed at its inception can be attributed to the fact that so many decent people were able to keep this thing under control. But yet, as the organization grew larger and larger, and, finally, by means of base corruption succeeded in taking over the government, then this hideous sore broke from its restricted area and defiled the entire body. At first the opponents sought, in the main, the safety of seclusion, while the German intelligentsia fled deep into their cellars, there to live in shadows hidden from the light of the sun, only to find that, little by little, they were suffocating. And now we stand at the end of all of this. It all depends now whether one is prepared to accept the necessity of opposition; whether one is willing to make others see where the trouble lies; not to rest for a moment until the very last person is convinced of the utter necessity of fighting against this system. If such a wave of discontent goes through the land; if one can feel it in the atmosphere itself; when not just a few are prepared to participate, then will this wretched system be destroyed in one final, powerful, smiting blow. An end with terror is still better than terror without end.

It is not given to us to realize the final meaning of historical events. Yet if this horrible catastrophe has some mysterious bearing on our salvation then it can be explained only as follows; that by suffering we are cleansed; that from out of the deepest night comes the light; that freed of his own illness, a man is finally able to shake off the yoke which weighs upon this world.

It is not our intention here to write about the Jewish question, not even to present any defense; no, we wish only to call your attention briefly to the fact that since the defeat of Poland 300,000 Jews have been killed in the most brutal fashion. In this we do see the most horrible crime against the dignity of man for which there is no parallel in the whole of human history. The Jews are also human beings—discuss the question as you will—and such a thing was done to human beings! Perhaps some may say: the Jews have earned such a fate—an opinion which can only be regarded as a very uncautious assumption. But even accepting this fact, how would this same person react to the fact that the entire aristocratic youth of Poland has been destroyed? (God forbid that this is not yet a fact!) You may well ask: how could such a thing be? All the male offspring of aristocratic families between the ages of fifteen and twenty have been sent to forced labor battalions in various concentration camps of Germany. All girls in this same age group have been transported to Norway to the brothels operated for the S.S. ... Why is it that we tell you all of this—things which you know already; or perhaps you know even worse crimes done by this underworld clique? Because this arouses a further question which touches us most deeply; a question which must give us all pause. Why does the German people appear to be so apathetic in the face of such monstrous, nay criminal inhumanity to man? Scarcely anyone seems to have any scruples. The fact is simply taken in and then forgotten. And then the German people resumes its stupid and incorrigible sleep, giving these Fascist criminals courage and opportunity to continue this madness—and, indeed, this they will do. Can this be a sign of the complete barbarization of the Germans, a return to primitive passions? In the face of such action is there no chord struck with cries out against this? Can we be sunk into the sleep of death from which there be no awakening ever? Such does it appear and such it may well be if the Germans do not rise out of this lethargy; if they do not protest whenever possible against this clique of criminals; if they are not prepared to suffer along with these hundreds of thousands of victims. Not only must we feel compassion. Oh no, much, much more. We must feel our share of this guilt [*Mitschuld*]. For by our apathetic behavior we Germans have given these low creatures the possibility to do what they have done. We have suffered this 'government' which has heaped boundless guilt upon us in that we could even permit that such a government be allowed to exist! Everyone wants to exonerate himself of this guilt by association, and, this done, proceeds to fall asleep with a good conscience. But *they* cannot be exonerated. They are all *guilty, guilty, guilty!* And yet it is not too late to rid ourselves of this the most mis-begotten of all governments in order that more guilt is not heaped upon us. Now that our eyes have been fully opened by events in this past year; now that we know with whom we are dealing, now is the time to root out this brown horde.

Until the outbreak of the war it might have been said that the greater part of the German people were dazzled by the National Socialists who hardly showed themselves in their true form. But now that we see them for what they are, the German people have the single and highest duty—one might better say holiest duty—to exterminate these beasts.

'Where the administration passes unobtrusively, the people are happy. Where the administration is everywhere in evidence, such a people's spirit is broken. Happiness is built upon suffering. Ah! yet happness is but a veil for misery. Where will it end? That we cannot know. Order changes into chaos; good changes into evil. The people are confused. Has it not ever been thus?

'An exalted being is at once forthright but not offensive; sharp but not cruel; upright but not ruthless. He is clear but does not wish to dazzle.'

Lao-tse.

'Who undertakes to rule the land and to fashion it after his own desires will not reach his goal. That is all.

'A state is a living organism; it cannot be forced. Whoever adds to it, ruins it; and who would overpower it, loses it.

'Among all creatures some lead, others follow; some blow warm, some blow cold; some are strong, some weak; some succeed, others fall by the wayside.

'An exalted being sets aside all exaggeration, presumption and encroachment on others.'

Lao-tse.

We ask you to reprint this with as many copies as possible and to pass it on. [70]

White Rose Leaflet, Nr. III

Salus publica suprema lex.

All ideal politics are utopias. A state cannot be constructed purely on theory; rather it must grow and mature even as does man. But that does not obviate the fact that at the beginning of a given culture the prototype of a state is there. The family is as old as man himself; and from this unity did man, endowed with reason, create

---

[70] Inge Scholl, *Die Weisse Rose,* 90-94. The reader's attention is drawn particularly to the statement of the problem of evil and the problem of human suffering.

his state built upon justice and providing the commonweal as the highest law. The state ought to be analagous to the divine order. The greatest of all utopias is the *Civitas Dei*, the prototype which all should seek to imitate in the final analysis. It is not our purpose here to judge the various possible expressions of this polity: democracy, contitutional monarchy, monarchy, etc. ... Only one thing must be said once and for all: every man has a right to an honest and workable government which guarantees the freedom of the individual and insures the prosperity of all. For man, according to God's will, is free and independent to try to arrive at earthly happiness in personal things within the orbit of civil society where we live and work together. Our present 'state' is a dictatorship of evil. 'Oh! we've known that for a long time,' I can hear you say, 'and we have no need to have this thrown up at us once again.' But I ask you: if you know this, why do you not rise up; why do you endure this until, little by little, open and covertly, one area of your rights after another is robbed from you, until one day you will find that there is nothing left to you—nothing but a mechanized contraption of a state operated by criminals and drunkards? Are your spirits so completely overpowered that you have forgotten that it is not only your right but, indeed, your *moral duty* to overthrow this system? If a creature no longer has the strength to demand his rights, then he must perforce go under. Indeed, we would deserve to be scattered throughout the whole world like sand in the wind if in this twelfth hour we did not raise ourselves up and show the courage which we have up until now lacked. Do not bury your cowardice under the cloak of cleverness. Every day which passes and finds you unwilling to resist this diabolical scheme, your guilt increases accordingly in a parabolic curve ever higher and higher.

Many of you who read these pages will wonder how you can best express your opposition. There seem to be no possibilities open to you. We would like to try and show that everyone is in the position to do something to get rid of this system. We do not suggest individual opposition in the manner of an embittered hermit; that will not destroy the foundations of this 'government,' nor make the rising against them any easier. Rather we ask for the cooperation of energetic men of conviction, people who understand that they can reach their goal if they try. We have no great collection of such means. There is only one which we have to offer: passive resistance.

The meaning and purpose of passive resistance is the destruction of National Socialism. In this fight there must be no shuddering at any path or action which lies open to us, no matter what it may be. At *all* points National Socialism must be attacked whenever possible. An end must be found to this state which violates all the canons of polity. A victory for Fascist Germany in this war would have the most shattering consequences. For the Germans today must seek not first and foremost the military defeat of Bolshevism, rather the defeat of the National Socialists. This *without any question* must be our first task. The profound necessity of this last fact we will demonstrate in coming broadsheets.

Every convinced opponent of National Socialism must ask himself: How can I do my part in fighting against the present 'state'? How can I deal it a telling blow? Through passive resistance—nothing more. It is quite clear that we are not able to indicate to everyone exactly how he can best do this. That you must work out for yourself. All we can do is to suggest certain common methods and devices.

Sabotage armaments and war industry plants; sabotage gatherings, meetings, festivals, organizations, anything which National Socialism has created. Hinder the smooth operation of the war machine—a machine which operates only for war, and to save and preserve the National Socialist Party and its dictatorship. *Sabotage* is possible on the level of higher learning, whether it be in the university, higher schools, laboratories, institutes or wherever it is they seek to perpetuate this war by employing the techniques of scholarship. *Sabotage* all these efforts along cultural lines which promote the Fascist 'view.' *Sabotage* all branches of the creative arts, no matter how remote their connection with National Socialism may seen. *Sabotage* all publications, all newspapers which are in the pay of the 'government' and continue to spread their ideas, this great, brown perversion of truth. Don't give one red cent to these street-collectors (even though they may appear to be collecting money in the name of some worthy purpose). That is only camouflage. In reality such sums as are collected never are seen by the Red Cross nor those who need it. The government doesn't need the money; it is not financially dependent on such collection.

Besides the presses turn out paper money in reams! The people must be held in suspense; the bridle must not be lifted! Don't give anything to metal, clothing or such-like collectors! Try to get those you know in the lower classes to see how ridiculous a continuation of this senselss war is; to show them how far their economic and intellectual slavery under the National Socialists has gone; to convince them how far the destruction of all moral and religious values has gone; and to get them to participate in passive resistance.

From Aristotle's *Politics*:

'Further it pertains to the essence of tyranny to try to see that nothing remains secret of what any subject says or does; but everywhere to have spies who will eavesdrop—further, to incite everyone, to set friend against friend, the common people against the aristocracy, and the rich against each other. Then it is a part of such tyrannical measures to make the subjects poor, in order to pay the police and also in order that the poor will have no time in which to think of plots.

'—Indeed, also such income taxes as the Syracuseans laid on; in five years under Dionysius the citizens of this state had given out their entire wealth. Needless to say, the tyrant is inclined always to start wars—'

Please reprint and pass on! [71]

White Rose Leaflet Nr. IV.

It is an old bit of wisdom—a thing one cannot say often enough to children—that he who will not listen must feel. A bright child will burn his fingers only once on a hot stove. In the past weeks Hitler has victories both in Russia and in Africa to which he can point. The result of this has been a certain increase of optimism in certain sections of the population, while in other parts there is an increase of despair and pessimism to a degree hitherto unknown amongst Germans. Everywhere amongst the opponents of Hitler—which is to say amongst the better half of the German people—one hears complaints, words of discontent and discouragement,

---

[71] *Ibid.*, 95-99. The readers attention is drawn particularly to the discussion of an organic polity as well as the discussion of passive resistance and of German guilt.

phrases which, often as not, end up with: 'In spite of everything, can Hitler ....'

Meanwhile the German attack on Egypt has been stopped; Rommel must bide his time in a very dangerous and exposed position. But the advance in the east goes forward, an apparent advance, that is, which is purchased at incredible cost to such an extent that one can hardly term it an advantage. Thus do we war against any optimism.

And who is it that counts the dead: Hitler or Goebbels? We can answer that: neither of them. In Russia thousands are falling daily. It is harvest time and the reaper moves swiftly amongst the ripened corn. Mourning covers every house in our land and there is no one to dry our mothers' tears. Hitler only lies to those from whom he has taken their most precious possession, having driven them to a meaningless death.

Every word that comes from Hitler's mouth is a lie. When he says peace, he means war; if in some wicked fashion he calls upon the name of the Almighty, he means the power of evil, the fallen angel, Satan himself. His very mouth is a stench-ridden cavern of Hell,—his power, utterly infamous. To be sure, we must fight against the National Socialist terror-state with rational means; yet, whoever doubts the real existence of the demonic powers today, has failed almost completely to understand the metaphysical background of this war. Behind concrete experiences, behind physical perceptions, behind all material and logical considerations, we perceive the *irrational,* which is, in this case, the fight against the devil, against the representatives of the anti-Christ. At all times in human history the devils have hidden in the shadows, waiting for their hour, waiting for the moment when man will reject that order which has been sanctioned by God and based upon freedom, waiting for the moment when man will give in to the pressure of evil and tear himself from the power of that higher order. Having thus made the first awful step of his own free will, there follow with mounting speed, the second, the third—; yet at all times in human history, at the times of greatest need and crisis individuals have risen up: prophets, saints, and the like who have preserved their freedom; men who have trusted God and directed their lives towards Him, and with His help will endeavor to bring the people back again. To be sure, man is free; but without the true God he is

powerless against evil; he is like a ship without a rudder which
must give in to the storm's ravagings; he is like a child without its
mother; he is like a cloud floating aimlessly.

Can there be—I ask you this as a Christian—can there be the
slightest hesitation in this struggle for the preservation of your
most prized possessions? Can there be any intriguing on your part?
Can there be any setting aside of the discussion in the hope that
someone else will take up arms and defend you? Has not God,
Himself, given you the power and the courage to fight? We must
wage battles against the evil one where he is most powerful. His
power today is greatest in Hitler.

'So I returned and considered all the oppressions that are done
under the sun: and behold the tears of such as were oppressed,
and they had no comforter; and on the side of their oppressors
there was power; but they had no comforter.

'Wherefore I praised the dead which are already dead, more
than the living which are yet alive.' (Eccles: 4, 1-2).

Novalis: 'True anarchy is the real test of religion. Out of the
destruction of all that is positive, she raises up her glorious head
as the new creator of the world. . . . If only Europe would again
awaken; if only there were a science of politics! Ought there to be
some form of hierarchy. . . . as a basis for a union of states! . . . .
Blood will flow across Europe until the nations become aware of
their unfortunate madness which drives them only in circles and
hearkening to this sacred music and mellowed by its message they
will take up their peaceful occupations and a great festival of peace
will be celebrated with flowing tears in those sanctuaries still
smouldering in ruin. Only religion can reawaken Europe and assure her people of their rights and reinstate Christianity with new
visible glory in her earthly mission as the patron and founder of
world peace.'

We wish to indicate here that the White Rose is not in the pay
of any foreign power. Although we realize that the power of National Socialism can only be broken with military force, still what
we seek is a re-awakening of the badly scarred German soul from
the interior outwards. This rebirth must be accompanied by a clear
recognition of all the guilt which the German people has heaped
upon itself, and also a relentless fight against Hitler and his all
too many helpers: party members, Quislings, etc. . . With all

brutality a chasm must be formed separating the better part of the people from all that goes to make up National Socialism. For Hitler and his followers there can be no punishment on this earth which would expiate their crimes. But out of love for the coming generations, after the end of the war, such an example must be made so that never again will anyone have the slightest desire to try anything like this again. And don't forget the little villains of this system; remember their names that none may get away! They shall not be able in the last moment before this is over to change flags and pretend that nothing has happened. To give you some reassurance we are happy to say that there is no list of receivers of these leaflets of the White Rose written down anywhere. The adresses have all been taken from address books.

We will not be silent. We are your bad conscience. The White Rose will not leave you at peace! [72]

In these exhortations there is more than simple criticism of the by-now traditional German passivity in the face of such brutalities against Jews and Poles. There is a demand formulated from the Christian teaching of the worth and dignity of the individual in the face of his eternal destiny to establish a government which will guarantee to the individual freedom of action and freedom of religion. Whether or not the Munich Students were consciously reflecting the views of the Catholic Church is difficult to say; but the reader will not fail to recall that these sentiments were the very ones which Cardinal Faulhaber had championed so valiantly in his sermon on Passion Sunday, 1942—the same year in which most of the leaflets appeared. [73] These students were in earnest when they made their pleas to rid their country of the National Socialist "perversion of truth." Nothing could have been more extreme in its opposition to Nazi propaganda than the statement that a victory for Nazi Bolshevism was more dangerous than Russian Bolshevism. Final-

---

[72] *Ibid.,* 100-104.
[73] See *supra,* Chapter 11.

ly, and most important, the selections from Novalis express the students' real sentiments: "Only religion can reawaken Europe." There is the key to understanding the Munich Students Revolt.

c) FROM SUMMER 1942 UNTIL THE END

From August until probably some time in October the Medical Student Company was on active duty on the Russian front. Whether leaflets of the White Rose were distributed amongst their fellow soldiers we do not know. But some activity might be expected of such a group as Scholl, Schmorell and Probst. For one thing there must have been a certain amount of discussion among the troops as well as attempts to enlist the support of others. In this they were not without success; for it was during that period that Wilhelm Graf joined the group. [74]

Willi Graf, as he is generally known, was born in Kuchenheim in the Saarland on January 2, 1918. His father was in the wholesale wine trade and successful enough in this to provide a good education for his son in the *Gymnasium* at Saarbrücken. After his Work Service was completed he began the study of medicine at Bonn. [75] These meagre facts about his early life pale in significance when one observes the important place he gave to religion in his life. Like Hans Scholl he had belonged to a youth group banned by the National Socialists; his was, however, a Catholic group in Saarbrücken. For this he found himself imprisoned for a short time in 1938. [76] And beyond this there is very little known about him, except possibly an overall quality of reserve which expressed itself in a questioning if not doubting altogether the value of material and worldly success. The world, the devil, and National Socialism were all one in his mind. That was his attitude before he joined with the others. That original

---

[74] Trial of Munich Students, II, 8.
[75] R. Huch, "Willi Graf," *Die Wandlung*, III, (1948), 13.
[76] Inge Scholl, *Die Weisse Rose*, 28.

attitude may well have reflected the Hamlet-like indecision of many German intellectuals, particularly those who styled their passivity an inner emigration: the world was to be left to the devil. In his diary there is this curious passage which may shed some light on his character.

> Is this really the right way to go about it? Sometimes I believe firmly that it is, other times I have serious doubts. But in spite of it all, I shall do it . . . . even though it is such a bother. [77]

In any case, when the students resumed their academic life, he was among them, sharing unstintingly in all their anti-Nazi efforts. Exactly what his part was in all of this we will review in a moment. There were several important things which involved Hans Scholl immediately upon his return from Russia, and these should concern us now.

First of all there was the fact that Hans' father was just then being released from prison. He had been denounced for having called Hitler "God's scourge on humanity." [78] Hans was anxious therefore to see him. He wished to receive renewed strength and courage from the element of society which we know from his leaflets he regarded as basic. [79] We can well imagine what intense emotions must have mingled in the hearts of such people amidst all their sorrow and travail. It is no easy thing to appreciate fully the terrible struggle in body and mind which must have tormented those who had to fight in a war they knew was not theirs—worse: in one in which they knew they must not be victorious. Hans felt this struggle keenly. But he needed not only the spiritual strength coming from his family, he needed also material assistance to carry out his plans. He needed money to carry on the work of printing leaflets, buying envelopes,

---

[77] R. Huch, "Willi Graf," loc. cit., 40.
[78] Inge Scholl, Die Weisse Rose, 31-32.
[79] See supra, White Rose Leaflet, Nr. I; especially the quote from Schiller, and White Rose Leaflet, III,

postage stamps, etc. His own meagre stipend was hardly adequate. While at home he turned to an old friend of the Scholl family: Eugen Grimmiger.

Herr Grimminger was born July 29, 1892, in Crailsheim, Württemberg. [80] Perhaps he had more reason than others to be disgusted with the Nazis and to turn this disgust into opposition because of the fact that his wife was Jewish. [81] In any case Scholl and Schmorell visited him sometime in November and he learned then of their various activities. We may assume that he listened enthusiastically to their plans; for he acceded to their request, presenting them with five hundred marks. [82]

There were other matters which occupied Hans Scholl in Ulm. Just before leaving Munich for Russia the preceding July, he had given Hans Hirzel eighty marks to buy a mimeograph machine in Ulm and to reprint some of the leaflets. [83] In the fall Scholl visited Hirzel to find out what had been accomplished while he was at the front. There is no evidence that Hirzel had accomplished anything. However, it is recorded that they talked together and they planned certain anti-Nazi posters. And, later on, Hirzel was put in charge of the distribution of leaflets in the Stuttgart area where he was later to be arrested in 1943 with his sister, Susanne Hirzel. [84]

One other question had been bothering Scholl even before he had gone to the front in July, a question which was discussed at Eickemayers' at their farewell party. What was the situation in the universities? Were there like-minded souls? Could he seek them out and encourage them to participate in a general movement?

---

[80] Trial of the Munich Students, II, 16.
[81] *Ibid.*, 16.
[82] *Ibid.*, 17.
[83] *Ibid.*, 13.
[84] *Ibid.*, 11, 13.

Sometime in January, 1943, Scholl and Schmorell went to Chemnitz to look up a certain Dr. Harnack who had achieved some fame at the National Theatre in Weimar where he had been the director until May, 1941. [85] If, as Harnack claimed at the trial, he was deaf to the enthusiastic proposals of Scholl and Schmorell, it is an interesting coincidence that he should have spent a six-day furlough in Munich between the sixth and twelfth of February. He was introduced to Professor Huber on February 8 when there was a rather prolonged discussion of the German situation. Huber found Harnack far too much to the left, without ever saying that he thought him entirely Communistic. It is true that Harnack saw the various leaflets published by the students and may have known of Scholl's plan for the display of February 18th. [86] But there is no evidence that he gave any active support to the students. Scholl may have failed with Harnack; but he had other irons in the fire.

In early January, 1943, he arranged to have Willi Graf distribute the leaflets in a number of towns in the Rhineland. Graf went first to Bonn. There he hoped to find like-minded students, some of whom he had known in the days when he belonged to a Catholic youth group. He was well enough received and they took the leaflets; unfortunately for him and his efforts, his friends were forced to devote their full time to preparations for examinations. So he went next to his hometown, Saarbrücken. Needless to say, he delivered more leaflets there. But most particularly he sought an old friend of his, Heinrich Bollinger.

---

[85] Dr. Falk Erich Walter Harnack, born March 2, 1913, in Stuttgart; a nephew of Adolf von Harnack; a brother of Arnold Harnack, condemned to death for high treason in 1942. See Criminal case, 6J, 24/43, 3, and Trial of Munich Students, II, 20. There is no evidence that he was related to Ernst von Harnack mentioned by Pechel as an outstanding opponent of National Socialism. See his *Deutscher Widerstand* (Erlenbach-Zürich, 1947), 95.

[86] Trial of Munich Students, II, 20. Also, Kurt Huber, Defense speech, *loc. cit.*, 5.

He learned that he was then at Freiburg. [87] But Graf was to be disappointed again; he was forced to seek him out at Ulm. There they finally met. Bollonger did take the leaflets back to Freiburg and discussed them with a friend, Helmut Bauer, [88] but there is no evidence that the connections at Freiburg went beyond this. Yet that meagre contact cannot be regarded as without significance. The simple fact that the contacts had increased, however tenuous they were, was all the Munich Students could expect at that time. [89]

---

[87] Trial of Munich Students, II, 18. Dr. Heinrich Philipp Bollinger, born April 23, 1916 at Saarbrücken, at the time of his arrest an assistant at the *Institut für Philosophie und Erziehungswissenschaft*. See also Criminal case, 6J, 24/43 — 1H, 101/43, 2.

[88] Criminal Case, 6J, 24/43, 1H, 101/43, 2. Helmut Karl Theodor August Bauer, born June 17, 1919 in Sarrbrücken.

[89] There is no record in the trial nor in any other documents of a contact with students in Berlin. There are, however, two secondary sources which indicate a connection with the events in Munich. Unfortunately there is a confusion in the spellings, if, indeed, the same person is involved in both descriptions. Jürgen Wittenstein writes in *Blick in die Welt* 13, 15, as follows: "In Berlin wurde eine eigene Gruppe gebildet, mit der regelmässige Verbindung bestand. An ihrer Spitze stand Helmut Hartert, ein alter Freund von Hans Scholl, der sein in München begonnenes Studium in Berlin fortsetzte."
Professor d'Ester of the Journalism Faculty of the University of Munich has given to me a short memoir of one of his students: "Kampfgenossen: Herman Hart," Typescript, 11 pages:
"Einer meiner treuesten Kampfgefährten war mein Freund und Schüler Hermann Hart. Wenn je der Name bereits das Wesen eines Menschen kennzeichnet, so war es bei Hart der Fall. *Hart* war sein Wille, es gab keine Gegensätze zwischen seiner Weltanschauung und seinem Leben. *Hart* war er aber auch nur gegen sich selbst. Dagegen von einer gewinnenden Liebe zu anderen, mochten sie auch in fremden, feindlichen Lagern stehen. Ein Sohn des weinfreudigen Maintales, aus dem mit Mauern umwehrten Volkach über Würzburg stammte er. Sein Vater betrieb eine Druckerei und gab auch eine Zeitung heraus. Die *Volkacher Zeitung* war eine jener in Deutschland so beliebten und für die Erhaltung des Stammesbewusstseins so wertvollen Heimatzeitungen. Nachdem Hart sich ein gediegenes Wissen auf Gymnasium und Universität angeeignet hatte, bewarb er sich bei mir um eine Dissertation. Sein besonders für alle Fragen der Presse, aber auch sein kritischer Blick für geschichtliche

But if the contacts with students at other universities appear to have been without results, the students were none the less as active as ever in Munich. They tightened their own ranks and relied much more on the advice of Professor Huber. Hans Scholl

Entwicklungen liessen ihn als besonders geeignet erscheinen, die Geschichte der ältesten katholischen Zeitung zu schreiben, der *Augsburger Postzeitung.* Er hat sich dieser Aufgabe mit ausserordentlichem Geschick entledigt. Seine Darstellung gibt nicht nur ein erschöpfendes Bild der wechselvollen Geschicke einer der führenden deutschen Zeitungen, sie liefert zugleich ein Stück Welt- und Kulturgeschichte durch die bewegte Zeit der Aufklärung und der französischen Revolution. Sorgfältiges Quellenstudium und strenge objektive Auswertung der riesigen Stoffmassen einen sich mit einer übersichtlichen Darstellung und einer gepflegten Sprache. So ist ein Standartwerk der deutschen Pressegeschichte entstanden, ein Vorbild für ähnliche Arbeiten ... Hart stellte sich und seine Zeitung ganz in den Dienst einer antinationalsozialistischen Propaganda. Wir hatten ausgemacht, dass ich ihn mit der nötigen Munition versähe. Ich las in der Zeit der Parteikämpfe täglich etwa 40 Zeitungen aller Parteien und Landstriche. Darin fand sich viel und oft recht schlagkräftiges Rüstzeug für die Entlarvung des frevelhaften Spiels von Lüge und Gemeinheit mit der gewissenlose aber gerissene Propagandisten wie Goebbels das deutsche Volk zu umgarnen wussten. In den Lokalblättern wurden so manche Einzelheiten verzeichnet, die mehr als lange Leitartikel der nationalsozialistischen Propaganda den Boden unter den Füssen wegzogen. So wurde aus Koblenz berichtet, dass Goebbels sein luxuriöses Auto in einer Garage eingestellt habe und mit einer Autodroschke zur Wahlversammlung gefahren sei, um den Schein der vielgepriesenen Selbstlosigkeit zu wahren. Jede Woche ging eine Sendung 'H.M.' nach Volkach. Diese Bezeichnung für 'Hitler-Munition' wählten wir, weil schon damals die Post bespitzelt wurde. Bis in die Nazi-herrschaft konnte sich das Hitler-feindliche Blatt halten, es fiel dann der Uniformierungssucht der Partei zum Opfer. Hart ruhte aber nicht, er begann mit einer Arbeit, über die er strengstes Stillschweigen beobachtete, von dem seine besten Freunde selbst erst nach seinem Tode erfuhren. Er schrieb eine Abrechnung mit den Verbrechern des Dritten Reiches unter dem Titel 'Attila der Letzte.' Er nutzte seine Stellung in dem Büro eines Berliner Nachrichtendienstes, um aus der Weltpresse all das Treiben der Nazis enthüllenden Notizen und Artikel abzuschreiben, um daraus eine Anklageschrift von unwiderstehlicher Überzeugungskraft zu formen. Er war sich der ungeheuern Gefahr dieses Beginnens bewusst, denn, hätte die Gestapo nur einen Teil dieser Arbeit gefunden, wäre Hart in das K.Z. gekommen. Er knüpfte auch schon früh Beziehungen zu dem Scholl-Kreis an: Einzelheiten wissen wir leider nicht, da er auf begreiflichen Gründen strenges Stillschweigen bewahrte."

had, as promised, written to him while in Russia, and written, it seems, a rather shocking account of his impressions of the eastern front. Naturally, when he returned he was anxious to discuss his impressions and their broader implications. A few days before Christmas, 1942, he and Schmorell went to Professor Huber's home in Gräfelfing. Then it was that he confessed that he was the author of the White Rose leaflets. [90] After Christmas, the three met again in Gräfelfing during which time they discussed the various contacts with students at other universities. [91]

The students also arranged for more evenings like those held the previous spring. On one of these occasions Scholl and Huber fell into disagreement over the word *Führerstaat*. It seems Scholl objected to that notion altogether, a position Huber found considerably more "radical" than he had previously noticed. [92] On another occasion, one morning late in January, Hans invited Professor Huber to come to his rooms where he read his two proposed leaflets. The first, written by Schmorell, Huber rejected as sounding much too Communistic. [93] The other, written by Scholl, entitled "To all Germans" and written under the caption: "Leaflet of the Resistance Movement" was wholly acceptable, except for the phrase the "Resistance Movement" which sounded a bit overpowering to Professor Huber.

And so another leaflet was ready for printing and distribution; another voice out of that wilderness which was Germany under Nazi tyranny; another and more powerful articulation of the

---

[90] Kurt Huber, Defense speech, 3.

[91] Frau Clara Huber recalls that at one of these visits Professor Huber and the students were allowing their discussion to become far too animated. She recalls hearing Hans Scholl call out that "if it must come to the shedding of blood, then let it come!" — or some similar phrase. Frau Clara Huber was anxious about the consequences of such public declamation and urged all of them to come into the house. [Told to the author by Frau Professor Huber.]

[92] Kurt Huber, Defense speech, 4.

[93] *Ibid.*

problem of what is good and what is evil for Germany and for Europe. Here imperialism is denounced in all its forms; a sweeping condemnation of German unification based on the hegemony of Prussia; a clarion call for the victory of federalism not only in Germany but, one feels, in all of Europe; and a belief in moderate socialism which must imply a respect for those basic rights and liberties so long claimed by the adherents of western civilization. Here, then, is Hans Scholl's last testament written sometime in January, 1943:

A Call to All Germans!

The war proceeds to its expected end. It is just as it was in 1918: while the armies in Russia are being driven back and while in the west the invasion plans are prepared, the government tries to attract attention to the growing success of submarine warfare. America's peak in arms production has not yet been reached; yet even now they have surpassed all other production known in the history of man. With all the certainty of a mathematician, Hitler is driving the German people into the abyss. *Hitler cannot win the war; he can only lengthen it!* His guilt and that of his abetters has surpassed all measurement. But a just punishment is coming ever closer!

But what are the German people doing? They see nothing and they hear nothing. Blindly do they follow these seducers to perdition. 'Victory at all costs!' is inscribed on their banners. Hitler says he will fight until the last man; but the war is already lost.

Germans! Do you wish for yourselves and for your children the same fate which the Jews have suffered? Do you wish to be judged as your evil leaders will be judged? Would you have us now and forever the most despised and rejected of all people in the world? No! Then cut yourselves off from those National Socialist criminals! Show by your deeds that you think otherwise! A new war of liberation has begun. The better half of the people is on our side. Divest yourself of the mantle of indifference which has until now covered your heart! *Decide, before it is too late!*

Do not believe this National Socialist propaganda about Bolshevism—a method they have of getting you to join up with them. Do not believe that Germany's salvation is bound up completely with a victory for National Socialism! No clique of criminals will ever be victorious. Do not hesitate to remove yourself in time from all which is part and parcel of National Socialism! After this war is over a terrible but just judgment will come on all those who were so cowardly and lacked the will to come out in the open.

What has this war—a war which was never a national war—taught us?

The idea of imperial power, wherever it may exist, must be shown for all time to be unprofitable. A one-sided Prussian militarism must never again be allowed to succeed to power. The only possible basis for a new development is the closest cooperation of European peoples. An effective centralism such as one found in the Prussian domination of Germany and the attempt, further, to dominate all of Europe must be nipped in the bud. The Germany which will exist after this is over can only be federal in its make-up. Only a healthy federal constitution will fill weakened Europe with new life. The working class will be freed from their condition of degrading slavery by a reasonable socialism. The vicious lie of an economic autarchy must be banished from Europe. Every nation, every individual has a right to the wealth of this world.

Freedom of speech, freedom of religion, protection of individual citizens against the criminal whims of totalitarian states—these are the foundations of a new Europe.

Support the Resistance Movement. Spread the leaflets. [94]

Several thousand of these leaflets were printed, of which a few hundred were sent by mail to people in Munich whose names were taken from a student address book. Several thousand copies were scattered about the streets of Munich. [95] A second batch was run off, this time numbering over three thousand. [96] These were to be mailed to various persons living in towns in southern Germany. But to do that it was thought wiser to mail them from the towns themselves, thus to give the impression that

---

[94] Inge Scholl, *Die Weisse Rose,* 105-107.
[95] Trial of Munich Students, II, 10.
[96] *Ibid.,* 11.

a chain of students was involved. The chief couriers were Sophie Scholl and Alexander Schmorell. He took large numbers to Salzburg, Linz and Vienna, posting some in Vienna to Frankfurt am Main; she took charge of Augsburg and brought them to Stuttgart where Hans and Susanne Hirzel were in charge of distribution. Two thousand leaflets were given to Hirzel in Ulm to be addressed for that place and for Stuttgart. He was assisted also by Franz Müller, particularly in addressing the envelopes. [97] The names of all those who received these leaflets we shall never know, because they were selected quite at random. And there were actions in the city of Munich which we may assume were observed by thousands. One morning in February, 1943, the population awoke to find public buildings on the Ludwigstrasse and the Leopoldstrasse painted with the words: "Down with Hitler." "Hitler the mass-murderer." "Freedom!" [98] That was the work of Scholl, Schmorell and Graf, done, probably, during the nights of February 3rd, 8th and 15th. [99]

Two things done by the Nazis stimulated the Munich Students to their final action. The first was a student assembly called by Gauleiter Giessler at the *Deutsches Museum*. Here the audience was incensed, as they were forced to listen to lewd jokes and shameless attacks on women students who, in the opinion of Giessler, ought not to be wasting their time studying when they could be bearing children for their country. [100] There was a good deal of booing at that and in the scuffle which followed several Nazis were beaten up. (The Nazis were used to such reactions. Professor Huber cites in his defense speech an occasion when the Medical Student Company at Munich greeted

---

[97] Criminal case, 6J 24/43 — 1H, 101/43; Franz Joseph Müller, born September 8, 1924, in Ulm.
[98] Trial of Munich Students, I, 3, and II, 15.
[99] Trial of Munich Students, II, 16.
[100] Inge Scholl, Das Andere Deutschland, 5.

military people as well as *Statthalter* von Epp with an ovation, while the Nazis, when they spoke, were greeted with stony silence. [101])

That took place in early February. But it can hardly be compared with the shock which all Germans received when they learned of the collapse of Stalingrad. It was only then that the Germans learned officially how much had been lost. From all accounts, Professor Huber was absolutely shaken. He realized then, if never before, how hopeless the situation was. On the evening of the seventh of February he sat down and wrote until early the next morning. The result of that night became known as the Manifesto of the Munich Students. It is related directly to the events in the *Deutsches Museum,* described above, and, of course, to Stalingrad. In it can be found, to be sure, chiefly a complaint against the disappearance of values and ideals which Professor Huber rightly claimed had been associated once so closely with the German universities. But the reader will notice that there is a direct appeal to the German students to stand up for their ideals; to annihilate "these torturers and thus aid in the building of a new, spiritual Europe;" and, to fight to restore "freedom and honor as members of a morally responsible nation." The broadsheet follows now in its entirety.

Fellow Students!

The nation is profoundly shaken by the defeat of our troops at Stalingrad. Three hundred and thirty thousand Germans have senselessly and irresponsibly been led to death and destruction

---

[101] Kurt Huber, Defense speech. In this connection see Ulrich von Hassell, *Diaries* (Garden City, N.Y., 1947), 49. He describes an incident which took place at the University of Munich, July 4, 1939. "A Party speaker was hissed out of one student gathering; in another he was bombarded with eggs, and the affair resulted in about ten students being sent off to Dachau. The halls of the university were plastered during the night with inscriptions: "Down with Hitler," and with slogans comparing Hitler with Napoleon, whose rule also had a quick end."

through the cunning strategy of a World War I corporal. Our
Führer, we thank thee! The German people grow restive. Shall we
continue to entrust the fate of our armies to a dilettante? Shall
we offer up what is left of the German youth to the base instincts
of the Party clique? Never. The day of reckoning of the German
youth with the most loathsome tyranny ever to be visited upon our
people is at hand. In the name of German youth we demand from
this Adolf Hitler government the return of our personal freedom—
our most treasured possession—that which he has filched from us
in a most wretched fashion.

We grew up in a state which ruthlessly muzzled every free expression of opinion. During those most important years of our
development the H.J., S.A., and S.S. have tried to regiment us,
to revolutionize us, and to drug us. "Ideological education"
(*"Weltanschauliche Schulung"*) is the name they use for their
contemptible method of drowning in a mass of empty phrases
every attempt to think independently. A special crop of leaders
(*"Führerauslese"*) is being groomed in Nazi camps by current
Party bosses who are educating them to be the godless, shameless,
unscrupulous exploiters and murderous leaders of the next genera-
tion. Of course, those of us who work with our minds will be expected to bend everything in the service of this new race of mas-
ters. Front line troops will be ordered about by student leaders
and *Gauleiteraspiranten* as if they were nothing but school boys.
Gauleiters are able to mock in an indecent manner the honor of
our women students. German women studying at the University of
Munich have given the right answer to any such besmirching of
their honor, and, indeed, German students have stood up and defended their colleagues.

That is the beginning in the struggle for our right of self-determination, without which any really creative work is impossible. We
all owe a vote of thanks to our brave comrades who have set such
a shining example for us!

For us there can only be one cry. Fight against the Party! Renounce your membership in Party organizations where all political
expression has been muzzled. Quit those courses offered by leaders
of the S.S. or other Party stool-pigeons! This is a matter of no less
importance than objective truth as well as academic freedom! Nor
will we be terrified by any threats, no, not even the threat to close

the universities. This is something which concerns each and every one of us now and for the future: our freedom and honor as members of a morally responsible nation.

Freedom and honor! For ten long years Hitler and his crowd have perverted, degraded and twisted these two glorious German words beyond recognition as indeed only a dilettante could do who might take the most prized possessions of a nation and toss them before swine. Just what freedom and honor means to them they have shown in these ten years during which time they have destroyed all material and intellectual freedom as well as blotted out every trace of morality from the German people. Surely the most stupid German has had his eyes opened by this horrible blood bath which has drenched all of Europe and continues now, daily, the same process, all in the name of freedom and honor of the German nation. The name of Germany will forever be besmirched unless the youth arise seeking at the same time vengeance and expiation by annihilating these torturers and thus aid in the building of a new spiritual Europe. Fellow Students! The German people look to us! As in 1813 the people looked to us to destroy the Napoleonic terror, so today in 1943 they look us to destroy the terror of National Socialism. Beresina and Stalingrad are burning in the east; the dead of Stalingrad adjure us.

'Rise up my people; the signal fires are ablaze!'

Our people are ready to revolt against the enslavement of Europe by the Nazis and look to the triumph of a new faith in freedom and honor. [102]

On February 9th, Professor Huber met Scholl and Schmorell in town and gave them the "Manifesto." As they read through the papers they were more than pleased, that is except for one sentence: "Stand by our glorious army." Hans drew a line through this. A quarrel ensued. Professor Huber demanded that if the manifesto were printed it should include his entire thought or that it should not be used at all. He left considerably irritated and did not see the students again. As it happened Professor

---

[102] Inge Scholl, *Die Weisse Rose,* 108-110. The reader will recall the phrase, "the signal fires are ablaze," was one used by Fritz Gerlich, Fr. Naab and Cardinal von Faulhaber.

Huber was engaged with affairs in Kempten which kept him there from about February 10th until February 17. The next thing he knew was that there had been a "revolt" of students at Munich. [103] The rest we already know: how, on that sunny Thursday morning, February 18, 1943, Hans and Sophie Scholl took a small case full of copies of Professor Huber's manifesto to the university to distribute in the lecture rooms before classes began. After placing them in all the rooms they found there were still copies left over. These they took to the top floor, opened one of the windows overlooking the courtyard and emptied the case. When the porter discovered that the leaflets were falling from the upper storey, he ordered all doors of the University locked. Hans and Sophie Scholl were prisoners. In an effort to save Christoph Probst from being involved, Hans tried to destroy his projected broadsheet which was then in manuscript form; but this was not successful.

The three, Hans, Sophie and Christoph, soon found themselves at *Gestapo* headquarters of Munich. They remained there, answering questions, until Freisler, the president of the People's Court, arrived from Berlin. He conducted the trial in the Palace of Justice before a hand-picked audience of Nazi officials. The trial was brief. Freisler announced that the penalty of death to be paid by the Scholls and Probst would halt any possible "stab-in-the-back" of the German war effort. [104] Hans Scholl tried to assume the entire guilt upon himself, but he was ordered by the court to keep silence. The three were dispatched quickly to Stadelheim prison to be executed.

According to witnesses close to the history of these events, both Hans and Sophie asked to be received into the Catholic Church before their execution. That was, however, not permitted

---

[103] Kurt Huber, Defense speech, 5.
[104] Trial of Munich Students, I, 4.

because, according to German church law, some notice has to be given if one wishes to change his religion. [105] Christoph Probst, not yet having been baptized, was accorded this rite by Father Speer, chaplain at Stadelheim, on the morning of his excution. Immediately afterwards he wrote this letter to his mother:

Munich, February 22, 1943

My dearest Mother:

Please do not be frightened by the fact that I did not come to you as planned last Saturday, nor be frightened by the events which I now must relate. Instead of getting my usual pass last Saturday, I was arrested and brought to Munich. Through an unfortunate development I have been brought here to the *Gestapo* prison. But please don't think I am exaggerating when I say things could not be better with me. The treatment is good and life here in this cell looks so pleasant to me that I have no particular anxiety about being here for a longer time. The only thing which bothers me is that I may have caused you to suffer by my actions. However difficult this exterior separation from my beloved wife and children may be, nonetheless I am drawn to them that much more inwardly. By this inner bond I strengthen myself. Your love is now more precious than ever. Oh that I now should cause you this anxiety! I shall try later on to explain all of this to you. For now I must think of my duties as a father—I must think of my children. The whole thing is so much bound up with our destiny that I must beg of you not to chastize me as irresponsible. You all know—mother, sister, wife and children—that I live only for you. I cannot express how much I have felt your love—how much your love has helped my little Vincent; how much you have helped little Herta. But I am doubly thankful when I realize that you must be as peaceful as I am; that you are not cast down by sorrow; that you will lose neither trust nor hope even when difficult things may come. You are my only mother, the loveliest ever; how could I bear to bring bitterness into your life? But you know that our destiny in this world is fixed and nothing we can do will change

[105] Georg Smolka, Letter to the author, Wessling, Bavaria, November 2, 1948. Also from conversation with Frau Clara Huber, February, 1951.

it. But no words, dearest mother, can express my innermost thoughts now. I feel above all the indestructibility of love. Today the future seems less secure than ever; and yet it disturbs me now less than ever. For myself I have no fears, only for you, my wife and children. I hope I shall always be able to help you when you need me. But should that possibility be deprived us for a while, may I still hope that things will go as well with you as if I were there as your protector. And even though something destroy me, may I hope that these gentle, guiltless creatures may live; I cannot imagine that they should suffer. How things will turn out, I do not know. I only know that nothing is too difficult for us to endure.

All good wishes to Heinz! Oh Mother! You have endured so much with Herta and now I become your child of sorrow. But we do know that mothers are more important for the children than the father.

I do not feel separated from you. I feel you are close by me, my own dear mother. I embrace you and remain, always, your son,

Christel [106]

He wrote another letter which was not allowed to leave the *Gestapo* files, wherein he said he was dying "without any feeling of hate." [107] There need be no remarks here to prove the extent to which he was motivated by the power of love; his letters are quite sufficient evidence. It was his fate to complete that love by death.

Sophie was the first to mount the scaffold, followed by Christoph. Hans Scholl before placing his head on the block called out in a full, clear voice: *"Es lebe die Freiheit!"* [108] These events took place four days after their arrest.

The second trial began on Monday, April 19. At that time Professor Huber, although he had been assigned a defense lawyer, took it upon himself to speak his own plea—a plea which was intended to cover the others as well. The first part is de-

---

[106] Christoph Probst, Letter to his mother, Frau K. Klublatt, Tegernsee.

[107] Dieter Sasse, *op. cit.,* 3.

[108] Inge Scholl, *Die Weisse Rose,* 80.

voted to a history of how he came to be involved with the group.
He then turned to a discussion of the Manifesto, the one written
on February 7th. If one remembers that the trial was a Nazi
show-piece to which various dignitaries were invited, his candid
description was itself an eloquent example of opposition. He
said, in part:

> As far as the text of the broadsheet is concerned I should like
> to mention again that it was written from the standpoint of those
> students who had gone to the front and found that their freedom
> had been so encroached upon. There is not a false assertion in it.
> History will charge Hitler with the full responsibility for Stalin-
> grad. The remarks about the demonstration of the youth against
> the Party I will still maintain as fact. I will retract not one word.
> During the past ten years the Party has effectively destroyed any
> sense of moral obligation as well as freedom in the coming gene-
> ration; the entire educative process has been bolshevized. And yet
> the professors at our universities have as a whole passively stood
> by while the bolshevization in education and upbringing has taken
> place. This powerful accusation I make now as I have made it
> before against the German universities. It does not exclude the
> possibility, however, that many professors, some of whom were
> members of the National Socialist Party, have done what they could
> to set aside the worst restrictions of the government. Yet that does
> not alter the overall guilt of the German academicians. They have
> clearly shown that they no longer control in any real sense the
> education of the German youth.

After remarks on several particular points in the prosecution
brief, Professor Huber concluded his speech as follows:

> I might say here that the prosecution's brief has presented the
> kernel of my attack quite fairly. As is maintained, I did insist in
> Schmorell's home that the NSDAP was moving more and more
> to the left. No patriot who has observed and followed the intel-
> lectual life of the Party as closely as I have during this past decade
> can quarrel about this definite move to the left. But may I call
> as a witness to the fact that I have for long watched this definite
> tendency and had occasion to seek out ways to stem this tide with
> the President of the Bavarian Academy of Sciences, Professor

Dr. K. A. von Müller. I have been able to tell him confidentially my scruples and observations at all times. I know also that my thoughts are shared by a great many National Socialists. That is why I believe an expression of these ideas in Schmorell's home or anywhere is perfectly in order. And I realize fully that our real task right now is to stop this tendency toward the left. All this propaganda in the newspapers about the danger of Bolshevism is at bottom worthless unless we do something about the growing Bolshevism within Germany itself. For myself, I had only this one means at my disposal of making my opinions felt, a means not of resistance but rather of contradiction. As a German citizen, as a German university professor, and as a political being, I consider it not only my right but indeed my moral duty to work within the present political framework and to fight any threats to the commonweal. I think I speak for all the young academicians here when I say that our action was in every sense a moral action aimed at this tendency; against Bolshevism which daily increases within the National Socialist state. To use every means at one's disposal to awaken the slumbering consciences of our fellow citizens and to bring them back to appreciate an unwritten code of justice universally enforced, this is nothing short of one's patriotic duty.

Let me conclude. What I intended was to awaken the group of students not by means of an organization but simply by words; not to excite them to an act of violence, but rather to give them moral insights into the existing evils of political life. A return to clear, moral principles, to a *Rechtsstaat,* to a mutual trust of one's fellow creatures: these are not illegal actions; quite the contrary, they represent a re-establishment of legality. I asked myself, in the sense of Kant's categorical imperative, what would happen if what I did were to become a general practice? To that there is only one answer: then and only then would order, security, respect for our state system return in our political life. Each and every morally responsible citizen should raise his voice against the threatening mastery of might over right, of caprice over free will. We would return to many of the principles advocated by the Party ten years ago. During the past ten years they have, often as not, not only not been fulfilled, but rather their opposites have been enforced. The demand for self-determination of even the

smallest minorities is gone in Europe today, not to mention the
preservation of natural and racial characteristics. The fundamental
rights in an effective commonweal are destroyed by the systematic
undermining of trust among men. No more horrible judgment
can be passed on society than the one which we must all make:
that no one feels secure, neither from his neighbor; no, not even
a father from his son! This is what I wanted to explain and had to explain.

All exterior legality has an outer ridge beyond which it becomes
invalid and immoral. Then it becomes a subterfuge of a cowardice
which does not dare oppose state violation of justice. A state which
stifles every free expression of opinion and places under the most
terrible punishments every, yes every, morally justifiable criticism;
when every proposal for improvement is labeled a plan for high
treason, then an unwritten, German, Teutonic right which has
always existed and must continue to exist is broken.

I ask and plead with you in this hour to let me speak for these
young accused, to speak for their creative right in the truest sense
of the word, not to dictate by force, but rather to let the clear
voice of their consciences speak out. And this spirit was probably
the most ideal which one can imagine. The striving for absolute
justice, cleanliness, truthfulness in the life of the state. For myself,
however, I claim that our most urgent need is a return to the
fundamental basis of a *Rechtsstaat,* that is a true German *Führerstaat.* Failing to respond to this can only lead to the downfall of
the German spirit and ultimately of the German people. I have
attained one goal: namely, to bring this warning and exhortation
not to the attention of one little discussion group but to the attention of responsible people in the highest position of the Judi-
ciary. I risk my life for this exhortation, for this conjuration to
conversion. I demand the return of freedom for us Germans. We
do not wish to spend our short lives in the chains of slavery—even
if they were golden chains of prosperity. I leave behind a broken
wife and two unhappy children in want and sorrow. Could you
not allow my unfortunate family at least a small stipend for living
which would compare to that which is due a German professor?
You have taken from me the rank and privileges of a professor,
along with my well-earned doctorate with its *summa cum laude*
and then reduced me to the level of the lowest criminal. No con-

viction of high treason will ever be able to rob me of my inner
worth as a professor or the conviction I hold as to my philosophy
of life and my attitude towards politics. History will justify my
actions and my desires; upon that do I rely as upon a rock. I
hope to God that the spiritual powers which justify it may be
brought forth from my own people in time. I have acted as I had to
act, prompted by a voice from within. I take the consequences
upon myself following the injunction of J. G. Fichte:
'And thou shouldst act as if the fate of all things German depended upon thee and thine action alone and the responsibility
were thine.' [109]

When the trial was about to come to an end, Freisler announced the sentences: Alexander Schmorell, Professor Huber
and Willi Graf would pay for their actions with their lives.
Eugen Grimminger, because he had aided the students with
money, received ten years in the penitentiary. Heinrich Bollinger
and Helmut Bauer, having had knowledge which they did not
report, received a penitentiary sentence of seven years each. Hans
Hirzel and Franz Müller, although only boys, received five-year
prison sentences; Heinrich Güter, having knowledge which he
did not report, was sentenced to eighteen months in prison.
Gisela Schertling, Katharina Schüddekopf, and Traute Lofrenz
each received one year in prison. Falk Harnack was able, somehow, to get away without any punishment. [110] Later Hans Carl
Leipelt was sentenced to death for having tried to aid the Scholls
and Frau Professor Huber. He was executed January 29,
1945. [111]

Professor Huber and Alexander Schmorell were not executed
until July 13, 1943. During the time in prison Professor Huber
busied himself with the final chapters of his study of Leibnitz. [112] In his last letter to his wife, Kurt Huber gives voice

[109] Kurt Huber, Defense Speech. Full text in Appendix K.
[110] Criminal case, 6J, 24/43; 1H, 101/43, 3.
[111] Clara Huber, op. cit., 29.
[112] Cf. Kurt Huber, Leibnitz (Munich, 1953).

again to his patriotic sentiments. He wrote, in part: "Rejoice with me! I am dying for my country, for a just and beautiful fatherland which will most assuredly emerge after this war." [113] In his very last postscript there is a toast to his wife and to his fatherland. More than the others, he considered this sacrifice of his life in terms of his loyalty to Germany, something not likely to be recognized by the students who found concepts such as nationalism completely perverted and made meaningless by ten years of National Socialism. This is, perhaps, the significant difference between the Professor and the students, a thing he quite poignantly brings out in the conclusion of his *Defense*. The students could no longer put their trust in the ideals of a safe and sound German nation. They wanted to seek again for those ideals and values of Christianity as the basis for the new society.

Willi Graf waited for his execution until October 8, 1943, for what reason, we do not know. We do know that he faced death with perfect Christian resignation. [114]

d) CONCLUSION

Thus ended the Munich Student Revolt. Almost at once knowledge of their action spread throughout the world. Reports in leading newspapers, journals as well as books assumed a generally positive appreciation of the students' effort. Particularly interesting in this regard is a novel by Alfred Neumann, *Six of Them*, [115] a novel which seems to a remarkable degree to have caught the spirit of wartime Munich. However, Neumann has done a certain amount of damage to the personalities of the Munich Students' Revolt: his characterizations sometimes violate seriously the real temper of the Munich Students.

---

[113] Clara Huber, *op. cit.*, 36.
[114] R. Huch, "Willi Graf," *loc. cit.*, 357.
[115] A. Neumann, *Es waren ihrer Sechs* (Stockholm, 1945).

The broader significance, however, is the general interest, one might almost say enthusiasm which the action seems to have aroused within Germany and abroad. The news was eagerly awaited. The eulogies of Pechel and Rothfels are fairly accurate when they say that the Munich students tried to "save the youth of Germany" or that they "tried to purify themselves and the name of Germany." Although outwardly a failure, it had deep repercussions. In this one respect it resembles all efforts to overthrow the Nazi regime, even the July 20th plot, whose instigators sought mainly to preserve Germany from needless destruction and inevitable dismemberment. [116] To anyone outside the group who planned the army coup of 1944, the entire episode might spell disaster and failure. Meinecke in his *Die Deutsche Katastrophe* has written of a visit with Beck in May, 1944, in which there was some feeling of futility of the plan to seize control. Yet the "cup of sorrow had to be emptied to its dregs." Meinecke continues:

> I rather imagine now that the attempt of July 20, 1944, was carried through on that basis even though they knew it was hopeless; some attempt had to be made to save Germany—some display before the inevitable mass arrests took place. [117]

The same is true of the Munich Students Revolt. One cannot miss that note of hopeful despair which permeates the lives and writings of the students. There seems to be no doubt that Hans Scholl knew what he was doing when he emptied the case containing the leaflets into the University courtyard. [118] The necessity and efficacy of that gesture may be questioned if one will. Yet Hans knew that the time was almost up. One public display

---

[116] Cf. Trial of Major War Criminals (Nürnberg, 1948), XII, 248-249.

[117] Meinecke, *Die deutsche Katastrophe* (Wiesbaden, 1949), 149.

[118] Dieter Sasse, Bericht über die Münchner Studenten, 3. "Kurz darauf erfuhr Hans Scholl durch einen Verbindungsmann zur Gestapo, dass seine Verhaftung unmittelbar bevorstand."

would be worth more than a thousand *Leaflets of the White Rose*. He and Sophie and the others offered themselves as victims; they were the sign which the world had long awaited. That was how the Munich students chose to bring themselves, their ideas and ideals "into the open." [119] The Munich students believed that words, the right words, would bring man to obey his conscience. This close union of ideas and ideals with themselves made them what they were; for, as they said over and over, and on this they were all in agreement: Germany's problem would be solved only if the people chose to reject the force of evil by repudiating Naziism, and only if they would devote themselves entirely to the practice of a Christian life. They were, plainly speaking, Christian idealists.

---

[119] See Leaflet of the White Rose, Nr. V, *supra,* 187-188.

CHAPTER V

THE FINAL EFFORT

a) THE BAVARIAN HEIMATBEWEGUNG

There can be little doubt that Hitler's failures in war encouraged opposition which, had he continued to be successful, would have continued to lie dormant. That is why it is often remarked that those interested in finding positive examples of opposition to Hitler ought not to select those moments when the German people were threatened with final destruction and probable dismemberment, but should rather inquire about attitudes held at moments of great national triumph, such as, for example, the period between the fall of France and the invasion of Russia. And yet we know from the study of various groups which opposed National Socialism that effectiveness cannot be the sole criterion in judging either the existence or the quality of such opposition. The opposition to Hitler from the Catholic Church was fairly consistent in Bavaria; even if the force of that opposition was severely crippled by the force of National Socialism, the opposition was none the less real. Freiherr von Harnier and his followers continued the plans for a restoration begun in those February days of 1933 by people like the Guttenberg brothers, one of whom could write so eloquently of his despair in fighting a war on the wrong side. At the same time Karl Ludwig zu Guttenberg was not one to presume that there was any easy way out of that trap in which Hitler had so successfully caught the German people. And again, in understanding the idealistic effort of the Munich Students, so encouraged by the sentiments of Muth and Haecker that between Christians and

Nazis there was an unbridgeable gap, we are nonetheless confronted with the difficult fact that Professor Huber finally succumbed to Party membership in that fateful year of 1940. These apparent contradictions are not the only problems one must face in writing the history of opposition to Hitler.

As the war progressed, bitterness became more and more pronounced among the people; but, as we shall see, the National Socialists kept an eye on this bitterness and acted accordingly. Opposition was treated mercilessly by the Nazis to the very last days of the war. It was this very fierceness and brutality on the part of the Nazis that gave an appreciable dimension to attempts such as those military efforts in southern Bavaria which sought to bring about a cessation of hostilities. These last are more commonly known as *Freiheits-Aktion Bayern*. Stillborn through this affair was, it had interesting antecedents which must concern us first.

In the summer of 1943 the Allies invadede Europe by way of Sicily, the first of a long series of invasions which had been promised since the fall of France. With Hitler's fortress no longer secure in the west, it could only be a matter of time before Germany would be forced to surrender all conquests made since 1940 and, probably, undergo occupation of her own territories. It was this prospect which stirred Germans to action, and not only Germans of the higher command in Berlin. Echoes were heard in Bavaria.

The arrest of monarchists in 1939 as well as the more recent Student Revolt had produced much uneasiness in the Bavarian capital. Now, as 1943 wore on, there were more demonstrations, and leaflets appeared showing some of the bitterness of the students at Munich, but somehow lacking the same ideological basis. One such which has survived was signed by the "Bavarian Section of the German Movement for Liberty." It follows in its entirety:

Bavarians!

From the very start you have not been deluded by the lies and deceptive promises of this man; you have withstood any attempt to deify him. Most of you have not fallen in with this Hitlerian salute, and this is having its effect now. Indeed, what shame must all of those feel who wished him health (*"Heil"*)— such a one who has brought only disease. (*"Unheil"*) Munich is called (by the Nazis) the "capital of the movement". From out of this infamous phrase you Bavarians should produce one which does you credit. Show everyone how Munich and Bavaria are the centers of the opposition.

Give good example to all Germans:
Don't use the Hitler salute.
Don't even reply when these grave-diggers of our people force you to respond to their "Heil Hitlers."
Stay clear of all National Socialist gatherings.
Don't give any money to these thievish street-collectors; every penny you give means more war and helps these brown apes to prolong their lives at the expense of the German people.
Don't tolerate these S.A. parades—these multidisplays which only besmirch your streets. Their last hour has struck! Once again: boycott them. Neither respond to them, nor greet them, nor give them any assistance whatever.
Destroy that symbol of their success and victory over the Germans: the swastika.
Away with this Party symbol, the sign under which the German people has lost justice.
Those who still wear the swastika show that they belong to those who would perpetuate this slavery; they will meet their proper fate on the day of reckoning.
Do not fear an occupation of our land by the English or the Americans. In spite of everything, they will be much more humane and just than this tyranny which we have endured long enough and which has cost the lives and limbs of hundreds and thousands of your sons and relatives. [1]

---

[1] Günther Weissenborn, *op. cit.*, Broadsheet of September, 1943, p. 313-314.

There is nothing unusual in this broadsheet, following as it does the pattern well established by the *Leaflets of the White Rose* and so many others. Yet, one cannot overlook this obvious reference to the end of the war: that an enemy occupation will not be as unbearable as the current regime.

There were Bavarians who were even more explicit about their hopes with the Allies, if and when they arrived. Von Hassell was "disturbed" by "these people, who were once idealistic National Socialists [who] now realize the imminence of the catastrophe and have only one idea: how can we save ourselves personally, and our Bavaria, from this chaos and from the reponsibility for what has happened?" And von Hassell goes on to transmit their point of view by adding, "Prussia can bear that burden! They hope naïvely that Bavaria will receive somewhat better treatment from the enemy. They want to join up with the Austrians, perhaps under a monarchy." [2]

That turns out to be a fairly accurate description of not only a "naïve" Bavarian point of view, but also the language of a disillusioned Prussian. Von Hassell, doubtless, was much closer to the thinking of Karl Ludwig zu Guttenberg: that there could be no special pleas for any particular Germans. But the fact is these Bavarians whom he is describing did feel that there was not a little in common between Prussianism and National Socialism.

Whether or not when he wrote those things von Hassell and his friend, Berthold, had an ex-consul by the name of Dr. Gebhard Seelos in mind, we shall never know. Dr. Seelos, whether

---

2 Ulrich von Hassell, *The von Hassell Diaries, 1938-1944,* (New York, 1949), 341. The reader's attention is invited again to that passage in von Hassell's *Diary* written in October, 1941: "The Third Reich which was designed permanently to unite the Germans had immeasurably deepened the breach between north and south. An unprecedented hatred toward Prussia was rampant in Bavaria and Austria." 216.

or not he was a "disillusioned Nazi," had been discharged from the Foreign Service on suspicion of disloyalty. [3] He and a former mayor of Regensburg, Dr. Hipp, got together and worked out the ideological basis for a movement which was to establish a new relationship between the states of Germany, one which was meant to give the preponderance to the south. [4] Their efforts were finally put on paper in August, 1943 and intended to serve as the argument preparatory to the issuing of a Bavarian declaration of independence. Even though it is tediously redundant throughout, their statement is presented here in its entirety because it captures in as concise a form as one can find something which is very real in southern Germany: the utter damnation of things Prussian. More explicit than this, with its implication of the need to separate Bavaria from such contagion, is the whole thesis that there could be no successful National Socialism without Prussianism. Nor is this the only statement of this thesis: Hans Scholl amongst others was not afraid to defend it in Munich a few years earlier. What follows, then, is unmistakably the sentiment of opposition which von Hassell dismissed so cavalierly in his diary.

BAVARIAN MEMORANDUM

INTRODUCTION

Germany has collapsed because it was Prussian. Germany has completely fallen to the National Socialists because Prussianism and National Socialism are the same sort of things.

The ancient opposition of Bavaria to Prussia is joined now with an opposition against the Nazi criminals, a fire which will not be

---

[3] *Wer ist Wer* (Berlin, 1951).

[4] See an unsigned typescript, *Bericht über die antinationalsozialistische Tätigkeit der bayerischen Heimatbewegung*, 8 p.p., now located in the Hoover Library, Stanford University, under the catalogue number, TS ww 1939, underground movements, G3, B, 355. This document will hereafter be referred to as, *Bericht, Seelos*.

extinguished. The stamping out of National Socialism means for Bavarians the elimination of everything Prussian from Bavaria. Fourteen hundred years independent, we will shake off the short-lived, unhappy, Prussian-German rule and once again announce the sovereignty of Bavaria.

I. BAVARIA'S TRADITION AS A STATE

Territory

Since the invasion in the sixth century of the Germanic tribes into the area between the Alps and the Bohemian forest, Bavaria has stood as an independent state with far-reaching, sovereign rights, not only in the Franconian empire and in the Holy Roman Empire but also as a state in Bismarck's empire. Since its foundation Bavaria has experienced no important territorial changes. In 1803 due to the dissolution of petty secular and ecclesiastical powers at the hands of Napoleon I, Bavaria was enlarged by the addition of Swabia and Franconia. According to the census of 1934 Bavaria comprised 77,800 qkm. with a population of 8,200,000.

Inhabitants

Bavaria was peopled from the start by the Bajuwaren (Boiern, Baiern) with some additions by the Franconian and Swabian groups who also belonged to the West Germanic tribe of the Semmonen. The Bavarian population is thus unified. Bavaria has never known dissensions between the newly arrived and the first settlers, between conquerors and conquered.

Government

When in 550 A.D. Bavaria chose to join in the Franconian empire, she retained her own rulers, the house of Agilolfinger, until 778. There then followed a series of other rulers. From 1180 until 1918 Bavaria enjoyed continuous rule by the ancient house of Wittelsbach, a fact which built up strong ties and traditions in the people.

Interest in the state

Because of this peculiar continuity of territory, people, and government—a situation we find in no other European state with the same kind of continuity—the feeling for the state amongst

Bavarians is strongly developed. This is so deeply imprinted here because all three of the components for the existence of a state have been brought about neither by the force of princes nor by the force of chance. Because Bavaria existed for centuries, long before the idea *'deutsch'* ever came up; and because Bavaria's strength as a state was always effective even when the Reich was weak, so it is easy to understand that for a Bavarian the concept 'Bavaria' is much more real than is the concept 'Deutschland.'

II. CHARACTERISTICS OF BAVARIA

Bavaria in her life as a state displays such positive marks that her revival and continuance as a factor for the people of central Europe seems not only something to be wished for but something which is necessary.

1) Bavarian history distinguishes itself by the complete absence of any imperialism. After the peaceful colonization of the Ostmark (later called Austria) between 600-800, Bavarian expansion ceased. Since then there have been neither losses nor expansions. Within the Reich, Bavaria has never striven for supremacy. Although, next to the Habsburgs and the Wettins, the Wittelsbachs are numbered amongst the oldest and most influential of the German reigning houses, they never sought the imperial crown. Should one happen to have been elected emperor, in contrast to other houses, the Wittelsbachs never increased their own power or sought by their reign to benefit their own house. Needless to say, however, when Bavaria was attacked or her freedom endangered, the Bavarians met such attacks and defended themselves tenaciously.

2) So it is that Bavaria never came to develop a great military power, nor did she produce any great generals. To be sure, in the Bavarian capital there is the famous *Feldherrnhalle* with the two statues of Generals von Tilly and von Wrede; but the first was no Bavarian, and the second was no general.

3) Because of the thousand year unity of the population with the ancient aristocracy and ruling house, there never existed a sharp class struggle, nor could revolution develop. We find already in the fourteenth century constitutional rights for the estates. In 1818 the Wittelsbachs introduced a constitution—among the very first of the German princes. Yet much more important than written

constitutions was this ancient feeling of oneness between the governing and the governed, clear indications of, and requirements for a true democracy. The Bavarians have long since rejected every kind of class rule and every encroachment on their traditional and personal activity. And should they have known such unpopular influences, they would free themselves from it with all their energy. This is clearly shown in recent times by the rapid cleaning-up of the revolutionary unrest of 1919, the squelching of the Hitler putsch of 1923, and the ever-increasing rejection of the National Socialist regime since 1933—a thing which has made Munich the capital of the opposition (*Hauptstadt der Gegenbewegung*). This healthy political instinct of the Bavarians, which relies on its tried and true methods, has been cultivated and built up by a thousand years of tradition.

4) Although Bavaria is not a rich country, it nonetheless possesses healthy economic conditions. The most important factor is farming which occupies over one-third of the population. Of the tillable soil, the average holding runs between five and one hundred hectars. This comprises 82.7 per cent of all the holdings as against 65.4 per cent for the comparable group in Prussia. Of holdings above one-hundred hectars there are only 4.2 per cent as against 24.7 per cent of all holdings in Prussia. There are 2,400,000 hectars of forest, covering about one-third of the country. Considering the ever growing importance of wood as a raw material this represents an important item of natural wealth. The industrial activity in Bavaria is neither concentrated in one definite industry nor is it fortunately concentrated in one definite area. Half of Germany's hydro-electric power (1936 figures) comes from Bavaria. (2.4 milliards KWH).

Because of this sound economic basis, Bavaria has been able to weather crises. In the winter of 1932-33 Bavaria had 6.7 per cent of the population unemployed as opposed to 9.5 per cent (of population unemployed) in Prussia. Nor has the social question ever been so sharp here as it is in northern Germany.

5) The health of this society is closely bound up with this happy economic situation. The ratio of one hundred and five persons per one square metre is far better than the national average of one hundred and forty one. The five large cities display normal size and distribution in relationship to the population as a whole:

Munich, 829,000; Augsburg, 185,000; Nürnberg, 423,000; Würzburg, 108,000; Ludwigshafen, 144,000. Yet the city population is only 19.9 per cent of Bavarian population as opposed to the national average of 30.2 per cent.

6) The Bavarians have developed a keen sense for the beautiful life in their land where the hands of man and nature work so harmoniously. It was from this optimistic world-view coupled with a deep religious conviction that there developed in Bavaria the last great European style: the Bavarian rococo, whose creations decorate the cities and hamlets of this land. Everywhere in Bavaria one observes the joy of songs and laughter. The passion-play at Oberammergau has attained international recognition. Artists flock to Munich which has become a center of European cultural activity.

7) Bavaria stands as a state *without foreign ambitions, without inner tensions, of ancient democratic spirit, economically sound, without serious social problems, with a healthy population, a guardian of culture and the home of a strong religious tradition.*

III. The Incorporation of Bavaria into Prussia

Because Bavaria's sense of her position was much too great, her incorporation into the Prussian-dominated Reich could only take place little by little; an all-out action (on the part of Prussia) would have endangered the ultimate success (of Prussia).

So it was that Prussia first sought domination over Bavaria's economic life. The Prussian-German customs union of 1833 served to be the first step toward a unified political system under Prussian leadership, just, indeed, as Motz, the Prussian Minister of Finance, had predicted in 1829. This also aided the Prussian Junkers who were at that time able to unload wheat in Bavaria which had regularly been shipped to England but was then being curtailed by new corn laws in the latter country. These economic advantages with the attendant industrial expansion of Bavaria drowned out all the voices which warned against further economic union with Prussia to the exclusion of Austria.

After the close of the war of 1866 between Prussia and Bavaria, Prussia went one step further and forced Bavaria into a military alliance, an event which gave Prussia greater influence through military reforms and controls within Bavaria.

Using this alliance, Bismarck manoeuvered Bavaria into the War of 1870 against the will of the majority in the Bavarian Legislature. Bismarck did not shy from any means of political or economic pressure; flattery, intrigue, propaganda, bribery were used to get Bavaria into the Prussian-German Reich. Still Bismarck had to leave those old rights of foreign representation, army, finance, etc., to Bavaria alone.

Because of the success of the War of 1870-71; because of the prosperous times; because of the development of a materialistic frame of mind; gradually Prussia came to dominate Bavaria, a thing which could only be overcome inside Bavaria or by a violent effort to shake off this control. Encroachments into Bavarian matters would never be tolerated by the ruling family.

Unfortunately this tendency was not clearly seen in Bavaria: her very existence was threatened; she could no longer decide in matters of war and peace. Thus it came that preparations for war lay in the all-powerful Prussian General Staff over which there was no parliamentary control. Foreign policy was in the hands of the Prussian Minister President who was also the German Reich Chancellor. Thus it was that the accession of William II to power, with his offensive manner in foreign affairs and his typical Prussian ways, was so repugnant to the Bavarians. Yet Bavaria possessed no constitutional means to check William II with any success. So it was that Bavaria, without any opportunity to voice a contrary opinion, found herself in a life and death struggle in 1914.

In retrospect, we see now that what was begun by Bismarck was continued by the Versailles treaty. The treaty considered Germany as an *Einheitsstaat* and not as a *Bundesstaat*. Looking for quick success, the Allies sought them in a financial centralization which destroyed part of Bavarian independence. Again, looking for political security, the Allies took away the territorial rights of southern Germany and delivered them to Prussia. Now for the first time Prussia's capital really became the capital of the Reich, whilst Munich sank to the level of a provincial city. Thus by not understanding the internal situation in 1919, the Allies strengthened Prussian and to a very large extent minimized the anti-Prussian powers.

After the Revolution of 1918 the Bavarians tended to support the native political parties. Dr. Heim, the Catholic farm leader, organized the Bavarian People's Party. There was also a Bavarian League of Farmers. And although these two parties controlled nearly half of the Bavarian votes; and although Bavaria did not feel at home in a Reich dominated by Prussia; due to a lack of responsible and determined leadership, there was no unified Bavarian movement and no strong influence on the national government now so completely dominated by Prussia. It was possible to notice new breaches of Bavarian rights.

The flare-up in 1923 which resulted from Berlin's usurpation of Bavarian troops directed against the Bavarian state remained only an episode.

But the final blow to Bavarian independence was struck by the law of 1933 after the Berlin National Socialists had taken over Bavaria. Bavaria now became, according to the constitution, a province of the Reich. A *Reichsstatthalter* (General v. Epp) was to see to it that the interests of the Reich would be protected in Bavaria. On all levels of public life Prussian arrangements and directions were introduced; Prussian officials, soldiers, and police were established in Bavaria. Bavaria was subdivided into Party districts, thus trying to defeat Bavaria's territorial unity. But since even this was not enough to destroy *Bayerntum*, at the beginning of the war in 1939 masses of non-Bavarians were moved in by the Nazis, whilst Bavarians were deported to other parts of Germany in an effort to achieve this goal.

It was exactly this exaggerated effort on the part of these Prussian-National Socialists to destroy Bavaria that unleashed a strong reaction. The effort on the part of Bismarck to destroy Bavaria and now continued by the Nazis, had enlivened Bavarian opposition. The demand for self-determination came from all sections of the population and all parts of the country in such strength that its fulfillment is a democratic demand.

IV. PRUSSIA AS THE OPPOSITE OF BAVARIA

In order to appreciate fully Bavaria's characteristic ways and the uncompromising disavowal of Prussian rule, it is necessary to observe the totally different foundation upon which the Prussian state is built and to observe the other factors which have formed the Prussians.

1) Prussia did not come about naturally. Prussia has no foundations in race, geography, or history; its real foundation is in the will to power of the House of Hohenzollern. Prussia is a mechanically constructed *Fürstenstaat*. Prussia gave its name to the Electorate of Brandenburg in 1701 and acquired the rest of its territory in 1815 and 1866.

2) There is no Germanic tribe in Prussia. (The Prussians are rather a mongrel-folk of German conquerors and Slavic subjects which have been assimilated by centuries of harshness and complete lack of consideration for others). After the partition of Poland (c. 1800) Prussia was half Slavic and did not really get a Germanic character until after the Congress of Vienna.

3) The triumph of despotism in that territory had serious consequence in Prussian society. The division between the colonists of the twelfth and thirteenth centuries and the rejected Slavic population continued until 1918 when the three-class electoral system was finally revoked. And meanwhile the Junkers maintained their political power in spite of the Constitution of 1848. By means of administrative devices they were able to keep the rural population in subjection and uncritical. In Prussia, meanwhile, a proletariat had arisen, and, this as a result of the peasant conditions on the estates of the East Elbian Junkers. The proletariat was now, however, a huge army of industrial workers without bonds of traditions or feelings for hearth and home. They began to fight for greater political freedom and against their status as slaves to the Junkers with their militaristic conception of the authority of the state. Such antitheses between aristocracy and common folk, military and civilian, city and country are unknown in Bavaria.

4) The latent inner tension in the Prussian state had been overcome in the Hohenzollern epoch by an active interest in foreign affairs. The Prussian state which in her zeal for power was always going beyond the limits which were placed on her by her national conditions, had to remain in motion in order to insure her own existence. Hardly had her enormous army won new territories than the size of the army would be doubled, in order to keep in balance the potential war booty with the potential number of enemies. Because Brandenburg-Prussia was a poor country, the Prussians had to work hard and save penuriously. All activity was

focused on one goal: the maintenance of the army. The Prussains always believed themselves specially called to perform in a spirited way some new and additional command. The fulfilment of this military goal kept encroaching on the civilian aspect of the state and began to influence the entire mental outlook of the people. That that which pertains to civilization should suffer through all of this, is only natural.

5) Even philosophy had to serve to bolster the state and keep the subjects in a position of unquestioning obedience. The state stood as the greatest reality, beyond good and evil; the actions of the state did not rely upon personal judgments or upon the voice of a single conscience. The masses were forced to keep in step and so they acquired a philosophy which paralysed the individual's critical sense from within.

6) The Prussians have only undertaken to look beyond their own frontiers to a more German conception when their egocentric state has been in danger. Do Prussian generals or politicians think of common German goals or German idealism? They do so only to weaken the possibility of an even more serious opposition to their power. After the defeat at Jena in 1806 the attempt at re-form lasted until 1819. This was followed by the worst sort of Junker restoration. The democratic spirit of Weimar, born in 1919, was already repressed in Prussia by 1933. The Nazis with their radical excesses continued the same Prussian policy.

V. Bavaria's Disavowal of Everything Prussian

The above description of Prussia ought to show convincingly enough the difficulty, if not the impossibility of any unity between Prussia and Bavaria. Because of her inherent drive to expand at the expense of smaller states, any effort to go-along with Prussia could only mean political suicide. After long experience and dread-ful suffering at her hands, we reject everything Prussian.

We refuse to participate in the egocentric, Prussian drive for power.

We refuse to go-along with Prussia's anti-German policies which have destroyed the old German Reich and replaced it with this Bismarckian and Nazi Reich which have so reduced *Deutsch-tum.*

We refuse to have our relations with other states determined by the Prussian methods of threats, provocations, boastings, suppressions and perfidy.

We Bavarians reject the Prussian deification of the state, giving it an autonomous morality.

We reject Prussian militarism which would force everything to follow in its pattern. We will not have it that from the cradle to the grave we are just soldiers on furlough.

We reject that Prussian bureaucracy which seeks to control everything.

We Bavarians reject Prussia because this state is against all true freedom. We reject Prussia because it destroys individuality.

We reject Prussia because it is, at bottom, undemocratic, and because it conceives the purpose of the state to keep its citizens in a kind of *Kadaver* obedience, and refuses to let them develop into responsible and free-willing agents in the government.

We Bavarians reject the Prussian system of education, training as it does only the will to respond to orders. In our schools we emphasize the whole man, an education in Christian humanism, and with the aim that all shall participate in political life.

We reject Prussia because Prussians imagine that they can control and master all things in this world with their rationalism. We put the power of feeling and the operation of the soul in the forefront.

We will not allow our culture, so deeply rooted in our home country, to be dominated by soulless Berlin.

We reject above all the Prussian system which either persecutes religion or makes it a tool of the state. Contrary to this system, we seek a life dominated by the spirit of Christianity.

We reject Prussia because even its positive achievements: the sense of duty, diligence, sufficiency, order, even these are perverted to the use of the state.

We reject Prussia because the law of that state is restlessness, movement, action, all of which contradict our *harmonic* Bavarian concept of life which holds fast to the natural order in all things.

We can reject the Prussians with such conviction, because we have come to know them so well during the period of Nazi domination, they have left their mark in speech, mannerism, gestures, accents, appearance even in the smallest villages of our country.

We reject the Prussians because we have seen in National Socialism the full scale of all the worst features of Prussianism. We reject Prussianism because the spiritual and social collapse in central Europe has been accelerated by the Prussians. We must recall our own values and rebuild on that firm, well-balanced, democratic basis a people's state and a *Rechtsstaat*, a thing impossible under Prussia.

XI. BAVARIAN AIMS

1) We wish for the independence of Bavaria, because only in as independent state can we fulfil our duties properly.

2) We aim for a re-constituted Bavaria as conscious Germans. The concept *"Deutsch"* has been besmeared by the concept "National Socialist"—which itself was falsified by Prussianism. The concept *"Deutsch"* must be fashioned anew. We Bavarians want to go back to the early foundations of the Reich, back to the historic connection of tribe and country. The unification and regimentation under Prussia and National Socialism put an end to the material and spiritual values, once the pride of Germans.

3) We want to find a greater national framework which will give us Bavarians freedom for our Bavarian needs. We Bavarians do not wish to turn back the wheel of history one hundred years and develop our local eccentricities. We want to go along with other well-knit German states into a greater unity of states and take our place in the rebuilding of Europe. We must, however, first re-build Bavaria because we know this land and have been entrusted with this task. Only with such a foundation will we know how to fit into a greater unity.

4) Therefore we Bavarians seek a partnership with the Austrians who have our same blood and who stand akin to us in so many ways. We also seek ties with Württemberg, Baden and Hesse. Free from every nationalistic feeling, Bavaria will be glad to work with non-Germanic people who are equally anxious to see a healthy group of central European states. Confident of our own strength we have not the least fear of invasions from outside.

5) We will not ask the question just now exactly what form the state ought to assume because this can be decided later. How-

ever, we feel that the Bavarian people and her history seem more prone to monarchy as the best form.

6) Aware of the strength and breadth of the Bavarian movement, we reject all efforts to force an artificial state-form upon us and pledge ourselves to the future of a democratic, christian, independent state of Bavaria. [5]

---

[5] Unsigned, undated typescript in Hoover Library, Stanford University, Stanford, California: Ts WW 1939, Underground Movements, G3 B 356, 12 pages. On the first page, directly above the phrase, *Bayerisches Memorandum*, we read: "Made up as a secret broadsheet, 1942." Again on the final page we find, this time in German: "1942 von der Widerstandsgruppe Dr. Seelos verfasst und in tausenden von Exemplaren verbreitet! Diese Widerstandsgruppe war eine der aktivsten, als sie nach der Kapitulation in einigen Orten als Bayer. Heimatpartei in Erscheinung trat, wurde sie von der CSU überspielt. Die Konseption der Bayern-Partei ist auf drei Widerstandsgruppen zurückzuführen." On page 2 of the *Bericht, Seelos, op. cit.,* we read: "Zum Verständnis der Notwendigkeit und Berechtigung eines eigenen bayerischen Staates bei den Deutschen und bei den Besatzungsmächten wurden die geschichtlichen, völkischen, wirtschaftlichen, kulturellen und politischen Grundlagen Bayerns in dem beiliegenden 'Bayerischen Memorandum' (vom August 1944) dargelegt, das Anfang Mai, 1945 dem Hauptquartier der 3. Amerik. Armee in Regensburg übermittelt worden ist." A letter from Gebhard Seelos, Generalkonsul for the Bonn Government, dated Istanbul-Beyogolu, June 22, 1954, to Mrs H. R. Boeninger, Curator of the Western and Central European Collections, Hoover Institute and Library, Stanford University, Stanford, California, reads in part as follows: "Das Bayerische Memorandum wurde von mir in der zweiten Hälfte des Jahres 1943 in München-Moosburg verfasst. Der Inhalt des Memorandums ist nur aus der damaligen Lage verständlich und aus dem Willen, mit allen Mitteln zu einem Ende der national-sozialistischen Herrschaft zu kommen. Das Memorandum ist in Maschinenschrift an die Untergruppen der bayerischen Heimatbewegung verteilt worden. Inwieweit es die eine oder andere Gruppe auch im Druck verbreitet hat, ist mir unbekannt. Unter den damaligen Mitgliedern befanden sich zahlreiche spätere Angehörige der Bayernpartei, aber auch der CSU."

There is a very strong possibility that the document in the Hoover Library may be a facsimile of the original Seelos effort which he dates as 1943. The author derives this opinion by noting the strong emphasis on the word "democracy" scattered throughout the Memorandum. Also, the reader cannot fail to notice the phrase, "... während der Naziherrschaft bis ins letzte Dorf von Mensch zu Mensch genügsam kennengelernt haben ..." (p. 11). In spite of this fact, the document (or the one similar to it) probably was written

It is entirely outside the scope of our purpose here to test the validity of these charges against Prussia. It is enough to read and appreciate the point of view expressed. Suffice it to say, it is not an opinion held by Bavarians only. [6] These Bavarians were trying to realize their heart-felt ambition to break the ties of the Prussian-dominated Reich. They saw their opportunity with the advance of the Allied armies across France into Germany. No amount of dissembling in words must ever obscure the plain truth: there was a direct relation between what these people were willing to undertake and the successful advance of the "enemy." Who were those involved in this action?

b) FREIHEITS-AKTION BAYERN

Although there were a number of such individuals, apparently friends of Seelos and Hipp, the real burden of the work fell upon men who were part of the German army in and around Munich. [7]

In Freising, there was an armored battalion of three thousand men under Major Braun; in Munich, the Translators Company under Captain Gerngruss; at the *Frontleitstelle* in Munich, there were certain personnel, among them a Sergeant Rieger—all of

---

during the war and does reflect the ideological basis of the *Bayerische Heimat-bewegung*, which played its part in the motivation of the *Freiheits-Aktion Bayern*.

[6] Erich Meissner has championed this view in two works published in England, *Germany in Peril* (London, 1942) and *Confusion of Faces* (London, 1946).

[7] According to the *Bericht, Seelos*, there were a number of *Vertrauens-männer* in towns throughout southern Bavaria, "die ihrerseits den Kreis der Anhänger ständig erweiterten. Solche Kreise bestanden in München, Neuburg, Eichstätt, Mühldorf, Pfarrkirchen, Schrobenhausen, Wolfratshausen, Murnau, Tegernsee, Garmisch-Partenkirchen, Markt Obersdorf, Immenstadt, und vielen anderen Orten." The *Bericht* then lists the following persons: Regierungsrat Hamberger in Augsburg, Dr. Elsen in Regensburg, Redakteur Kolmsperger in Moosburg, Oberverwalter Schneider in Moosburg, Dr. Eggensberger in Doel-lingen, Diplomlandwirt Eichinger in Dornhasselbach, Dr. v. Werz in Hirschau.

these could be counted on to assist in a *coup*. [8] They assumed this to be their major task: to carry out a military *coup* successfully, and then to hand over the government to the *Bayernbewegung*. [9] This done, Dr. Seelos and Dr. Hipp would then, presumably, put into effect the ideas found in the *Bavarian Memorandum*: a separation of Bavaria from the Reich.

Toward the end of 1944, Munich had a garrison of about twenty thousand troops under General Vogler. Any action which Dr. Seelos and his group proposed would have to reckon with General Vogler. With incredible audacity, Sgt. Rieger of the Munich *Frontleitstelle* arranged an interview between Dr. Seelos and General Vogler on February 12, 1945, with the curious outcome that the General agreed to use his troops to take over the city, arrest the Party leaders, and participate in the establishing of a separate Bavaria. [10] These facts seem all the more astounding when one realizes that Vogler, as an S.S. general, was directly responsible to Heinrich Himmler.

The plan, scheduled for March, collapsed when General Vogler was ordered out of Munich. Fortunately for those immediately involved, knowledge of the proposed *coup* remained secret, and, as a result, there was no needless death toll. The same, however, was not true for those events which took place one month later and are linked with the very last days of the war in and around Munich.

From the headquarters of the German Seventh Defense Command someone in a fairly responsible position sent Lt. Malke and Lt. Feller to General Patton's headquarters. They informed the Americans that there would be no resistance to their advance south of the Danube. This was one part of a final action which

---

[8] *Bericht, Seelos,* 3.
[9] *Bericht, Seelos, Ibid.*
[10] *Ibid.,* 4.

was to involve the arrest of Nazi leaders and the assumption of power by anti-Nazis, at least until the Americans arrived. [11] On April 28, 1945, Major Braun's armored battalion seized the radio station at Erding. [12] This action was combined with events which were moving rapidly forward inside Munich at the Translators Company on the Ludwigstrasse. [13] For several hours this group claimed to have the government of the city in their hands and promptly broadcasted the end of hostilities over the Erding radio, now in friendly hands. Capt. Gerngruss is reported to have given the signal for all Bavarians to rise against the Nazis, an event which had terrible consequences for some. [15]

Throughout southern Bavaria enthusiastic supporters heard this message of final deliverance and emerged from their homes shouting with joy. In Bad Wiessee Harold Dohrn was one of these; he began at once to proclaim the end of the long nightmare, only to find that this action was to be his last. He was arrested on the spot by S.S. troopers, brought to Munich, tried, and shot on the evening of the twenty-eighth. [16] Similarly in Altötting, Landrat Kehrer heard the announcement of the war's end, ordered the local Party leaders jailed, and with five others commissioned a new government for the city. These claimed to be representatives of the *Freiheits-Aktion* and included Verwaltungsinspektor Seidel, Müllermeister Joseph Bruckmeier, Lagerverwalter Riehl, Buchhändler Wehnert, and Administrator Vogel. They met the

---

[11] This information given to me (July, 1951) in an interview with Major Braun, former commanding officer of the armored battalion stationed outside of Munich in April 1945.
[12] *Bericht, Seelos*, 4.
[13] Weisenborn, *op. cit.*, "Report by Dr. Rupprecht Gerngruss, 126-127.
[14] *Bericht, Seelos*, 4.
[15] Weisenborn, *op. cit.*, 127.
[16] Dieter Sasse, Bericht über die Münchner Studenten 1943, Typescript, 5. Harold Dohrn was the father-in-law of Christoph Probst, who had been executed for his part in the Munich Student Revolt, February 22, 1943.

same end as did Harold Dohrn: an S.S. company was dispatched to restore order in Altötting and the five were shot out of hand with considerable brutality. [17] Meanwhile, in Munich the entire Translators Company was arrested, and several of the instigators of the Putch were tried and convicted of treason. Only the arrival of the Americans saved them from death. [18]

With the arrival of the American forces, the number of Hitler's opponents swelled to include nearly the entire population of Bavaria. What these people meant when they informed all and sundry *"dass wir immer dagegen waren"* is not a subject which admits to scientific study. The reaction to this on the part of some thoughtful persons was the rather cynical judgment that Germans who had actually opposed Hitler had carried their opposition with them to the grave. But this is clearly allowing opposition to be a matter on which the Nazis could be the sole judges; that the Nazis recognized their opponents and then honored them with martyrdom. A situation such as the *Freiheits-Aktion Bayern* is instructive to the student of such opposition because the quality and dimension of this opposition can more easily be verified. It brings into clearer focus also those events which have been considered in detail in previous chapters of this study.

Many who earned death in those last days, (or who can be credited with heroic deeds in violation of orders by mad Party leaders) were motivated simply by human compassion. For example, when the officers at the command post in Munich, knowing that the end was not far distant, awarded furloughs to Bavarians to return to their homes, they might have been motivated by a

---

[17] For more complete details of this episode, see *Traunsteiner Nachrichten,* September 9, Sept. 21, Sept. 23, 1950, and the *Münchner Abendzeitung,* Sept. 18, 1950, 2, which are newspaper reports of the proceedings at the trial of the S.S. officers who carried out the reprisal.

[18] Interview with Major Braun, (July, 1951). Of the group, a Major Caracciola was shot on April 28th.

concern for the soldier and his family rather than by a desire to attack Berlin. Or when the commander of a prisoner-of-war camp evaded an order which might mean that troops under him would end up in concentration camps, this can be clearly understood in terms of human compassion. [19] Actions which in themselves were motivated by a desire to put an end quickly to what was already a lost war, cannot be labeled opposition unles such action was coupled with an ideology which offered something to replace the Nazi regime. It is this which makes it necessary, therefore, to see Dr. Seelos' long protocol. The convictions that southern Germany was a unit incompatible with northern Germany; that a Prussian-dominated Reich would always lead to trouble for Germany and Europe; that Prussia gave form and force to National Socialism; that Bavaria ought to be independent— these convictions Dr. Seelos shared not only with many of his immediate associates but with others whose efforts to oppose Hitler have been discussed earlier in this work. And these same convictions give us the real basis for a better understanding of what has been called *Freiheits-Aktion Bayern*, the final effort of Hitler's conservative opponents in Bavaria.

---

[19] *Bericht, Seelos,* 3.

APPENDICES

Appendix A

A NAZI VIEW OF ACTIVITIES OF THE JESUITS

Being a confidential report prepared by Max Köglmeier for Ministerialrat Schneidewand in the Kultusministerium, Munich, dated December 19, 1940.

Auffallend und bezeichnend für die zentrale Lenkung der Jugendpropaganda der Kirche ist auch die Tatsache, dass die *starke Werbung der Kirche unter den HJ-Führern der mittleren und höheren Schulklassen von denselben jesuitischen Kreisen ausgeht, die auch die Propaganda an der Universität betreiben.* (Vor allem gehört hierher der Pater Kronseder S.J.)

Diese aktive Propaganda der Kirche selbst zieht immer weitere Kreise und nimmt immer deutlichere Formen an. Seitens der Gaustudentenführung wird mitgeteilt, das die kath. Studenten von der Studentenseelsorge regelmässig angeschrieben werden. Auch neu eingeschriebene Studenten, deren Ansicht aus den gedruckten offiziellen Verzeichnissen nicht entnommen werden kann, da diese erst sehr spät erscheinen, werden in dieser Weise angeschrieben. Die Herkunft dieser Adressen hat man teils bei den Adressensammlerinnen zu suchen, die von der Kirche systematisch vor und nach Gottesdiensten am Eingang der Kirche aufgestellt werden und die die Kirchgänger um Adressen angehen, *teils in einem raffiniert aufgebauten und reibungslos funktionierenden Nachrichtendienst, der ein regelrechtes Meldesystem durch Vertrauensleute der Kirche innerhalb der Studentenschaft eingerichtet hat.* Durch diese Vertrauensleute werden alle die Studenten, die nicht schon ohnehin durch ihre Heimatpfarreien in München vor- und angemeldet sind, in „zufälligen" Gesprächen „erfasst" und der Kirchenbehörde, in diesem Falle der kath. Hochschulseelsorge München, gemeldet. Dieser Nachrichtendienst der Kirche aus den aktiven Katholiken der Studentenschaft gibt auch den höheren Stellen regelmässig Berichte über die allgemeine „Lage" der Studenten, über die Reaktion der Studenten auf die kath. Propaganda-aktionen und brauchbare Hinweise zu weiterem propagandistischen Vorgehen. *Die in diesem Nachrichtendienst organisatorisch eingesetzten kath. „Jugendführer" bilden meist auch als „Gruppen- und Obergruppenführer" die Mittelpunkte der sich immer zahlreicher bildenden kath. Zirkel* innerhalb der Studentenschaft. Diese Zirkel werden ausschliesslich von der kath. Hochschulseelsorge in München organisiert und geleitet. Sie versammeln sich allwöchentlich zu Zusammenkünften, an denen 6-12, zuweilen auch 30-35 Studenten, übrigens auch Schüler höherer Schulen teilnehmen. Die meisten dieser Zirkel stehen unter dem Protektorat und der aktiven Leitung des Paters Friedrich Kronseder S.J., der Montag, Dienstag, Mittwoch und Freitag von 11-13 Uhr Sprechstunden hält, am Samstag von 17.30 bis 20 Uhr Beichtgelegenheit bietet und innerhalb der regelmässigen Veranstaltungen der Hochschulseelsorge neben seinen „Zirkeln" am Sonntag um 17 Uhr „neutestamentarische Vorträge" in St. Michael für Studenten hält. Die Zirkel dieses Paters erfreuen sich neben den Zirkeln anderer Pater, wie des Dr. Franz J. Müller S.J., besonderer Beliebtheit bei den Studenten. Die Zirkel Kronseders finden am Montag um 20 Uhr und am Samstag um 20 Uhr mit jeweiligen Parallelzirkeln statt und setzen sich nach aussen hin die Aufgabe der Erklärung der hl. Schrift. *In Wirklichkeit führt Pater Kronseder die ihn besuchenden Zirkel,* d.h. lose gehaltenen Gemeinschaften von meist 6-12 Studenten und einigen Schülern, in locker geführtem und *souverän beherrschtem Gespräch durch alle „Weltstoffe", Arbeitsdienst, Wehrmacht, Berufe, Lebensverhältnisse usw, um dann mit humoristischen Wendungen in geschickter Weise auf seine weltanschaulich-kirchlichen Zwecke zu kommen. Da er Studenten zu „betreuen" hat, arbeitet Kronseder mit Vorliebe und für neutrale und harmlose Gemüter* unbemerkbar auf dem Gebiete der Wissenschaft. Seine reichhaltige Bibliothek, die keineswegs vordringlich theologisch ist und meist rein wissenschaftliche Werke enthält, stellt er den Studenten vorbehaltlos zur Verfügung. *Da die Zirkel nach Altersstufen, d.h. im grossen und ganzen nach Semestern eingeteilt sind und unter Berücksichtigung der einzelnen Studienzweige geleitet werden, haben sie ein unmittelbares Interesse für die Studenten in Hinsicht auf ihre Berufsvorbereitung, ja selbst auf ihre Examina.* Auch aussenstehende wissenschwache Studenten wenden sich an diese Zirkel, um durch die gemeinsame Aussprache mit dem wissensmächtigen Pater ihr Fachwissen zu erweitern. Der persönliche Einfluss und der persönliche Zusammenhang dieser Zirkel hat zur Folge, dass die Propaganda der Kirche über die engeren Kreise der Zirkel hinaus (die übrigens mindestens 300 (Studenten) Studierende erfassen) in die Hochschule und in die höheren Schulen weiterwirkt.

Appendix B

THE TRIAL OF P. RUPERT MAYER, S.J.

Being the trial of Father Mayer before the Sondergerichtshof, Munich.

1 b KMs-So. 32/37(144)
16 c Js.So. 548/37

Im Namen des Deutschen Volkes!

Das Sondergericht für den Bezirk des Oberlandesgerichts München bei dem Landgerichte München I erlässt in der Strafsache gegen MAYER Rupert, Jesuitenpater in München, wegen Verg. g.d. Ges. v. 20.12.34 u.a. auf Grund der Hauptverhandlung von 22. und 23. Juli 1937, in der öffentlichen Sitzung vom 23. Juli 1937, an der teilgenommen haben:

1. der Vorsitzende: Landgerichtsdirektor Dr. Wölzl,
2. Die Beisitzer: Landgerichtsräte Schwingenschlögl und Dr. Wachte,
3. der Erste Staatsanwalt Dr. Grosser,
4. der stv. Urkundsbeamte: Referendar Schmieg, folgendes

U r t e i l :

MAYER Rupert, geboren am 23. Januar 1876 in Stuttgart, ledig, Jesuitenpater in München, z. Zt. in Untersuchungshaft, wird wegen eines fortgesetzten Vergehens gegen § 130a StGB. in Tateinheit mit einem fortgesetzten Vergehen gegen das Gesetz vom 20. Dezember 1934 zur Gefängnisstrafe von sechs Monaten ab 6 Wochen Untersuchungshaft, sowie zur Tragung der Kosten verurteilt.

G r ü n d e :

I.

Der Angeklagte ist nach 1½ jähriger Tätigkeit als weltlicher Priester im Jahre 1900 in den Jesuitenorden eingetreten. Er hat am

Weltkriege als Militärpfarrer teilgenommen und zwar seit Januar 1915 als Divisionspfarrer, hat dabei wiederholt in vorderster Linie sein Leben eingesetzt und wurde dafür im Jahre 1915 mit dem EK II, dem Bayerischen Militärsverdienstkreuz mit Krone und Schwerter, mit dem EK I und im Jahre 1916 mit dem Ritterkreuz des würt. Friedrichsordens und dem Franz-Joseforden ausgezeichnet. Im Dezember 1916 wurde er im Gefechtsbereich eines von ihm seelsorgerisch betreuten Regiments durch einen Schrapnellschuss derart verwundet, dass der linke Fuss amputiert werden musste. Der Angeklagte ist dann in der Folgezeit in München als Seelsorger tätig gewesen und zu einem weit über München hinaus bekannten Kanzelredner geworden. Er gibt selbst an, dass er in manchem Monat ca. 70 Predigten gehalten hat. Er ist aber darüber hinaus in den Jahren 1919 bis 1932 in politischen Versammlungen linksgerichteter Parteien, insbesondere der KPD., als Diskussionsredner aufgetreten, um der in der maxistischen Lehre liegenden Gefahr für die Religion entgegenzutreten. Er kam während dieser Zeit auch mit dem Nationalsozialismus in Berührung und begrüsste die Bewegung, bis er annahm, dass sie geeignet sei, der katholischen Religion- und Weltanschauung Abbruch zu tun. Er wurde auch anlässlich seines 25-jährigen Priesterjubiläums im Jahre 1924 vom Führer durch ein Handschreiben beglückwünscht.

Die religiösen Bedenken brachten schliesslich den Angeklagten in einen immer stärker werdenden Gegensatz zum Nationalsozialismus, und diese Einstellung fand etwa vom Jahre 1934 ab in mehr oder weniger scharfer Form ihren Ausdruck in den Predigten, die der Angeklagte insbesondere in der St. Michaelskirche in München, aber auch an anderen Orten, hielt. Er wurde deshalb auch im Mai 1936 durch die Staatsanwaltschaft München I verwarnt.

II

In den Monaten Januar mit Mai 1937 befasst sich der Angeklagte in seinen in München und auswärts gehaltenen Predigten wiederholt mit dem Schulwesen, mit den Methoden im Kampf um die Bekenntnisschule, mit dem Pressewesen, insbesondere mit der Berichterstattung über die Verfahren gegen die katholischen Geistlichen und Ordensleute wegen sittlicher Verfehlungen, mit dem NS-Schrifttum und mit dem Nationalsozialismus als solchem. 9 dieser Predigten führten dazu, dass der Angeklagte vom 5. bis 10. Juni 1937 in Polizeihaft genommen wurde, dass gegen ihn Anklage wegen eines fortgesetzten Vergehens des Kanzelmissbrauchs in Tateinheit mit einem fortgesetzten Vergehen gegen § 2 des Heimtückegesetzes erhoben wurde und dass er am 10. Juni 1937 wegen Wiederholungsgefahr in Untersuchungshaft genommen wurde, weil er am 9. Juni 1937 der Geheimen Staatspolizei gegenüber die Erklärung abgab, er werde auch weiterhin in der von ihm bisher geübten Art und Weise predigen, selbst wenn die staatlichen Behörden, die Polizei und die Gerichte seine Kanzelreden als strafbare Handlungen und als Kanzelmissbrauch bewerten sollten.

In der Hauptverhandlung wurde folgender Sachverhalt festgestellt:
1. (Anklage Ziffer 1a): Am 3. Februar 1937 hielt der Angeklagte abends in der St. Josefskirche in München vor Angehörigen der Männerkongregation eine Predigt, in der er sich mit dem Ergebnis der Schuleinschreibung an den Volksschulen in München und späterhin mit der Begründung des Papsttums befasste. Er begann diese Predigt nach seinem eigenen Geständnis mit folgendem Worten: „Am lezten Montag wurde ein Sieg gefeiert, aber so ein Sieg ist noch nicht gefeiert worden, solange die Welt besteht! Ich muss schon sagen: ein Sieg war das, der denen, die ihn gefeiert haben, gewiss nicht zur Ehre gereicht. Ein Sieg war das, ein Terror! Dieser Sieg war ein Pyrrhussieg, ein Gewaltsieg!".
2. (Anklage Ziffer 1b): Am 29. März 1937 hielt der Angeklagte in der bis auf den letzten Platz besetzten Klosterkirche in Ursberg eine Predigt, in der er sich zunächst mit der geschichtlichen Entwicklung der christlichen Kirchen befasste und dann zu der Frage „Bekenntnisschule oder Gemeinschaftsschule" überging. Er kam dabei auf die Schuleinschreibung in München zu sprechen und äusserte nach seinem eigenen Geständnis folgendes: „In München sind die katholischen Erziehungsberechtigten gegen alles Recht und Gesetz um die katholiliche Bekenntnisschule gebracht worden, da haben alle städtischen und Parteidienststellen zusammengeholfen, mündlich und schriftlich". Er äusserte dann weiter: „Das Reich schliesst Konkordate, und diese treiben das Gegenteil", und schloss die Predigt mit den Worten: „Aus Gewissensgründen achten wir die rechtmässige Obrigkeit. Wir lassen uns in unserer Treue von niemandem übertreffen. In allen politischen, wirtschaftlichen, sozialen Fragen arbeiten wir mit allen Volks-

genossen zusammen, aber in religiösen Fragen sagen wir zu den anderen „Finger weg!"

Der Hauptleiter Schön aus Burtenbach bestätigte als Zeuge diesen Inhalt der Predigt, behauptete aber, dass der Angeklagte nicht von städtischen, sondern von staatlichen Stellen gesprochen habe. Das Gericht hielt das nicht für erwiesen, weil es immerhin möglich ist, dass sich der Zeuge verhört oder im Stenogramm verschrieben hat.

3. (Anklage Ziffer 1c): Am 11. April 1937 traf der Bishof von Augsburg begleitet von zahlreichen Geistlichen in der Stadtpfarrkirche in Weissenhorn ein und hielt dort auch eine kurze Ansprache. Ausser ihm sprach noch zweimal der Angeklagte. Er befasste sich in der zweiten Predigt (die erste Predigt ist nicht Gegenstand der Anklage) mit der geschichtlichen Entwicklung der christlichen Kirchen, mit dem, was die katholische Kirche mit der evangelischen Kirche gemeinsam habe, und schliesslich damit, dass die Reichsregierung das Konkordat abgeschlossen habe, um dem deutschen Volke die religiösen Kämpfe zu ersparen, dass das aber manchem Gegner der Kirche nicht passe. Er fuhr dann fort: „Ja, habt Ihr noch nichts gehört von den Schulkämpfen? Die Menschen sollen genötigt werden, ihre Kinder in der Schule entkonfessionalisieren zu lassen". Er kam dann auf die Schuleinschreibung in München zu sprechen und äusserte dabei: „Es wurde in den Schulen gelogen, dass sich die grössten Balken bogen". Er sprach dann davon, dass die Art und Weise, in der der Kampf um die Gemeinschaftsschule und gegen die Bekenntnisschule geführt worden sei, mit dem als Reichsgesetz geltenden Konkordat nicht vereinbar sei, führte Beispiele zum Beweise seiner Auffassung an und äusserte dann wörtlich: *„Die Sache hat einen ernsten Hintergrund; es kommt einem gerade vor, als ob die Reichsregierung das Konkordat abgeschlossen habe, um es sabotieren zu lassen von den untergeordneten Stellen".*

Der Angeklagte gibt zu, von einer Sabotage des Konkordats gesprochen und auch die sonstigen Äusserungen gebraucht zu haben, er bestreitet aber ganz entschieden, gesagt zu haben, die Reichsregierung habe das Konkordat geschlossen, *um* es sabotieren *zu* lassen. Er könne der Reichsregierung eine solche Absicht nicht unterstellen und habe sich daher auch nicht so geäussert. Dem steht aber entgegen, dass die Zeugen Gendarmeriehauptwachtmeister Meck und Wildegger unter Eid und trotz wiederholten Vorhalts bekundeten, dass die Äusserung bstimmt dem Sinne nach so gelautet habe, wie sie oben angeführt ist, dass der über die Predigt erstattete, diesen Satz enthaltende Gendarmeriebericht mindestens in diesem Punkt dem Wortlaut nach sich mit dem decke, was von mehreren Stenografen über diesen Punkt mitgeschrieben worden sei, und schliesslich, dass auch der *Zeuge Gabs*, der als Kriminalinspektor der Gestapo dieser Predigt anwohnte, unter Eid bekundet hat, er habe die Worte „um zu" gehört.

Angesichts dieses übereinstimmenden Beweisergebnisses hatte das Gericht keinen Anlass, dem Eventualantrag der Verteidigung auf Ladung des Dekans Schmid von Weissenhorn und einer der von ihm mit der stenografischen Aufnahme der Predigt beauftragten Frauen stattzugeben. Der Antrag wurde damit begründet, dass der Dekan in in einem „Gedenkblatt an den Bischofstag der Männer in Weissenhorn 11.4.37" die Äusserung über das Konkordat nur in der vom Angeklagten eingeräumten Form wiedergegeben habe und dass dieses Gedenkblatt unter Zugrundelegung des von ihm veranlassten Stenogramms abgefasst worden sei. Dieses Gedenkblatt ist aber keine wörtliche Wiedergabe der Predigt, sondern ein Auszug aus ihr. Es kann schon deshalb keinen Anspruch auf Beweiskraft erheben. Auch der Einwand des Angeklagten, er habe doch auch in anderen Predigten von einer Sabotage des Konkordats durch untergeordnete Stellen gesprochen, ohne der Reichsregierung den Vorwurf der Unaufrichtigkeit zu machen, war nicht stichhaltig, weil diese Tatsache keineswegs ausschliesst, dass der Angeklagte doch in der den Gegenstand der Anklage bildenden Predigt vom 11. April 1937 seine Auffassung über diesen Punkt so formuliert hat, wie es von den Zeugen bekundet wurde.

4. (Anklage Ziffer 1d): Am 18. April 1937 hielt der Angeklagte abends in der Pfarrkirche in Kirchheim für die katholischen Jungmänner und Männer eine gutbesuchte Predigt, in der er davon sprach, dass das Schicksal der Kirche in den Händen der Jungmänner liege, und dann wörtlich anführte „Man will die Schule entkonfessionalisieren lassen, sie darf auch nicht mehr christlich sein. Man sagt, man habe noch Religionsunterricht; in einem Jahr hat das Christentum in der Gemeinschaftsschule vollständig aufgehört, dann weht ein antikatholischer, antichristlicher Geist".

Er sprach dann über den Kampf um die Gemeinschaftsschule und äusserte dabei: „Was in dem Schulkampf gelogen wurde von den untergeordneten Stellen, da wurde gelogen, dass sich die Balken bogen. .... Wie man es diesen Menschen (die für die Bekenntnisschule eintraten) gemacht hat, sie wurden Volksfeinde und Landesverräter, die nicht da mittun wollen, das hörte man überall durch. Wenn einer diesen *Staatsbetrug* nicht ausüben wollte, dann hat man ihm dieses Schimpfwort zugerufen". Er schloss denn mit einer längeren Mahnung an das Landvolk, im Kampf um die Bekenntnisschule zusammenzustehen.

Der Angeklagte gibt diese Äusserung zu.

5. (Anklage Ziffer 2 und 2c):

Am 23. Mai 1937 hielt der Angeklagte abends in der St. Michaelskirche in München anlässlich der Lichterprozession der Männerkongregation eine Predigt, in der er sich zunächst mit den Aufgaben der Kongregation befasste und dann auf den Schulkampf in München zu sprechen kam. Er äusserte dabei bei seinem eigenen Geständnis wörtlich: „Wäre ich im Lager unserer Gegner, ich hätte mich über einen mit so unredlichen Waffen erfochtenen Sieg nicht freuen können. Ich hätte mich eines solchen Sieges geschämt. Mit roher Gewalt kann man kein Recht zerstören und vernichten". Er sprach dann über die sittlichen Verfehlungen von Geistlichen und Ordensleuten und brachte sein Bedauern darüber zum Ausdruck, wies darauf hin, dass der Prozentsatz der sittlich entgleisten Priester und Ordensleute doch ein sehr geringer sei und fuhr dann fort: „Aber das ist noch etwas ganz anderes, was man jetzt dem katholischen Volk vorzulügen sucht. Liebe Freunde, was uns weh tut, das sind die Berichte über diese Skandalprozesse. Denn da müssen wir das eine sagen: Wir haben jetzt Beweise in der Hand, die genügen, um uns jeden Glauben an einen grossen Teil der deutschen Presse zu nehmen und endgültig zu rauben. Wir wussten schon, dass man in dieser Presse für katholische Dinge überhaupt kein Verständnis hat. So einseitig, so unwahr und gehässig und so verlogen hat man immer über die katholische Kirche geschrieben!" Er führte dann 2 Beispiele an, darunter die Presseberichte über die Ermordung des Klosterzöglings in Manage (Belgien), behauptete, dass die Art der Berichterstattung über die Sittlichkeitsprozesse eine schwere Schädigung des Vertrauens zum Priesterstand und zur Kirche zur Folge habe und erklärte dann wörtlich: „Man sagt so gerne zu uns: Ihr könnt zufrieden sein; denn in Spanien hätte man Euch schon längst an die Wand gestellt. Ich sage aber ganz ruhig: Dem Tode habe ich schon hundertemale ganz bewusst in die Augen geschaut. Das bin ich gewöhnt. Das ist nicht so schlimm. Aber wenn man einen Menschen geistig tötet, wenn man ihn kaput macht vor der Welt, das ist das Furchtbarste, was man sich vorstellen kann". Alsdann wies er nach Betonung des Grundsatzes der Treue gegenüber dem Staat nochmals darauf hin, dass durch die deutsche Presse ein Hassfeldzug gegen Priester und Ordensleute gehe und fügte hinzu: „Darum, liebe Freunde, ist es aus und vorbei mit dem Glauben an den Grossteil der deutschen Presse, wenn sie berichtet über religiös-sittliche Verhältnisse, über christlich-katholische Belange".

Der Angeklagte gibt auch diese Äusserung zu. Der Zeuge Wilhelm meinte gehört zu haben, dass der Angeklagte gesagt habe, dass man in diesen „Prozessen" für katholische Dinge kein Verständnis habe, er musste aber die Möglichkeit einräumen, sich verhört zu haben. Das Gericht folgte deshalb der Darstellung des Angeklagten und nahm an, dass er von dieser „Presse" gesprochen hat, zumal das auch mehr in den Zusammenhang hineinpasst.

6. (Anklage Ziffer 2a):

Am 24. Januar 1937 hielt der Angeklagte in der St. Michaelskirche in München nach dem Hochamt eine Predigt, in der er sich über die Presseberichte zum Fall „Schülle" beklagte und dabei ausführte: „Die Zeiten sind vorbei, wo wir geglaubt haben, was in der Zeitung steht. Was über religiöse Dinge in der Zeitung steht, das glauben wir grundsätzlich nicht". Er wandte sich dann gegen die Methoden des Kampfes um die Gemeinschaftsschule, wies darauf hin, dass eine Beeinflussung durch Versammlungen, Vorträge und Jugendkundgebungen zu erwarten sei, warnte davor, das zu glauben, was darüber in den Zeitungen stehe, und schloss mit den Worten: „Glaubt überhaupt keiner Zeitung, wenn sie sich mit sittlich-religiösen Dingen befasst! Hört nicht darauf! Lest keine Zeitungen! Und jetzt, wenn Ihr hinaus geht, dann möchte ich, dass eine religiöse Welle von der Kirche aus sich auf die Strasse ergiesst und von der Strasse aus in die einzelnen Häuser".

Der Angeklagte gab auch diese Äusserungen zu.

7. (Anklage Ziffer 2b):

Am 2. Mai 1937 hielt der Angeklagte in der St. Michaelskirche in München nach dem Hauptgottesdienst eine sehr stark besuchte Predigt, in der er sich mit den Presseberichten über die Strafverfahren gegen katholische Geistliche und Ordensleute wegen sittlicher Verfehlungen befasste und dabei ausführte: „Aber, meine Lieben, es ist nicht alles wahr, was in der Zeitung steht. Die Art und Weise der

Darstellung ist so übertrieben und es wird so aufgebauscht, und das, was in den christentums- und katholikenfeindlichen Zeitungen steht, das wird erst recht aufgebauscht und ausgeweitet ... Dann lesen wir überall von 1000 Sittlichkeitsverbrechen von Priestern und Ordensleuten! Die Zahl ist bei weitem übertrieben und soviel ich weiss sind es höchstens 500 Fälle, von denen ich gelesen habe, vielleicht sind es aber auch nur 250. — Warum liest man das überhaupt nur bei katholischen und evangelischen Kreisen? Von den anderen hört und liest man nie etwas. *Wer in Glashaus sitzt, soll nicht mit Steinen werfen*"! Er wandte sich dann gegen verallgemeinernde Werturteile in der Presse und fügte hinzu: „*Wir sind keine Revolutionäre, aber wenn das so weitergeht, dann werden wir katholischen und evangelischen Geistlichen eine ganz gewaltige Stinkbombe hineinwerfen müssen.* Wir lassen uns dass nicht mehr gefallen, wir werden jetzt dagegen rücksichtslos kämpfen." Der Angeklagte gibt auch diese Äusserungen zu.

8. (Anklage Ziffer 3a):

Am 26. Januar 1937 hielt der Angeklagte abends in der St. Theresienkirche in München eine „Predigt für Männer und Jungmänner über Probleme der Zeit". Er befasste sich darin mit dem Nationalsozialismus und seinem Schrifttum, führte Klage darüber, dass der „Stürmer" ein Bild gebracht habe, auf dem sich ein Priester und ein Bolschewist die bluttriefenden Hände reichen, und fuhr fort: „In der Marxistenzeit habe ich viele Hetzschriften gelesen weil man das nicht bekämpfen kann, was man nicht kennt. Meine lieben Freunde, ich muss sagen, es ist mir damals oft ein Ekel aufgestiegen, und es ist mir reichlich schwer gefallen, diesen Schmutz zu lesen. Aber das, *was an nationalsozialistischer Literatur heute empfohlen wird, von massgebender Stelle heute empfohlen wird, das ist ekelerregender denn je*". Er wandte sich in diesen Zusammenhang noch gegen die neuerliche Verbreitung des Pfaffenspiegels. Gegen Ende der Predigt betonte er noch, dass er das alles nicht sage, um die Zuhörer gegen den Staat aufzuhetzen oder weil er sich gegen den Staat auflehne. Der Angeklagte räumt auch diese Äusserungen ein.

9. (Anklage Ziffer 3b):

Am 24. Januar 1937 hielt der Angeklagte in Ainach eine sehr gut besuchte Predigt, in der er alsbald auf die nationalsozialistische Weltanschauung zu sprechen kam. Er führte dabei aus: „Es wird heute viel von nationalsozialistischer Weltanschauung gesprochen, drum müssen wir sie von unserer Seite aus ansehen. Ich beschäftige mich seit Monaten mit dem nationalsozialistischen Schrifttum, doch bin ich mir nicht klar geworden, was man darunter versteht. Euch, liebe Freunde, wird es auch so gehen". Er wandte sich dann dagegen, dass in nationalsozialistischen Schulungskursen gegen die Kirche und den christlichen Glauben gekämpft werde, dass im Theater und im Rundfunk ein kirchenfeindliches Stück gebracht worden sei, dass die Presse einen Bericht über einen im Konzentrationslager Dachau befindlichen Geistlichen und dessen Eingeständnis sittlicher Verfehlungen gebracht habe, obwohl sich gar kein Priester dort befunden habe, und fuhr fort: „Nach diesen Beweisen könnte man glauben, dass der Nationalsozialismus der erbitterste Gegner der Kirche sei. Demgegenüber steht die Erklärung der Reichsregierung vom Frühling 1933, das Konkordat und der Programmpunkt 24. Da kennt man sich nicht mehr aus, was richtig ist".

Der Angeklagte gibt zu, diese Äusserungen gebraucht zu haben.

Dass der Angeklagte, wie die Anklage annahm, behauptet hat, der Nationalsozialismus „sei" der grösste Feind der Kirche, konnte nicht festgestellt werden.

III.

1. Bei der rechtlichen Würdigung dieses Sachverhalts unter dem Gesichtspunkt des § 130 a StGB. hatte das Gericht zunächst zu prüfen, was *objektiv* der Sinn der Äusserungen des Angeklagten gewesen ist. „Es kam dabei nicht entscheidend darauf an, welchen Sinn der Angeklagte seinen Worten geben wollte, sondern darauf, welcher Sinn ihnen nach der natürlichen Auffassung der Zuhörer bei Berücksichtigung ihrer geistigen Aufnahmefähigkeit, des Zusammenhangs der Äusserungen und der Umstände, unter denen sie gemacht wurden, zukommen musste". (vergl. Urteil des Reichsgerichts von 20. Oktober 1936 I D 350/36 — JW. 1937 S. 699 Nr. 13). Dabei musste auch berücksichtigt werden, unter welchen Zeitverhältnissen die Äusserungen gefallen sind und welche — wenn auch sprachlich nicht zum Ausdruck gekommene — Gedankenverbindungen den Äusserungen zugrunde lagen und den Zuhörern erkennbar waren (vergl. Urteil des Reichsgerichts von 1. August 1935 5 D 505/35 — JW. 1935 S. 3383 Nr. 12).

Davon ausgehend kam das Gericht zu folgenden Feststellungen.

Die Äusserungen des Angeklagten zum Schulkampf (Predigten

1-5) gingen eindeutig dahin, dass im Kampf „Gemeinschaftsschule oder Bekenntnisschule" Lüge und Gewalt zum Siege der Anhänger der Gemeinschaftsschule geführt hätten, dass sich auch die Lehrkräfte zugunsten der Gemeinschaftsschule an diesem Kampf beteiligt und der hemmungslosen Lüge als Kampfmittel bedient hätten (bes. Predigt 2, 3 und 4), dass es eine Schande sei, sich eines mit solchen Mitteln erfochtenen Sieges zu freuen (bes. Predigt 1 und 5) und dass die Schuleinschreibung rechtlich nicht wirksam sei (Predigt Nr. 5 „Mit roher Gewalt kann man kein Recht zerstören und vernichten"). Die Predigt 3 enthielt aber darüber hinaus den Vorwurf, die Reichsregierung habe schon beim Abschluss des Konkordats vom 20. Juli 1935 die Absicht gehabt, sich nicht daran zu halten, sondern es durch die untergeordneten Stellen sabotieren zu lassen (,,Die Sache hat einen *ernsten Hintergrund: es komt einem gerade vor, als ob die* Reichsregierung das Konkordat abgeschlossen habe, *um* es sabotieren *zu* lassen, von den untergeordneten Stellen"). Kein unbefangener Zuhörer von normalem Urteilsvermögen konnte der festgestellten Äusserung eine unverfänglichere, die Reichsregierung nicht oder weniger belastende Deutung geben. Der Kriminalinspektor Gambs hat allerdings bekundet, dass er auf Grund seiner genaueren Kenntniss des Angeklagten und weil er diesem eine derartige Unvorsichtigkeit nicht zutraute, als Zuhörer zu der Annahme kam, der Angeklagte habe nur untergeordneten Stellen den Vorwurf der Sabotage machen wollen und sich dabei im Ausdruck vielleicht vergriffen. Auch er hat aber bekundet, dass ein anderer Zuhörer sehr leicht zu einer anderen Auffassung kommen konnte. Dass der Angeklagte in der gleichen Predigt *vorher* davon sprach, dass die Reichsregierung dem deutschen Volke die religiösen Kampfe ersparen wollte und deshalb das Konkordat angeschlossen habe, steht zwar im Widerspruch mit dem später gegen die Reichsregierung erhobenen Vorwurf, konnte aber dessen Wirkung auf die inzwischen durch scharfe Angriffe gegen die Methoden des Schulkampfes und die angeblichen Ziele der Gemeinschaftsschule misstrauisch gewordenen Zuhörer nicht abschwächen oder gar aufheben. In der Predigt 4 wurde der Vorwurf erhoben, die Schuleinschreibung sei das Ergebnis eines Betrugs und der Staat habe an diesem Betrug mitgewirkt. (,,Wenn einer diesen Staatsbetrug nicht ausüben wollte"). Der Angeklagte hat erklärt, dass er das Wort „Staatsbetrug" gebraucht habe, um damit entsprechend dem Sprachgebrauch seiner schwäbischen Heimat zum Ausdruck zu bringen, dass es ein grosser Betrug, „ein Mordsbetrug" gewesen sei, wie man auch einen recht grossen Menschen oft als „Staatskerl" bezeichne. Dieser Vergleich hinkt. Wer als Staatskerl bezeichnet wird, wird damit wohl in keinem Falle in Beziehung zu dem Staate gebracht. Wenn aber im Zusammenhang mit einer scharfen Kritik über den Schulkampf behauptet wird, die untergeordneten Stellen hätten gelogen, dass sich die Balken bogen, und wenn das alles als „Staatsbetrug" bezeichnet wird, dann wirkt dieses Wort auch in einem schwäbischen Ort wie Kirchheim auf einen natürlich auffassenden Zuhörer als Vorwurf des Betrugs, begangen durch den Staat.

Die Predigten 3 und 4 enthielten noch den Vorwurf, es sei beabsichtigt, die Kinder durch die Gemeinschaftsschule um ihre Religion zu bringen. Schon das Wort „entkonfessionalisieren" musste bei der Mehrzahl der Zuhörer diesen Eindruck hervorrufen. Wer keine höhere Schulbildung genossen hat und mit den Schlagworten im Schulkampf nicht vertraut ist, hört aus dem Worte „entkonfessionalisieren" nur heraus, dass die Schulkinder um ihr religiöses Bekenntnis gebracht werden sollen. Die Predigt 4 führte auch noch aus, dass in einem Jahre das Christentum in der Gemeinschaftsschule vollständig aufgehört habe und dass dann ein antikatholischer, antichristlicher Geist wehe. Darin liegt der Vorwurf, die Gemeinschaftsschule diene der Beseitigung der christlichen Bekenntnisse.

Die Predigten 6 und 7 und der zweite Teil der Predigt 5 erhoben gegen die Presse den Vorwurf der Unzuverlässigkeit und Unwahrhaftigkeit bei der Behandlung religiös-sittlicher Dinge. Die Zuhörer mussten den Eindruck bekommen, als sei mehr oder weniger alles unwahr und entstellt, was in der Presse über die Strafverfahren gegen katholische Geistliche und Ordensangehörige wegen sittlicher Verfehlungen berichtet wurde. Die Predigt 6 gipfelte sogar in der Aufforderung, gar keine Zeitungen mehr zu lesen. Die Predigt 7 ging noch einen Schritt weiter. Sie deutete an, dass die nationalsozialistischen Kreise allen Anlass hätten, zu schweigen, weil bei ihnen auf sittlichem Gebiet vieles nicht in Ordnung sei, und enthielt die Androhung von Enthüllungen solcher Verfehlungen (Wer im Glashaus sitzt, soll nicht mit Steinen werfen ... Wenn das so weitergeht, dann werden wir ... eine ganz gewaltige Stinkbombe hineinwerfen müssen"). Damit war aber auch zwangsläufig zum Ausdruck gebracht, dass die Regierung in den Reihen ihrer Anhänger nicht nach dem Rechten sehe. Was der Angeklagte über Spanien und im unmittelbaren Zusammenhang damit über sich selbst gesagt, brachte nach Ansicht des Gerichts nur zum Ausdruck, dass er selbst lieber getötet als ehrlos gemacht werden wolle. In der Predigt 8 wurde die nationalsozialistische Literatur mit dem marxistischen Schrifttum verglichen und als noch ekelerregender bezeichnet. Es wurde ferner den „massgebenden Stellen" vorgewurfen, derartiges auch noch zu empfehlen. Dieser Vorwurf richtete sich in seiner Allgemeinheit nicht nur gegen irgendwelche unterordneten Stellen von Partei oder Staat, sondern gegen die Staatsführung als solche. Zum mindesten musste die Äusserung bei den Zuhörern den Eindruck erwecken, als richte sie sich gegen die Regierung selbst.

Die Predigt 9 wies darauf hin, dass entgegen der Regierungserklärung, entgegen dem Konkordat und entgegen dem Punkt 24 des Parteiprogramms überall kirchenfeindliche Tendenzen erkennbar seien, dass man sich daher nicht mehr auskenne und meinen könne, der Nationalsozialismus sei der erbitterste Feind der Kirche. Was der Angeklagte in der Predigt 9 über den Nationalsozialismus als solchen ausführte, bezog sich erkennbar nur auf den religiösen Teil dieser Weltanschauung. Auf ihn bezieht sich auch die Äusserung des Angeklagten, er sei sich nicht klar geworden, was man unter nationalsozialistischer Weltanschauung verstehe.

Man könnte daran denken, dass die oben näher begründete Annahme, die Predigt 8 habe sich gegen die Staatsführung als solche gerichtet, dadurch widerlegt sei, dass der Angeklagte am Schluss dieser Predigt ausführte, er sage das alles nicht, um die Zuhörer gegen den Staat aufzuhetzen oder weil er sich gegen den Staat auflehne. Dieser Schlusssatz hat aber den erkennbar gegen die Staatsführung erhobenen Vorwurf, ekelerregende Literatur zu empfehlen, keineswegs eingeschränkt, sondern zeigt nur, dass der Angeklagte sich selbst bewusst war, dass seine vorausgehenden Ausführungen als Angriff gegen die Staatsführung gewirkt hatten.

2. Es war nun weiter zu prüfen, ob durch die festgestellten Äusserungen *Angelegenheiten des Staates* zum Gegenstand einer Erörterung gemacht wurden und, wenn ja, ob dies in einer den öffentlichen Frieden gefährdenden Weise geschehen ist.

Sieht man die einzelnen Predigten daraufhin an, so muss man feststellen, dass sich in den zum Gegenstand der Anklage gemachten Punkten die Predigten 1-5 mit dem *Schulwesen* und die Predigten 6-9 und die Predigt 5 in zweiten Teil mit dem *Pressewesen* befassten.

Eine Erörterung über das Schulwesen liegt nicht nur vor, wenn über die Schulen als solche, über ihren Aufbau, ihren Lehrplan, über die das Schulwesen regelnden gesetzlichen Normen oder über die Zusammensetzung und das Wirken der an den Schulen tätigen Lehrkräfte gesprochen wird, sondern auch dann, wenn, wie in vorliegendem Falle, der Schulkampf, seine Methoden und seine wirklichen oder vermeintlichen Ziele im Vordergrund der Erörterung stehen. Auch hier werden Angelegenheiten besprochen, die den Staat als solchen angehen, bei denen es sich um seine Rechte und Pflichten, seine Interessen und Aufgaben handelt, die durch die Gesetze des öffentlichen Rechtes geordnet und gestaltet werden. (vergl. schon RGStr. Bd. 27 S. 430). Dass auch die Anordnungen untergeordneter Stellen nicht von dem Begriff der Staatsangelegenheiten ausgeschlossen sind, hat schon ein Urteil des Reichsgerichtes in Strafsache Bd. 18 S. 406 hervorgehoben.

Die Verteidigung hat eingewendet, nicht Staat und Partei hätten den Schulkampf geführt, sondern ein im Vereinsregister eingetragener Verein, die „Deutsche Schulgemeinde". Dem ist entgegenzuhalten, dass sich der Angeklagte keineswegs auf eine Kritik von Massnahmen der Deutschen Schulgemeinde beschränkt hat und dass überdies das Schulwesen und seine Entwicklung auch dann Angelegenheiten des Staates sind und bleiben, wenn sich vorübergehend oder dauernd irgendwelche öffentlich-rechtlichen oder privatrechtlichen Verbände für bestimmte schulische Ziele kämpferisch einsetzen und damit an der Gestaltung und Umformung des Schulwesens mitwirken. Dass das Schulwesen auch eine Angelegenheit der katholischen Kirche ist (vgl. bes. Art. 21, 23 ff. des Reichskonkordats v. 20. Juli 1933), ändert nichts an der Tatsache, dass es in erster Linie eine Angelegenheit des Staates ist.

Auch das Pressewesen gehört zu den Angelegenheiten des heutigen Staates, der von dem Grundsatze hemmungsloser Pressefreiheit abgerückt ist und in der Presse eines der bedeutsamsten Mittel sieht, das Volk im nationalsozialistischen Geist aufzuklären und zu schulen. Daraus und aus der Erkenntnis der Gefahren, die die uneingeschränkte Pressefreiheit für die Einigkeit und Geschlossenheit eines Volkes mit sich bringt, ist die mannigfaltige Einflussnahme auf die Presse und ihre Überwachung zu erklären. Daraus erklären sich auch die Bestimmungen des Schriftleitergesetzes von 4. Oktober 1933, das im § 1 dem Schriftleiter „eine in ihren beruflichen Pflichten und Rech-

ten vom Staat durch dieses Gesetz geregelte öffentliche Aufgabe"
zuweist. Das Reichsgericht hat in der von der Verteidigung vorge-
legten Entscheidung von 1. Juni 1937 1 D 174/36 ausgesprochen,
dass durch die geschichtliche Wendung zum nationalsozialistischen
Staat der Bereich des staatlichen Lebens erweitert wurde, dass daher
z.b. alles, was über den Begriffsinhalt von Blut, Boden (und) Rasse
sowie über ihre Auswirkungen und Anforderungen für das Leben
der Gesamtheit und des Einzelnen ernsthaft öffentlich vorgetragen
oder gelehrt wird, in der Regel die nationalsozialistische Bewegung
und daher auch den von ihr getragenen nationalsozialistischen Staat
angeht und dass zu den „Angelegenheiten des Staates" auch die Ordnung des Pressewesens, sowie die Einflussnahme auf die Verbreitung
insbesondere *der* Presse gehört, die das Volk in nationalsozialistischen
Geiste aufklären und schulen will. Das Reichsgericht hat in diesem Urteil weiter ausgesprochen, dass selbst Angelegenheiten, mit
denen sich der Staat bisher noch nicht befasst hat, dadurch im Sinne
des § 13 STGB. in den Kreis „der Angelegenheiten des Staates" her-
eingezogen werden können, dass sie der Sprecher z.b. durch die
Behauptung, der Staat habe gegenüber dieser oder jener Angelegenheit eine bestimmte Einstellung oder Wirkungsweise, zum Staate in
Beziehung bringt. Davon ausgehend, kann es keinem Zweifel unter-
liegen, dass sich nicht nur die Kritik der Presseberichte über die
Strafverfahren gegen katholische Geistliche und Ordensleute, sondern
auch die Kritik sonstiger Veröffentlichungen der nationalsozialistischen Zeitungen und Zeitschriften, aber auch die allgemeine Kritik
des NS-Schrifttum mit Angelegenheiten des Staates im Sinne des
§ 130 a StGB befasst hat. Dass der Angeklagte wiederholt seine
Kritik auf die Veröffentlichungen über religiös-sittliche Dinge beschränkt hat, ändert daran schon deshalb nichts, weil der Staat an
den von diesem Begriff umfassten Dingen und an den Veröffentlichungen darüber nicht weniger interessiert ist.

Bei der Prüfung der Frage, ob der Angeklagte *in einer den öffent-*
lichen Frieden gefährdenden Weise gesprochen hat, war davon auszu-
gehen, dass eine solche Gefährdung vorliegt, wenn das *Gefühl* der
Sicherheit, das unter dem Schutz einer sicheren Rechtspflege eines
machtvollen Staates bei allen Staatsangehörigen vorhanden zu sein
pflegt, in seinem Bestand gefährdet wird, *oder* wenn der *Zustand* der
allgemeinen Rechtssicherheit durch die Gefahr der Entstehung von
Unruhen oder von Angriffen auf die Rechte anderer bedroht wird, und

dass in beiden Fällen auch schon das Herbeiführen einer entfernten Gefahr hinreichend ist (vgl. das oben angeführte Urteil des Reichsgerichts vom 1. Juni 1937 und die dort angezogene Rechtssprechung). Eine Entscheidung des Reichsgerichts in Strafsachen Bd. 18 S. 314, die sich mit Äusserungen wie „Rechtsbeugung" und „Unterdrückung" zu befassen hatte, führt aus, dass es eine Gefährdung des öffentlichen Friedens bedeute, wenn in einer die Leidenschaften erregenden Weise die gegenwärtigen Rechtszustände als ein verwerfliches und wieder zu beseitigendes Unrecht hingestellt werden und durch solche Erörterungen die Gemüter verhetzt werden und Unfriede ausgesät wird. Dass es nicht allein auf die in einer *einzelnen* Äusserung liegende Gefahr, sondern auch darauf ankommt, dass sie gerade von der in § 130 a StGB angeführten *Stelle* aus geschieht und in der darin liegenden Gefahr, ist in dem bereits einmal erwähnten Reichsgerichtsurteil vom 20. Oktober 1936 hervorgehoben. Eine solche Gefahr kann durch den Inhalt der Äusserung, aber unter Umständen auch schon durch ihre Form, herbeigeführt werden.

Unter Berücksichtigung aller dieser Gesichtspunkte kam das Gericht zu der Überzeugung, dass der Angeklagte in allen Fällen den öffentlichen Frieden und zwar das Gefühl der Rechtssicherheit gefährdet hat. Der Angeklagte hat in den 9 Predigten, soweit er sich mit Angelegenheiten des Staates befasste, nur negative Kritik geübt und zwar in äusserst scharfer Form. Er hat seine hinsichtlich des Schulkampfes erhobenen Vorwürfe ebenso verallgemeinert wie seine Vorwürfe gegen die Presse und gegen das NS-Schrifttum. Er hat dem Staate Hinterhältigkeit (Predigt 3), Betrug (Predigt 4), Schonung verbrecherischer Anhänger (Predigt 7) und Förderung von Schund- und Schmutzschriften (Predigt 8) vorgeworfen. Diese und die anderen in Ziffer III 1 näher bezeichneten Vorwürfe waren geeignet, in den den Worten des Angeklagten blind vertrauenden Zuhörern nicht nur Unruhe und inneren Widerstreit hervorzurufen, sondern darüber hinaus das Vertrauen zum Staate und zur staatlichen Rechtsordnung in der schwersten Weise zu erschüttern und zwar weit über das religiös-sittliche Gebiet hinaus. Das gilt von jeder der 9 Predigten. Auch wo der Angeklagte nur unter Anführung von Beispielen davon sprach, man könnte meinen, der Nationalsozialismus sei der erbitterste Feind der Kirche, man kenne sich da nicht mehr aus was richtig sei (Predigt 9) waren seine Äusserungen geeignet, bei den Zuhörern allgemeine Unzufriedenheit und allgemeines Misstrauen nicht nur gegen die Partei, sondern auch gegen den von ihr getragenen Staat hervorzurufen und das Ansehen staatlicher Stellen zu untergraben.

Die Verteidigung berief sich darauf, dass im Urteil des Reichsgerichtes vom 1. Juni 1937 ausgeführt sei, eine packende Predigt oder eine andere öffentliche Aussprache über weltanschauliche oder religiöse Fragen könne die Gewissen der Zuhörer bis in den tiefsten Grund aufrühren und in grosse sittliche oder religiöse Erregung oder Unruhe bringen; solche Erscheinungen des geistigen Kampfes der Weltanschauungen oder der religiösen Bekenntnisse, der nach aller geschichtlichen Erfahrung gerade der deutschen Volksseele immerein Bedürfnis gewesen sei und bleiben werde, brauchten den öffentlichen *Rechtsfrieden* nicht zu stören oder in eine auch nur entfernte Gefahr zu bringen. Damit kann sich aber der Angeklagte nicht entlasten. Er hat sich nicht nur mit weltanschaulichen und religiösen Fragen auseinandergesetzt. Er hat sich zu Äusserungen hinreissen lassen, die unmittelbar in den politischen Tageskampf eingriffen und in ihrer Wirkung einer Misstrauenserklärung und z.t. auch einer Kampfansage gegen den Staat gleichkamen.

3. Dass der Angeklagte in allen 9 Predigten als Geistlicher in Ausübung seines Berufes in einer Kirche und vor mehreren gesprochen hat bedarf keiner weiteren Erörterung. Das Gericht kam auch zu der Überzeugung, dass der Angeklagte vorsätzlich gehandelt hat. Vorsatz liegt schon vor, wenn der Prediger das Bewusstsein hat, seine Äusserungen seien geeignet, den öffentlichen Frieden zu gefährden und wenn er seine Äusserungen auf diese Gefahr hin gebraucht. Dieses Bewusstsein hatte der Angeklagte zweifellos. Er wusste als erfahrener Kanzelredner, wie sich derartige Predigten bei den Zuhörern auszuwirken pflegen, er wusste, welch uneingeschränkte Autorität er bei der grossen Masse seiner Zuhörer genoss, er wusste, dass diese Zuhörer seine Äusserungen nicht nur als Kritik an einzelnen von ihm beispielsweise angeführten Vorkommnissen, sondern, um ein Schlagwort zu gebrauchen, als Kritik am ganzen „System" auffassten und dass damit die Gefahr einer schweren Erschütterung des Vertrauens zum Staat und zur staatlichen Rechtsordnung heraufbeschworen wurde. Er hat dies in Kauf genommen. Er gab selbst an, er habe es als eine Aufgabe angesehen, die Leute mit Misstrauen gegen die Berichtstattung über religiöse Dinge in der völkischen Presse zu erfüllen. Dass von diesem Misstrauen zum Misstrauen gegen

die Presse überhaupt und von da aus zum Misstrauen gegen den die Presse überwachenden Staat nur ein kleiner Schritt ist, war dem Angeklagten sicherlich bewusst. Das gleiche gilt vom Schulkampf. Auch hier konnte es dem Angeklagten nicht entgehen, dass seine Charakterisierung des Schulkampfes, seine Prophezeiungen über die Entwicklung der Gemeinschaftsschule, seine Angriffe gegen die untergeordneten Stellen, gegen die städtischen Lehrkräfte, letzten Endes zum tiefsten Misstrauen gegen den heutigen Staat führen mussten, mindestens aber sehr leicht führen konnten. Dass der Angeklagte in der einen oder anderen Predigt den Zuhörern Treue zum Staat empfahl, war nicht geeignet, die Wirkung seiner das Vertrauen zum Staate erschütternden Äusserungen merklich abzuschwächen, denn Treue setzt Vertrauen voraus. Dazu kommt, dass der Angeklagte, wie bereits dargetan, in vier Predigten (Predigt 3, 4, 7, 8) die Staatsführung unmittelbar angegriffen hat. Das konnte ihm selbst in der Erregung nicht entgangen sein. Wenn er das Wort Staatsbetrug in dem von ihm angegebenen Sinne gebraucht hat, so kam ihm nach Überzeugung des Gerichts doch sofort zum Bewusstsein, dass viele Zuhörer dieses Wort anders auffassen konnten und in dem Zusammenhang sogar anders auffassen mussten. Er hätte denn die Pflicht gehabt, sich zu berichtigen. Wenn er das unterliess, so hat er schuldhaft gehandelt. Das Gleiche gilt für die anderen 3 Äusserungen, inbesondere von der Äusserung über das Konkordat in der Predigt 3.

4. Es steht somit fest, dass der Angeklagte in allen 9 Fällen den äusseren und den inneren Tatbestand des § 130 a StGB. erfüllt hat.

IV.

Der Reichsminister der Justiz hat durch Entschliessung vom 17. Juni 1937 Nr. III g[11] 5611 a/37 die Strafverfolgung aus §2 des Gesetzes vom 20. Dezember 1934 angeordnet. Es war daher auch zu prüfen, ob und inwieweit der Angeklagte sich gegen diese Gesetzbestimmung verfehlt hat.

Es ist bereits wiederholt ausgeführt, dass sich 4 Äusserungen des Angeklagten in den Predigten 3, 4, 7 und 8 unmittelbar gegen die heutige Staatsführung richteten und welche Vorwürfe sie enthielten. Die in Frage kommenden Stellen sind schon in Ziffer II des Urteils durch Unterstreichung gekennzeichnet. Dass diese Äusserungen geeignet waren, das Vertrauen des Volkes zur politischen Führung zu untergraben und dass sich der Angeklagte dessen auch bewusst war, bedarf keiner weiteren Ausführung mehr. Es darf insoweit auf Ziffer

III 2, 3 des Urteils verwiesen werden. Was dort über die Gefährdung des öffentlichen Friedens und über das Bewusstsein der Friedensgefährdung gesagt wurde, ist auch eine Begründung dafür, dass diese Äusserungen zersetzenden Charakters waren und dass sich der Angeklagte dessen bewusst war. Dass keine der leitenden Persönlichkeiten namentlich genannt wurde, ist rechtlich bedeutungslos. Diese 4 Äusserungen waren aber auch *nach Form und Inhalt* hetzerisch. Sie liessen die Absicht erkennen, bei den Zuhörern Misstrauen und Unzufriedenheit gegen das Verhalten der Staatsführung auf den in den Äusserungen berührten Gebieten hervorzurufen und wirkten damit hetzerisch. Auch hier gilt wieder, dass es Pflicht des Angeklagten gewesen wäre, unbedachte Entgleisungen richtig zu stellen und dass er durch die Unterlassung einer solchen Richtigstellung schuldhaft gehandelt hat. Nach der bisherigen Rechtsprechung zu § 2 des Gesetzes vom 20. Dezember 1934 wären diese 4 Äusserungen auch dann als Hetzreden im Sinne dieser Strafbestimmung angesehen worden, wenn sie in einem ähnlichen Zusammenhang an anderer Stelle und nicht von einem Geistlichen gebraucht worden wären. Im vorliegenden Falle aber darf insbesondere nicht übersehen werden, dass der Angeklagte als hochgebildeter, erfahrener Kanzelredner weit mehr als irgend ein anderer auch unter Wahrung der Belange der Kirche in der Lage gewesen wäre, selbst in der grössten seelischen Erregung sich bei seinen Äusserungen die Mässigung aufzuerlegen, die von ihm als Prediger verlangt werden muss. Die 4 Predigten waren jedermann zugänglich und von einem grösseren durch keinerlei engeren Beziehungen zusammengehaltenen Personenkreis besucht. Der Angeklagte war sich dessen bewusst. Er hat somit in 4 Fällen öffentlich über leitende Persönlichkeiten des Staates und deren Anordnungen hetzerische Äusserungen gemacht, die geeignet waren, das Vertrauen des Volkes zur politischen Führung zu untergraben (§ 2 Abs. 1 des Gesetzen vom 20. Dezember 1934).

V.

Der Angeklagte und die Verteidigung haben sich noch darauf berufen, dass ein Fall religiöser Notwehr vorgelegen sei, die Notwehr sei auch nicht überschritten worden, denn das Mass der Abwehr werde durch das Mass des Angriffs bestimmt. Es wurde dazu aufgeführt, dass im Schulkampf entgegen den der Kirche im Konkordat

gegebenen Zusicherungen auf die Eltern in unzulässiger Weise ein-
gewirkt worden sei, um sie zu bestimmen, entgegen ihrer inneren
Überzeugung ihre Kinder zur Gemeinschaftsschule anzumelden, dass
sich die unrichtigen Presseberichte über katholische Geistliche und
Ordensleute und die gegen die Kirche und ihre Diener gerichteten
Artikel so gehäuft hätten, dass der Angeklagte keine andere Wahl
gehabt hätte, als im Interesse der Kirche und des katholischen Glaubens von der Kanzel aus in entschiedener Form zu diesen Vorkommnissen Stellung zu nehmen, zumal Vorstellungen kirchlicher Stellen
bei den zuständigen Reichsbehörden erfolglos, ja sogar unbeantwortet
geblieben seien.

Nun hat allerdings das Reichsgericht anerkannt, dass auch zugunsten juristischer Personen des privaten oder öffentlichen Rechts Notwehr geübt werden könne, wenn rechtswidrige Angriffe gegen ihre
geschützten Rechtsgüter erhoben werden (RG. Str. Bd. 63 S. 220).
Voraussetzung für die Annahme einer Notwehrhandlung ist aber
immer, dass sich die Verteidigung gegen den Angreifer richtet und
nicht die Rechte Dritter verletzt. Äusserungen, die sich in ihrer Wirkung gegen den Staat richten, die geeignet sind, den Staat zu schä-
digen, Kanzel*missbrauch* und zersetzende Hetzreden sind auch dann
keine Notwehr, wenn einem Angreifer gegenüber Notwehr (auch
Ehrennotwehr) zulässig wäre. Schon aus diesem Grunde muss dem
Angeklagten abgesprochen werden, dass seine Äusserungen als Not-
wehrhandlungen zu gelten haben.

Artikel 33 des Reichskonkordats weist auf den Weg hin, der der
Kirche offensteht, wenn sie einzelne Bestimmungen des Konkordats
für verletzt hält. Es geht aber nicht an, dass die einzelnen Priester je
nach ihren Gutdünken von der Kanzel aus das Kirchenvolk in den
Kampf der Meinungen verwickeln und unter Inanspruchnahme der
kirchlichen Autorität in eine innere Kampfstellung zum Staate
bringen.

Dem Angeklagten kann auch nicht zugebilligt werden, dass er in
vermeintlicher Notwehr gehandelt habe. Er kannte auch sehr wohl
die Grenzen, die ihm bei seinem Wirken als Prediger durch die Gesetze des Staates gezogen waren.

Da schon aus allen diesen Gründen der Einwand der Notwehr
ausscheidet, war der Angeklagte schuldig zu sprechen.

Soweit Verfehlungen gegen den Gesetz vom 20. Dezember 1934
vorliegen, stehen sie in Tateinheit mit den Verfehlungen gegen §

130 a STGB., da durch ein und dieselbe Handlung beide Strafgesetze verletzt wurden.

Das gericht hat angenommen, dass der Angeklagte aus einem einheitlichen von vornherein auf den Gesamterfolg gerichteten Vorsatz heraus gehandelt hat, da er selbst angibt, dass er sich auf Grund seiner religiösen Überzeugung für verpflichtet hielt, in der von ihm geübten Art und Weise zu predigen und da er sogar noch am. 9 Juni 1937 erklärt hat, er werde weiterhin so predigen, gleichviel wie seine Predigten strafrechtlich bewertet werden.

Der Angeklagte war deshalb wegen eines fortgesetzten Vergehens nach § 130 a StGB, in Tateinheit mit einem fortgesetzten Vergehen nach § 2 des Gesetzes vom 20. Dezember 1934 zu verurteilen.

VI.

Straferschwerend kam in Betracht, dass der Angeklagte schon einmal verwarnt wurde, dass es sich um insgesamt 9 Predigten handelt, die zur Verurteilung führten, dass die Äusserungen des Angeklagten ihrem Inhalt nach und teilweise auch ihrer Form nach besonders schwerwiegend und gefährlich waren, dass die Zuhörermenge jeweils eine sehr grosse war und dass demgemäss auch die staatsabträgliche Wirkung der Äusserungen eine äusserst weitgehende war, dass sich der Angeklagte bewusst war, dass das Kirchenvolk seinen Äusserungen eine weit stärkere Bedeutung beimass als den Äusserungen irgend eines mehr oder weniger unbekannten Geistlichen.

Strafmildernd fiel ausser der Straflosigkeit ins Gewicht, dass der Angeklagte sich im Felde äusserst tapfer benommen hat, dass er schwer kriegsbeschädigt ist, dass er unter vollen Einsatz seiner Persönlichkeit gegen den Kommunismus aufgetreten ist, dass er sich offen zu seinem Äusserungen bekannt hat und dass er nicht aus grundsätzlicher Abneigung gegen den Staat, sondern auf Grund religiöser Besorgnisse zu seinen Äusserungen gekommen ist.

Die Strafe war gemäss § 73 StGB, aus § 2 des Gesetzes vom 20. Dezember 1934 zu entnehmen. Eine Gefängnisstrafe von 6 Monaten erschien schuldentsprechend. Es erschien angezeigt, ihm die Untersuchungshaft in Höhe von 6 Wochen auf die Strafe anzurechnen.

Kosten: §§ 464, 645 StPO.

Der Vorsitzende: Die Beisitzer:

(L.S.) gez. Dr. Wölsl   Schwingenschlögl   Dr. Wachter
Landgerichtsdirektor   Landgerichtsräte

Appendix C

BROADSHEET OF THE RHÄTIA FRATERNITY

Being an explanation to members of this Fraternity of differences wich exist between them and the Nazi Party.

Vertraulich
unter Burschenwort!

ERKLÄRUNG.

Veranlasst durch Vorkommnisse bei einer Burschenprüfung fasste der Phil.-Ausschuss am 19. II. 31 einstimmig den Beschluss, eine Erklärung sämtlichen Bundesbrüdern zu übermitteln:

Schon wiederholt mussten wir in Erfahrung bringen, dass Bundesbrüder nicht nur sich persönlich in der nationalsozialistischen Partei betätigen, sondern auch noch versuchen dafür innerhalb der Verbindung Stimmung zu machen.

Zunächst weisen wir darauf hin, dass nach unseren Satzungen S. 11, Abs. II **Parteipolitik von der Verbindung fern zu halten ist.**

Darüber hinaus unterstehen wir als **katholische** Verbindung selbstverständlich den Weisungen, die unsere Bischöfe in grundsätzlichen Fragen der Weltanschauung geben.

Sämtliche bayerische Bischöfe haben im Einklang mit den übrigen deutschen und einem Grossteil ausserdeutscher Bischöfe öffentlich erklärt, dass die nationalsozialistische Weltanschauung in wichtigen Fragen nach ihrem Programm und nach den Äusserungen massgebender Führer im Widerspruch zur kath. Weltanschauung stehe. Unser 1. Prinzip aber verlangt von jedem Rhaeten das vorbehaltlose Bekenntnis zur katholischen Weltanschauung und damit auch den Gehorsam gegenüber den grundsätzlichen Weisungen unserer Bischöfe.

Unser 2. Prinzip verlangt von uns besondere Pflege der Liebe zum bayerischen Volk und Vaterland. Auch der wohlwollendste Beurteiler der nationalsozialistischen Bewegung wird nicht behaupten können, dass innerhalb dieser Bewegung allenthalben ein besonderes Eintreten für die Interessen des bayerischen Landes und Volkes gewährleistet sei. Wer aber einer **bayerischen** Verbindung den Burscheneid geleistet hat und sich innerhalb oder ausserhalb derselben im gegensätzlichen Sinne betätigt, kommt in Konflikt mit seinem Burschenwort. Aus tiefstem Verantwortungsbewusstsein heraus muss der Phil. A. S. um die Reinerhaltung der Prinzipien besorgt sein. **Er ist der Überzeugung, dass die nationalsozialistische Weltanschauung mit den beiden ersten Prinzipien unserer Verbindung im Widerspruch steht und desshalb ein guter Rhaete nicht gleichzeitig Nationalsozialist sein kann.**

Wir bitten alle Bundesbrüder uns im Kampfe um die Reinerhaltung unserer Prinzipien nach Kräften zu unterstützen.

I. A. des Phil.-Ausschusses:

L. Bruner, Oberstudiendirektor
Phil.-Senior.

Appendix D

A LETTER TO MEMBERS OF RHÄTIA

A policy letter sent to all members of this Bavarian Fraternity which explains in detail their cultural and political differences with the National Socialists; dated, November, 1932.

Die Gründungsphilister an alle Rhäten!

Die Versendung des von 22 Conphilistern unterzeichnten Rundschreibens an alle Philister „Sie lassen die Verbindung nicht zur Ruhe kommen" erfüllen im Zusamenhang mit anderen Vorkommnissen uns Gründungsphilister mit ernstester Sorge, weil wir den Geist bedroht sehen, von dem seinerzeit wir Gründungsphilister beseelt waren. Wir wenden uns daher in Folgendem an sämtliche Bundesbrüder:

Wenn man die Correspondenzblätter der Aktivitas und des Philisteriums und die Jahrgänge unserer Verbindungsschrift des „Herold", in denen die Geschichte der Rhätia aufgezeichnet ist, durchmustert, so wird man kaum finden, dass je viel von Politik und politischen Parteien die Rede ist, obwohl es auch dazumal schon viele Parteien gegeben hat. Eine Stellungnahme zu politischen Fragen oder eine Einflussnahme einer einzelnen Partei auf die Verbindung zu propagandistischen Zwecken hat nie stattgefunden. Und das war im Interesse des Friedens in der Verbindung und der Reinerhaltung unserer Prinzipien gut so. Über die Prinzipien der Verbindung gab es nie einen Meinungsstreit, weil jeder die Notwendigkeit derselben für den kath. bayerischen Akademiker kannte und sich der Verpflichtung bewusst war, die er mit seinem Eintritt in eine katholische bayeriche Studentenverbindung für das ganze Leben auf sich genommen hatte.

Das wurde nun anders, seitdem eine neue Partei, die nationalsoizialistische Arbeiterpartei auf den politischen Plan getreten ist. Aus ihrem Agitationsbedürfnis heraus kam es, dass auch Mitglieder der NSDAP in unserer Verbindung Agitationszellen errichten wollten, um von hier aus Mitglieder für die Partei zu gewinnen. Es ist im Interesse der historischen Wahrheit und zum Verständnis der späteren Vorgänge wichtig daran festzuhalten, dass *nicht die baye-riche Volkspartei und ihre Anhänger aktive Politik in die Verbindung hineingetragen haben, sondern Angehörige der NSDAP.* Wir legen besonderen Wert auf die Feststellung!

In den beiden Schriftstücken „Adiatur et altera pars" (1931) und „Sie lassen die Verbindung nicht zur Ruhe kommen" (Oktober 1932) offentbart sich ein organisierter Widerstand gegen den Phi-listersenior, die Philistervorstandschaft und den Philister-Ausschuss, denen mit überwältigender Mehrheit beim Philister-Convent des 50. Stiftungsfestes durch die Wahl das Vertrauen ausgesprochen worden ist.

Von den Verfassern der beiden Rundschreiben wird mit unseren Prinzipien jongliert wie mit Bällen und ihr Inhalt veranlasst uns Gründungsphilister, die wir durch 50 Jahre die Verbindungsgeschich-te miterlebt haben, unsere mahnende und warnende Stimme zu er-heben und uns schützend vor unsere Philistervorstandschaft und den Philisterausschuss zu stellen, in deren Rücken der Dolchstoss geführt werden sollte. Unsere toten Freunde sollen uns nicht dereinst den Vorwurf machen können, dass wir das Werk unserer gemeinsamen Jugendideale im Stiche gelassen oder zu träge und zu feige gewesen wären, den Kampf um dasselbe zu führen. Wir werden, solange noch ein Tropfen katholischess und bayerisches Blut in unseren Adern rinnt, das ihren toten Händen entfallene rotweissblaue Banner hoch-halten und die in ihm versinnbildeten hehren Prinzipien der Rhätia vor jeder Verflachung und vor jedem Angriff schützen und vertei-digen, so wahr uns Gott helfe!

Der wichtigste Punkt in dem ganzen Streitkomplex ist die Be-antwortung der Frage:

Wie stehen die noch in der Rhätia gebliebenen und wie standen die ausgeschiedenen nationalsoz. Philister zum bekannten Erlass der Bischöfe und damit zum 1. Prinzip?

Haben sie den Erlass mit kath. Demut und mit kath. Gehorsam und mit dem Respekt aufgenommen, wie er den Äusserungen der auf hoher kirchlicher Warte stehenden Nachfolger der Apostel ge-hört? Wir wissen uns totsicher einig mit unseren verstorbenen Freun-den, wenn wir diese Frage verneinen! Missachtung und Kritik an Bischöflichen Lehrentscheidungen sind nicht katholisch und führen auf Wege, wie sie dem religiösen Individualismus eigen sind, der immer von der Kirche verurteilt werden musste.

Wenn die Bischöfe erklären:

*„Was der Nationalsozialismus Christentum nennt,
ist nicht mehr das Christentum Christi!"*

und wenn sie sagen, dass in dem kulturpolitischen Programm Irrlehren enthalten sind, so haben sich die *Angehörigen der kath.
Studentenverbindung* vorbehaltlos auf die Seite der Bischöfe zu stellen.
Sie haben sich zu prüfen, ob sie sich nicht selbst auf einem Irrwege
befinden. *Gerade Philister* müssen der Aktivitas ein leuchtendes Vorbild katholischer Treue und Disziplin geben.

Ehe wir daran gehen, die Schlussfolgerungen aus unseren Ausführungen zu ziehen, möchten wir uns noch kurz mit dem letzten
Rundschreiben befassen, das zur Beantwortung von 3 Fragen an den
Philister *Dr. Stoll* auffordert, von dem besonders hervorgehoben
wird, dass er keiner politischen Partei angehöre. Ob Philister *Dr.
Stoll* einer politischen Partei angehört oder nicht, erscheint uns in
Bezug auf den Kernpunkt der Frage völlig belanglos. Der Philisterausschuss hat die Frage der Zugehörigkeit zu der NSDAP. nicht vom
Standpunkte der Parteipolitik, sondern vom Gesichtspunkte der Weltanschauung aus betrachtet. Bezüglich unseres 1. Prinzipes, also auch
bezüglich des Erlasses der Bischöfe, kann es bei einem Rhäten keinen
neutralen oder parteilosen Standpunkt geben.

Völlig unverständlich aber ist uns Gründungsphilistern und dem
allergrössten Teile unseres Philisteriums, dem Philisterium einer
*katholischen und bayerischen Verbindung, die an Hass grenzende
Abneigung des Philisters Dr. Stoll und seiner Gesinnungsgenossen*
gegen eine politische Partei, die ebenfalls *Katholizität und Bayerntum* auf ihre Fahne geschrieben hat, gegen die BVP. Warum verteilt
der Verfasser des Rundschreibens Licht und Schatten so ungleich?
Warum alles Licht den Angehörigen der NSDAP und allen Schatten
den BVP. Philistern? Warum? — Dr. Stoll lehnen wir als Unparteiischen glattweg ab!

Der Titel „Sie lassen die Verbindung nicht zur Ruhe kommen" ist
hetzerisch und verstösst gegen die Fundamente der auch für eine
Verbindung unerlässlichen Disziplin und besonders gegen unser Prinzip der Lebensfreundschaft. Die ganze Darstellung über die Vorgänge
in der Verbindung ist tendenziös gefärbt. Von dem Prinzip der
Lebensfreundschaft gegenüber den Angegriffenen entdeckt man in
dem Schreiben keine Spur mehr.

Im übrigen sind wir einverstanden mit der Meinung des Zirkulars, dass die Studenten auf die Universität geschickt werden zum Studieren und nicht zum Politisieren. Sie sollen sich in der Politik unterrichten über die Zeitströmungen, aber nicht aktive Politik treiben. Eines aber wundert uns, dass angesehene Mitglieder unseres Bundes ihren Namen unter ein solches Schriftstück zu setzen den Geschmack hatten. Man kann diese Tatsache nur damit erklären, dass die Philister ihre Namen zur Verfügung stellten, ohne das Schreiben in dieser Aufmachung vorher zu kennen. Tatsächlich haben mehrere von den Unterzeichnern schon gegen den Missbrauch ihres Namens protestiert.

Wir kommen zum Schluss und fassen unser Urteil über die Vorgänge in der Verbindung und über das, was wir zum Besten der Verbindung für notwendig halten, in objektiver Weise in folgende Sätze zusammen:

1) Es ist Tatsache, dass die derzeitige Störung des Friedens in der Verbindung durch den Versuch verursacht wurde, eine nationalsozialistische Agitationszelle in ihr zu errichten.

2) Es ist Tatsache, dass von den Mitgliedern der BVP., die schon jahrzehntelang der Verbindung wertvolle Dienste geleistet haben, keinerlei Partei-Agitation in derselben getrieben wurde.

3) Der Philistersenior und der Philisterausschuss haben korrekt gehandelt und verdienen unseren Dank und unsere Anerkennung, dass sie durch ihre Massnahmen für die Aufrechthaltung der Prinzipien in der Verbindung gesorgt haben. Wir erwarten, dass sie auch weiterhin mit starker Hand eine Verflachung unserer Prinzipien hintanhalten.

4) Wir verurteilen das jüngst in Umlauf gebrachte Zirkular wegen Disziplinlosigkeit, wegen schwerer Verletzung des 4. Prinzipes, die in dem Vorwurf der Parteilichkeit gegen die führenden Persönlichkeiten liegt, die seit Jahr und Tag in uneigennützigster Weise mühevolle, Zeit und Kraft raubende Arbeit für die Gesamtheit der Verbindung geleistet haben.

5) Wir erwarten, dass die nationalsozialistischen Philister, solange die unkirchlichen Programmsätze der NSDAP. Geltung haben, entweder ihren Austritt aus der Partei, oder, falls sie sich dazu ausser Stande erklären, aus dem Philisterium der Rhätia betätigen, da in diesem Falle ihr Verbleiben in der Verbindung eine schwere Belastung der Rhätia gegenüber der Kirche und dem kirchentreuen bayerischen Volke bedeuten würde.

Gerne benützen wir diese Gelegenheit, dem Phil. Ausschuss unseren freudigen Dank für die Erwerbung des prachtvollen Verbindungsheimes auszusprechen. Möge die Verbindung in ihrem schönen Haus Tage des Glückes und der Freude erleben, Tage, die gegründet sind auf unseren Wahlspruch:

Cum fide virtus!

Das wünschen allen Rhäten mit Brudergruss und Handschlag

Die Gründungsphilister:

Sanitätsrat Lübsche, Glsn

München, den 24. Nov. 32. Leonh. Schmid, Pfarrer.

Appendix E

LETTER OF KARL LUDWIG FREIHERR ZU GUTTENBERG

Being a letter from Baron zu Guttenberg to the Kreisleiter of Neustadt a.d. Saale, explaining his refusal to join the Nazi Party; dated, September 5, 1937.

Auf der Salzburg, den 5. Sept. 1937
Post Bad Neustadt an der fr. Saale

Herrn

Kreisleiter A. Ingebrand

Bad Neustadt a/Saale

Betr.: Aufforderung vom 26.8.1937

PERSÖNLICH

Die Berufung in die N.S.D.A.P. durch den Herrn Kreisleiter ist mir als Zeichen des Vertrauens eine aufrichtige Freude. Ich sehe in diesem Schritt, wie in dem Vorschlag, der ihn veranlasste, eine Anerkennung meiner positiven Einstellung zu den Aufgaben des neuen Staates, meines Bemühens, im Rahmen der eigenen bescheidenen Wirkungsmöglichkeiten die Pflichten zu erfüllen, welche die Zeit unserem Volke auferlegt und deren Inangriffnahme vielfach erst durch den Einsatz und den Sieg der N.S.D.A.P. ermöglicht wurde. Diese Einstellung und dieses Bemühen war für mich auf Grund der Tradition meiner Familie und meines eigenen Entwicklungsganges eine Selbstverständlichkeit, gerade deshalb ist es mir aber eine freudige und dankbar empfundene Genugtuung, dass diese Haltung durch die zuständigen Stellen eine positive Wertung findet und die Gemeinsamkeit, welche der Dienst an der Gegenwart und Zukunft unseres Volkes gibt, auch in dem neuen Schritt des Herrn Kreisleiters Ausdruck gefunden hat.

Wenn ich daher heute meinen Dank für die Berufung in die N.S.D.A.P. ausspreche und bitte, diesen Dank auch jenen zu übermitteln, welche meinem Vorschlag ihre Zustimmung gegeben haben, so möchte ich dabei vor allem betonen, dass ich auch in Zukunft in meinem Aufgabenkreis alles versuchen werde, um den nationalen, staatlichen und völkischen Zielen zu dienen, die ja auch Ziele der

Bewegung sind: mögen diese Aufgaben nun aus meinen Beziehungen zu unserer engeren Heimat erwachsen oder im Zusammenhang mit den besonderen Pflichten stehen, welcher der Historiker bei der Pflege der grossen geschichtlichen Traditionen unseres Volkes zu erfüllen hat.

Die Ausführungen sind mir deshalb ein Bedürfnis, weil ich der ehrenden Berufung in die Partei selbst noch nicht Folge leisten kann. Jede Entscheidung, die man nach reiflicher Überlegung vornimmt, muss man ganz vertreten können, sonst ist der Sache nicht gedient, der sie gilt. Art und Form, mit welcher religiöse und kirchliche Fragen innerhalb der Partei zeitweise behandelt und zu lösen versucht werden, lassen sich aber mit meinem Empfinden so schwer in Einklang bringen, dass ich ein erspriessliches Wirken für meine Person in der Partei selbst zur Zeit noch nicht zu sehen vermag. Diese Fragen und ihre Lösung sind von so tiefgehender Bedeutung für das gesamte Volk wie für den Einzelnen, dass man sie bei einer grundsätzlichen Entscheidung nicht ausser acht lassen kann. Ich hoffe aber, dass die Hinderungsgründe, welche für mich aus der Behandlung dieser Fragen erwachsen, mit der Zeit gegenstandslos werden. Bis dahin möchte ich meinerseits den Aufnahmeantrag zurückstellen.

Dass mir diese Entscheidung nicht leicht gefallen ist, davon bitte ich überzeugt zu sein, ich fühlte mich aber zu der Offenheit verpflichtet, die bei wichtigen Dingen immer Voraussetzung des Handelns sein soll.

Heil Hitler!

Dr. Karl Ludwig Fr. zu Guttenberg.

Appendix F

A POLITICAL STATEMENT OF FREIHERR ZU GUTTENBERG MADE, NOVEMBER 7, 1944

Being a statement prepared by Baron zu Guttenberg in answer to the inquiry of Standartenführer Huppenkothen. A commentary on this statement has been adde oy Therese Freifrau zu Guttenberg.

9. Nov. 44

ZUSAMMENASSUNG MEINER ANGABEN

VOR

STANDARTENFÜHRER HUPPENKOTHEN AM 7. NOV. 1944

Mein Einsatz für die Idee der Monarchie geschah aus der Überzeugung, dass die Anerkennung erblicher Gewalt am klarsten das Organische im Staatsaufbau zum Ausdruck bringt und der monarchische Gedanke — bei aller oft mangelnden Übereinstimmung zwischen Idee und Wirklichkeit — daher am sinnfälligsten das Wesen konservativer Staatsauffassung umschreibt. Dabei war für mich eine Selbstverständlichkeit, dass gerade dieser Gedanke nicht einer bestimmten Partei zugehört. So habe ich mich auch immer bemüht, unsere Veröffentlichungen von jeglicher Parteibindung fernzuhalten. Wie überhaupt m.E. konservative Einstellung niemals mit einem bestimmten Personenkreis zusammenfällt, sondern eine allgemeine menschliche Haltung darstellt, deren erhaltende Art neben den fortschrittlichen, jugendlich-revolutionären Bestrebungen auch für ein Staatswesen immer von Bedeutung sein wird. Erst aus Zusammenklang und Auseinandersetzung beider Kräfte schien mir geschichtliches Leben zu erwachsen, jedoch die zu starke Zurückdrängung einer dieser Grundeinstellungen nach den Erfahrungen der Geschichte zu schweren Erschütterungen zu führen. Aus dieser Überzeugung heraus wollte ich, nachdem 1933 die revolutionären Kräfte des Nationalsozialismus die Führung übernommen hatten, im Rahmen meiner Zeitschrift die erhaltenden und das Erbe unserer Geschichte bewahrenden Ideen pflegen. Was den monarchischen Gedanken anbelangte, so sollte er von Verunglimpfungen freigehalten und in

seiner Bedeutung für die deutsche Geschichte gezeigt werden. ¹ Wesentlich erschien mir dabei nicht, ob diese Idee wieder einmal ihre
Verwirklichung finden würde, sondern dass überhaupt in dem grossen
Umbruch das Verständnis für derartige Gedanken wacherhalten
blieb. — Bei der Zusammenstellung der „Weissen Blätter" sollte
nur dem Positiven Raum gewährt werden.

Nicht im Angriff gegen
andersgeartete Kräfte sollte der eigene Standpunkt zum Ausdruck
kommen, sondern Erbe und Tradition, wie sie aus der christlich-
abendländischen Gedankenwelt erwachsen sind, in Geschichte, Idee
und Lebensform dargestellt werden.

In diesem Sinne habe ich sowohl über die Zeitschrift „Monarchie",
die bis Februar 1934 erschienen ist, wie über die „Weissen Blätter",
deren Erscheinen im Mai 1934 genehmigt wurde und bis 1943 an-
dauerte, mit führenden Persönlichkeiten der N.S.D.A.P. gesprochen.
Die Zeitschrift hatte einen bescheidenen, aber ihr sehr zugetanen
Leserkreis. Durch diesen Umstand und durch das Beschaffen der
Aufsätze, wodurch ich mit verhältnismässig vielen Berufs- und Ge-
legenheitsautoren zusammenkam, wurde mein Name für eine Anzahl
von Menschen fest mit der Vorstellung einer von ihnen positiv bewerteten christlich-konservativen Haltung verbunden. Dieser Eindruck dürfte sich häufig im Gespräch noch vertieft haben.

Ich nehme an, dass von derartigen Persönlichkeiten meine Einberufung zum O.K.W. angeregt wurde, um mir auf Grund meiner
Vorbildung auch einen entsprechenderen Einsatz zu verschaffen, als
beim Zahlmeister der Würzburger Landesschützen. Ich sah jedenfalls selbst in meiner Einberufung nach Berlin eine Folge meiner
redaktionellen Tätigkeit. Der damalige Oberst Oster, der die Einberufung veranlasste, sowie Dr. v. Dohnanyi waren mir weder
persönlich noch dem Namen nach bekannt. Auch der Leiter der
Abteilung Ausland, ein Jahrgangskamerad meines Bruders, war mir
bis dahin unbekannt. Von der Abteilung war ich früher nur dem Ge-
sandten Dr. Kiep begegnet, der auch ein Leser der „W. Blätter"
war und meine Mitarbeit bei der Gruppe begrüsste. Von Persön-

---

¹ Bis hierher tatsächliche Einstellung meines Mannes. Von „Wesentlich"
bis „blieb":
In früheren Jahren war mein Mann unbedingt für die Errichtung von Mo-
narchien, von 1941 ab etwa rückte dieser Gedanke gegenüber der Vording-
lichkeit der Ablösung des Nationalsozialismus gegen ein anderes Regime in
den Hintergrund.

lichkeiten, von denen ich später feststellte, dass sie zur Abwehr Beziehungen hatten, kannte ich noch Botschafter von Hassel, der uns 1937 anlässlich einer Arbeitsdienstleistung seiner Tochter zu Hause aufsuchte und der von da ab ein sehr interessierter Mitarbeiter der W. Bl. wurde; ausserdem nach Generaloberst Beck, dem ich 1939 mit der Bitte um einen Beitrag für die W. Bl. aufgesucht hatte. Wenn Beck auch trotz einer später neuerlich vorgebrachten Bitte diesen Beitrag auch nicht geschrieben hat, so war er doch über die Zeitschrift unterrichtet und erkannte mir gegenüber ihren Inhalt sehr zustimmend an. Es ist also auch möglich, dass von einer diesen Seiten auf mich aufmerksam gemacht wurde. [2]

Ich selbst war glücklich über die neue Verwendung als Referent der Gruppe I Abtl. Ausland, besonders als es sich zeigte, dass ich meine Aufgabe ohne grössere Beanstandungen durch meine Vorgesetzten erfüllen konnte.

Mitte 1940 wurde für uns ganz unerwartet die Beschlagnahmung der Schwarzenberg'schen Besitzungen — Familie meiner Frau — ausgesprochen und war meine Freizeit in der Folge durch Besuche der Familie, Rücksprache mit Anwälten etc. im Hinblick auf diese Angelegenheit voll ausgefüllt. In diesem Zusammenhang kam ich auch durch Vermittlung Dohnanyis zu Admiral Canaris, der mir seine Unterstützung bezüglich des Erbteils meiner Frau zusagte. [3]

Gegen Mitte 1941 wurde ich dann unverhofft zu Oberst Oster

---

[2] Her von Hassel, den wir beide kannten un der in Weissen Blättern mitgearbeitet hatte, veranlasste über General-Oberst Beck die Einberufung meines Mannes zum OKW Berlin im Frühjahr 1940. Es ist richtig, dass der damalige Oberst Oster sowie Herr von Dohnanyi zu diesem Zeitpunkt mit meinem Mann noch nicht bekannt waren. Es war zwischen mir und meinem Mann besprochen worden, den Grund — bei evtl. Verhören — anzugeben, dass mein Mann wohl wegen seiner redaktionellen Tätigkeit zum OKW einberufen worden sei. Allenfalls sollte auch noch seine Doktorarbeit über die Zeitgenössische Presse über Lenin als Begründung Erwähnung finden.

[3] Mein Mann wurde bei Frau Admiral Gebhardt in Berlin-Kl. Machnow einquartiert, welche mit dem Ehepaar *Canaris* befreundet war und wodurch mein Mann auch deren ausserdienstliche Bekanntschaft machte. Mein Mann wollte offensichtlich diese uns beiden befreundete Dame nicht nennen, da sie sowieso gefährdet war.

Zu den zu bearbeitenden Meldungen gehörten auch Auslandsnachrichten, jedoch m.W. durch eine bestimmte Stelle vorher ausgewählt.

gerufen und aufgefordert, bei Z. die Stelle von Spitzy (zu übernehmen), der sich zur Truppe gemeldet habe. Meine Aufgabe bestünde in der Sichtung eingehender Meldungen und Berichte und einem entsprechenden Vortrag über deren wesentlichen Inhalt. Daneben kämen vielleicht gelegentlich noch gewisse Adjudantur-Aufgaben. Ich verliess meine Stellung bei Ausland sehr ungern, sah aber in der Berufung zu Z. das nach der Hierarchie des Amtes an der Spitze stand, eine besondere Anerkennung. 4 Der gedanke, dass es sich bei dem

---

4 Unrichtig! Mein Mann wurde in die Zentrale versetzt, um mit den massgebenden Herrn dieses Amtes unauffällig zusammensein zu können. Er selbst wäre eigentlich lieber in der Gruppe I, Abt. Ausland geblieben, weil er das Gefühl hatte, dort nicht so ins Blickfeld gerückt zu sein und unauffällig mehr leisten zu können, als an der exponierten Stelle in der Zentrale. Es war ihm selbstverständlich vollkommen klar, dass viele Herren des Amtes für den Umsturz arbeiteten.

Die Zusammenarbeit mit dem damaligen Oberst Oster, Herrn v. Dohnanyi und Herrn Justus Delbrück war für meinen Mann aber eine sehr erfreuliche, da die Herren sich in politischer Hinsicht vollkommen einig waren.

Diese Erkenntnisse stimmen, nur waren sie schon früher da und wurden nur durch die Tátigkeit im OKW unterbaut und vertieft.

Mein Mann hatte in seinem Aufgabenkreis die Lage im Nahen Osten zu bearbeiten. In diesem Zusammenhang erhielt er den Auftrag (es musste im Frühjahr 1941 gewesen sein) einen Bericht abzufassen, der von Keitel benötigt werde für einen Lagebericht bei Hitler. Mein Mann erledigte diese Aufgabe pflichtgemäss und versuchte auf Grund seiner Informationen ein klares Bild zu geben. Als er am anderen Morgen ins Amt kam, herrschte dort furchtbare Aufregung.

Keitel habe verlangt zu erfahren, wer diesen unglaublichen Bericht gemacht hätte. So etwas könne er doch „dem Führer nicht vorlegen". Dieser würde toben. Der Bericht sei umzuschreiben und „rosig zu färben". Mein Mann, den ich mittags traf, war ausser sich, hatte sich aber fügen müssen und sagte mir, nun gebe es für ihn nur noch eines, nämlich die Arbeit für den Umsturz.

An dieser Stelle möchte ich noch bemerken, dass mein Mann sehr lang absolut gegen ein Attentat war. Nicht aus religiösen Hemmungen, sondern weil er die Ansicht vertrat, dass Hitler damit unter Umständen zum Märtyrer werden könne. Er hätte gehofft, Hitler gefangen nehmen zu können und dann vor ein Kriegsgericht zu stellen. Selbst wenn bei dieser Gefangennahme Hitler umkäme, müsste man eine Gerichtverhandlung gegen ihn abhalten. Im Mai 1944 war mein Mann sehr deprimiert und äusserte mir gegenüber, es werde zu viel geredet, aber zu wenig getan.

Aufgabengebiet von Z.B. um eine aus dem Rahmen des Amtes fallende Sonderorganisation handeln könne, ist mir nie gekommen, und ich war bis zuletzt überzeugt, auf meinem Posten eine Aufgabe des Amtes zu erfüllen. Diese Aufgabe sah ich darin, aus dem Vielerlei des einlaufenden Materials das Wichtigste herauszusuchen und an Hand des Gesamtmaterials eine möglichst klare Lagebeurteilung- entsprechend der Z.B. vorliegenden Nachrichten, inbesondere der „militärpolitischen Lage", zu geben. Ich war stets bemüht, dieses Bild völlig objektiv zu geben und glaubte mich dadurch in der Lage, die mir in diesem Kriege zugewiesene Aufgabe ganz erfüllen zu können. Gleichzeitig mit dieser Tätigkeit, d.h. durch sie, bekam ich Kenntnis von Vorgängen, die mir in ihren Auswirkungen für die Kriegsführung äusserst gefährlich erschienen und die ich mit meinem Bilde von Deutschland nicht in Einklang zu bringen vermochte. Auch der mich umgebende Personenkreis hatte das gleiche Urteil über diese Vorgänge. Dazu kam eine wachsende Sorge um den Ausgang des Krieges, bedingt durch russische Erfolge an der Ostfront und die immer klarer werdenden Kriegsvorbereitungen der USA mit all ihren Folgen. Wirtschaftliche Engpässe im Inneren ergänzten das Bild. Diese Lage wurde häufig besprochen.

In dieser Zeit — ich nehme an, Ende 1941, lernte ich Dr. Gördeler kennen und suchte ihn dann im Hospitz am Anhalter Bahnhof auf. Meine Absicht war, von ihm — wie längst vorgesehen — einen Aufsatz für die W. Bl. zu erbitten. Bei dieser Gelegenheit kamen wir auch auf die allgemeine Lage zusprechen, da ich das mir im Amte zugängliche Material durch mündliche Informationen nach Möglichkeit zu ergänzen trachtete. Gördeler äusserte sich auf Grund wirtschaftlicher Überlegungen äusserst pessimistisch. Er sah eine Katastrophe, ich glaube, in längstens drei Monaten voraus und vertrat die Ansicht, dass die Generäle etwas unternehmen müssten, um einen Systemwechsel zu erreichen. Denn seinem Urteil nach bekämpfte die Entente vor allem den Nationalsozialismus und wäre bei einem Systemwechsel ein für Deutschland tragbarer Friede zu erlangen. Wie dies Dr. Görderler im Einzelnen zum Ausdruck brachte, ist mir ebenso wie der Termin meines Besuches nicht mehr erinnerlich. [5]

---

[5] Ich glaube, dass dies stimmt, wenn auch schon früher ein Verbindung über gemeinsame Bekannte bestanden hat.

Persönlich teilte ich seine Beurteilung besserer Friedensaussichten für eine andere Regierung jedenfalls nicht, da ich überzeugt war, dass die Entente, war sie dazu erst in der Lage, jedes wie immer regierte Deutschland völlig niederringen und mit Bedingungen belegen würde, die Versailles weit in den Schatten stellen dürften. Dagegen schien es mir auch erforderlich, dass massgebende Männer, die eine ernsthaft begründete Sorge oder Kritik vertraten, dies auch — unter Einsatz ihrer ganzen Person — gegenüber ihrer vorgesetzten Stelle taten, die Spitzen der Generalität also gegenüber der obersten Führung. Dies setzte aber in diesem Falle eine einheitliche Beurteilung der weiteren Kriegsentwicklung voraus. Je mehr ich mich aber in mein Aufgabengebiet einarbeitete, desto skeptischer wurde ich gegen die Möglichkeit einer bindenden Schlussfolgerung aus einer noch so erschöpfenden Lagebeurteilung. Ich bekam dadurch auch eine ganz andere Einstellung zu Ansichten, wie sie z.b. von Gördeler ausgesprochen wurden und kam zu der Überzeugung, dass trotz alle Engpässe etc. weder Art noch Zeitpunkt eines Kriegsendes vorauszusagen wäre und jederzeit völlig unerwartete Wendungen eintreten könnten. Jede termingebundene und bestimmte Voraussage über die zukünftige Entwicklung auch auf Grund des besten Nachrichtenmaterials schien mir von da ab einfach abwegig. 6 Damit kam ich auch zu der Gewissheit, dass bezüglich der Kriegsaussichten kein *gemein*samer Schritt der höheren Generalität, der allein zu tiefgreifenden Folgen hätte

---

Gördeler sah immer einen baldigen Zusammenbruch voraus, eine Ansicht, die mein Mann nicht teilte, weshalb eine engere Zusammenarbeit nicht statt-fand.

6 Dies stimmt, wenn auch mein Mann diese seine Ansicht hier etwas für die Gestapo umgedreht hat. Bis Stalingrad war mein Mann der Ansicht, die Alliierten würden im Verfolg eines Militärputsches gegen Hitler zu Friedens-verhandlungen bereit sein, wobei er Schwierigkeiten darin sah, dass in einer Übergangszeit die russische Front gehalten werden müsste, da von dort her Gefahr drohe. Er fusste dabei wohl auf seinen ziemlich umfassenden Studien für seine Doktorarbeit. Nach Stalingrad hat mir mein Mann fast wörtlich gesagt, nun ist es wohl zu spät, um mit den Alliierten zu verhandeln. Die Lawine ist jetzt ins Rollen gekommen und das Geschehen bricht nun über uns herein. Die Alliierten haben es ja nun gar nicht mehr nötig, mit uns zu ver-handeln, selbst wenn das Regime wechselt, denn eine Niederlage ist wohl gewiss, und so werden die Alliierten lieber auf diesen Zeitpunkt warten, selbst wenn eine andere Regierung drankäme.

führen können, zu erwarten sei, weil eben zu einer einheitlichen Beurteilung dieser Aussichten gar keine Möglichkeit bestand. [7] Ein Staatsstreich einzelner Generäle schien mir aber schon gänzlich ausgeschlossen, weil dieser ein Mitwirken der Truppe voraussetzte, das meiner Ansicht nach völlig ausserhalb jeder Möglichkeit lag. Keine Formation, sowohl Offiziere wie Mannschaften, konnten m.E. dazu bewegt werden, gegen den Führer Stellung zu nehmen.

Aus diesen Gründen war ich der Meinung, dass von Seiten der Generäle während des Krieges bestimmt nichts erfolgen würde und damit den Überlegungen Goerdelers jede Voraussetzung fehle. [8] Sollte jedoch tatsächlich ein Verlust des Krieges eintreten, dann hielt ich es für möglich, dass Männern wie Gördeler und Beck die Aufgabe zufallen würde, dem dann bestimmt aufbrandenden Kommunismus nicht allein das Feld zu überlassen. Denn dass ein Kriegsverlust auch einen Wechsel des Systems zur Folge haben würde, dies schien mir nicht zu bezweifeln.

Dabei war mir persönlich bewusst, dass ein jeder einzelne alles zu tun habe, um einem Kriegsverlust entgegenzuwirken und dass sich keiner dem Vorwurf aussetzen dürfe, an seinem Platze in dieser Hinsicht etwas unterlassen zu haben. Denn ein verlorener Krieg würde derart unsagbar Schweres bringen, dass alle anderen Überlegungen daneben in den Augen der Nation vollkommen zurücktreten müssen. [9] Nur wenn der Kriegsverlust schicksalhaft, nach Einsatz aller Möglichkeiten doch eintreten sollte, schien mir eine Umgestaltung zu erwarten, deren Fragen aber bestimmt in einem solchen Falle fast zur Gänze durch den verständnis- und rücksichtslosen Willen der Sieger und nicht durch das deutsche Volk gelöst würden. [10] Immerhin interessierte es mich, dass meiner Erinnerung nach Gördeler

---

[7] Diesen Schritt hatte mein Mann wohl in den ersten Kriegsjahren erhofft, dann aber nicht mehr erwartet, da die verblüffenden Erfolge an den verschiedenen Fronten für Offiziere und Mannschaften verblendend wirken mussten.

[8] Das stimmt und war die Ansicht meines Mannes.

[9] Dies ist so aufzufassen, dass mein Mann es für ehrlos gehalten hätte, zu desertieren. Bei einer solchen Handlungsweise liegt die Grenze zwischen wirklicher Einstellung und persönlicher Feigkeit zu nahe beieinander.

[10] Die Meinung über den Ausgang eines Krieges hat bei meinem Mann auch geschwankt und äusserte er sich, dass er nicht wisse, was ärger sei: ein

damals erwähnte, ihm bekannte ehemalige Arbeitsführer wären der
Ansicht, die Arbeiterschaft würde an einem Wiederstehen der
Monarchie keinen Anstoss nehmen. Wie Goerdeler selbst über diese
Frage dachte, ist mir dabei nicht ganz klar geworden, da er die zwei
oder dreimal, die ich mit ihm zusammen war, über die schon ge-
schilderten Ansichten hinaus keinerlei Angaben machte und mir
auch nie entsprechende schriftliche Ausführungen zu lesen gab. Und
später habe ich eben Gördeler nicht mehr gesprochen, da ich in An-
betracht seiner einfach unzutreffenden Informationen und der sich
daraus ergebenden Lagebeurteilungen von mir aus keine weiteren
Begegnungen suchte. Jedenfalls glaube ich, dass er bei aller grundsätzlichen Bejahung der monarchischen Idee der Auffassung nicht
widersprach, dass bei einem Systemwechsel, der ja m.E. nur bei
Kriegsverlust eintreten konnte, eine Monarchie ganz unvorstellbar
wäre. Müsste doch sonst der Eindruck entstehen, dass die furchtbare
Not, die dann die Nation bedrücken würde, dazu gedient habe, die
Wünsche eines früheren Herrscherhauses zu befriedigen — von der
aussenpolitischen Unmöglichkeit ganz abgesehen! — 11.
Irgend einen konkreten Plan über die Herbeiführung eines System-
wechsels habe ich aber niemals von Gördeler oder von irgend einer
anderen Seite erfahren. Ich habe auch niemals in einem derartigen

---

verlorener Krieg, der nicht nur für Deutschland, sondern für die ganze Welt
unsagbar Schweres bringen müsse, weil er bis zum letzten geführt würde, oder
ein unverhoffter Sieg Deutschlands, welcher für alle Nichtnationalsozialisten
entsetzlich werden müsse.
Mein Mann war der Ansicht, dass die Situation in Deutschland aus dem
Auslande nicht zu beurteilen sei, dass auch die Emigranten kein richtiges Bild
der Lage geben könnten. Sie würden aus dem Schweren, das sie erfahren
hätten, eine furchtbare Abneigung gegen Deutschland behalten. Deutschland
würde daher von den Alliierten kein Verständnis für viele Vorgänge erwarten
dürfen. Es ist für viele schwer, sich zu widersetzen, eine Aufklärung der
breiten Masse über die furchtbaren Auswüchse des nationalsozialistischen
Systems kaum durchzuführen.
Vielleicht ist die Einstellung meines Mannes am deutlichsten zu erkennen,
dass er mir, ich glaube im Jahre 1942, sagte: es sei letzten Endes gleich, wer
siege, ob Hitler beseitigt würde oder nicht, sein furchtbares Erbe bleibe doch
in der Welt und das sei der Hass, den er gesät habe.
11 Stimmt nur bedingt, da mein Mann gerade in der Person eines geeigneten
Herrschers eine Mittelsperson zu den Alliierten zu erblicken glaubte, ohne
dabei an einen bestimmten Mann zu denken.

Zusammenhang einen Auftrag ausgeführt oder erhalten. Wie ich schon ausführte, war ich auf Grund meiner Überlegungen auch fest davon überzeugt, dass ein Schritt von Seiten der Generäle nicht erfolgen würde und glaubte deshalb an keinerlei Veränderung der Lage auf Grund innerer Vorkommnisse. Ich führe dies alles natürlich nicht an, um meinen Ansichten irgendwelche besondere Bedeutung beizumessen, sondern nur um zu zeigen, wie sehr für mich die reine Betrachtung und Beurteilung der Lage und der weiteren Entwicklung im Mittelpunkt stand, der auch m.E. alle ernsthaften Gespräche dienten, die ich während meiner Tätigkeit bei Z. führte. [12]

Von Agram aus versuchte ich auf ähnliche Weise, jene Informationen zur Lage zu erlangen, von denen ich annahm, dass sie General Glaise von Horstenau in seiner Eigenschaft als Deutscher Bevollmächtigter General interessieren würden. Ich war daher bemüht, ein möglichst umfassendes und vielseitiges Bild zu erhalten und suchte dazu alle Quellen, die mir von meiner Tätigkeit bei Z. her bekannt waren, heranzuziehen. So suchte ich z.B. auch Gehre auf, der stets über sehr gute Unterlagen zu einer Lagebeurteilung verfügte. Irgendwelche Andeutungen, die mich auf Ereignisse wie die des 20. Juli schliessen liessen, wurden mir dabei in keinem Falle gemacht. — [13].

Standartenführer Huppenkothen habe ich gebeten, ob er mich nicht selbst über die noch ungeklärten Fragen vernehmen könnte. Ich bitte dies nicht als Anmassung aufzufassen, ich glaube nur, dass ich eher Fragen nach Zusammenhängen und Persönlichkeiten beantworten kann, als Gespräche wiedergeben, an deren Inhalt ich mich einfach nicht mehr entsinne und die ich bestimmt desshalb oft unzutreffend wiedergebe. Der Grund dazu, mein ungemein schlechtes Gedächtnis, ist wirklich keine Ausflucht, sondern hat mir im Leben schon genug Schwierigkeiten bereitet. [14]

---

[12] Unrichtig! und nur für die Gestapo geschrieben!

[13] Mein Mann wurde nach Agram versetzt, da im Amt und in den befreundeten Kreisen die Befürchtung entstanden war, er sei der Gestapo unangenehm aufgefallen. General Glaise-Horstenau, der meinen Mann persönlich sehr schätzte, wollte ihn als seinen Adjudanten mitnehmen nach Agram, doch wurde er zu dem Zeitpunkt in Berlin nicht freigegeben von seinem Amt. Ein halbes Jahr später nahm ihn General Glaise dann doch nach Agram, obwohl der Posten besetzt worden war, um meinen Mann aus dem Blickfeld der Gestapo zu bringen.

[14] Unrichtig! Mein Mann war durch eine Geheimmeldung verständigt, dass

Jedenfalls bitte ich darum, mir meinen Wunsch nach persönlicher
Vernehmung durch Standartenführer Huppenkothen nicht zu ver-
übeln und mir wenigstens vor einer Weiterführung der Vernehmung
Gelegenheit zu geben, mit St. Huppenkothen kurz über diese Niederschrift zu sprechen.

(Die beiden letzten Abschnitte nahm Commissar Sonderegger in
eine Schreibmaschinenabschrift, die ich unterzeichnen musste, als
nicht zur Vernehmung gehörend, *nicht auf*. Er erklärte, sie würden
Huppenkothen im Original vorgelegt und kämen dann auch zu meinem Akt. Zeuge der Weigerung, diese Abschnitte in die Abschrift
aufzunemen, war Commissar . . .). [15]

---

er sich bereit halten solle. Er hatte mir einmal gesagt, er werde nicht unmit-
telbar dabei sein, aber innerhalb der nächsten ein bis zwei Tage nach dem
Umsturz in Berlin sein, da dort für ihn eine Verwendung vorgesehen sei.
Über die Art derselben hat er mir nichts mitgeteilt.

[15] *Bemerkungen:*
Im Sommer 1943 war mein Mann im Zusammenhang mit der Verhaftung des
Herrn von Dohnanyi im Frühjahr d. Jhrs. von Agram aus zu Verhören nach
Berlin beordert worden. Diese Verhöre fanden beim Reichskriegsgericht statt
und wurden von Oberstaatsanwalt Roeder geführt. Sie dauerten etwa drei
Tage, doch war mein Mann auf freiem Fuss. Die Verhöre waren äusserst un-
angenehm. Das Protokoll wurde unrichtig geführt, nur dem Umstand, dass
Roeder zum Essen ging und seine Sekretärin unter Anleitung meines Mannes
das Protokoll umschreiben liess, war zu danken, dass mein Mann das Protokoll
unterschrieben konnte, ohne dabei gegen seine eigene Überzeugung zu handeln.

Appendix G

ARREST LIST OF MONARCHISTS, 1939

Being a list of persons arrested in September and October, 1939 for complicity in the von Harnier Circle. This document is Appendix I to the Gestapo report, prepared by Weintz: "Die Illegale Monarchistische Bewegung in Bayern." This is followed by Appendix II in that same document which is a list of so-called "Functionaries" in that movement.

Anhang I.

VERZEICHNIS DER FESTGENOMMENEN.
(Stand: 20. Oktober 1939)

1) ABELE, Florian, geb. am 5.1.1889 in Iggingen, verw. Fräser, wohnhaft in München Wilhelm Hertzstr. 8 a/I
   Festnahme: 4.8.1939

2) ALLEKOTTE, Kurt, geb. am 14.9.1896 in München, verh. Förster, wohnhaft in Haar b. München, Forststr. 40
   Festnahme: 16.8.1939

3) ARNOLD Johann, geb. am 27.6.1900 un Kreuzholzhausen, verh. Maurerpolier, wohnhaft in Obermenzing, Adolf Wagnerstr. 10.
   Festnahme: 30.8.1939

4) BADER Johann, geb. am 17.11.1867 in Steinheim, verh. Polizeiwachtmeister a.D., wohnhaft in München, Hirschgartenallee 30
   Festnahme: 12.8.1939
   Entlassung: 12.8.1939

5) BAUBERGER Johann, geb. am 21.1.1913 in München, led. Gärtner, wohnhaft in München, Dachauerstr. 184/0
   Festnahme: 4.8.1939

6) BAUER Luitpold, geb. am 25.1.1908 in Freihung, verh. Former, wohnhaft in München, Herzog Rudolfstr. 15/0
   Festnahme: 4.8.1939

7) BERCHTENBREITER Xaver, geb. am 20.10.1887 in Hirschbach,

verh. Reichsbahnsekretär a.D., wohnhaft in Lindau i.B. Kölberweisweg 8
Festnahme: 4.8.1939
Entlassung: 15.8.1939

8) BERNHARDT Albert, geb. am 19.6.1909 in Wiesau, led. Gärtner, wohnhaft in Mitterndorf, Hs. Nr. 56
Festnahme: 30.8.1939

9) BETZ Michael, geb. am 8.5.1873 in Kinding, verh. Oberpostschaffner a.D., wohnhaft in München, Clementstr. 55/3
Festnahme: 9.10.1939
Entlassung: 11.10.1939

10) BETZ Willibald, geb. am 17.9.1912 in München, led. Architekt, wohnhaft in München, Clementstr. 55/III
Festnahme: 19.8.1939

11) BOSBACH Wilhelm, geb. am 25.1.1887 in Köln-Mühlheim, verh. Zigarrenhändler, wohnhaft in München, Augustenstr. 53/3
Festnahme: 4.8.1939
Entlassung: 2.9.1939

12) CHRAMBACH Erich, geb. am 10.12.1888 in Dresden, verh. Rittmeister a.D. und Landwirt, wohnhaft in Schalterbachhöfl, Ld. Krs. Deggendorf Nr. 53 1/3
Festnahme: 5.8.1939

13) DANNER Kaspar, geb. am 23.10.1883 in Jachenau, verh. Bauer, wohnhaft in Petern, Ld. Krs. Tölz Nr. 27
Festnahme: 29.8.1939

14) DENK Josef, geb. am 6.1.1902 in Mittenheim, led. Hilfsarbeiter, whonhaft in Oberschleissheim, Schlageterstr. 17
Festnahme: 9.8.1939

15) DENK Ludwig, geb. am 26.12.05 in Mittenheim, led. Hilfsjäger, wohnhaft in Oberscheissheim, Schlageterstr. Dorfmeisterhaus
Festnahme: 4.8.1939

16) DIRSCH Philipp, geb. am 20.2.1910 in Obermässing, led. Kupferschmied, wohnhaft in München, Schommerstr. 7
Festnahme: 8.8.1939

17) DONAUBAUER Michael, geb. am 14.1.1886 in Mändlfeld, verh. Mesner, wohnhaft in München, Reisingerstr. 23
Festnahme: 7.9.1939

18) DREHER Franz Xaver, geb. am 5.5.1905 in Schwabsoien, led. Maurermeister, wohnhaft in München, Nördl. Waldstr. 25
Festnahme: 13.8.1939

19) EBERTH Franz Xaver, geb. am 23.1.1895 in Grafing, verh. Reichsbahnbetriebswart, wohnhaft in Rimsting b. Rosenheim, Bahnhof
Festnahme: 5.8.1939

20) EWERLING Martin, geb. am 29.11.1876 in Reinheim. verh. Verbandssekretär, wohnhaft in München, Jägerstr. 30/II
Festnahme: 4.8.1939

21) FACKLER Franz Xaver, geb. am 20.10.1895 in München, gesch. kaufm. Angestellter, wohnhaft in München Schmidstr. 2/I
Festnahme: 4.8.1939

22) FAHRNER Gebhard, geb. am 21.6.1896 in Frommenhausen, verh. Schneidermeister, wohnhaft in München, Würmstr. 5
Festnahme: 4.8.1939

23) FELCH Franz, geb. am 9.5.1907 in München, verh. Filmvorführer, wohnhaft in München, Hiltenspergerstr. 45/4
Festnahme: 19.9.1939

24) FEICHTMAYER Karl, geb. am 12.11.1900 in Landsberg, verh. Techniker, wohnhaft in München, Gundelindenstrasse 7/3
Festnahme: 28.8.1939

25) FELLNER Alois, geb. am 1.8.1898 in München, led. Angestellter, wohnhaft in München, Bismarckstr. 30
Festnahme: 19.8.1939

26) FICHTL Wilhelm, geb. am 29.3.1905 in München, led. Privatlehrer, wohnhaft in München, Kurfürstenstr. 17/II
Festnahme: 14.10.1939

27) FINK Josef, geb. am 13.9.1916 in München, led. Chemigraph, wohnhaft in München, Schulstr. 46/4
Festnahme: 11.8.1939
Überstellung an das Kriegsgericht München: 19.9.1939

28) FISCHER Christoph, geb. am 30.4.1875 in Landshut, verh. Zahlmeister a.D. wohnhaft in München, Maria Wardstr. 116
Festnahme: 4.8.1939

29) FISCHER, Baul, geb. am 28.6.1880 in Scheles, verh. Mechaniker, wohnhaft in München, Ettenhüberstr. 8/0
Festnahme: 4.8.1939

30) FUCHS Alois, geb. am 18.9.1903 in Berchtesgaden, verh.

Schlossdiener, wohnhaft in Berchtesgaden, Schlossplatz 6
Festnahme: 4.8.1939

31) GAMPERL Dr. Georg, geb. am 21.4.1898 in Aresing, verh. Chemiker, wohnhaft in Kaufbeuren
Festnahme: 9.8.1939
Entlassung: 31.8.1939

32) GANGWOLF Alois, geb. am 16.11.1882 in Landshut, verh. Schreinergehilfe, wohnhaft in München, Schulstr. 44/2
Festnahme: 8.8.1939
Entlassung: 19.8.1939
Neuerliche Festnahme: 12.10.1939

33) GEDON Fridolin, geb. am 28.7.1876 in München, verh. Kunstmaler, wohnhaft in München, Franz Josefstr. 20/0
Festnahme: 12.9.1939

34) GÖTZ Martin, geb. am 19.91911 in Pforzheim, led. kathol. Geistlicher, wohnhaft in Burgkirchen
Festnahme: 24.8.1939

35) HALLINGER Michael, geb. am 2.9.1893 in Salberg, verh. Maurerpolier, wohnhaft in Berchtesgaden, Toni Kurzstr. 12
Festnahme: 27.8.1939

36) HARLANDER Andreas, geb. am 15.7.1903 in München, verh. Fliessenleger, wohnhaft in München-Obermenzing, Herzog Johannstr. 11
Festnahme: 11.8.1939

37) v. HARNIER ADOLF, geb, am 14.4.1903 in München, verh. Rechtsanwalt, wohnhaft in München, Hohenstaufenstr. 5
Festnahme: 3.8.1939

38) HEISERER Hans, geb. am 2.6.1893 in Aufkirchen, led. Metzger, wohnhaft in Schleissheim, Schlosshof 1
Festnahme: 11.8.1939

39) HEISERER Dr. Ulrich, geb. am 2.7.1904 in Aufkirchen, wohnhaft in Fürstenfeldbruck, Hindenburgstr. 20/0
Festnahme: 5.8.1939

40) HÖRL Gregor, geb. am 20.7.1903 in Ampertshausen, verh. Maurergeschäftsinhaber, wohnhaft in Schleissheim, Rotdornstr. 135 1/2
Festnahme: 15.8.1939
Entlassung: 16.8.1939

41) HÖSS Augustin, geb. am 14.9.1909 in Oberaudorf, led. kath.

Geistlicher, wohnhaft in Kolbermoor
Festnahme: 24.8.1939
42) HUBER Franz, geb. am 30.3.1895 in Fürbach, verh. Mesner,
wohnhaft in München, Antwerpenerstr. 20/0
Festnahme: 4.8.1939
43) HÜTT Benno, geb. am 19.5.1880 in Deutenhausen, verh. Bauer,
wohnhaft in Schleissheim, Schlageterstr. 15
Festnahme: 12.8.1939
44) JUNG Georg, geb. am 21.12.1882 in Aha, verh. Oberlehrer,
wohnhaft in München, Orffstr. 12/1
Festnahme: 25.9.1939
45) JUNGMANN Johann, geb. am 29.10.1887 in Unterhütte, led.
kath. Geistlicher, wohnhaft in Neufarn Nr. 121, Pfarrhof
Festnahme: 12.8.1939
45) KAIFER Albert, geb. am 25.3.1893 in Hafenhofen, verh. Geschäftsführer, wohnhaft in Augsburg-Neusäss, Gartenstr. 22f
Festnahme: 2.9.1939
47) KANZLER Rudolf, geb. am 26.2.1873 in Wasserburg, getr. leb.
Oberamtmann a.D., whonhaft in München, Orleanstr. 55/4
Festnahme: 18.9.1939
48) KIENING Karl, geb. am 6.3.1908 in München, verh. Sekretär,
wohnhaft in Feldmoching, Eibenstr. Gths.
49) KNOBLAUCH Ferdinand, geb. am 22.6.1874 in Lustadt, verh.
Geheimrat, wohnhaft in Pasing, Aubingerstr. 5
Festnahme: 1.9.1939
50) KNOTT Daniel, geb. am 8.11.1885 in Eggstätt, verh. Kaufmann, wohnhaft in Eggstätt
Festnahme: 18.8.1939
51) KORNBERGER Bruno, geb. am 4.10.1893 im Haimhausen, verh.
Baupolier, wohnhaft in München-Trudering, Kreuzerweg 2/0
Festnahme: 8.8.1939
52) KOTTER Johann, geb. am 31.12.1883 in Grasbrunn, verh. Land-
und Gastwirt, wohnhaft in Grasbrunn
Festnahme: 19.8.1939
53) KRANZ Josef, geb. am 17.3.1883 in Ganzenhausen, led, Pfarrer, wohnhaft in Schleissheim, Kirchplatz 271
Festnahme: 28.8.1939
54) KRIECHBAUM Josef, geb. am 4.3.1873 in Rankham, verh. Bauer,
wohnhaft in Eggstätt

Festnahme: 18.8.1939
Entlassung: 8.9.1939
55) Kröner Hans, geb. am 29.91896 in München, verh. Mechaniker, wohnhaft in Schleissheim, Effnerstr. 4
Festnahme: 4.8.1939
56) Landstorfer Ludwig, geb. am 22.2.1879 in Trudendorf, verh. Postsekretär, wohnhaft in München, Augsburgerstr. 14/1
Festnahme: 4.8.1939
57) Leichmann Adolf, geb. am 19.3.1901 in München, verh. Monteur, wohnhaft in München, Corneliusstr. 18/0
Festnahme: 24.8.1939
58) Link Karl, geb. am 27.10.1872 in Grossheubach, verh. Kaminkehrermeister, wohnhaft in München, Mannheimerstr. 12/0
Festnahme: 20.8.1939
59) Lorenz Sebastian, geb. am 10.1.1894 in Welnzach, verh. Gastwirt, wohnhaft in Schledorf, Nr. 50
Festnahme: 29.8.1939
60) Lotter Konrad, geb. am 7.4.1889 in Nürnberg, verh. Feinmechaniker, wohnhaft in Unterbrunn Nr. 52
Festnahme: 5.10.1939
Entlassung: 6.10.1939
61) Maier Franz Xaver, geb. am 16.12.1891 in Erding, verh. Gastwirt, wohnhaft in Erding, Kordohnhausstr. 1
Festnahme: 7.9.1939
62) Marey Max, geb. am 17.9.1894 in Rosenheim, verh. Messerschmied, wohnhaft in Rosenheim
Festnahme: 18.8.1939
Entlassung: 1.9.1939
63) Messmer Eduard, geb. am 7.2.1907 in Saarbrücken, verh. Bankbeamter, wohnhaft in München, Tettenbachstr. 12/2
Festnahme: 14.10.1939
63) Naegele Richard, geb. am 22.3.1894 in Bieringen, eld. kathol. Stadtpfarrer, wohnhaft in München, Dom Pedrostr. 39
Festnahme: 13.8.1939
65) Niederbuchner Johann, geb. am 25.11.1877 in St. Georgen, verh. Sägewerks- und Mühlenbesitzer, wohnhaft in St. Georgen, Hs. Nr. 74
Festnahme: 9.9.1939

Entlassung: 26.9.1939
66) NOLL Leonhard, geb. am 18.4.1893 in München, verh. Kaufmann, wohnhaft in München, Nymphenbürgerstr. 109
67) NÖPL Josef, geb. am 25.1.1884 in Jandelsbrunn, led. Leinenfabrikant, wohnhaft in Wagscheid;
Festnahme: 21.8.1939
68) NUTZINGER Anton, geb. am 3.4.1909 in München, led. Büroangestellter, wohnhaft in München, Nymphenburgerstr. 203/0
Festnahme: 11.8.1939
69) OSTERMAIER Josef, geb. am 27.12.1907 in München, verh. Maschinenbauer, wohnhaft in München, Zielstattstr. 55/1
Festnahme: 4.8.1939
70) PERZL Josef, geb. am 5.2.1909 in Gurnobach, led. Landwirt, wohnhaft in München, Maria Wardstr. 30/0
Festnahme: 10.8.1939
71) PFAFFINGER Josef, geb. am 22.3.1890 in Bernau, verh. Spinnereiarbeiter und Gütler, wohnhaft in Kolbermoor, Staatstr. 8
Festnahme: 19.8.1939
72) PFLÜGER Bruno, geb. am 13.5.1914 in München, led. Theologiestudent, wohnhaft in München, Sailerstr. 28/1
Festnahme: 4.8.1939
73) PFLÜGER Ernst, geb. am 5.3.1903 in München, led. Uhrmacher, wohnhaft in München, Sailerstr. 28/I
Festnahme: 4.8.1939
74) PFLÜGER Friedrich, geb. am 17.6.1900 in München, verh. Opernsänger, wohnhaft in München, Kuglmüllerstr. 22/0
Festnahme: 4.8.1939
Entlassung: 19.8.1939
75) PFLÜGER Heinrich, geb. am 4.6.1908 in München, led. Elektromonteur, wohnhaft in München, Sailerstr. 28/I
Festnahme: 4.8.1939
76) PFLÜGER Karl jun., geb. am 16.11.1901 in München, led. Ordenspriester, wohnhaft in Köln, Stolkgasse 6
Festnahme: 29.9.1939
77) PFLÜGER Karl sen., geb. am 31.1.1869 in Rottweil, verh. Kaufmann, wohnhaft in München, Sailerstr. 28/I
Festnahme: 4.8.1939
Entlassung: 31.8.1939

78) PFLÜGER Luitpold, geb. am 3.6.1912 in München, led. Kooperator, wohnhaft in Neiche b. Indersdorf
Festnahme: 7.8.1939

79) PFLÜGER Wilhelm, geb. am 9.3.1906 in München, led. kath. Geistlicher, wohnhaft in Goldach b. Erding Nr. 95
Festnahme: 5.8.1939

80) PFNÜR Anton, geb. am 28.5.1890 in Salzburg, verh. Bahnhofschaffner, wohnhaft in Schwöbeck am Königsee
Festnahme: 27.8.1939

81) PLETZER Max, geb. am 9.5.1885 in München, verh. Malermeister, wohnhaft in Schleissheim Nr. 170
Festnahme: 15.8.1939
Entlassung: 16.8.1939

82) PONGRATZ Josef, geb. am 27.2.1899 in Berbing, verh. Steinmetz, wohnhaft in München, Heubergstr. 14/0
Festnahme: 4.8.1939

83) PRENNER Nikolaus, geb. am 18.11.1884 in Altersham, verh. Bauer, wohnhaft in Altersham
Festnahme: 12.10.1939

84) PRESTEL Johann, geb. am 27.6.1913 in München, verh. Mauergehilfe, wohnhaft in München, Entenbachstr. 2/0
Festnahme: 4.8.1939

85) PURZER Andreas, geb. am 20.3.1907 in Lustheim verh. Landwirt, wohnhaft in Lustheim Nr. 35
Festnahme: 11.8.1939
Entlassung: 22.8.1939

86) PÜSCHEL Adolf, geb. am 20.3.1896 in München, verh. Vertreter, wohnhaft in München, Antwerpenerstr. 29/0
Festnahme: 19.8.1939

87) RAMSAUER Albert, geb. am 5.5.1896 in Ebenrind, verh. Melker, wohnhaft in Schleissheim, Staatsgut
Festnahme: 4.8.1939

88) RANK Josef, geb. am 27.5.1895 in Miesbach, verh. Bauer, wohnhaft in Gasse b. Gmund Nr. 133
Festnahme: 4.8.1939

89) REINDL Ludwig, geb. am 25.3.1891 in Hohenkemnath, getr. lebend Betriebleiter, wohnhaft in München, Schäftlarnstr. 166/0
Festnahme: 4.8.1939

90) RITTER Wilhelm, geb. am 13.4.1888 in Ingelstadt, verw. Geschäftsführer, wohnhaft in München, Olgastr. 6/0
Festnahme: 18.8.1939

91) RITTHALER Anton, geb. am 22.4.1904 in München, led. Schriftsteller, wohnhaft in München, Clemensstr. 22/III
Festnahme: 19.9.1939
Entlassung: 20.9.1939

92) RUHL Heinrich, geb. am 23.6.1871 in Bauerschwend, verh. Versicherungsdirektor a.D., wohnhaft in München, Jakob Klarstr. 10/III
Festnahme: 26.9.1939
Entlassung: 28.9.1939

93) SCHLAMMER Jakob, geb. am 30.12.1912 in München, led. Gärtner, wohnhaft in München-Moosach, Gärtnerstr. 2/I
Festnahm: 18.8.1939

94) SCHMAUS Josef, geb. am 8.11.1882 in Neukelheim, verh. Angestelltenrentner, wohnhaft in München, Ismaningerstr. 64/I
Festnahme: 4.8.1939
Entlassung: 10.8.1939

95) SCHMID Johann, geb. am 29.9.1894 in Viehbach, verh. Zimmerer, wohnhaft in Lohhof, Ingolstädterstr. 5 1/2
Festnahme: 11.8.1939

96) SCHMID Josef, geb. am 5.4.1911 in Weilheim, verh. Elektromeister, wohnhaft in München, Damaschkestr. 5
Festnahme: 4.8.1939

97) SCHUSTER Franz, geb. am 10.1.1905 in München, verh. Gärtner, wohnhaft in München, Nederlingerstr. 74a
Festnahme: 11.8.1939

98) SCHUSTER Josef, geb. am 7.3.1890 in Oberlindhart, verh. Reichsbahnlokführer, wohnhaft in München, Cammerloherstr. 71/0

99) SCHUSTER Karl, geb. am 13.3.1905 in München, led. Benefiziat, wohnhaft in München, Kenedystr. 1/I
Festnahme: 12.8.1939

100) SENGER Karl Oskar, geb. am 18.8.1890 in Passau, verh. prakt. Arzt, wohnhaft in München, Briennerstr. 28a/III
Festnahme: 26.9.1939

101) SENNINGER Max, geb. am 8.3.1909 in Pasing, led. Kaplan, wohnhaft in München, Pelkovenstr. 60
Festnahme: 10.8.1939

102) SEUTTER v. Lötzen Wilhelm, geb. am 31.12.1901 in Lindau, verh. Kraftwagenführer, wohnhaft in München-Grünwald, Südl. Münchenerstr. 16
Festnahme: 4.8.1939

103) v. SIGRITZ Heinrich, geb. am 1.10.1885 in München, verh. Landwirt, wohnhaft in Reichersbeuren b. Tölz
Festnahme: 4.8.1939
Entlassung: 26.8.1939

104) SOMMER Karl, geb. am 14.11.1890 in Berchtesgaden, verh. Gärtnereigeschäftsführer, wohnhaft in Berchtesgaden, Adolf Hitlerstr. 5
Festnahme: 27.8.1939

105) STARK Johann, geb. am 20.7.1884 in Oberheid, verh. Baumeister, wohnhaft in München, Agricolastr. 57
Festnahme: 6.9.1939

106) v. STENGEL Margarete, geb. am 10.2.1898 in München, led. Bildhauerin, wohnhaft in München, Glückstr. 10/4
Festnahme: 19.8.1939
Entlassung: 25.8.1939
Neuerliche Festnahme: 7.9.1939

107) STIEGLER Heinrich, geb. am 3.11.1881 in Rieden, verh. Schreinergehilfe, wohnhaft in München, Trappentreustr. 34/III
Festnahme: 4.8.1939
Entlassung: 11.8.1939

108) STRASSER Hans, geb. am 11.6.1900 in Aufham, verh. Bauunternehmer, wohnhaft in Eggstätt
Festnahme: 18.8.1939

109) STÜRMANN Dr. Josef, geb. am 6.8.1906 in Münster i. Westf., led. Bankangestellter, wohnhaft in München, Ohmstr. 10/2
Festnahme: 4.8.1939

110) UTZ Georg, geb. am 9.7.1876 in Arnsdorf, verh. Behördenangestellter, wohnhaft in München, Friedrichstr. 31
Festnahme: 18.8.1939

111) VOGL Josef, geb. am 14.6.1885 in Wies, verh. Fräser, wohnhaft in Mitterdarching
Festnahme: 18.8.1939

112) VOGL Lorenz, geb. am 17.4.1901 in München, verh. Kaufmann, wohnhaft in München, Baldurstr. 79/0
Festnahme: 11.8.1939

113) VAAS Sebastian jun., geb. am 7.9.1902 in Bürstling, verh. Bote, wohnhaft in Schliersee.
Festnahme: 18.8.1939

114) VAAS Sebastian sen., geb. am 16.1.1877 in Mitterharthausen, verh. Bergmann, wohnhaft in Hausham, Kiesbacherstr. 23
Festnahme: 7.9.1939

115) WEBER Adolf, geb. am 5.8.1875 in Hohenwart, verh. Seifenhändler, wohnhaft in München, Luisenstr. 45/0
Festnahme: 4.8.1939

116) WEINZIERL Peter, geb. am 3.1.1890 in Weindfing, verh. Heizer, wohnhaft in Lustheim Nr. 54
Festnahme: 11.8.1939

117) WEISS Franz, geb. am 29.11.1889 in Laufen, gesch. Schreinermeister, wohnhaft in München, Adlzreiterstr. 17/I
Festnahme: 12.8.1939

118) WEISS Heinrich, geb. am 4.7.1887 in Laufen a.S., verh. Gartenverwalter, wohnhaft in Schleissheim, Altes Schloss 1
Festnahme: 4.8.1939

119) WENDLINGER Karl, geb. am 17.11.1912 in Reichenhall, led. Hilfsarbeiter, wohnhaft in München, Trivastr. 22/0
Festnahme: 23.8.1939

120) Westenkirchner Josef, geb. am 4.12.1901 in Tann/Ndb., verh. Heizer, wohnhaft in Schleissheim, Feldmochingerstr. 2
Festnahme: 12.8.1939

121) WIEDEMANN Johann, geb. am 16.10.1899 in Kassenbeuren, verh. Schreinermeister, wohnhaft in München, Werneckstr. 17
Festnahme: 18.8.1939

122) WISMETH Josef, geb. am 3.2.1900 in Schlicht, verh. Zuschneider, wohnhaft in München, Wilramstr. 61/0
Festnahme: 8.8.1939

123) WOLLSCHLAGER Benedikt, geb. am 3.2.1877 in Thonhausen, verh. Schuhmachermeister, wohnhaft in Schleissheim, Hindenburgstr. 116 1/2
Festnahme: 11.8.1939

124) ZIPPELIUS Karl Georg, geb. am 8.2.1889 in München, verh. Maler, wohnhaft in München, Schulstr. 6/4
Festnahme: 4.8.1939
125) ZOTT Josef, geb. am 16.3.1901 in München, verh. stadt. Bauaufseher, wohnhaft in München, Geroltstr. 24/I
Festnahme: 4.8.1939

Anhang II.

VERZEICHNIS DER FUNKTIONÄRE

(Stand: 1. August 1939)

I. Landesleitung

1) Landesleiter: Adolf Frhr. von Harnier
2) Mitglieder der Landesleitung: a) Josef Zott, b) Franz X. Fackler, c) Wilhelm Seutter v. Lötzen

II. Hauptkreisleitungen.

1) Hauptkreisleiter von München-Oberbayern: Josef Zott
2) Hauptkreisleiter von Niederbayern: Erich Chrambach
3) Hauptkreisleiter von Schwaben: Albert Kaifer

III. Kreisleitungen.

1) Krieslieter von München: Josef Zott
Stellvertreter: Franz Xaver Fackler
2) Kreisleiter von Oberbayern: Wilhelm Seutter v. Lötzen

IV. Hauptbezirksleitungen.

1) Hauptbezirksleiter von München-Ost: Michael Fischer
Stellvertreter: Josef Pongratz
2) Hauptbezirksleiter von München-Süd: Ed. Angermeier
Stellvertreter: Josef Ostermeier
3) Hauptbezirksleiter von München-West: Gebhard Fahrner
Stellvertreter: Joh. Bauberger
4) Hauptbezirksleiter von München-Nord: Heinrich Pflüger
Stellvertreter: Florian Abele
5) Hauptbezirksleiter von München-Mitte: Philipp Dirsch

V. Bezirksleitungen.

1) Bezirksleiter von München-Neuhausen: Karl Zippelius
2) Berirksleiter von München-Thalkirchen: Ludwig Reindl
3) Bezirksleiter des Chiemgaues: Franz Xaver Eberth

VI. Ortsgruppenleitungen.

1) Ortsgruppenleiter von Schleissheim: Hans Kröner
   Stellvertreter: Albert Ramsauer
2) Ortsgruppenleiter von München-Schwabing: Fl. Abele
3) Ortsgruppenleiter von Berchtesgaden: Alois Fuchs

VII. Zellenleitungen.

1) Zellenleiter von München-Moesach: Johann Bauberger
2) Zellenleiter von München-Schwabing: a) Franz Huber, b) Karl Feichtmayer

VIII. Stützpunktleitungen.

1) Burgkirchen: Martin Götz
2) Eggstätt: Daniel Knott
3) Fürstenfeldbruch: Dr. Ulrich Heiserer
4) Gmund a. Tegernsee: Josef Rank
5) Goldach b. Freising: Wilhelm Pflüger
6) Grasbrunn b. München: Johann Kotter
7) Haar b. München: Kurt Allekotte
8) Kolbermoor: Josef Pfaffinger
9) Langgries: Otto Fischer
10) Lohhof: Johann Schmid
10) Mitterdarching: Josef Vogl
12) München-Pasing: Ferdinand Knoblauch
13) München-Trudering: Josef Schmid
14) Neufahrn: Johann Jungmann
15) Passau: Bruno Pflüger
16) Petern: Kaspar Danner
17) Schlehdorf: Sebastian Lorenz
18) Schliersee: Sebastian Vaas jun.
19) Wegscheid: Josef Wöpl

Appendix H

ADOLF FREIHERR VON HARNIER'S REPLY TO THE PROSECUTION

Being Baron von Harnier's reply to the brief of the prosecution, dated, March 13, 1944.

Adolf Freiherr von Harnier   München, 5.5.1944.
Rechtsanwalt

Betrifft: Harnier u.A. wegen Vorbereitung zum Hochverrat u.a.
7 J 32/44.

Die Anklage des Oberreichsanwalts vom 13.3.1944 gibt mir Veranlassung zu der folgenden Erwiderung:

A. *Allgemeines zu meiner Person.*

„Ich bin Untertan der Krone Bayern und deshalb meinem König und Vaterland zu bedingungsloser Treue verpflichtet. Daran hat die Revolution von 1918 so wenig geändert wie die Gesamtheit der auf sie gefolgten staatsrechtlichen Erscheinungen" (Rede des Kard. v. Faulhaber auf dem Katholikentag München 1921).

Trotz der Widerrechtlichkeit der Revolution von 1918 und ihrer tatsächlichen Erfolge bin ich als Staatsbürger der Obrigkeit zu Gehorsam verpflichtet, die effektiv Gewalt über mich hat; diese tatsächliche, organisierte, legale Staatsordnung stellt zwar nur ein provisorisches, vorübergehendes Surrogat minderen Rechtes im Verhältnis zur allein rechtmässigen und nur in ihrer tatsächlichen Wirksamkeit gestörten Staatsordnung dar, doch bin ich als Privatmann wegen der auf dem christlichen Sittengesetz beruhenden Gehorsamspflicht nicht befugt, eigenmächtig und im Widerspruch zu bestehenden Gesetzen, etwa gar durch Gewaltanwendung staatsrechtliche Veränderungen, selbst solche in Richtung auf die Wiederherstellung der legitimen Staatsordnung, herbeizuführen.

Damit scheidet für mich als überzeugten Katholiken der blosse Gedanke an irgendwelche illegale Handlung und gar an Hochverrat aus dem Bereich der Möglichkeiten begrifflich aus.

Ich bin dagegen auf Grund natürlichen Menschenrechtes als erwachsener und steuerzahlender Staatsbürger unter jedwedem staatsrechtlichen Zustand der öffentlichen Verhältnisse meines Vaterlandes befugt, ja moralisch sogar verpflichtet, an den letzteren Interesse und entsprechend meinen individuellen Fähigkeiten tätigen Anteil zu nehmen. Solcher Betätigung kann nur im Einzelfall durch Verfassung und sonstige Gesetzgebung eine praktische, nie aber eine grundsätzliche, das Recht als ein Ganzes umfassende Grenze gesetzt werden.

Die Gesetzeslage in Deutschland nach 1933 hat sehr einschneidende Beschränkungen der politischen Betätigungs-Möglichkeiten der Staatsbürger gebracht; sie hat dieselben aber selbst in praktischer Beziehung nicht bei weitem völlig und noch viel weniger theoretisch aufgehoben. Insbesondere sind auch seit 1933 mannigfache Volksabstimmungen erfolgt, in denen der Regierung Billigung oder Missbilligung einzelner politischer Akte, ihrer Politik in cumulo und sogar ihres eigenen Bestandes auszusprechen war.

Ergibt somit die Untersuchung, dass einerseits von Seiten der derzeitigen Staatsgewalt das politische Aktivitätsrecht der Staatsbürger nicht aufgehoben sein kann, so steht andererseits der obigen Ausführung über die Folgen des Naturrechts und des christlichen Sittengesetzes entsprechend fest, dass auch der dem rechtmässigen Herrscher zur Treue verbundene Untertan trotz Unterbrechung in der Wirksamkeit der Herscher-Rechte unter den jeweils obwaltenden Umständen grundsätzlich staatsrechtliche Pflichten anerkennen und Rechte ausüben darf. Dies wurde zur Behebung jeglicher Zweifel und Gewissenskonflikte ausdrücklich in dem Eidesentbindungs-Manifest Weiland König Ludwigs III vom 13.11.1918 ausgesprochen.

Dieser Auffassung hat das tatsächliche Verhalten aller in Betracht kommenden Personen unseres öffentlichen Lebens seit 1918 entsprochen; ich verweise insbesondere darauf, dass in Bayern seit dem November 1918 die Staatsgewalt mit der einzigen Ausnahme des kurz im Amt gewesenen Ministerpräsidenten Hoffmann ausnahmslos in Händen von erklärten königstreuen Ministerpräsidenten gelegen hat, wozu seit März 1933 auch noch die Herren General v. Epp, Ministerpräsident Siebert und weitere nationalsozialistische Amtsinhaber zu rechnen sind. Im übrigen Deutschland verweise ich insbesondere auf Haltung und Handlung des verstorbenen Feldmarschalls von Hindenburg, dessen grundsätzliche *und* tatsächliche Einstellung — mutatis mutandis — grundsätzlich die meinige ist.

Ich bin im übrigen nicht nur auf Grund meiner Untertanenpflicht treuer Diener meines Königs und Vaterlandes, sondern ich bin auch in akademisch-staatsphilosophischer Beziehung überzeugter Monarchist; damit spreche ich aus, dass ich — jenseits meiner Person und meines Verhältnisses zu meinem bayerischen und deutschen Vaterland — die monarchistische Staatsordnung für die glücklichste aller bisher in der Geschichte der Menschheit bekannt gewordenen Staatseinrichtungen halte.

B. *Allgemeines zur Vorgeschichte.*

Auf Grund meines seit jeher bestehenden politischen Interesses an Politik habe ich schon frühzeitig am öffentlichen Geschehen Anteil genommen und vielfältige Gelegenheit gehabt, Erfahrungen auf diesem Gebiet zu sammeln, so war ich z.b. im [Jahre] 1922 nach der Ermordung Rathenau's persönlicher Begleiter des mir verwandschaftlich verbundenen, 1924 verunglückten Vize-Reichskanzler's Dr. Helfferich in Berlin, der damals im Mittelpunkt der Nachkriegspolitik stand, so habe ich 1928 meinen Aufenthalt in London genommen und dort eine staats- und völkerrechtliche Dissertation vorbereitet und so habe ich in den folgenden Jahren im Kreis der von der Krone berufenen Bevollmächtigten meinem Vaterland zu dienen begonnen. Ausser der Mitarbeit bei der Arbeitsstelle für konservatives Schrifttum habe ich mich gelegentlichen Dienstleistungen bei dem Präsidenten des Heimat- u. Königsbundes, Reichsrat Freiherrn zu Guttenberg, gewidmet; vor allem aber habe ich an vielfachen Beratungen teilgenommen, die fortdauernd stattfanden und der Unterrichtung der politischen Ratgeber der Krone dienten. Der Heimat- u. Königsbund, eine ganz eigenmächtige Gründung des verstorbenen Genossenschafts-Organisators Geheimrat Heim, war kaum eine wirkliche Organisation, dagegen in den letzten Jahren aus ungeeigneten Händen auf Weisung der Krone in jene des Freiherrn zu Guttenberg übergegangen und diente im Wesentlichen nur als Unterlage für die Veranstaltung von Volksversammlungen und anderen politischen Demonstrationen, zu denen die sonstigen, wirklich durchgebildeten Organisationen der sog. Vereinigten Vaterländischen Verbände Bayern's (Kriegerbund, Stahlhelm usw.) das Massenaufgebot stellten.

Sehr früh vor dem Ende der parlamentarisch-demokratischen Phase der Republik erkannte die Krone Umfang und Dynamik der nationalsozialistischen Bewegung und entschloss sie sich, auch dieser politischen Folge-Erscheinung des Umsturzes von 1918 noch ihren ungehinderten Verlauf zu lassen. Auf Weisung der Krone ist deshalb der Heimat- u. Königsbund im Sommer 1933 freiwillig aufgelöst worden. In gleicher Linie lag, dass auch die Krone selbst als äusseres Zeichen ihrer Politik fairer Chance für das neue Regime ihren Kabinett-Chef verabschiedete und von einer Neu-Ernennung absah. In gleicher Linie lag, was den Heimat- u. Königsbund betraf, dass sich die Mitglieder seiner bisherigen Leitung in das Privat- oder Berufsleben zurückzogen und einander gegenseitig nicht mehr aufsuchten, sondern ausgesprochen mieden, um ja keinen Zweifel darüber aufkommen zu lassen, dass dem neuen Regime ungehindert freier Lauf eingeräumt werde. So hat sich der stv. Landesleiter Generalmajor F. Feser wieder in den Dienst der Wehrmacht zurückbegeben und einen Lehrauftrag an der Universität Würzburg für wehrpolitische Fragen übernommen, so hat sich der Geschäftsleiter Major Neuffer völlig zurückgezogen, um bald zu sterben, so hat der Generalsekretär Dr. Graf eine Stellung in einem Versicherungsunternehmen angenommen und so haben die verschiedenen Kreisleiter in den Provinzen meiner Beobachtung nach jede Beziehung untereinander abgebrochen.

Allein Baron Guttenberg hat im Auftrag der Krone noch weiter Beziehungen zu politischen Seiten unterhalten und zwar solchen des neuen Reg'me's. Seine Verbindung zur SA-Führung hat ihm auch nach dem 30.6.1934 Verhaftung, Untersuchung und bedingungslose Rechtfertigung seiner Rolle gebracht. Er wurde nach ganz kurzer Zeit bereits wieder in Freiheit entlassen.

Ich selbst habe nur noch ganz selten politische Freunde meines Standes gesehen. Vielmehr habe ich von Januar 1933 bis Weihnachten 1936 vollkommen zurückgezogen in der Oberpfalz gelebt. Meine Enttäuschung über die charakterliche Haltung sehr vieler naher und nächster Gesinnungsfreunde, Verwandter, Angehöriger usw. meines Geburts- und Berufs-Standes war so gross, dass ich den Gedanken, mich jemals mehr einer öffentlichen Aufgabe zu widmen, damals aufgegeben habe. Ich habe auch in der Oberpfalz, meiner engeren Heimat, in der ich als Mitglied des Kreisausschusses des Heimat- u. Königsbundes eine sehr grosse Zahl politisch interessierter Menschen kenne, keinerlei politische Beziehung mehr aufrechterhalten, am wenigsten die Mitglieder des aufgelösten Heimat- u. Königsbundes irgendwie aufgesucht, zusammengefasst oder wie immer organisiert.

Die Entfaltung irgendwelcher Bestrebungen in Richtung der Wie-

derherstellung der rechtmässigen Staatsordnung, soweit solche Bestrebungen ausserhalb der nationalsozialistischen Partei Platz gegriffen
hätten, hätte, mindestens damals, die Absichten der Krone, wie ich
wusste, gestört; ich hätte sie schon aus diesem Grund für unerlaubt
gehalten und unterlassen. Ich erinnere hier daran, dass damals ausgesprochene Legitimisten in erheblicher Zahl in der vordersten Linie
der Politik standen und keinerlei Hehl aus ihren Absichten bezüglich
der endgültigen Staatsordnung machten: FM v. Hindenburg. Gö-
ring, Röhm, Epp, Siebert, Graf Quadt.

Es bestand kein theoretischer Grund, dem nationalsozialistischen
Regime wegen seiner programmatischen Antecedentien mit mehr
Voreingenommenheit vom legitimistischen Standpunkt aus gegenüber-
zustehen oder entgegen zu treten als dem parlamentarisch-demokratischen, denn per Saldo waren hier wie dort annähernd gleich viele
und entwicklungsfähige Kräfte zugunsten der Restoration vorhanden
und am Werk.

In der Praxis hat sich das Bild allerdings ziemlich bald verschoben,
indem sich sämtliche „Kräfte" in der nationalsozialistischen Partei als
völlig bedeutungslos gegenüber der allein entscheidenden, nichts weniger als legitimistischen Person des Partei-Führers erwiesen und
indem sich zu dem Übergang von der Neutralität in der Staatsord-
nungsfrage zur Gegnerschaft gegenüber der Restauration noch Erscheinungen gesellten, die angesichts ihrer Zahl und Schwere unmöglich mehr anders denn als Korruption bezeichnet werden können —
Korruption, die vor allem deshalb jedem Denkenden als schwerer
Schaden erscheinen musste, weil ihren einzelnen Fällen von Seiten
der Führung zugestandenermassen nicht gesteuert wurde und wird.
Diese Begleiterscheinung hat von Haus aus gar nichts mit dem
Nationalsozialismus als solchem zu tun; vielmehr hatte ja gerade
dieser die sittliche Erneuerung des Staates nach seiner Schädigung
durch die Parlaments-Wirtschaft auf seine Fahnen geschrieben gehabt. Umso krasser wirkte dann das in der Praxis hervortretende
Gegenteil. Vielleicht habe ich in meiner Berufstätigkeit ausser meinen
Beobachtungen als Privatmann mit einem besonderen Mass an solchen
Unerfreulichkeiten zu tun gehabt; jedenfalls erscheint mir dieser moralische Schaden, den unser Volk und Staat nehmen, als ein Verhängnis schwerster Art für Bestand und Zukunft Deutschlands und ich
habe nichts, am wenigsten Gefahr für meine Person, gescheut, wo es
galt oder möglich war, dem Recht Anwalt zu sein.

Einer der unglaublichsten Fälle, der noch dazu von der nationalsozialistischen bayer. Staatsregierung Epp-Siebert in voller Öffent-
lichkeit durch die Presse behandelt worden ist, ist der heute noch
nicht erledigte Fall des gewesenen Landesbauernführers Staatssekre-
tärs Luber und seiner passiven Bestechung zum Schaden der Staatskasse. Bekannt ist ferner, wie, bsonders in Kreisen kleiner Leute,
die gleich Pilzen aus dem Boden schiessenden „Gauleiter-Villen"
Empörung erzeugt haben. In München, wo die jetzigen Amtsinhaber
noch aus früherer Zeit weiten Bevölkerungskreisen in bescheidenster
Aufmachung in Erinnerung sind, haben vor allem die Villen Ley,
Hess, Fiehler, ferner Frick, Bouhler usw. böses Blut gemacht.

Es ist also neben der immer schärfer gewordenen politischen Ge-
gensätzlichkeit besonders diese, an sich mit keinem besondern politischen Programm notwendig verbundene Begleiterscheinung des
neuen Systems, die die Gegensätze bitter hat werden lassen.

Diese Verhältnisse in der öffentlichen Stimmung habe ich ange-
troffen, als ich im Winter 1936/7 nach München übersiedelt bin.

C. *Allgemeines zur politischen Frage.*

Mit den unter A und B bezeichneten staatsrechtlichen Massgaben
habe ich den öffentlichen Verhältnissen in Deutschland auch seit
1918 lebhaftes Interesse entgegengebracht. Davon ist jedoch jeglicher
Fanatismus im abträglichen Wortsinn, wie er in der Anklageschrift
mir in meinem Verhältnis zum Nationalsozialismus unterschoben wird,
zu unterscheiden. Es bedarf wohl kaum erst der Versicherung, dass
kein ausgebildeter Jurist auf Gebieten, die diejenigen seiner besonderen Berufsausbildung sind, von Fanatismus besessen ist. Uner-
schütterliche Kühle und Sachlichkeit sind ihm vom ersten Tag seiner
theoretischen und praktischen Studien an zur Richtschnur beruflichen
und sogar ausserberuflichen Daseins geworden.

Ich habe nach 1918 keinerlei engere Beziehung oder gar Bindung
zu einer politischen Partei oder Organisation auf mich genommen,
weil mir trotz der Fülle wohllautender Programme keine Gewähr
dafür geboten zu werden schien, dass dem allerersten und wichtigsten
politischen Erfordernis, dem Recht, Genüge getan werde. In den
Heimat- u. Königsbund bin ich erst eingetreten und in ihm habe
ich erst Mitarbeit geleistet, als dies auf Weisung der Krone unbedenklich und erwünscht war.

Von den Parteien habe ich der Bayer. Volkspartei am nächsten gestanden; doch habe ich trotz der grossen Zahl persönlicher Beziehungen keine weitere Annäherung gesucht, weil sie ganz besonders ihre programmatische Loyalität gegenüber der Krone in der Praxis verleugnet hat.

Je länger das demokratisch-parlamentarische Fiasko dauerte und seinem sicheren Ende zustrebte, desto fester begründete sich meine Meinung, dass diese Ausübung der öffentlichen Gewalt, selbst wenn sie noch einmal unter rechtmässiger Staatsordnung versucht werden wollte, eine in Deutschland undurchführbare Regierungsweise darstelle; der deutsche Volks-Charakter eignet sich hierfür nicht. Ich halte eine andere Art der Anteilnahme des regierten Volkes an der Regierung für erforderlich. Ich habe deshalb lang vor 1933 bereits die Auflösung der politischen Parteien Deutschlands herbeigewünscht — allerdings ausnahmslos aller Parteien, auch der nationalsozialistischen. In der Verurteilung des Parteien-Systems alter Prägung bin ich also gleiches Zieles wie der Nationalsozialismus gewesen und habe die Erreichung dieses Zieles, wenn auch nicht ihre Methode, vorbehaltlos begrüsst. Alle Behauptungen, die sinngemäss mich in Gegensatz dazu bringen wollen, sind deshalb widersinnig und schon aus diesem Grund unrichtig.

Mein Widerspruch richtet sich aber auch gegen jegliche Art von Staat im Staat, die zur Privilegierung ausgewählter Menschenkreise oder politischer Tendenzen im öffentlichen Leben führt. Ich bin deshalb nicht nur Gegner des jetzigen Ein-Parteien-Systems und insoweit des Nationalsozialismus, sondern auch jeder sonstigen politischen Organisations-Bildung. So wenig ich demgemäss in Abrede stelle, in diesem Fragenbereich ein offener Gegner des Nationalsozialismus „in allen (gesetzlichen) Züchten und Ehren" zu sein, so sehr bin ich aus grundsätzlichster Überzeugung heraus unfähig (im ideellen Sinn), irgendwelche politische Organisationen zu gründen, zu unterstützen oder in irgendwelchem sonstigen Sinn zu begünstigen. Der diesbezügliche Vorwurf ist also schon deshalb und an sich vollendeter Widersinn.

In den Bereichen der Kulturpolitik befinde ich mich als Christ und Katholik in dem naturgegebenen Gegensatz zur Praxis des neuen Systems, soweit sie die kirchlichen Angelegenheiten betrifft. Auch in anderen Beziehungen, vor allem in Dingen der Freiheit des Geisteslebens, befinde ich mich in scharfem Gegensatz zu den Massnahmen des neuen Regime's.

In Sachen der Wehrpolitik habe ich die Wiederaufrichtung einer allein durch Deutschland bestimmten und begrenzten Wehrmacht vorbehaltlos begrüsst; hier stimme ich mit den Strebungen des Nationalsozialismus durchaus überein. Meine Stellungnahme zu den wenigen vorverzeichneten Fragen-Komplexen zeigt beispielhalber, dass ich dem nationalsozialistischen Regime so wenig voreingenommen gegenübergestanden habe und stehe wie dem vergangenen demokratischen und vollkommen grundsätzlich und sachlich mein Urteil bilde. Da ich in nicht wenigen Fragen-Bereichen der nationalsozialistischen Politik die Zustimmung nicht versagen kann, richtet sich der Vorwurf der Anklage von selbst, ich hätte im Sinne der einschlägigen Bestimmungen des Strafgesetzes aus fanatischem Hass heraus gegen das System masslos und wahrheitswidrig gehetzt, verleumdet usw.

D. *Verfahrens-Methoden der Polizei und der Anklagebehörde.*

1. Das Anklage-Material entstammt im Wesentlichen der Berichterstattung der Gestapo-Spitzl Fischer Michael (S. 22, 24, 42 der Anklageschrift) und Paulus (S. 45).

Beide Spitzl sind mir persönlich bekannt geworden; sie sind inferiorster geistiger Qualität und keinesfalls fähig, auch nur halbwegs zuverlässig Sinn und Wortlaut einer mehrstündigen Unterhaltung zahlreicher Menschen aus dem Gedächtnis wiederzugeben.

Die Spitzl haben spät Abends nach dem Auseinandergehen vom nächsten Fernsprech-Automaten aus die Staatspolizei-Leitstelle München angerufen und dem Nachtdienst-Beamten ihre sog. Berichte in die Feder (Stenogramm) diktiert. Dabei haben sie keinesfalls mehr weder Inhalt und Umfang der vielfältigen Äusserungen richtig wiedergeben, noch den einzelnen Teilnehmern zuteilen können.

Mir waren beide Spitzl von ihrem Erscheinen an als wenig erfreulich aufgefallen und ich habe sie deshalb G.s.D. so sehr gemieden, als es mir ohne auffallende Zurücksetzung möglich war. Nie habe ich mit einem der Beiden allein eine Unterhaltung geführt.

2. Nach der Verhaftung aller Beteiligten im August 1939 hat der Spitzl Fischer die Frauen einiger Verhafteter aufgesucht, sich als Angehörigen der im übrigen in Haft befindlichen Freunde ausgegeben und unter der Vorgabe, Unterstützung für mittellose Frauen und Familien Verhafteter durchführen zu wollen, Geldbeträge zu durchschnittlich fünfzig Reichsmark herausgeschwindelt. Bekannt ist

mir heute nur noch sein Besuch bei Frau Pongratz, die ich anwalt-
lich vertreten habe.

Einen überzeugenderen Beweis für den charakterlichen Unwert
dieser Kreaturen und ihres „Materials" kann man sich schlechterdings
nicht wünschen. Hierher ist übrigens zu verwerten: Goebbels, „Vom
Kaiserhof zur Reichskanzlei", 5. Aufl., Fr. Eher Nachfolger, Seite
88, Tagebuch-Eintrag v. 26.4.32 über Hochverrats-Anklage und
Spitzl-„Arbeit".

3. Über die Vernehmungen bei der Gestapo samt Begleiterschein-
ungen wird mündlich zu sprechen sein.

4. Die Anklage hätte nach Gesetz sämtliche belastende und ebenso sämtliche *ent*lastende Tatbestandsmerkmale vorzutragen; davon
ist die Anklageschrift in ihrer Tendenz, aber auch in konkreten Einzelheiten weit entfernt.

Die Anklage hat vor allem den für meine Entlastung geradezu
ausschlaggebenden Spitzlbericht über eine Zusammenkunft vom 10.
Januar 1939 glatt unterdrückt, während sie sonst sämtliche Berichte
in zeitlicher Reihenfolge wohlgeordnet bringt. Ich weiss mit Sicherheit, dass ich diesen Bericht nicht nur bei der Gestapo Dank der
Arglosigkeit des vernehmenden Beamten feststellen konnte, dass er
sodann bei meiner Vernehmung durch den Ermittlungsrichter LGR
Rehse von uns diskutiert wurde, sondern dass mindestens ich, wenn
nicht auch Rehse, ihn in das Protokoll ausdrücklich aufgenommen
haben. In den Rehse-Protokollen ist nur ein ganz kurzes Stück von
mir über meine grundsätzliche Auffassung selbst diktiert; die Stelle
über den Bericht vom 10.1.1939 lässt sich also unschwer eruieren.

Die Anklage hat ferner die mir von Vernehmungsbeamten und m.E.
auch von Rehse mehrfach erwähnte unmutige Äusserung Zott's über
mich aus etwa Ende 1938 oder Anfang 1939 unterschlagen: „Wenn
uns jetzt der Baron auch nicht mehr hergeht (ich hatte wegen beruflicher Überlastung mehrfach abgesagt), dann renn ich ihm das
Messer (einen Hirschfänger, den er zufällig zur Hand hatte) hin-
ein!"

Die Anklage hat schliesslich meine und mindestens auch Fackler's
Aussage, dass nicht nur Flugblätter von mir von vornherein sondern
nach Prüfung der gesetzlichen Verhältnisse auch die Versendung geschlossener Nachrichtenbriefe an auswärtige Gesinnungsfreunde als
nicht unbedenklich abgelehnt worden sind, vollkommen unterschlagen und die unzutreffende Behauptung aufgestellt, ein Defekt einer

Schreibmachine habe die Versendungs-Absicht nicht ausführen lassen.
Inwieweit noch in anderen Fällen die Anklageschrift dem Akten-Inhalt zuwider Behauptungen aufgestellt oder Entlastungs-Beweise unterdrückt hat, bedürfte sorgfältiger Prüfung.

E. Der Inhalt der Anklageschrift im Einzelnen.

Kapitel I. (5) Die Bemerkungen zu meinem „politischen Werdegang" sind zutreffend.

Über die Mit-Angeschuldigten weiss ich nichts, weil ich sie sämtlich nur primitiv-oberflächlich kennen gelernt habe, soweit sie mir nicht völlig unbekannt sind wie z.b. Kaplan Schuster.

Kapitel II. (7) Mit diesen Vorgängen habe ich nicht das Leiseste zu tun gehabt.

Kapitel III. (15) Von den behaupteten Beziehungen des Zott zu Kreisen der Kommunistischen Partei, seinen Fahrten in die Schweiz usw. habe ich keine Ahnung gehabt.

Es interessiert hier, dass Zott in diesen Kreisen den Spitzl Fischer (22) kennen gelernt hat, der sich mir als „Mitarbeiter" des gewaltsam geendeten Redakteurs Dr. Fritz Gerlich vom „Geraden Weg" vorgestellt hat; er wollte als betont katholisch und als Vertrauensmann des Fürsten Waldburg-Zeil gelten, der am „Geraden Weg" finanziell interessiert war. Fischer scheint von der Gestapo nach 1933 in kommunistische Kreise zur „Arbeit" vorgeschickt worden zu sein. Offiziell wollte er 1937/39 in der Nacht-Redaktion der Münchener Neusten Nachrichten beschäftigt gewesen sein.

Kapitel IV. (22) Die Darstellung ist, was mich betrifft, grundsätzlich falsch.

So wenig wie früher habe ich mich 1936/7 jemandem „angeschlossen" — am allerwenigsten diesem Kreis mir sozial beträchtlich untergeordneter Männer.

Bei meiner Übersiedlung nach München um Weihnachten 1936 hat mich Weiss, den ich bei der Baronin Stengel kennen gelernt hatte, gebeten, ich möchte mich um sie verlassene Schar loyal gesinnter ehemaliger Angehöriger der aufgelösten nationalen Verbände annehmen, da ihnen ihre „patentierten, unwandelbaren, nie wankenden Führer" auf Nimmerwiedersehen abhanden gekommen seien und sie in schmählichster Weise hätten sitzen lassen. Es handelte sich nach Weiss darum, dass ich diesen verwaisten und politisch Obdachlosgewordenen „politische Seelsorge" leisten sollte, indem ich mich

in entsprechenden Abständen mit ihnen treffen und Stand und Entwicklung der politischen Verhältnisse erläutern sollte.

Vor mir haben sich dieser Leute, die zu anständig waren, als dass
sie sich ihrer Gesinnung zuwider in die Partei-Formationen gedrängt
und dort ihren Vorteil gesucht hätten, nur noch der vormalige Stahl-
helm-Angehörige und Direktor der Handwerkskammer München,
Geheimrat Knoblauch, der vor- (44) malige Kreisleiter des Heimat-
u. Königsbundes in Niederbayern, Rittmeister Erich Chrambach (22),
mein persönlicher Freund, und endlich der Fabrikbesitzer Joseph
Nöpl (45) angenommen. Wie eng der Kontakt zwichsen Knoblauch
und der Weiss-Gruppe war, weiss ich nicht; ich habe Knoblauch
einmal auf einem Bier-Abend gesehen und kennen gelernt. Chrambach und Nöpl haben ihre Wohnsitze ausserhalb von München und
sind deshalb vor und auch während meiner Zeit in regelmässigen
Abständen, aber natürlich seltener als ich, zu Zusammenkünften gekommen.

Ich habe mich Weiss grundsätzlich bereit erklärt, mich seiner
Gruppe anzunehmen, wenn er mit die Erfüllung meiner Bedingungen
zusichern wolle:

1. Kein Teilnehmer dürfe von Seiten der Polizei politisch bean-
standet worden sein; dies verneinte Weiss ausdrücklich.

2. Er dürften keinerlei Personen-Verzeichnisse bestehen oder entstehen, da sie zu dem Verdacht führen könnten, eine Organisation
wolle im Widerspruch zu dem Parteigründungs-Verbot gebildet
werden.

3. Aus dem gleichen Grund dürfe keinerlei politisches Programm,
Ziel oder ähnliches vorhanden sein, woraus auf irgendwelche kon-
krete Absichten geschlossen werden könne.

4. Endlich dürfe zwischen den Beteiligten keine wie immer gear-
tete Verpflichtung, persönlicher, politischer oder finanzieller Natur
be- oder entstehen.

In pectore habe ich als Ergänzung zu diesen Bedingungen noch die
Vorbehalte gemacht,

5. an keiner Zusammenkunft teilzunehmen, zu welcher ich nicht
jeweils eigens gebeten würde, um nur ja nicht den Eindruck einer
„Führung", d.h. einer von mir ausgehenden Initiative, zu erwecken,

6. grundsätzlich keinerlei finanzielle, in Bayern sonst durchaus
übliche Wohltätigkeit im Rahmen der Zusammenkünfte zu üben,
um ja keinen „Freibier-Patriotismus" zu züchten.

Kapitel V. (24) Ich bin nicht „wieder"-erschienen, sondern habe

meiner Erinnerung nach um Weihnachten 1936/Neujahr 1937 zum
ersten Mal einer Gasthaus-Zusammenkunft angewohnt.

Von Tarnung war keine Rede; es wurde nur auf die entsprechende
„Distanz" von anderen Gasthaus-Besuchern gesehen, um „Heim-
tücke"-Komplikationen auszuschliessen, falls von dem einen oder
anderen Teilnehmer gelegentlich ein allzu volkstümlicher Krafts-
ausdruck gebraucht werden sollte.

(25) Über die Tätigkeit, die Weiss vor meiner Zeit entfaltet hat,
weiss ich nichts. Es ist aber ausgeschlossen, dass er Gedankengänge
entwickelt und gar politische Zukunft-Programm entwickelt hat, weil
ihm mit jeglicher Bildung auch jegliche politische Erfahrung und
ebenso die hinreichende Beherrschung der deutschen Sprache fehlt,
um sich an solche Aufgaben zu wagen. Weiss hat im Rahmen seiner
grundanständigen Gesinnung mit seinen Freunden die politischen
Verhältnisse diskutiert und die Hoffnung auf baldige Wiederher-
stellung der rechtmässigen Staatsordnung wachgehalten.

(26) Ich habe bei den Zusammenkünften, denen ich anwohnte,
soweit möglich, insbesondere also in den Wohnungen einzelner Teilnehmer, zusammenhängend über die jeweiligen politischen Verhältnisse und besondere Tagesereignisse gesprochen. Anschliessend oder
überhaupt ausschliesslich wurde von sämtlichen Beteiligten diskutiert
und wurden an mich sehr viele Fragen und Bitten um Auskünfte
gerichtet. Hierüber habe ich nach bestem Vermögen Auskunft er-
teilt. Von irgendeiner „pol. Ausrichtung einer Bewegung" war selbstverständlich keine Rede; sie war ebensowenig grundsätzlich ange-
strebt, wie sie erzielt worden ist. In sehr vielen Fällen erinnere ich
mich, dass die verschiedensten Meinungen über Diskussions-Gegen-
stände aufeinanderplatzten und bestehen blieben. Am wenigsten habe
ich irgend jemanden meine oder eine bestimmte Anschauung aufzu-
oktroyieren versucht. Allgemeine Diskussions- u. Ausgangs-Basis der
Veranstaltungen war lediglich die grundsätzliche Übereinstimmung
in der christlichen Weltanschauung und der Treue zu König und
Vaterland.

(26) Gegen die Behauptung unwahrer oder gröblicher Entstellung
von Behauptungen, gehässiger Äusserungen, Hetze usw usw verwehre
ich mich auf das Entschiedenste. Hier handelt es sich um einen systematischen Lügenfeldzug der gewerbsmässigen Spitzl, vor allem
Fischer's, deren Spitzl-Verdienst stand und fiel mit der Vorlage hinreichend pikanter Berichte; als hierzu die Möglichkeit durch unsere

Verhaftung weggefallen war, suchte und fand Fischer Ersatz durch seine Betrügereien bei den Frauen der Verhafteten, bis ihm auch dieses Handwerk durch die Polizei (wahrscheinlich discretissime, um ihn nicht als Kronzeuge zu entwerten) gelegt wurde. Die mir im Einzeln in den Mund gelegten „Greuel" bestreite ich entschieden.

Kapitel VI (29) Das Phantasie-Produkt über den „organisatorischen Aufbau" entbehrt, soweit ich in Betracht komme, jeglicher Basis. Ich habe jede Art von Organisation glatt abgelehnt und jedem Anderen angelegentlich widerraten, insbesondere dem Angesch. Zott, der einige Mal in dieser Beziehung anfragte, als er Veranstalter der Zusammenkünfte an Weiss' Stelle geworden war. Wie kategorisch ich meine Ablehnung aussprach, ergibt sich daraus, dass selbst der Spitzl Fischer nicht umhinzukönnen glaubte, in seinem Bericht vom 10.1.1939 eine (der mehreren, im Lauf der Zeit erfolgten) Aussprachen über diesen Punkt samt meiner ausdrücklichen Weigerung zu erwähnen. Es ist beschämend für den Verfasser der Anklage, dass er dieses wichtigste sämtlicher Dokumente unterschlagen hat.

Richtig ist, dass vielfach zwischen den Leuten Erörterungen stattfanden, wie sie ihre Zusammenkünfte am geeigneten instradieren könnten. Sämtliche Beteiligte waren berufstätig, in sehr bescheidenen finanziellen Verhältnissen, ohne Telephon oder ständig Anwesende (Dienstboten) in ihren Wohnungen und nicht selten mit dem Lesen und Schreiben nicht besonders vertraut; diese vielfachen Mängel haben deshalb dem jeweiligen maitre de plaisir, Weiss und nachmals Zott, die Arbeit der Verständigung über eine beabsichtigte Zusammenkunft sehr erschwert. Auch hingen meiner vagen Beobachtung nach die einzelnen Teilnehmer ursprünglich nur nach ihren jeweiligen früheren Organisationen und ohne Rücksicht auf ihre Wohngegend zusammen. Hier hat schon Weiss, vor allem aber dann Zott Wandel zu schaffen gesucht und die berüchtigte Einteilung der Stadt München und der Umgebung in verschiedene Bezirke, Kreise oder Ähnliches vorgenommen. Ich habe mehrfach diese Erörterungen mitangehört, aber nur mit halbem Ohr hingehört, weil mich das gar nicht weiter berührte. Ich habe mich nur einmal infolge eines Versehens der Veranstalter versetzt gefunden und habe daraufhin auf bessere Verständigung gedrungen, weil ich damals bereits stark beruflich in Anspruch genommen war und mir solche Zeitverluste nicht mehr erlauben konnte.

Die ungewöhnlich innige Beziehung zwischen Gross-Stadt und Land, die sich München im Gegensatz zu anderen Städten bewahrt hat, hat vorliegend zur Folge gehabt, dass der Weiss'sche Kreis auch über das Stadtgebiet auf einige Stellen Oberbayerns hinausreichte. Schleissheim mit seinen mehreren Teilnehmern fällt dabei jedoch aus, weil es als vormaliger Dienstsitz des Weiss und als Vorstadt von München nicht im gedachten Sinn als Land zu rechnen ist. Gerade die am flachen Land und fern aller Verkehrsmöglichkeit mit politisch Interessierten lebenden Menschen haben seit der Unterdrückung der Presse- und sonstigen Äusserungs-Freiheit ein besonders starkes Bedürfnis nach Fühlung und Unterrichtung gezeigt. Daraus erklärt sich die Fortdauer, nicht aber, wie die Anklage behauptet, die Neuaufnahme von Beziehungen zu etlichen Leuten am Land. Grundsätzlich habe ich jede Ausweitung des Kreises Weiss abgelehnt — vor allem die Konvertierung völlig Fremder. Wäre mir an der Schaffung einer Bewegung gelegen gewesen, so hätte ich selbstverständlich als erstes in meiner engeren Heimat Oberpfalz und sodann in Anknüpfung der früheren Heimat- u. Königsbund-Organe in den übrigen Provinzen begonnen, im übrigen erfahrene und mir als vertrauenswürdig bekannte Personen zu „Organen" gemacht. Tatsächlich habe ich mich nie auch nur erkundigt, wer wer ist, wer erscheint, welchen Berufs, welcher politischen Vergangenheit usw usw jeder einzelne Teilnehmer ist; ausser von den Mit-Angeschuldigten kenne ich noch heute fast von keinem anderen Teilnehmer auch nur den Namen!

Kapitel VII. (31) Die „propagandistischen Massnahmen" waren 1937 so wenig die allermindesten wie in den Jahren 1938 und 1939. Gelegentlich der Fertigstellung der Ley-Villa in München-Geiselgasteig ging durch ganz München eine ebenso hohe Welle der Empörung wie anlässlich der Hess- und Fiehler-Villen. Ganz besonders haben sich auch ausgesprochen Alte-Kämpfer-Kreise der NSDAP über diese Ausgeburt der vormals zu Propaganda-Zwecken gepredigten Selbstlosigkeit aufgehalten. Es lag deshalb nahe, dass gelegentlich eines Treffens Fackler auf die Sache zu sprechen kam und in seiner jokosen Art *unverkennbar* als Witz den Besuch aller Huber und Maier bei ihrem Genossen Ley oder Kameraden Ley entwarf. Ich erinnere mich im Gegensatz zu den sonstigen, viele Jahre zurückliegenden Gesprächen dieser Unterhaltung sehr gut und erwähne den Fall ausdrücklich, um an der Person Fackler's die Bösartigkeit und Gewissenlosigkeit des professionellen Lügners Fischer darzutun.

(32) Die Herstellung und Verbreitung von *Flug*-Blättern ist gelegentlich erörtert, von mir jedoch aus dem Stegreif abgelehnt worden, weil ich dieselbe für im Widerspruch zu den bestehenden strafrechtlichen Bestimmungen befindlich wusste. Ich habe auch zu keinerlei Vorbereitung von Flug-Schriften, -zetteln oder dergleichen die Hand gereicht. Weder Gross-, noch Kleinvervielfältiger-Apparate habe ich je gesehen.

(33) Dagegen haben wir des öfteren, angeregt durch auswärtige Besucher, die Möglichkeit der Herausgabe geschlossener Nachrichtenbriefe an Freunde auf dem Land erörtert, weil diese nur sehr selten die Möglichkeit zu Reisen nach München und zur Fühlungnahme mit Gleichgesinnten hatten und dringend wünschten, das zu hören und mitzuerleben, was jenseits der VB-Schlagzeile in der Welt geschah.

Es handelt sich dabei nicht um Aufrufe oder ähnliche Propaganda-Produkte, sondern um ausgesprochene politische *Sach*-Nachrichten nach Art von Fachblättern einzelner Berufsgruppen. Auch diese Nachrichten-Briefe sind jedoch nicht entstanden, sondern unterblieben, weil ich mir vorbehalten hatte, die strafrechtliche Seite der Sache eigens zu prüfen, und mich diese Prüfung zu der Überzeugung geführt hat, dass das Vorhaben nicht völlig über jeden Zweifel erhaben sei. Das ist der alleinige Grund für den Verzicht auf die Nachrichtenblätter, der von den auswärtigen Gesinnungsfreunden lebhaft bedauert wurde, nicht aber der von der Anklage auf Seite 37 behauptete Schaden einer mir völlig unbekannten Schreibmaschine, der sich ja erforderlichenfalles hätte unschwer beheben lassen. Besonderer Zeuge meiner Ablehnung der Nachrichten-Briefe ist Fackler, dem ich als politisch Meist-Erfahrenen meine rechtlichen Bedenken ausführlicher als den übrigen dargelegt habe, um den Verdacht auszuschliessen, ich weigerte mich nur aus Mangel an persönlicher Bereitwilligkeit.

(33) Den Weiss'schen Aufruf glaube ich mich zu erinnern, nicht dagegen, was mit ihm geschah. Ich habe ihm vor allem deshalb keine Aufmerksamkeit geschenkt, wie ich heute annehme, weil er mir schwach und zugleich im Inhalt völlig unbedenklich erschienen sein dürfte. Ich wüsste auch heute nicht, was gegen ihn einzuwenden wäre; jedenfalls steht er hinter der „Boden-verwurzelten Heimat-Treue" des Völkischen Beobachters in dessen Wahlkampf zum Bayer. Landtag im Frühjahr 1932 *meilenweit* zurück.

(35) Mein „Aufsatz-Entwurf" ist kein Entwurf zu einem Aufsatz, sondern aus dem Stegreif am Schluss einer Zusammenkunft niedergeschriebene Kurz-Skizze zu erörterten, ganz heterogenen Themen, aus der für den Fall der Herausgabe von Nachrichten-Briefen berichtende und belehrende Texte auszuarbeiten gewesen wären. In der wiedergegebenen Fassung waren sie selbstverständlich für keinerlei Verwertung bestimmt. Es handelte sich im Einzelnen um Folgendes: a) Die Einleitung befasst sich in gemeinverständlicher Ausdrucksweise mit der immer stärker zutage getretenen Korruption und wiederholt zunächst in deutscher Sprache das bekannte „Quo usque tandem..." Cicero's gegen die Catilinarischen Getreide-Schiebungen zum Schaden des Staates.

Sodann nimmt der Wortlaut, was ohne Kenntnis der vorhergegangenen Unterhaltung und Torsenhaftigkeit der Text-Skizze allerdings kaum verständlich ist, die Person Hitler's gegen den Vorwurf persönlicher Anteilnahme an Korruptions-Affären in Schutz und macht ihm nur den Vorwurf des Irrtums über die moralische Berechtigung seines vielerwähnten und -umfochtenen Führer-Gefolgschafts-Treue-Komplexes gegenüber seinen unwürdigen Gefolgsleuten innerhalb der NSDAP. Der Ausdruck Irrer ist gewählt, weil ich bei den Beteiligten Verständnis für den Sinngehalt von „Komplex" nicht voraussetzen durfte und andererseits bewusst termini technici wie Geisteskranker, Verrückter, nicht wählen konnte, da ich der Person Hitler's nicht entfernt geistige Defekte zuschreiben will, dagegen überzeugt bin, dass es sich bei ihm um Übersteigerungen gewisser Vorstellungen von Treue, Kameradschaftspflicht usw handelt, die sein Weltbild und Mitmenschen-Bild teilweise verschieben. Hitler sieht nach meiner Beobachtung in der blossen Tatsache frühzeitigen Anschlusses an weniger seine politischen Bewegung als seine Person einen so überaus wertvollen Tugend-Akt des Betreffenden, dass er das als ausreichende Rechtfertigung erachtet, spätere „geringe Schönheitsfehler" seiner „Getreuen" zu übersehen oder wenigstens zu amnestieren. Ich verweise hierher auf die Partei-gründungs-Jubiläums-Rede 1942 (?) im Hofbräuhaus-Saal, in der sich dem Sinn und ungefähren Wortlaut nach folgende Bemerkung fand: „Wenn ich in der Einnerung an die seinerzeitige Parteigründung mich im Kreis meiner damaligen Kameraden umblicke, so freut es mich, auch heute noch ausnahmlos in ihnen wirkliche Mannsbilder zu erkennen, mögen sie auch hier und da einmal eine rauhe Schale zeigen!"

Es ist naheliegend, dass dem menschlichen Charakter nichts so
gefährlich als eine derartige Bagatellisierung und Vorweg-Amnestie
„rauher Schalen" und ihrer Opfer werden muss. Im Einzelnen belege
ich die Vorwürfe der Schädigung der Staatskasse mit dem Bestech-
ungs-Fall Landesbauernführer Georg Huber als klassischem Beispiel,
in welchem es nicht einmal der bayer. Staatsregierung Epp-Siebert
gelungen ist, trotz öffentlichster Behandlung des Skandals in der
Presse Abhilfe zu schaffen, Huber vielmehr für dauernd einen Ruhe-
Gehalt von monatlich neunhundert Reichsmark von Darré zugespro-
chen erhielt und den umfochtenen Besitz heute noch im Eigentum
hat. Der Verrat an den Interessen der Nation bezieht sich beispiels-
halber vor allem auf Süd-Tirol, das ein Opfer der Freundschaft mit
Mussolini wurde — ähnlich Lothringen und Elsass im Verhältnis zu
Frankreich und die Garantie-Offerte an England für das Common-
wealth. Die Ermordung von Menschen exemplifiziert vorzüglich auf
den 30.6.1934, d.h. nicht auf die mehr oder minder formelle Exe-
kution Schuldiger als die Ermordung Unschuldiger *ohne* Aburteilung
der Mörder durch das ordentliche Gericht. Die Vergewaltigung endlich bezieht sich auf die Aufhebung aller verfassungsmässigen wichtigen Grundrechte des Menschen durch die nationalsozialistische
Regierung.

Am Schluss der Präambel, die übrigens nicht für die eventuell
herauszugebenden Nachrichten-Briefe gedacht war, sondern einen
Niederschlag der Stimmung im eigenen Kreis darstellt, erfolgt die
Aufforderung zur Rettung des Staates nach besten Kräften — also
nicht, wie die Anklage im Schluss-Resumé zu unterstellen versucht,
auf illegalen Wegen, sondern über die gebotenen Gelegenheiten der
Volksabstimmung.

b) Die aussenpolitischen Streiflichter bedürfen kaum der Erläu-
terung.

Das Fiasko Ribbentropp's in London ist haargenau so verlaufen,
wie im Text vorausgesagt. Eine einzige Variante hat sich insofern
ergeben, als Ribb, die Stiege nicht hinunter-, sondern hinaufgefallen
und an Neurath's Stelle im Februar 1938 zum Reichsaussenminister
ernannt worden ist. Gegenstand meines Angriff's war weit weniger
sein Misserfolg in London, der jedem anderen Beauftragten hätte
zustossen können, als die Tatsache der Verwendung eines so krassen
beruflichen Aussenseiters und Dilettanten in so besonders schwieriger
und entscheidender Funktion und ferner der besondere diplomatische

Missgriff, ausgerechnet an den Londoner Posten einen Mann zu delegieren, der sich dortselbst bereits in einem zwar durchaus ehrenwerten, aber nach ungeschriebenen Geschmacks-Regeln der „Welt" als bescheiden bewerteten Beruf (commis voyageur) betätigt hatte. Angesichts des empfindlichen froid, das sich zwischen Ribb. und den offiziellen englischen Kreisen ausgebreitet hatte, war es vollends ein affront für London, dass Ribb. Nachfolger Neurath's wurde. Der Angriff gegen Weber bezieht sich auf die Tatsache, dass sich diese Gestalt in Paris und später auch noch in Budapest als Repräsentant des Deutschen Reiches auf Vollblutzucht-Konferenzen hatte zeigen dürfen. Hieran ist auch in fast sämtlichen Kreisen der Regierung und NSDAP eine gleich scharfe Kritik geübt worden. Die Skizze bezüglich Ungarn's dürfte irrelevant sein. Die Phase der Mussolinischen Schimpfereien über Deutschland von Herbst 1933 (Konferenz Hitler-Muss. in Venedig) bis Herbst 1935 (Verständigung Hitler-Mussolini nach Ausbruch des Abessinien-Krieges) ist in der Presse nicht zum vollen Ausdruck gelangt, trotzdem aber unbestrittene Tatsache; auch über Hitler selbst ist im Anschluss an Venedig eine bösartige Bemerkung Mussolini's bekannt geworden. Bezüglich Hess' ist übrigens das amtliche Kommuniqué über seine politische Unreife und Uneignung gelegentlich seiner Flucht nach England im Mai 1941 in der deutschen Presse völlig gleichartig. Der Wurm-Fortsatz meiner Skizze auf S. 37 ist nicht von mir.

Kapitel VIII. (37) Ich habe es von Anfang an grundsätzlich abgelehnt, dem Weiss-schen Kreis irgendwelche erwähnenswerte Geldmittel zuzuführen, damit nicht der Eindruck irgendeines weiterreichenden Zweckes oder Zieles entstehen könne. Ich aber selbst habe nur verhältnismässig geringfügige Beträge gespendet, wie das die Herren Knoblauch, Chrambach, Nöpl bereits vor mir getan hatten. Durch die Vorbereitung der Zusammenkünfte und durch die Mittellosigkeit einiger Teilnehmer war ein ganz geringer Geldbedarf vorhanden, der mir ursprünglich auch nicht bekannt gewesen war. Um diesen zu decken, musste nach meiner Meinung die Selbsthilfe der Teilnehmer ausreichen; auf diese habe ich sie deshalb in der Tat verwiesen. Gerade dadurch und durch die Weigerung Grossbeträge von finanzkräftiger Seite einzuholen, habe ich jeden Verdacht illegaler Absichten hintangehalten und eventuellen, mir ja ursprünglich gar nicht bekannten Heiss-Spornen von vornherein jede Möglichkeit benommen.

Schon während der Weiss-Ära waren die Leute bestrebt, gegen Spenden Quittungs-Marken zu verteilen, die den Spenden und Spendern für spätere Zeiten als politisch-moralische Alibi's dienen sollten. Ich habe dieses Streben seiner Tendenz wegen sehr begrüsst und in ihm die bei der breiten Masse unseres Volkes so schmerzlich vermisste charakterliche Sauberkeit und Opferwilligkeit gesehen. In ähnlicher Weise sind mir die Spenden-Bemühungen unter Zott erschienen, ich habe lediglich vollkommen Freiwilligkeit in Gemässheit meiner ursprünglichen Bedingung empfohlen und meiner Erinnerung nach auch tatsächlich beobachtet. Im übrigen habe ich den Geldangelegenheiten keine Beachtung geschenkt.

Es sei hier erwähnt, dass ich zwar nie Gasthaus-Zechen für Andere bezahlt oder sonst andere Beträge als die in der Anklage genannten gespendet habe, dass ich aber in anderer Weise, vor allem als Anwalt, einzelnen Hilfsbedürftigen aus dem Weiss-Zott'schen Kreis gern jede Hilfe gewährt habe. In einem einzigen Fall bin ich von einem angeblich in Verlegenheit geratenen Mann des Kreises um fünfzig Reichsmark angepumpt worden.

(38) Die Verteilung der Rupprecht-Bilder wird von der Anklage wiederum in polemischer Absicht und entgegen den Aussagen auf den Kopf gestellt. Weiss klagte mir eines Tages, die offizielle Politik unterdrücke so systematisch alle Lebenszeichen unseres Königshauses, dass schon kaum ein Uneingeweihter mehr vom Leben des Königs wisse und ihn von Angesicht mehr kenne; es seien wahrscheinlich auch keine Bilder der Mitglieder des Königshauses mehr aufzutreiben. Daraufhin liess ich mir vom Hofphotographen Greiner dreihundert Bilder Sr. Majestät in schöner Ausführung liefern und schenkte sie dem Weiss zur Verteilung unter seinen Kreis; dabei kam mir m.E. nach der Gedanke, er könne sich dafür jeweils eine Spende von den Empfängern ausbitten. In dieser kausalen Reihenfolge geschah also die Beschaffung der Bilder, ihre Überlassung an Weiss und die Weitergabe an die Einzelnen gegen Spenden.

Kapitel IX. (38) Zu der wiederholten Falschdarstellung der vermeintlichen Organisation ist meinen Bemerkungen zu Kapittel VI auf meiner Seite 10 nichts hinzuzufügen. Richtig ist allein die Tatsache, dass ich, als gesellschaftlich darin erfahren, dem Weiss die Weigerung seiner Freunde mitteilte, wegen seiner ungeordneten Familienverhältnisse (die mir völlig unbekannt gewesen waren) weiter mit ihm zu verkehren und das ich vorschlug, Zott möge doch in Zukunft an Weiss' Stelle die Zusammenkünfte vereinbaren. Im weiteren Verlauf mag Zott vielleicht mehr und hinter meinem Rücken von Einteilung usw gesprochen haben. Sobald jedoch die rechtlich zu beachtende Grenze verbotener Organisation auch nur entfernt auftauchte, habe ich ihm Paroli geboten, wie der Spitzl-Bericht vom 10.1.39 gerade wegen seiner sonstigen systematischen Hetze gegen mich so glaubhaft ausweist.

(40) Von einer ehrenwörtlichen Schweigeverpflichtung ist mir nicht das Mindeste erinnerlich.

(41) Es ist sehr wertvoll, dass die Anklage im ersten Absatz diesmal selbst von Nachrichtenblättern und nicht von Flugblättern spricht; das entspricht der Wahrheit, nur liegt der Fall wesentlich früher.

(42) An den Flugblatt-Entwurf Zott kann ich mich nicht erinnern. Sollte ich es zu Gesicht bekommen haben, so habe ich seine Verbreitung auf jeden Fall inhibiert, weil ich grundsätzlich *Flug*blätter von allem Anfang abgelehnt hatte.

Kapitel X. (43) Zu diesem aus unerklärlichen Gründen wiederholten Finanz-Thema verweise ich auf meine Bemerkungen auf obiger Seite 13 zu Kapitel VIII, die das Wesentliche zu dieser völlig unwesentlichen Begleiterscheinung enthalten. Die Aufbauschung erklärt sich offensichtlich aus dem Auftrag, aus einem Nichts einen Elefanten zu machen.

(45) Ich habe (letzter Absatz) nicht „darauf" zweimal Geldbeträge von Chrambach und Nöpl durch *meine* Bemühungen er„fochten"; beide Herren haben längst vor mir in regelmässigem Verkehr mit dem Weiss'schen Kreis gestanden und ihm der Landessitte entsprechend von Zeit zu Zeit als „noble Hunde" Spenden zukommen lassen und hätten sicher viel häufiger an Zusammenkünften teilgenommen, hätten sie ebenfalls in München gelebt. Ich habe in Erinnerung, dass gelegentlich beide Herren zufällig zugleich in München waren und mich besucht hatten. Da am Abend eine Zusammenkunft war, sind wir zu Dritt dorthin gegangen und nach deren Ende wiederum zu Dritt noch in den Ratskeller, um uns über unsere privaten, berufsgeschäftlichen und auch noch über politische Gegenstände zu unterhalten. Ich habe Nöpl überhaupt erst durch Weiss kennen gelernt und Nöpl ist danach erst mein ständiger Mandant mit seinem Unternehmen geworden. Diese sämtlichen Beziehungen waren und sind so absichtslos wie nur möglich.

Kapitel XI. (46) Auch zu dieser Wiederholung bereits abgehandelter Gegenstände beziehe ich mich auf meine Ausführungen auf der obigen Seite 9 zu Kapitel V.

In der Erziehungs-Anstalt Birkeneck war ich seit langer Zeit eingeladen. Ich habe selbstverständlich dort nicht über Möglichkeiten der Restoration in Bayern gesprochen; das hätte Eulen nach Athen tragen geheissen. Ich habe überhaupt nicht „vorgetragen", sondern habe mit den Geistlichen über Fragen der Kulturpolitik, insbesondere über die Grenzen gesprochen, die der unkirchlich-christlichen Erziehungsmethode der staatlichen Jugend-Behörden gesetzt sind. Der Besuch war veranlasst durch Kaplan Pflüger der dortigen Nachbar-Pfarrei, einen Bruder des Mit-Angeschuldigten Pflüger. Der Besuch war ebenso absichtslos, was politische vermeintliche Ziele betrifft, wie es meine Beziehung zum Kreis Weiss-Zott war. Es handelt sich nur um eine zufällige persönliche Verbindung durch die Brüder Pflüger, die zum Kreis Weiss führte, und die ebenso zufällig in sonstigen Beziehungen hätte vorhanden sein können. Der Vortrag der Anklage über den Besuch in Birkeneck zeichnet sich auch durch beträchtliche Unsicherheit der aufgestellten Behauptungen aus, weil an diesem Besuch kein Spitzl teilgenommen hat und die Gestapo deshalb auf das Resultat ihrer Vernehmungs-„Kunst" begrenzt war.

Kapitel XII (49) Ich verwahre mich auf das Entschiedenste gegen die bodenlose Unverschämtheit, mir Lügenhetze zu unterschieben, nur weil sonst meine Verurteilung und Ausschliessung aus der Anwaltschaft nicht möglich ist. Ich habe dank der in meinem Stand üblichen strengen Erziehung weder die Gewohnheit zu lügen, noch zu hetzen, noch zu verleumden, noch in sonstiger Weise durch blosse Unsachlichkeiten mit dem ganz allgemeinen Wahrheitsgebot in Konflikt zu geraten.

Eine unfreiwillige und gerade deshalb völlig unverdächtige Probe meiner Dialektik bietet die Skizze zu einem Nachrichten-Brief (35/6), die in ohne Zweifel scharfer Polemik sich doch von jeder hetzerischen, standeswidrigen Äusserung enthält und allein Ironie und Sarkasmus ihre umso wirksamere Waffen führen lasst. Die gleiche Skizze erbringt den weiteren Beweis dafür, dass meine Voraussagen, wenn sie überhaupt geschahen, durchaus Hand und Fuss hatten. Ich habe noch mehr als in meinen eigenen Lebens- und Standesbereichen in dem sozial beträchtlich unter mir befindlichen Kreise Weiss-Zott einen vorzüglich Umgangston beobachtet und dadurch auch für die anderen Teilnehmer inauguriert. Es ist ausgeschlossen, dass einer der Beteiligten das nicht vorbehaltslos bezeugt, er sei denn ein bezahlter Spitzl, der den Auftrag hat, um jeden Preis Material gegen mich zu beschaffen.

Ich verwahre mich also gegen jeden Vorwurf über die von mir geführte formelle Sprache und ich verwahre mich gleichermassen gegen jeden Vorwurf bezüglich des sachlichen Inhalts alles dessen, was ich im irgendwelcher Beziehung geäussert habe. Ich habe zu allen politischen Themen und Fragen gesprochen, die aktuell waren und mir vorgelegt wurden. Ich habe jede meiner Äusserungen aus alter Gewohnheit gerade im Hinblick auf die besondere Qualität meines Zuhörerkreises „einfacher Leute" einem doppelten Filter in förmlicher und sachlicher Beziehung unterworfen und bestreite deshalb die Berechtigung auch des leisesten Vorwurfes in dieser Hinsicht. In aller Regel habe ich besonders in heiklen Themen, die Personen oder Sachen betrafen und deren Verhältnisse mir aus besonderem beruflichen oder sonstigen Grund authentisch bekannt waren, jede Äusserung überhaupt vermieden, höchstenfalls mich aber darauf beschränkt, den Umlauf eines einschlägigen Gerüchtes zu bestätigen.

Es ist mir heute natürlich nicht mehr möglich, zu jedem einzelnen, von der Spitzl-Berichterstattung mir angedichteten Punkt bejahend oder verneinend mit Eidesanerbietung Stellung zu nehmen. Ich beschränke mich deshalb darauf, die krassesten und mir noch erinnerlichen Fälle aufzureifen:

(50) Ich habe *nie* zum Eintritt in Partei-Organisationen und deren „Zerbröckelung" aufgefordert, sondern habe es im Gegenteil stets als Anstandspflicht jedes charaktervollen Menschen bezeichnet, die Zugehörigkeit zu politischen Parteien usw auch auf die Gefahr von Zurücksetzung, Schädigung und erst recht von Vorteils-Verlusten hin dann zu verzichten, wenn sie im Widerspruch zur wirklichen, inneren Überzeugung wäre. Diese ist der passive Widerstand, den ein Mann von Ehre gleichgültig unter welchem System zu leisten hat.

(51) Ich habe mich nie mit dem Thema der vielerörterten Geisteskrankheit Adolf Hitler's befasst, es sei denn mit seinem bewussten Treue-Komplex wie oben Seite 12 zu Kapitel VII dargelegt.

(52) Ich habe Epp nie Gesinnungslump genannt, weil er das subjektiv nicht ist; dagegen habe ich ihn Judas (35) genannt und ebenso ist möglich, dass ich erklärt habe, ich würde ihm nie mehr

die Hand reichen (28), weil er tatsächlich Treue und Gehorsam seinem königlichen Herrn gegenüber in eklatanter Weise gebrochen hat und heute noch bricht, *obwohl* er sich zu gleicher Zeit rühmt, treuester Diener seines Königs und Herrn zu sein und seiner politischen Funktion unter Hitler als oberstes Ziel die Wiederaufrichtung des bayerischen Trones anzustreben. Äussere Beweise dieser Epp'schen „Politik" sind die beiden Audienzen, die Epp im März und September 1933 bei Sr. Majestät erwirkt hat, sowie die berühmte, vom Herbst 1933 meiner Erinnerung nach datierende Rede, in der er Adolf Hitler dankte für die Titulierung einer SA-„Leib"-Standarte, „die die Tradition des kgl. Leibregiments übernommen habe und nur noch des Leibes bedürfe, den sie dann wieder wie vor 1918 mit Gut und Blut werde schützen dürfen.". Eine derartige Geistesverwirrung ist unmöglich mehr bei einem sonst ganz nüchternen, wenn auch bescheiden bemittelten Mann wie Epp anzunehmen; das ist das auf beiden Schultern tragen wollen, obwohl es unmoralisch ist und niemand zwei Herren dienen kann. Denn dass Adolf Hitler seit seiner Ernennung zum Reichkanzler nichts weniger als in Restauration gemacht hat, musste auch einem Epp klar geworden sein; trotzdem hat er nicht aufgehört, seinem Herrn den Judas-Kuss zu geben.

(53) Über Hitler's Abstammung kann ich nichts anderes geäussert haben, als dass in den k.u.k. Beamten-Familien Blut-Mischungen aller Völker der Monarchie an der Tagesordnung seien. Von besseren oder schlechteren, geschweige denn allerschlechtesten Rassen kann ich unmöglich gesprochen haben, weil ich von Grund aus die Überhebung einer Rasse über die andere als unmoralisch und ebenso die Blut-Mischung, deren Produkt ich selbst bin, dementsprechend verurteile bzw verteidige. Gerade wegen meines Gegensatzes zur nationalsozialistischen Rassen-Programmatik verwahre ich mich gegen die mir unterstellte Äusserung über Hitler's mir gänzlich unbekannte Abstammung. Auch von Schindluder kann ich nicht gesprochen haben; der Vergleich zwischen Volk und Theorie ist Unsinn.

(55) Während sämtliche Spizl-Auslassungen auf den Seiten 54 u. 55 ein nicht beachtenswerter Kauderwelsch sind, interessiert das unfreiwillige und selbstverständlich von der Anklageschrift geflissentlich nicht weiter verwertete Kurz-Zitat aus meiner angeblichen Rede, „die Monarchisten könnten abwarten ...". Sieht die Vorbereitung zum gewaltsamen Umsturz des Staatsordnung so aus? Vergleiche hierzu die „tats. und rechtl. Würdigung" (71)!

(55) *Schamlos* ist die Fälschung, die Spizl oder Anklage mit meiner Stellungnahme zur Heeresdienstfrage begangen haben. Schon die Wiedergabe in der Anklage beweist, dass der erste Teil meiner Stellungnahme, nämlich die Bejahung der Dienstpflicht, unterschlagen ist und nur mit dem zweiten, völlig entstellten Teil versucht wird, mir am Zeug zu flicken. Ich erinnere mich an diese Fahrner'sche Frage sehr gut und eben gut daran, dass ich ohne jede Einschränkung zur Erfüllung jedweder Militär-Pflicht aufgefordert habe. Ich habe den Militärdienst als Pflicht bezeichnet, der wir aus christlichem Sittengebot ebenso zu genügen hätten wie der Steuer- und jeder anderen Staatsbürgerpflicht — ohne Ansehen der uns genehmen oder nicht genehmen momentanen Regierung. Und ich habe die Dienstpflichterfüllung gefordert, weil wir auch keinerlei Anlass hätten, uns wegen einer vorübergehenden Regierugs-Konstellation aus dem innigen Zusammenhang mit dem Volksganzen loszulösen, selbst wenn es uns sitlich erlaubt wäre. Lediglich im Hinblick auf das Alter, bereits geleistete Dienste im Weltkrieg und die meist vorhandenen Familien meiner Zuhörer habe ich geäussert, ältere, lang im Krieg gediente Männer hätten nicht die moralische Pflicht, sich zu freiwilligen Patrouillen und dergleichen zu drängen, sondern könnten das jüngeren Jahrgängen und Ledigen als Erstberufenen überlassen.

(57) Pöbelhafte Ausdrücke wie „wahnsinnig gewordener Anstreicher" benutze ich aus den oben dargelegten Gründen unter keinen Umständen. Die Spitzl-Behauptung ist erlogen oder verwechselt.

(57) Nach dem ersten Absatz über die Zusammenkunft vom 15.9. 38 und dem zweiten über die (angeblich *so* gehäuften) Zusammenkunft vom 23.2.1939 fehlt die ausschlaggebend wichtige Berichterstattung vom 10.1.39 (Auch dieser Abend ist erst *vier* Monate nach dem letzten erfolgt).

(57) Ich kann Funk unmöglich einen Wirtschaftbolschewisten genannt haben, da er mir als Kapitalist von Kopf zu Fuss bekannt ist und ich mich lediglich gewundert habe, dass die sozialistische Arbeiterpartei ausgerechnet durch Hugenberge, Schimtt's Stausse, Schacht's und Funk's ihr antikapitalistisches Programm durchführen lässt und einen Gottfried Feder nach wenigen Monaten in zweitrangiger Position in die Wüste schickt.

(58) Über Hitler'sche Wutausbrüche in tausend verschiedenen Varianten habe ich soviel zu hören bekommen, dass ich schon deshalb

keinesfalls derartig leeres Stroh gedroschen habe. Von einem Arzt und einem dazu gehörigen katholischen Geistlichen in Dachau habe ich keine Ahnung; ich würde mich sonst bestimmt daran erinnern. *Kapitel XIII. (59)* Von dem gesamten Inhalt des Kapitels habe ich so wenig eine Ahnung gehabt, wie ich den mir auch als Münchener Anwalt nicht erinnerlichen Dr. Loritz oder den Kaplan Schuster gekannt habe. Letzteren habe ich erst in der Haft kennen gelernt. An sich bräuchte mich der Sach-Komplex nicht zu interessieren; trotzdem ist er ein überaus wichtiges Beweismittel für die von mir stets verteidigte völlige Absichtslosigkeit meiner Beziehung zum Weiss-Kreis.

Dass überhaupt einige Teilnehmer des Weiss-Kreises abgesprungen und zu Dr. Loritz gestossen sind, beweist deutlicher, als es irgend ein sonstiger Beweis könnte, dass „die monarchistische Organistion nicht nur keinen richtigen Zusammenhalt" gehabt hat, sondern überhaupt nicht vorhanden war, und dass dem Weiss-Zott-Kreis „die erforderlichen Geldmittel gefehlt" haben (60).

Diese völlig unwiderleglichen und ebenso schlüssigen Beweise für die Richtigkeit meiner Behauptung, dass von einer Organisation Harnier-Weiss-Zott keine Rede sein kann, zwar zur Belastung der davon betroffenen Loritz-Gefolgsmänner zu benutzen, sie aber für die unvoreingenommene Bewertung meiner Handlungsweise zu unterschlagen, ist eine der unerfreulichsten Seiten der Anklageschrift.

Zur Sache bemerke ich noch, dass in dem Kapitel die Jahre 1938 und 1939 vielfältig wechseln und offensichtlich, z.B. mindestens auf Seiten 59, 60, 63, 64, verwechselt sind. Für mich ist es eventuell von Interesse, ob dieser Anschluss der Schuster-Gruppe an Dr. Loritz bereits 1938 erfolgt ist, wo ich anfing, immer seltener Zusammenkünften anzuwohnen.

(66) Bezeichnend ist das gute Gewissen Fahrner's, der es nach der Polizei-Durchsuchung für angezeigt hielt, Dr. Loritz, nicht aber Zott zu verständigen.

(66) Dass auch Kaplan Schuster auf die ersten Anzeichen polizeilichen Einschreitens geflohen sein soll, belastet mich ebensowenig.

Mir ist Mitte Juli 1939 mein Auslandsreise-Pass von der Staatspolizeistelle München entzogen worden. Ich habe mich daraufhin im Pass-Zentralamt des Staatspolizei-Amtes in Berlin beschwert und die sofortige Rückgabe meines Passes verlangt. Die Entziehung meines Passes sah ich in anderem, beruflichen Zusammenhang.

Kapitel XIV. *(66)* Das Eingeständnis der Anklageschrift, dass sämtliche Beteiligte, also mindestens die Angehörigen des Kreises Weiss-Zott, übereinstimmend jede gewaltsame Absichten bezüglich eines Sturzes in Abrede gestellt haben, ist überzeugend.

(67) Ich habe nicht nur die Diktatur als eine rasch vorübergehende Episode in der Geschichte Deutschlands gehalten, sondern halte sie heute noch genau so und erst recht dafür. Sämtliche Lehren der Menschheitsgeschichte und alle eigenen Erfahrungen zwingen mich dazu. Über die „Dauer der Länge" habe ich niemals Prophezeihungen geäussert; kein Mensch ist zum Propheten à la Stopp-Uhr geboren. Auch spielen fünf Jahre hin oder her keine, im Rahmen unserer Geschichte erwähnenswerte Rolle.

Ich habe nie beabsichtigt, „einen Gedanken in eine Waagschale zu werfen", sondern ganz einfach dem Kreis einfachster, grundanständiger, rat- und fassungsloser Gesinnungsgenossen insoweit Helfer und Ratgeber zu sein, als sie mich jeweils ausdrücklich darum angehen würden. Das ist mir soziale Pflicht und zugleich Anlass zur eigenen politisch-moralischen Gewissenserforschung gewesen. Nichts ist so schwer, als vor einem Kreis ungebildeter, aber kritisch denkender, mit untrüglichem Instinkt für Charakterwerte ausgestatteter Arbeiter die Probe auf das Exempel des eigenen guten Gewissens zu bestehen. Dass ich diese Probe bestanden habe, beweist mir, dass die einzige Unmuts-Äusserung mit dem Messer-hinein-rennen (Zott) über mich gefallen ist, weil die Befürchtung aufgekommen war, ich könnte mich von dem Kreis der Arbeiter zurückziehen. Das ist und bleibt mein Stolz neben der Genugtuung, den Leuten in schwerer Zeit Wegweiser gewesen zu sein.

Dass ich die Leute nicht unverantwortlich verhetzt habe, beweist mir der Übergang der aktiveren zu der Loritz-Organisation wegen meiner Lendenlahmheit.

(69) Während die übrigen angeblichen Einwendungen wegen ihrer Entstehung keinen Wert beanspruchen können, ist von Bedeutung, dass Seutter die unter Ziffer 6 gebrachte Verteidigung als Protokoll hat durchsetzen können.

Kapitel XV. *(70)* Der Inhalt dieses Abschnittes ist das Erbärmlichste an Konstruktion in usum delphini, das sich denken lässt.

(70) Die Nicht-Benennung der angeblich vorhandenen Zeugen ausser dem auf mich nicht bezüglichen und mir völlig unbekannten Früchtl ist typisch für das Bestreben, das charakterlich und geistig

gleich unterwertige „Personal" nach Möglichkeit nicht preiszugeben; die Schönheitsfehler sind doch zu arg. Natürlich ist die Behandlung der Glaubwürdigkeit dieser „Zeugen" entscheidend wichtig, insbesondere die Betrügereien des Fischer.

(71)Die logischen salti mortali, die mich wegen der nicht in einem *einzigen* Fall behaupteten oder gar erwiesenen hetzerischen Äusserungen und wegen der mir anerkanntermassen völlig unbekannten Beziehungen Zott's zur Kommunistischen Seite ans Messer der Hochverrats-Vorbereitung liefern wollen, sind so abwegig, dass sie kaum der Erwiderung bedürfen. Von einer „katholisch-kommunistischen Einheitsfront" zu sprechen, ohne zu erröten, zeugt von einem geistig-moralischen Tiefstand, wie er auch in den Breitegraden des Geistes von Potsdam unvorstellbar sein sollte.

(71) Der Angriff gegen die Teilnehmer der demokratischen Organisation, die doch nach dem Inhalt der Anklageschrift mit Lanze und Spiess und recht eindeutigen Ankündigungen zu Feld gezogen sein sollen, ist verblüffend schwach und zurückhaltend und sein Verhältnis zu dem auf mich gerichteten Angriff angesichts der Anklage-Behauptungen geradezu auf den Kopf gestellt. Auch hier tritt deutlich das Bestreben hervor, das (aus *ganz* anderen Gründen) hauptsächliche Karnickel Harnier ohne jede Rücksicht auf den wirklichen Sachverhalt an die Spitze zu stellen.

(72) Die weiteren Behauptungen über qualifizierende Wirkungen der entschieden bestrittenen Vorarbeiten für die à limine von mir abgelehnten *Flug*-Blätter und der geschenkten Rupprechtbilder haben gleichfalls keinerlei tatsächliche und rechtliche Basis. Sehr bezeichnend ist die Hilfs-Stütze die der Hochverrats-Vorbereitung-Anklage gegen mich gegeben wird, indem auch Verurteilung nach § 90 f StGB vorsorglich und subsidiär gefordert wird, damit ich unter allen Umständen mit einem formidablen Zuchthaus-Urteil zu Fall gebracht werden kann.

(72) Die Zitation aus dem VGH-Urteil vom 10.1.39 über die Organisations-Merkmale ist sehr wertvoll. Sie beweist, wie richtig meine Forderungen bezüglich der Vermeidung jedes Illegalitäts-Verdachtes waren (oben Seiten 8/9). Indem ich forderte, die bezeichneten Tatumstände zu vermeiden, habe ich den Wunsch und die feste Überzeugung gehabt, Wesensmerkmale jeder Organisation à limine auszuschliessen, die nicht hinweggedacht werden können, ohne dass mit ihnen der strafrechtliche Minimal-Tatbestand entfällt. Im

Gegensatz zu dem im Urteil vom 10.1.39 behandelten Sachverhalt ist durch meine Bedingung sowohl das *illegale* Erstreben eines Zieles, ein irgendwie bindender Zusammenschluss und vor allem jeder für-rende Wille samt Unterordnung der übrigen Meinungs-Träger aus-geschlossen geblieben. Die Abzweigung einiger Teilnehmer des Weiss-Zott-Kreises zu Dr. Loritz hinter dem Rücken der anderen Monarchisten beweist zur Evidenz die absolute Ungebundenheit aller Beteiligten. Die unbestrittene Tatsache, dass ich nicht eine einzige Zusammenkunft angeregt oder ohne ausdrückliche Einladung besucht habe, beweist den Mangel führenden Willens und eines Unterord-nungs-Verhältnisses welcher Art immer.

Appendix I

Judgment of Baron von Harnier and his friends by the Volksgerichts-hof, June 28, 1944

Abschrift
6 H 92/44
7 J 32/44

IM NAMEN DES DEUTSCHEN VOLKES
In der Strafsache gegen

1) den Rechtsanwalt Dr. Adolf Freiherr von Harnier aus München
   geboren am 14. April 1903 in München,
2) den staatlichen Gartenverwalter Heinrich Weiss aus München-Schleissheim, Altes Schloss Nr. 1,
   geboren am 4. Juli 1887 in Laufen an der Saale,
3) den Elektromonteur Heinrich Pflüger aus München,
   geboren am 4. Juni 1908 in München,
4) den Schneider Gebhard Fahrner aus München,
   geboren am 21. Juni 1896 in Frommenhausen,
5) den Kraftwagenführer Wilhelm Seutter von Lötzen aus Grünwald,
   geboren am 31. Dezember 1901 in Lindau am Bodensee,
6) den kaufmännischen Angestellten Franz Xaver Fackler aus München
   geboren am 20. Oktober 1895 in München,
7) Die Bildhauerin Margarete Elisabeth Freiin von Stengel in Rieden bei Reutte (Tirol)
   geboren am 10. Februar 1898 in München,
8) den Kaplan und Benfiziat Karl Schuster aus München
   geboren am 13. März 1905 in München,
von 1 bis 5 und zu 8 zur Zeit in gerichtlicher Untersuchungshaft,
wegen Vorbereitung zum Hochverrat
hat der Volksgerichtshof, 6. Senat, auf Grund der Hauptverhandlung
vom 13. bis einschliesslich 16. Juni 1944, an welcher teilgenommen
haben
   als Richter:
      Kammergerichtsrat Granzow, Vorsitzer,

Oberlandesgerichtsrat Fikèis,
Generalarbeitsführer a.d. Müler
Generalleutnant Canabis,
Staatssekretär Köglmaier,
als Vertreter des Oberreichsanwalts:
Landgerichtsrat von Zeschau,
für Recht erkannt:
Der Angeklagte Adolf von Harnier hat vor dem Kriege einer monarchistischen Organisation führend angehört und durch Lügenhetze das
Ansehen des deutschen Volkes schwer gefährdet.
Auch die übrigen Angeklagten mit Ausnahme von Schuster haben
dieser Organisation angehört. Fahrner ist über dies für eine demokra-
tisch revolutionäre Organisation tätig gewesen. Schuster hat die Tätigkeit eines Funktionärs dieser Organisation dadurch unterstützt, dass er
ihn mit Fahrner und Pflüger in Verbindung gebracht und seine Wohnung zu einer Besprechung zur Verfügung gestellt hat. Pflüger hat es
unterlassen, von dem Bestande der Organisation Anzeige zu erstatten.
Es werden deswegen verurteilt:
von Harnier zu 10 (zehn) Jahren, Weiss zu 2 (zwei) Jahren und 6
(sechs) Monaten, Pflüger zu 5 (fünf) Jahren, Fahrner zu 9 (neun)
Jahren Zuchthaus, Seutter von Lötzen zu 2 (zwei) Jahren, und 6
(sechs) Monaten, Fackler zu 2 (zwei) Jahren und 3 (drei) Monaten
Gefängnis, Margarete von Stengel zu 2 (zwei) Jahren und Schuster
zu 7 (sieben) Jahren Zuchthaus.
Die bürgerlichen Ehrenrechte verlieren von Harnier auf 10 (zehn),
Fahrner auf 9 (neun), Schuster auf 7 (sieben), Pflüger auf 5 (fünf),
Weiss auf 3 (drei) und Margarete von Stengel auf 2 (zwei) Jahre.
Die gegen Weiss, Seutter von Lötzen, Fackler und Margarete von
Stengel verhängten Freiheitsstrafen sind verbüsst. Den übrigen An-
geklagten werden je 4 Jahre 10 Monate der erlittenen Haft auf die
Freiheitsstrafen angerechnet.
Es werden eingezogen:
der Personenkraftwagen II A — 18602 (Wert 100 RM),
die Schreibmachine „Rheinmetall" (Wert 50 RM)
der Abziehapparat „Geha Rotary" Nr. (Wert 50 RM)
sowie die sichergestellten Beträge von 100 RM und 50 RM.
Die Verurteilten tragen die Kosten des Verfahrens.

Die Richtigkeit der vorstehenden Abschrift wird beglaubigt und die
Vollstreckbarkeit des Urteils bescheinigt.

Potsdam, den 28. Juni 1944

Dienstsiegel   gez. Schröder-Kay, Amtsrat
als Urkundsbeamter der Geschäftsstelle.

Beglaubigt:

gez.: Kramp, Sekretär
als Urkundsbeamter der Geschäftsstelle.

Für die Richtigkeit der Abschrift:
Straubing, den 24. Januar 1949
der Vorstand der Strafanstalt

Reickely
Verw.-Obersekretär

Appendix J

HEYDRICH'S LETTER CONCERNING CROWN PRINCE RUPPRECHT

Being a letter written to Amtsrat Paul Weber by Heydrich suggesting the withdrawal of citizenship rights from Crown Prince Rupprecht; dated, August 30, 1940.

Abschrift zu $\dfrac{\text{I } 2008/40 \text{ g}}{5013 \text{ c}}$

Reichssicherheitshauptamt   Berlin SW 11, den 30. August 1940
I A 11 — 281/40 g

An die
Abteilung I des Reichsministeriums des Innern
z. Hd. von Herrn Amtsrat Paul W e b e r o.V.i.A.
Berlin.

Betrifft: Aberkennung der deutschen Staatsangehörigkeit des Generalfeldmarschalls Exkronprinzen Rupprecht von B a y e r n, geb. am 18.5.1869 in München und Erstreckung der Ausbürgerung auf die Ehefrau Antonia geb. Prinzessin v. Luxemburg und von Nassau, geb. am 7.10.1899 auf Schloss Hohenburg und die Kinder Prinz Heinrich Franz Wilhelm v. Bayern, geb. 28.3.1922 auf Schloss Hohenburg, Prinzessin Irmgard Maria Josefa v. Bayern, geb. 29.5.1923 in Berchtesgaden, Prinzessin Editha Marie Gabriele Anna v. Bayern, geb. am 16.9.1924 auf Schloss Hohenburg, Prinzessin Hilda Hildegard Marie Gabriele v. Bayern, geb. am 24. 3.1926 in Berchtesgaden, Prinzessin Gabriele Adelgunde Marie Theresia Antonia v. Bayern, geb. am 10.5.1927 in Berchtesgaden, Prinzessin Sophie Marie Therese v. Bayern, geb. am 20.6.1935 in Starnberg am See, letzter inländischen Wohnsitz: München, Leuchtenberg-Palais, Odeonsplatz 4, bezw. Leutstetten b. Starnberg, jetziger Aufenthalt: Italien.

Bezug: Ohne
Anlagen: 1 Durchschrift.

Reichssicherheitshauptamt   Berlin SW 11, den 30.August 1940

I A 11 - 281/40 g

An die

Abteilung I des Reichsministeriums des Innern
z.Hd. von Herrn Amtsrat Paul **W e b e r** o.V.i.A.

Berlin.

—

Betrifft: Aberkennung der deutschen Staatsangehörigkeit des
Generalfeldmarschalls Exkronprinzen Rupprecht von
B a y e r n, geb. am 18.5.1869 in München und Erstreckung der Ausbürgerung auf die Ehefrau Antonia
geb. Prinzessin v. Luxemburg und von Nassau, geb.
am 7.10.1899 auf Schloss Hohenburg und die Kinder
Prinz Heinrich Franz Wilhelm v. Bayern, geb. 28.3.1922
auf Schloss Hohenburg, Prinzessin Irmgard Maria Josefa
v. Bayern, geb. 29.5.1923 in Berchtesgaden, Prinzessin
Editha Marie Gabriele Anna v. Bayern, geb. am 16.9.1924
auf Schloss Hohenburg, Prinzessin Hilda Hildegard Marie
Gabriele v.Bayern, geb. am 24.3.1926 in Berchtesgaden,
Prinzessin Gabriele Adelgunde Marie Theresia Antonia
v. Bayern, geb. am 10.5.1927 in Berchtesgaden, Prinzessin Sophie Marie Therese v.Bayern, geb. am 20.6.1935
in Starnberg am See, letzter inländischer Wohnsitz:
München, Leuchtenberg-Palais, Odeonsplatz 4, bezw.
Leutstetten b.Starnberg, jetziger Aufenthalt: Italien.

Bezug: Ohne

Anlagen: 1 Durchschrift.

—

I.

Der Exkronprinz Rupprecht v. **B a y e r n** hat sich in den

vergangenen Jahren viel im Ausland hauptsächlich in Ungarn und

Italien - aufgehalten. Nachdem er zuletzt vom 13.8. bis 1.10.1939

....

Dem Auswärtigen Amt sind zwei Durchschriften dieses

Schreibens übersandt worden.

Von dem Abschluß des Verfahrens bitte ich mich zu unter-

richten.

gez.Heydrich.

I.

Der Exkronprinz Rupprecht v. B a y e r n hat sich in den vergangenen Jahren viel im Ausland hauptsächlich in Ungarn und Italien — aufgehalten. Nachdem er zuletzt vom 13.8. bis 1.10.1939 bei seinem in Sarvar/Ungarn wohnhaften Bruder geweilt hatte, ist er nur für kurze Zeit nach Deutschland zurückgekehrt, um sich am 30.12.1939 erneut ins Ausland — nach Italien — zu begeben. Von dieser Reise, die angeblich auf Einladung des Italienischen Königs erfolgt sein soll, ist der Exkronprinz bisher nicht zurückgekehrt, obwohl er am 28.12.1939 vom Landrat in Starnberg lediglich einen bis zum 1.3.1940 für eine einmalige Aus- und Wiedereinreise gültigen Sichtvermerk erhalten hatte. Nach den von hier über die Deutsche Botschaft in Rom bezw. über den bei dieser tätigen Beauftragten der Sicherheitspolizei getroffenen Feststellungen hat der Exkronprinz Rupprecht von Bayern zeitweise in Florenz in der Villa Franchetti gewohnt, deren Inhaberin die deutschblütige, aber mit einem inzwischen verstorbenen Juden italienischer Staatsangehörigkeit verheiratet gewesene Baronin F r a n c h e t t i ist. Während die Pension Franchetti früher auch Mittelpunkt der Deutschen in Florenz war, ist in den letzten Jahren jede Verbindung zu der deutschen Kolonie abgebrochen. Nach den neuesten Feststellungen hält sich der Exkronprinz Rupprecht zur Zeit in einem Ort in der Nähe von Via Reggio auf.

Die Ehefrau des Exkronprinzen Rupprecht, Antonia v. Bayern, geborene Prinzessin von Luxemburg und von Nassau, hat sich im August 1939 zu ihrer Schwester, der Grossherzogin Charlotte v. Luxemburg, begeben, um dort ihre vier ältesten Töchter abzuholen, die sich bezeichnenderweise gemeinsam mit den Kindern des Grossherzogs v. Luxemburg seit etwa 2 Jahren in einem Internat in England befanden und nur während der Sommerferien zu ihren Eltern nach Deutschland bezw. Luxemburg zurückzukehren pflegten. Die Exkronprinzessin Antonia hat sich von Luxemburg aus auf Einladung ihrer Schwester noch eine Woche in der Schweiz aufgehalten und ist später nach München zurückgekehrt. Am 27.1.1940 hat sie ebenfalls Antrag auf Erteilung eines Aus- und Wiedereinreisesichtvermerks für sich und ihre Kinder für eine einmalige Reise nach Italien gestellt und ist dann mit ihren Kindern:

1) Prinz Heinrich Franz Wilhelm v. Bayern, geb. am 28.3.1922 auf Schloss Hohenburg,
2) Prinzessin Irmgard Marie Josefa v. Bayern, geb. am 29.5.1923 in Berchtesgaden,
3) Prinzessin Editha Marie Gabriele Anna v. Bayern, geb .am 16.9. 1924 auf Schloss Hohenburg,
4) Prinzessin Hilda Hildegard Marie Gabriele v. Bayern, geb. am 24.3.1926 in Berchtesgaden,
5) Prinzessin Gabriele Adelgunde Marie Theresia Antonia v. Bayern, geb. am 10.5.1927 in Berchtesgaden,
und
6) Prinzessin Sophie Marie Therese v. Bayern, geb. am 20.6.1935 in Starnberg am See,
nach Italien ausgereist, wo sie sich zur Zeit bei ihrem Ehemann aufhält.

Bezüglich des Aufenthaltes des Exkronprinzen Rupprecht und dessen Familie in Italien ist hier noch bekannt geworden, dass Rupprecht am 7.1.1940 vom Papst in Audienz empfangen worden ist, ohne vorher die Deutsche Botschaft beim Vatikan, wie sonst üblich, in Anspruch zu nehmen.

II.

Der Exkronprinz sowie dessen Familie haben durch ihre unmittelbar in der Spannungszeit vor Kriegsausbruch sowie während des Krieges unternommenen Reisen ins Ausland eindeutig unter Beweis gestellt, dass sie dem Kampf des deutschen Volkes zumindest gleichgültig gegenüberstehen und sich diesem nicht verbunden fühlen. Die Vermutung, dass sie sich in dem zur Zeit ihrer Ausreise noch nicht kriegsführenden Italien sicherer als in Deutschland glaubten und aus diesem Grunde das Reichsgebiet verlassen haben, bedarf hier keiner näheren Begründung. Welch schlechtes Beispiel Rupprecht als Chef des Hauses Wittelsbach mit seinem Verhalten gegeben hat, zeigt die Tatsache, dass sich — von ihm selbst, seiner Ehefrau und seinen Kindern aus zweiter Ehe abgesehen — zur Zeit zwanzig weitere Wittelsbacher im Ausland aufhalten. Der Umstand, dass der Exkronprinz Rupprecht lediglich einen bis zum 1. März 1940 befristeten Sichtvermerk erhalten hatte und sich nach wie vor in Italien aufhält, obwohl eine Verlängerung des Sichtvermerks weder erfolgt ist noch überhaupt beantrugt wurde, zeigt weiter, dass der Genannte glaubt, sich willkürlich über behördliche Anordnungen des national-sozialistischen Staates hinwegsetzen zu können. Auch dieses Verhalten beweist wiederum seine Interessenlosigkeit an dem Schicksalskampf des Deutschen Volkes. Dass das feindliche Ausland aus dem Ver-halten der Wittelsbacher und insbesondere des Exkronprinzen Rup-precht gewisse Rückschlüsse zieht und diese propagandistisch zum Nachteil des Deutschen Reiches verwertet, geht aus verschiedenen Presseveröffentlichungen und Rundfunksendungen hervor.

Weiter tauchte bei der im August 1939 aufgerollten illegalen mon-archistischen Bewegung „Bayernwacht", in der sich zur Zeit noch 81 Beschuldigte in Untersuchungshaft befinden, auch der Name des Exkronprinzen Rupprecht auf. Wie die daraufhin durchgeführten Er-mittlungen ergeben haben, hat der Genannte den Leiter der illegalen Organisation, den Rechtsanwalt Dr. Frhr. von Harnier, den er bereits seit Jahren kannte, wiederholt und eine aus drei weiteren Beschul-digten bestehende Abordnung einmal empfangen. Der Exkronprinz Rupprecht hat diesen Sachverhalt bei seiner am 4. Oktober 1939 durch die Staatspolizeistelle München erfolgten Vernehmung selbst zugeben müssen. Wie er dabei weiter erklärte, habe er sich zwar bis 1933 wiederholt Gedanken über die Möglichkeit einer Wiederher-stellung der Monarchie gemacht, nach der Machtübernahme aber erkannt, dass dieses Ziel wenigstens solange unerreichbar sei, als der nationalsozialistische Staat bestehe. Aus dieser Erkenntnis heraus habe er auch Personen, die ihm derartige, auf Wiedererrichtung einer Monarchie gerichtete Absichten unterbreiten, darunter auch den Frhr. von Harnier, stets zurückgewiesen.

Diese Einlassungen des Exkronprinzen zeigen, dass er schon auf Grund seiner Herkunft — absolut monarchistisch eingestellt ist und über die Bestrebungen der illegalen „Bayernwacht" wenigstens in grossen Zügen unterrichtet worden ist. Der Nachweis, die ihm vor-getragenen Absichten gebilligt und unterstützt zu haben, war auf Grund seines Leugnens und der Tatsache, dass die Festgenommenen zu seiner ihn belastenden Aussage nicht zu bewegen waren, nicht möglich. Im übrigen schwebt das Verfahren gegen v. Harnier u.a. zur Zeit noch beim Oberreichsanwalt beim Volksgerichtshof in Berlin.

In allerletzter Zeit ist der Name des Exkronprinzen Rupprecht auch in einer illegalen legitimistischen Organisation in Linz genannt worden.

Eine offen staatsfeindliche Betätigung konnte dem Exkronprinzen Rupprecht bisher nicht nachgewiesen werden. Doch sind die Gerüchte dass er mit illegalen monarchistischen bezw. legitimistischen Organisationen in Verbindung stehe oder zumindest derartige Bestrebungen fördere bezw. wissentlich dulde, seit Jahren nicht mehr verstummt. Bereits im Jahre 1936 soll der Genannte an Besprechungen im Ausland teilgenommen haben, die sich mit der Frage der Wiedereinsetzung einer Monarchie befassten.

III.

Der geschilderte Sachverhalt zeigt, dass der Genannte als Kristallisationspunkt aller monarchistischen bezw. legitimistischen Bestrebungen in Bayern und zum Teil auch in den angrenzenden süddeutschen katholischen Gebieten anzusehen ist. Diese Tatsache wird durch verschiedene Gerüchte die, sich mit seiner Person befassten, wie auch durch zahlreiche Ergebenheits- und Glückwunschschreiben sowie die seit Jahren beim Portier des Leuchtenberg-Palais ausgelegten Audienzbücher belegt, die die Namenszüge von Tausenden von Verehrern enthalten. Dass die schriftlichen Äusserungen der Ergebenheit nicht immer harmloser Natur waren, geht aus der Äusserung des Exkronprinzen Rupprecht anlässlich seiner bereits erwähnten Vernehmung hervor, er habe ihm von der „Bayernwacht" übersandte Ergebenheitsadressen und Glückwunschschreiben jeweils sofort verbrennen lassen.

Wenngleich dem Exkronprinzen eine ausgesprochen staatsfeindliche Betätigung bisher nicht nachgewiesen werden konnte, zeigt doch sein geschildertes Verhalten, insbesondere sein jetziger Aufenthalt in Italien, dass er sich nicht als zu dem im Nationalsozialismus geeinten deutschen Volk zugehörig fühlt und dass er dem nationalsozialistischen Staat feindlich gegenübersteht. Er hat damit die ihm gegenüber Volk und Reich obliegende Treuepflicht gröblich verletzt und die deutschen Belange erheblich geschädigt. Ich halte daher die Voraussetzungen für die Aberkennung der deutschen Staatsangehörigkeit und die Erstreckung der Ausbürgerung sowie die Vermögenbeschlagnahme und Verfallerklärung für gegeben und bitte, das Weitere zu veranlassen.

Dem Auswärtigen Amt sind zwei Durchschriften dieses Schreibens übersandt worden.

Von dem Abschluss des Verfahrens bitte ich mich zu unterrichten.

gez. Heydrich

Appendix K

PROFESSOR KURT HUBER'S DEFENSE SPEECH

Being the words spoken by Professor Kurt Huber in defense of his own and the students' action at the second trial of the Munich Students, April 19, 1943.

Verteidigung.

1. Ich bin mit S c h o l l an einem Abend bei Frau Dr. Mertens bekannt geworden, zu dem sie mich gebeten hatte. Es war eine Anzahl junge Mediziner und Studentinnen und einige Ältere aus ihrem Bekanntenkreis geladen. Sie las eine kleine Skizze über religiöse Erneuerung, die wegen gewisser Einseitigkeiten und ziemlich weltferner Einstellung bei den jungen Leuten auf Widerstand stiess. Im Verlauf der Diskussion ergaben sich scharfe Gegensätze zwischen Nord und Süd, deren Exponenten Scholl (Süd) und ein Dr. E l l e r m a n n waren, die ich zu überbrücken suchte. Beide machten mir einen sehr intelligenten Eindruck und man beschloss, wieder zusammenzukommen.

2. Ende Juli wurde ich von Scholl, den ich in der Zwischenzeit kaum einmal nach meinem Kolleg gesehen hatte, zu einer Zusammenkunft in H a r l a c h i n g geladen. Trotz beruflicher Überlastung sagte ich zu und traf Scholl um 6 Uhr abends an der Haltestelle Heilig Geist. Einige Tage vorher hatte ich ein Flugblatt „Weisse Rose" zugeschickt erhalten, das ich mit Prof. Dr. Karl A. v. *Müller* besprochen hatte. Dass Scholl der Verfasser war, konnte ich damals nicht wissen. S c h m o r e l l, in dessen Villa die Zusammenkunft stattfand, kannte ich noch gar nicht. Eine mir unbekannte Studentin, Frl. L a f r e n z, die mit Scholl und mir herausgefahren war, fragte mich kurz vor Ankunft in der Villa Schmorell, ob ich auch ein Flugblatt „Weisse Rose" erhalten habe, was ich bejahte. Dass Frl. Lafrenz, die ich ja nicht kannte, von der Autorschaft des Flugblattes damals schon wusste, habe ich erst bei der Vernehmung durch den Kommissar erfahren.

3. Die zwanglosen Erörterungen in Villa Schmorell, in denen frei-

lich Kritik an der politischen Lage, und m i t v o l l e m R e c h t, geübt wurde, nahmen bald das Thema „Nord-Süd" wieder auf und ich stellte mich in sehr wesentlichen Punkten der Anerkennung der politischen Leistung Preussens auf Seite Dr. Ellermann und empfahl sogar das Schrifttum der Erhebung Preussens 1813 zur Lektüre in der vollen Absicht, auf eine Gesundung und Vertiefung des politischen Niveaus in dem kleinen Kreis ernsthaft suchender Akademiker hinzuwirken. Wir waren uns darüber einig, dass die politische Erziehung durch Partei und Studentenführung in keiner Weise ernst zu nehmen war. Mit leeren Phrasen und Zwangspropaganda lassen sich ernsthafte deutsche Studenten auf die Dauer nicht „erziehen". Diese strikte und scharfe Ablehnung des niederen politischen Niveaus an der Hochschule war es, was alle Teilnehmer verband.

4. Nach dem Abend in Villa Schmorell sah ich Scholl nur öfters kurz nach meinem Kolleg mit einigen Studentinnen und Studenten zusammen, wobei nur kurze Worte gewechselt wurden. Als der Einsatz der Studenten in der Sanitätshilfe während des Sommersemesters bekannt gegeben wurde, lud mich die Gruppe Scholl nach dem Kolleg zu einem Abschiedsabend in das Atelier E i c k e n m a i e r. Ich hatte keinen Grund, abzusagen, da ich mit fähiger studentischer Jugend immer gern in Fühlung blieb. Gleich zu Beginn des Abends wurde die Frage erörtert, wie sich die Studentenschaft draussen verhalten soll. Damals empfahl S c h m o r e l l meines Wissens erstmals in vagen Formulierungen Widerstand, *was von uns anderen und auch von Scholl ausdrücklich abgelehnt wurde.* Ich selbst war der Ansicht, dass die Studenten sich ganz auf Seite der Wehrmacht gegen die drohende Vorherrschaft der SS und die „Politisierung" des Soldaten wenden sollten. Auch damals wusste ich n o c h n i c h t, dass Scholl die Flugblätter der „Weissen Rose" herausgegeben hatte. Ich bat Scholl, mir gelegentlich über seine Eindrücke von der russischen Front zu schreiben, was mir auch andere Studenten sehr verschiedener Richtung getan hatten. Ich selbst schrieb keine Briefe, da ich durch die dringliche Fertigstellung eines Manuskripts den ganzen Tag an die Maschine gebunden war. Von irgendwelchen B e s c h l ü s s e n zur Ausgabe von Flugblättern oder gar Anregungen zu Sabotageakten war in der Unterhaltung k e i n e R e d e. Wieder lag der Nachdruck der Kritik auf dem ideellen Kampf gegen das Vorgehen der Partei in den besetzten Gebieten, die Massenmorde, die Schiebungen und Ungerechtigkeiten in der Etappe, die Beschneidigung aller geis-

tigen und zumal auch der religiösen Freiheit. Dieser „Meinungsaustauch", mehr war es in meinen Augen nicht — dauerte nicht lange. Bald löste er sich in Einzelgespräche über die verschiedensten Dinge auf.

Ich verliess das Atelier gegen 10.40 Uhr und wurde von einem Innsbrucker Herrn zur Bahn begleitet. Ob n a c h meinem Weggang noch politische Gespräche geführt wurden, weiss ich nicht. Klar ist mir, dass unsere Besprechungen sich in nichts von einer v o l l b e- r e c h t i g t e n, j a n o t w e n d i g e n K r i t i k a n d e n b e d e n k- l i c h e n A u s w ü c h s e n d e s h e u t i g e n M a c h t s y s t e m s entfernten und auch die Möglichkeiten einer Besserung v o n i n n e n h e r a u s, durch Selbsterziehung und Einwirkung auf andere ins Auge fassten. Unsere Kritik war eine Kritik an offen zutage liegenden Rechtsverletzungen, zugunsten der Machtstellen in Partei und Staat, die die heutige Regierung niemals wird unterbinden können. Sie fühlt sich durch solche Kritik bedroht; aber sie kann durch keine Machtmittel der Welt verhindern, dass deutsche Menschen mutig und offen den Finger auf die schwärende Wunde legen und die drohende Gefahr mit klaren Worten aufzeigen.

Angesichts dieser Sachlage kommt es gar nicht darauf an, was der einzelne von uns in diesem und jenem Falle gesagt hat. Ich übernehme geschlossen für den damaligen Kreis die Verantwortung, dass er aus sittlichen Motiven, aus innerer Not und im Kampf um das Recht des Einzelnen wie der Gemeinschaft auf ihre politische Selbstbestimmung die Wege der Rück k e h r z u e i n e m d e u t s c h e n R e c h t s s t a a t erörtert hat. Dies heilige Recht nehme ich für alle in Anspruch.

5. Im Spätherbst berichtete mir S c h o l l aus dem Feld in einem Brief, der mich überraschte, über seine Eindrücke von der Front. Seine ehemals schärfste Kampfstellung gegen Russland, in der ich mit ihm besonders sympathisiert hatte, war einer wesentlich günstigeren, ja zum Teil positiven Wertung der russischen Verhältnisse gewichen. Er unterrichtete mich kurz vor Weihnachten darüber mündlich in einem kurzen Besuch in meiner Wohnung. Damals erfuhr ich erst von ihm, dass er die „Weisse Rose" herausgegeben hatte.

Nach Weihnachten wartete er öfters nach dem Kolleg auf mich. Mit dem Kreis um Scholl bin ich nie zusammengekommen. Er besuchte mich plötzlich eines Samstagnachmittags in meiner Wohnung und sprach unbestimmt von der Fühlungnahme mit anderen Hochschulen, die mich nicht weiter interessierte. Hingegen erörteten wir eingehender die Frage, wie wir uns positiv die R ü c k k e h r z u e i n e m r e c h t m ä s s i g e n F ü h r e r s t a a t im Einzelnen dächten. In der Ablehnung der alten parlamentarischen Demokratieen waren wir einig, ebenso in der Forderung eines rechtmässigen föderalistischen Moments und eines wirklich ständischen Aufbaus der Volksvertretung. Das Problem schien uns so dringlich, dass wir zu seiner Erörterung a l l e i n gelegentlich zusammenkommen wollten.

An einem Abend Ende Januar trafen wir uns erstmals in Scholls Wohnung. Die Schwester Scholls war zum Teil anwesend, beteiligte sich jedoch *nicht* am Gespräch, fast ebensowenig Schmorell, der später kam. Ich entwickelte im wesentlichen einige der in meinem „Politischen Bekenntnis" niedergelegten Gesichtspunkte der Rückkehr zu einem wirklichen Führerstaat. Scholl schien damals etwas radikaler und wollte das Wort „Führerstaat" ausgemerzt wissen. Doch war er meinen Ideen im übrigen durchaus zugänglich. Ich wirkte auf ihn nachdrücklich in antibolschewistischem Sinn ein.

Bei einem zweiten Besuch, um den mich Scholl eines Vormittags dringend ersuchte, las mir Scholl unvorbereitet in Anwesenheit Schmorells seinen Flugblattentwurf „An alle Deutschen" vor, ebenso einen Entwurf Schmorells, der in ein Konzept gegangen war. Schmorells Entwurf lehnte ich als kommunistisch klingend und im übrigen gar nicht klar und phrasenhaft strikt ab. Von Scholls Entwurf, der nicht fertig war, liess ich, wie in meiner Vernehmung dargestellt, den Anfang stehen, änderte an dem unfertigen Teil einige Sätze stilistisch und setzte an Stelle eines missverständlichen Satzes einen neuen ein. Ich verlangte die Entfernung der Überschrift „Blätter der Widerstandsbewegung". Ich konnte nicht annehmen, dass der Entwurf sofort ausgeführt wurde und die Grundlage eines Flugblattes würde.

Nach dieser Besprechung gingen wir in das Arbeitszimmer, wo die Schwester Scholl mit ein oder zwei Freundinnen etwas Tee gerichtet hatte. Politisches wurde mit keinem Wort berührt. Ich hatte keinesfalls den Eindruck, dass einer der Anwesenden von unserer Besprechung wusste. Später kam noch ein älterer, stark schwäbisch sprechender Herr. Ich muss ihn erwähnen, weil er bei der Gegenüberstellung in der Polizei b e s t r i t t e n hat, mich zu kennen. Die beiden bei der Gegenüberstellung anwesenden Kommissare sind Zeuge, dass der Herr bei der Gegenüberstellung auch in seinem Gebaren verriet, dass er mich kennen musste. Bei Eickenmaier — was allein nicht in Frage käme — kann ich mich nicht entsinnen, den Mann gesehen zu haben.

6. Etwa Montag, 8. Februar, bat mich Scholl nach dem Kolleg mir einen *Dr. Harnack* aus Berlin vorstellen zu dürfen. Ich lehnte sehr bestimmt ab. Am andern Morgen, 9. Februar, wartete er mich mit Harnack nach dem Kolleg ab. Ich konnte nicht wohl mehr ablehnen und ging mit in die Wohnung von Scholl. Harnack, der Volkswirtschaftler ist, legte ich nach kurzem Gespräch über die durch den Fall von Stalingrad geschaffene Lage auf seine Ansichten über den Wirtschaftsaufbau Europas fest. Er entwickelte in verschleierter Form ein im ganzen rein kommunistisches Programm, gegen das ich mich mit aller Schärfe wendete. Nach dem Weggang von Dr. Harnach warnte ich Scholl n a c h d r ü c k l i c h vor jeder weiteren Fühlungsnahme mit Harnack. Ich war mir nicht ganz klar, ob Harnack mehr idealistischer, theoretischer Kommunist sei oder ob er im Sinne einer Organisation arbeite. Persönlich machte er einen sehr gepflegten, intelligenten, durchaus nicht unsympathischen Eindruck.

7. Die Tage vorher war ich durch das Schicksal Stalingrads völlig niedergeschmettert. Es war allgemein bekannt, dass die Katastrophe nur der Unnachgiebigkeit Hitlers zu verdanken war und die militärische Leitung rechtzeitig gewarnt hatte. Es ging auch schon vorher aus der Absetzung von Halders hervor, der — wie ich wusste — in München war. Mit ausschlaggebend aber war für mich die im höchsten Grad unsittliche Ausschlachtung dieses Heldentums in der Parteipresse. Im selben Augenblick wagten Gauleiter und Studentenführer ihren unerhörten Angriff auf die Frontstudenten und den indiskutablen Angriff auf die Standesehre der Studentinnen. Keiner der Hochschulrektoren und Professoren wagte es, sich mutig und eindeutig auf die Seite der Studenten zu stellen. Das war für mich der Anlass, mich klar und aufrichtig von der Professorenschaft abzuheben. In den einleitenden Worten meiner Vorlesung nach dem Fall von Stalingrad, in denen ich zur Nachahmung des Heldentums ohne Phrase (der Kämpfer von Stalingrad) aufrief, liess ich bei meinen über 250 Hörern keinen Zweifel, dass ich die Behandlung dieser nationalen Katastrophe in der Partei aufs schärfste verurteile. Ebenso wenig waren Studentinnen und Studenten bei meiner Begrüssung am Tag nach der Studentenversammlung im unklaren, dass ich mich restlost auf ihre Seite stellte. Ebenso habe ich Präsident v.

Müller gegenüber privat in scharfen Worten gegen diese niederträchtige Behandlung von Studentinnen und Frontstudenten durch Parteiorgane Stellung genommen. Mich an den Rektor zu wenden, verbot sich bei dessen hinreichend bekannter Einstellung von selbst. Es ist unangebracht, mir dies als Feigheit auszulegen, wie es der Herr General der Polizei, von Eberstein, mir gegenüber getan hat. In solchen Fällen tritt von jeher das Flugblatt in die Funktion sich *öffentlich* Gehör zu verschaffen. Die rein technischen Voraussetzungen dazu waren gegeben. Scholl ersuchte mich dringend, jetzt selbst einzugreifen und im Namen und in der Tonart des Studenten einen Aufruf zu verfassen, der sich lediglich an die Studenten richten sollte. Er verlangte darin die Aufforderung, aus den Gliederungen der Partei auszutreten und bei berüchtigten Parteiprofessoren nicht mehr zu hören. Diese Forderung sei in den erregten Diskussionen der Studentenschaft i m m e r w i e d e r e r h o b e n w o r d e n. Zugleich ersuchte er mich um ein neuestes Studentenverzeichnis, da er den Aufruf *nur schriftlich versenden wolle.* Ich gab ihm am 9. Februar nach der Besprechung mit Harnack ein altes von 1941 mit dem Bemerken, dass es ihm gar nichts nütze, und zeigte ihm einen maschinengeschriebenen Entwurf, den ich in Eile z u h a u s e vor dem Kolleg geschrieben hatte. Scholl nahm das Blatt und s t r i c h mit Schmorell den entscheidenden Passus, der die Studenten zur restlosen Unterstellung unter die Wehrmacht aufforderte, durch. I c h e r w i d e r t e e m p ö r t, d a s s s i e d a m i t e i n F l u g b l a t t a u f e i g e n e V e r a n t w o r t u n g m a c h t e n u n d v e r l a n g t e, d a e r d a s B l a t t n i c h t m e h r z u r ü c k g a b, d i e s o f o r t i g e V e r n i c h t u n g m e i n e s E n t w u r f s. Ich verliess die Wohnung sehr ärgerlich u n d h a b e S c h o l l u n d S c h m o r e l l n i c h t m e h r g e s e h e n. In der Aufregung vergass ich, das Studentenverzeichnis zurückzufordern. Ein zweimaliger telefonischer Aufruf am Nachmittag blieb ohne Antwort. Zwei Tage darauf musste ich zu einem Vortrag nach Kempten fahren. Einen Tag nach meiner Rückkehr, meinem ersten Kollegtag, warfen die Geschwister Scholl die Flugblätter in der Universität ab.

8. Zum Text des Flugblatts betone ich, dass es v o m S t a n d p u n k t d e s i n s e i n e r F r e i h e i t b e e i n t r ä c h t i g t e n F r o n t s t u d e n t e n a u s geschrieben ist. Es behauptet jedoch nirgends eine Unwahrheit: Die volle Verantwortung Hitlers für Stalingrad wird die Geschichte feststellen, die Behauptungen über

die Entsittlichung der Jugend durch die heutige Parteierziehung h a l t e i c h u n e i n g e s c h r ä n k t a u f r e c h t. Ich nehme kein Wort davon zurück. Die Partei hat in den 10 Jahren ihres Wirkens d i e F r e i h e i t u n d s i t t l i c h e S e l b s t s t ä n d i g - k e i t d e r h e r a n w a c h s e n d e n d e u t s c h e n J u g e n d r e s t l o s z e r s c h l a g e n und das gesamte Erziehungswesen b o l s c h e w i s i e r t. Die deutsche Professorenschaft hat a l s G e s a m t h e i t der Vernichtung des deutschen Erziehungs- und Bildungswesens im bolschewistischen Sinn t a t e n l o s z u g e - s e h e n. Diesen schweren Vorwurf erhebe ich nach wie vor gegen die deutsche Hochschule. Er schliesst nicht aus, dass im einzelnen viele auch nationalsozialistische Professoren alles eingesetzt haben, um die schlimmsten Massnahmen der Regierung zu verhindern oder doch abzuschwächen. Das kann jedoch an der Gesamtschuld der Professorenschaft nichts Wesentliches ändern. Sie hat eindeutig gezeigt, dass sie die geistige Führung der deutschen akademischen Jugend nicht mehr in der Hand hat. Der Aufruf unterstellt mit allem Nachdruck den deutschen Studenten der deutschen Wehrmacht. Der Wortlaut der Anklageschrift, mein Entwurf habe sich, angeblich in nicht herabsetzendem Sinne auch mit der deutschen Wehrmacht befasst, entstellt dementgegen den Sachverhalt gänzlich. Der Entwurf betonte an der in meiner Vernehmung angegebenen Stelle, dass sich die Studenten an der Front und die Studenten und Studentinnen in der Etappe und in der Heimat, in der Verwundetenpflege, im Laboratorium, aber auch am Schreibtisch ganz und voll für das Vaterland geopfert hätten und fügte wörtlich bei: „Stelt Euch weiterhin alle restlos in den Dienst u n s e r e r h e r r l i c h e n W e h r - m a c h t !" Die Anklageschrift zitiert aus dem Zusammenhang gerissen den Ausdruck "unsere herrliche Wehrmacht" und will wissen, dass er übrigens im Widerspruch zum übrigen Text stehe. Das ist ein beispielloser Angriff auf meine Ehre. Von einem Widerspruch ist gar keine Rede, ganz im Gegenteil! Aber ich will mit den Worten der Partei ganz exakt festlegen, was hier „Wehrmacht" heisst!

Der Wortlaut der parteiamtlich redigierten Berichte aus dem Führerhauptquartier trennt immer scharf „Truppen und Verbände der Waffen SS" und „Truppen und Verbände der Wehrmacht"! Die Waffen SS, nicht die Wehrmacht, rückt in Charkow ein usw.. Also ist nach einer einfachen Logik d i e W a f f e n S S k e i n T e i l d e r W e h r m a c h t. Im selben Sinne beschränkt der Entwurf die

Forderung „Unterstellt Euch unserer herrlichen Wehrmacht!" Das schliesst den mindesten Widerspruch zu meiner vollberechtigten Kritik an der Jugenderziehung des SS in sich. Ich bestreite einen solchen Widerspruch auf das Entschiedenste! Von irgend einer, auch nur der leisesten Verkleinerung unserer Wehrmacht und der w i r k l i c h e n Heeresführung ist keine Spur. Nur in der Reinigung der Wehrmacht von zersetzenden Parteiinteressen zum w i r k l i c h e n Volksheer sieht es die Gewähr auch des militärischen Sieges. An dieser Reinigung in e r s t e r L i n i e mitzuarbeiten ist die Forderung, die der Aufruf an die Frontstudenten wie an Student und Studentin der Heimat und der Etappe stellt. Der Aufruf ist i m h ö c h s t e n S i n n n a t i o n a l, aber er kämpft mit Leidenschaft gegen die Parteipolitik im Heere. In ihr sieht er die tiefste Wurzel militärischer Misserfolge vom Ausmasse Stalingrads.

9. Nachdrücklich muss ich betonen, dass der Text des Flugblattes „An alle Deutschen", wie ihn mir Scholl vorlas, nach meinem Erinnern an k e i n e r Stelle eine Aufforderung zur V e r f a s s u n g s-ä n d e r u n g m i t G e w a l t enthielt. Einen kommunistisch klingenden Satz liess ich streichen und verlangte sehr bestimmt die Streichung der Überschrift „Blätter der Widerstandsbewegung" mit dem Bemerken, dass uns ein organisierter Widerstand „ganz fern liege". Die Kritik war meinerseits so oberflächlich kurz, dass ich d i e n i c h t sagen kann, ob der Entwurf und das Flugblatt sich decken. E b e n s o w e n i g fordert mein eigener Entwurf „Studentinnen, Studenten" auch nur indirekt z u r A n w e n d u n g v o n G e w a l t a u f. Am Tatbestand der reinen Machtherrschaft aber kann kein vernünftiger Mensch in einem Staate zweifeln, der alles Recht auf den Willen eines Einzelnen letztendig zurückführt. In einem Staate, der den „Wilhelm Tell" als staatsgefährlich vom Spielplan absetzen muss und den Marquis Poa nicht mehr die Bitte der Niederlande „Gebt uns Gedankenfreiheit" vortragen lässt. Ich habe die Überwindung dieser Tyrannis d u r c h d i e M a c h t d e s G e i s t e s verlangt. Durch die Macht des Geistes, n i c h t durch Gewalt! Das heisst: Durch die klare sittliche *Einsicht*, dass die heutige Anwendung der blossen Macht, dass die Vernichtung von Hunderttausenden aus blossen Machtinteressen, dass die Unterbindung jeder freien Meinungsäusserung, jeglicher gesunden Kritik mit der Würde eines Rechtsstaates wie eines Kulturvolkes unvereinbar ist.

10. Auch von der Bildung einer äusseren oder inneren Organisation

ist in dem Entwurf keine Rede. Er wendet sich an die akademische Jugend der Hochschulen. Er fordert zur klaren Ablehnung der unwürdigen Parteibevormundung. Das ist alles. Er wendet sich an eine von sich aus geschlossene Mehrheit. Auch das StgB kann nicht Organisation nennen, was keine Organisation ist. Wenn sie die einheitliche Äusserung eines Standpunkts eine Organisation nennen, dann hätten sie vor fünf Wochen sämtliche studentischen Teilnehmer an der Sven Hedinfeier wegen Hochverrats aburteilen müssen als sie bei der Ansprache des Rektors den Herrn Reichsstatthalter, die anwesenden Generale und den Akademiepräsidenten mit tosendem Beifall begrüssten, hingegen die Spitzen der Partei mit eisigem Stillschweigen übergingen. Das war die nicht zufällige Antwort auf die Beleidigung der Studentinnen durch Studentenführer und Partei.

Anmerkung: Zur Anklageschrift S. 9.

Ich war für Beschränkung auf Süddeutschland, weil eine Umkehr vom bolschewistischen Kurs nur von Süddeutschland ausgehen könne. Gegen süddeutsche Separationsideen habe ich mich schon in der Villa Schmorell so scharf und eindeutig ausgesprochen, dass sich die damals Anwesenden noch sehr wohl daran erinnern werden. Ich schlug damals sogar vor, das Schrifttum der preussischen Befreiungsbewegung, vor allem die Vorschläge v o n S t e i n s zu studieren.

Zu Seite 10. Wo ich mich „offenbar" zu unerhörten Beleidigungen in der Besprechung mit Scholl oder gar in der Vernehmung habe hinreissen lassen, ist mir unerfindlich.

Rede, Schluss.

Ich darf hervorheben, dass die Anklageschrift selbst den Kern meines Eingreifens ganz richtig angibt. In der Villa Schmorell — behauptet sie — habe ich betont, dass die NSDAP sich immer mehr nach links wende. Kein Vaterlandsfreund, der die geistige Bewegung in der Partei so genau und so sorgfältig wie ich im letzten Jahrzehnt verfolgt und beobachtet hat, kann mir im Ernst diese Linksbewegung bestreiten. Ich rufe aber als Zeugen, dass ich diese Linksbewegung längst kommen sah und mich dauernd mit der Frage einer Rückdämmung dieses Kurses beschäftigte, den Herrn Präsidenten der Bayer. Akademie der Wissenschaften, Professor Dr. K.A. v. Müller, an. Ich habe ihm in vertrautem Gespräch meine Bedenken und Beobachtungen in dieser Hinsicht laufend vortragen können. Ich weiss, dass meine Bedenken ein grosser Teil der Nationalsozialisten teilte. Ich halte daher das in der Villa Schmorell Ausgeführte auch heute in vollem Umfang aufrecht.

Ich war mir aber auch darüber klar, dass die Abstoppung dieses Linkskurses das oberste Gebot der Stunde ist. Alle Pressepropaganda gegen den Bolschewismus ist im Grunde unwahrhaftig, solange nicht der wachsenden Bolschewisierung des deutschen Staates und Volkes mit allen zulässigen Mitteln Einhalt getan wird. Es gab für mich nur das Mittel des offenen und öffentlichen Einspruchs, des W i d e r s p r u c h s, n i c h t d e s W i d e r s t a n d e s. Als deutscher Staatsbürger, als deutscher Hochschullehrer und als politischer Mensch erachte ich es als Recht nicht nur, sondern als sittliche Pflicht, an der politischen Gestaltung der deutschen Geschicke mitzuarbeiten, offenkundige Schäden aufzudecken und zu bekämpfen. Ich glaube im Namen all der jungen Akademiker, die hier angeklagt sind, zu sprechen, wenn ich behaupte: Die Bekämpfung des i n n e r e n B o l s c h e w i s m u s, der im nationalsozialistischen Staat von heute immer bedrohlicher sich ausbreitet, war das sittliche Ziel unseres Handelns. Mit allen Mitteln der Aufrüttelung eingeschlafener Gewissen, der Einsicht in die Verkehrung einer ungeschriebenen, für jeden geltenden Rechtsordnung zu dienen, ist höchste vaterländische Pflicht.

Ich fasse zusammen: Was ich bezweckte, war die Weckung der studentischen Kreise nicht durch eine Organisation, sondern durch das schlichte Wort, nicht zu irgendeinem Akt der Gewalt, sondern zur sittlichen Einsicht in bestehende schwere Schäden des politischen Lebens. Rückkehr zu klaren sittlichen Grundsätzen, zum Rechtsstaat, zu gegenseitigem Vertrauen von Mensch zu Mensch; das ist nicht illegal, sondern umgekehrt die W i e d e r h e r s t e l l u n g d e r L e g a l i t ä t. Ich habe mich im Sinne von Kants kategorischem Imperativ gefragt, was geschähe, wennn diese subjektive Maxime meines Handelns ein allgemeines Gesetz würde. Darauf kann es nur e i n e Antwort geben! Dann würde Ordnung, Sicherheit, Vertrauen in unser Staatswesen, in unser politisches Leben zurückkehren. Jeder sittlich Verantwortliche würde mit uns seine Stimme erheben gegen die drohende Herrschaft der blossen Macht über das Recht, der blossen Willkür über den Willen des sittlich Guten. Wir würden im einzelnen zu manchen Forderungen zurückkehren, die die Partei noch vor zehn Jahren mit Recht gestellt hat. Sie haben sich im Laufe dieser Jahre nicht nur nicht erfüllt, sondern in ihr Gegenteil verkehrt. Die

Forderung der freien Selbstbestimmung auch des kleinsten Volksteils ist in ganz Europa vergewaltigt, nicht minder die Forderung der Wahrung der rassischen und völkischen Eigenart. Die grundlegende Forderung wahrer Volksgemeinschaft ist durch die systematische Untergrabung des Vertrauens von Mensch zu Mensch zunichte gemacht. Es gibt kein furchtbareres Urteil über eine Volksgemeinschaft als das Eingeständnis, das wir uns alle machen müssen, dass keiner sich vor seinem Nachbarn, der Vater nicht mehr vor seinem Söhnen sicher fühlt. Das war es, was ich wollte, musste.

Es gibt für alle äussere Legalität eine letzte Grenze, wo sie unwahrhaftig und unsittlich wird. Dann nämlich, wenn sie zum Deckmantel einer Feigheit wird, die sich nicht getraut, gegen offenkundige Rechtsverletzung aufzutreten. Ein Staat, der jegliche freie Meinungsäusserung unterbindet und jede, aber auch jede sittlich berechtigte Kritik, jeden Verbesserungsvorschlag als „Vorbereitung zum Hochverrat" unter die furchtbarsten Strafen stellt, bricht ein ungeschriebenes deutsches, germanisches Recht, das „im gesunden Volksempfinden" noch immer lebendig war und lebendig bleiben muss.

Ich bitte und beschwöre Sie in dieser Stunde, diesen jungen Angeklagten gegenüber in wahrem Wortsinn schöpferisch Recht zu sprechen, nicht ein Diktat der Macht, sondern die klare Stimme des Gewissens sprechen zu lassen, die auf die G e s i n n u n g schaut, aus der die Tat hervorging. Und diese Gesinnung war wohl die uneigennützigste, idealste, die man sich denken kann! Das Streben nach absoluter Rechtlichkeit, Sauberkeit, Wahrhaftigkeit im Leben des Staates. Für mich selbst aber nehme ich in Anspruch, dass meine Mahnung z u r B e s i n n u n g auf die allein dauerhaften Fundamente eines Rechtsstaates, z u r R ü c k k e h r zum wahren germanischen Führerstaat das oberste Gebot der Stunde ist, dessen Überhören nur den Untergang des deutschen Geistes und zuletzt des deutschen Volkes nach sich zieht. Ich habe das eine Ziel erreicht, diese Warnung und Mahnung nicht in einem privaten kleinen Diskutierklub, sondern an verantwortlicher, an höchster richterlicher Stelle vorzubringen. Ich setze für diese Mahnung, für diese beschwörende Bitte zur Rückkehr mein Leben ein. Ich fordere die Freiheit für unser deutsches Volk zurück. Wir wollen nicht in Sklavenketten unser kurzes Leben dahinfristen, und wären es goldene Ketten eines materiellen Überflusses.

Ich hinterlasse eine gebrochene Frau und zwei unglückliche Kinder in Not und Trauer. Wollen Sie meiner armen Familie wenigstens einen Lebensunterhalt gewähren, der meiner Stellung als deutscher Hochschullehrer entspricht. Sie haben mir den Rang und die Rechte des Professors und den „summa cum laude" erarbeiteten Doktorhut genommen und mich dem niedrigsten Verbrecher gleichgestellt. Die innere Würde des Hochschullehrers, des offenen, mutigen Bekenners seiner Welt- und Staatsanschauung kann mir kein Hochverratsverfahren rauben. Mein Handeln und Wollen wird der eherne Gang der Geschichte rechtfertigen; darauf vertraue ich felsenfest. Ich hoffe zu Gott, dass die geistigen Kräfte, die es rechtfertigen, rechtzeitig aus meinem eigenen Volke sich entbinden mögen. Ich habe gehandelt, wie ich aus einer inneren Stimme heraus handeln musste. Ich nehme die Folgen auf mich nach dem schönen Worte Joh. Gottlieb Fichtes:

> Und handeln sollst du so,
> Als hinge von dir und deinem Tun allein
> Das Schicksal ab der deutschen Dinge,
> Und die Verantwortung wär dein.

Appendix L

THE JUDGMENT OF THE MUNICH STUDENTS

*Being the judgment of the Volksgerichtshof of Professor Huber
and the students at the second trial of the Munich Students, April
19, 1943.*

Regl. Abschrift
6 J 24/43
1 H 1ɔ1/43

~ Jm Namen
des Deutschen Volkes

In der Strafsache gegen

1.) den Alexander S c h m o r e l l aus München, geboren am 16.
September 1917 in Orenburg (Rußland),

2.) den Kurt H u b e r aus München, geboren am 24. Oktober 1893
in Chur (Schweiz),

3.) den Wilhelm G r a f aus München, geboren am 2. Januar 1918
in Kuchenheim,

4.) den Hans H i r z e l aus Ulm, geboren am 3o. Oktober 1924
in Untersteinbach (Stuttgart),

5.) die Susanne H i r z e l aus Stuttgart, geboren am 7. August
1921 in Untersteinbach,

6.) den <u>Franz</u> Joseph M ü l l e r aus Ulm, geboren am 8. September
1924 in Ulm,

7.) den Heinrich G u t e r aus Ulm, geboren am 11. Januar 1925
in Ulm,

8.) den Eugen G r i m m i n g e r aus Stuttgart, geboren am 29.
Juli 1892 in Crailsheim,

9.) den Dr. <u>Heinrich</u> Philipp B o l l i n g e r aus <u>Freiburg, geboren am 23. April 1916 in Saarbrücken</u>,

1o.) den <u>Helmut</u> Karl Theodor August B a u e r aus Freiburg, geboren
am 19. Juni 1919 in Saarbrücken,

11.) den Dr. <u>Falk</u> Erich Walter H a r n a c k aus Chemnitz, geboren
am 2. März 1913 in Stuttgart,

12.) die Gisela S c h e r t l i n g aus München, geboren am 9. Februar
1922 in Pößneck/Thür.,

13.) die Katharina S c h ü d d e k o p f aus München, geboren am
8. Februar 1916 in Magdeburg,

14.) die Traute L a f r e n z aus München, geboren am 3. Mai 1919
in Hamburg,   zur

- 2 -
                    zur Zeit in dieser Sache in gerichtlicher Unter-
                    suchungshaft,
wegen Feindbegünstigung u.a.,
hat der Volksgerichtshof, 1. Senat, auf Grund der Hauptverhandlung vom
19. April 1943, an welcher teilgenommen haben
                    als Richter:
            Präsident des Volksgerichtshofs Dr- Freisler, Vorsitzer,
            Landgerichtsdirektor Stier,
            ₦-Gruppenführer und Generalleutnant der Waffen-₦ Breit-
                                                              haupt,
            SA-Gruppenführer Bunge,
            SA-Gruppenführer und Staatssekretär Köglmaier,
                    als Vertreter des Oberreichsanwalts:
            Erster Staatsanwalt Bischoff,
für Recht erkannt:
                    cAlexander S c h m o r e l l , Kurt H u b e r und Wilhel
G r a f haben im Kriege in Flugblättern zur Sabotage der Rüstung und
zum Sturz der nationalsozialistischen Lebensform unseres Volkes aufge-
rufen, defaitistische Gedanken propagiert und den Führer aufs gemeinste
beschimpft und dadurch den Feind des Reiches begünstigt und unsere Wehr-
kraft zersetzt.
                    Sie werden deshalb mit
                                        dem T o d e
bestraft.
                    Ihre Bürgerrechte haben sie für immer verwirkt.
                    Eugen G r i m m i n g e r hat einen feindbegünstigenden
Hochverräter Geld gegeben. Zwar kam ihm nicht zum Bewußtsein, daß er dadurch half, den Feind des Reiches zu begünstigen. Aber er rechnete damit
daß dieser das Geld benutzen könnte, um unserem Volk seine nationalsozialistische Lebensform zu rauben.
                    Weil er so einen Hochverrat unterstützt hat, bekommt er
zehn Jahre Zuchthaus und hat seine Ehre für zehn Jahre verwirkt.
                    Heinrich B o l l i n g e r und Helmut B a u e r haben
Kenntnis von hochverräterischen Umtrieben gehabt, das aber nicht angezeigt. Dazu haben sie fremde Rundfunknachrichten über Kriegsereignisse
oder Vorkommnisse im Innern Deutschlands zusammen angehört. Dafür bekom
men sie sieben Jahre Zuchthaus und haben ihre Bürgerehre für sieben Jahre
verloren.

                                                    Hans

- 3 -

Hans H i r z e l und Franz M ü l l e r haben -als unreife Burschen von Staatsfeinden verführt- hochverräterische Flugblattpropaganda gegen den Nationalsozialismus unterstützt. Dafür bekommen sie fünf Jahre Gefängnis.

Heinrich G u t e r hat von solchen Propagandaabsichten gewußt, das aber nicht angezeigt. Er wird dafür mit achtzehn Monaten Gefängnis bestraft.

Gisela S c h e r t l i n g , Katharina S c h ü d d e k o p f und Traute L a f r e n z haben dasselbe verbrochen. Als Mädchen bekommen sie dafür ein Jahr Gefängnis.

Susanne H i r z e l hat hochverräterische Flugblätter verbreiten helfen. Daß sie hochverräterisch waren, wußte sie zwar nicht; aber nur deshalb, weil sie in unverzeihlicher Gutgläubigkeit sich keine Gewißheit verschafft hat. Sie wird mit sechs Monaten Gefängnis bestraft.

Allen Angeklagten, die Zuchthaus oder Gefängnis bekommen haben, hat der Volksgerichtshof ihre Polizei-und Untersuchungshaft ganz auf ihre Strafe angerechnet.

Falk H a r n a c k hat zwar auch seine Kenntnis von hochverräterischen Umtrieben nicht angezeigt. Aber be ihm liegen so einmalig besondere Verhältnisse vor, daß man ihn wegen dieser Unterlassung nicht bestrafen kann. Er wird daher freigesprochen.

Die Richtigkeit der vorstehenden Abschrift wird beglaubigt und die Vollstreckbarkeit des Urteils bescheinigt.
Berlin, am 28. April 1943
Thiele, Amtsrat
als Urkundsbeamter der Geschäftsstelle.

Beglaubigt:

(Signature) Sekretär
als Urkundsbeamter d. Geschäftsstelle

BIBLIOGRAPHY

PRIMARY SOURCES

Unpublished Documents

Documents from the Berlin Document Center

Bamberg, das Erzbischöfliche Ordinariat. Letter, June 30, 1933, to the Bayer. Staatsministerium des Innern, complaining of needless arrests of Catholic priests and laymen.

Der Bayer. Ministerpräsident. Letter, October 24, 1940, to the Reichsminister des Innern, questioning the withdrawal of citizenship rights of Crown Prince Rupprecht.

Bayer. Politische Polizei. Letter, April 2, 1936, to all Polizeidirektionen, concerning the "Black Front."

Der Bayer. Staatsminister des Innern. Letter, October 23, 1940, to Ministerpräsident Ludwig Siebert, explaining the withdrawal of citizenship rights from Crown Prince Rupprecht.

Beer-Grunow, Heinrich. Letter, Paris, 1938, giving his reasons for withdrawal from Otto Strasser's "Black Front."

Geheime Staatspolizei, Berlin. Letter, July 13, 1939, to Geheime Staatspolizei, Würzburg, concerning Albert von Manstein.

———, Munich. Letter, January 20, 1939, to the Polizeipräsidium, Munich, concerning the clergy's obligation to salute.

———, ———. Report, November 9, 1939, of the events in the Bürgerbräukeller.

———, ———. Letter, March, 29, 1941, concerning Christoph Fischer, arrested for his part in an illegal monarchist group.

———, Würzburg. Letter, July 19, 1939, to Geheime Staatspolizei, Berlin, concerning Albert von Manstein.

———, ———. Letter, October 16, 1939, to the Landräte of Mainfranken, seeking information on Alfred Loritz.

———, ———. June 20, 1940, to the Landräte of Mainfranken, giving information of plots on the life of Adolf Hitler planned by "clericals and Marxists."

Gendarmerie-Station, Remlingen. Report, Nr. 1794, December 15, 1936, to the Bezirksamt Marktheidenfeld, concerning the insubordination of Franz Götz of Birkenfeld.

Gonnermann, Major, a. D. Letter, January 12, 1937, to von Epp, on the unfortunate state of affairs in Nazi Germany.

Gülchsheim, Evangelisch-Lutheranischer Kirchenvorstand. Letter, July, 23, to Staaatssekretär Hofmann, concerning the defamation of the local Protestant minister, H. Söllner, by the mayor, Voch.

Hitler-Jugend, Augsburg. Unterbahn I/B3, report, of Karl Waiblinger, June 21, 1934, denouncing a Catholic priest who tried to dissuade Waiblinger from interest in National Socialism.

Miltenberg, Bishop (of Würzburg). Letter, June 29, 1933, to von Epp, complaining of the arrest of thirty-eight priests.

N.S.D.A.P., der Stellvertreter des Führers, Munich. May 21, 1938, letter to the Gauleiter of Munich and Upper Bavaria, concerning the political views of Professor Kurt Huber.

von Redwitz, Freiherr. Letter, September 1, 1939, to the Kreisleiter of Starnberg, complaining of the occupation of Leutstetten by evacuees.

——. Letter. September 16, 1939, to the Kreisleiter of Starnberg, stating the income and value of the Crown Prince's castle at Leutstetten.

Der Reichsführer der S.S. und Chef der Deutschen Polizei. Letter, October 16, 1941, to Dr. Lammers, Chef der Reichskanzlei, refusing a passport to Franz von Bayern.

Der Reichsminister des Innern. Letter, October 8, 1940, to the Bavarian Ministerpräsident, concerning the withdrawal of citizenship rights from Crown Prince Rupprecht.

Das Reichssicherheitshauptamt. Letter, August 30, 1940, to the Reichsminister des Innern, concerning the withdrawal of citizenship rights from Crown Prince Rupprecht. An important source which discusses the von Harnier Kreis.

Der Reichsstatthalter in Bayern. Letter, October 21, 1940, to the Reichsminister der Innern, concerning the travel ban on members of the Wittelsbach family.

Das Sondergericht für den Oberlandesgerichtsbezirk Bamberg bei dem Landesgerichte Würzburg. File of over one hundred cases in the period from the summer of 1943 until the winter of 1945.

Die Staatskanzlei des Freistaates Bayern. Letter, March 15, 1934, to Ministerpräsident Siebert, concerning Graf von Strachwitz of Innsbruck's part in the "von Aretin plot" of February, 1933.

Die Sturmabteilung der N.S.D.A.P., Neuhaus a.d. Pegnitz. Report, June, 27, 1935, concerning local anti-Nazi sentiment.

Uffenheim, der Vorstand des Bezirksamts. Letter, December 4, 1934, to Präsidium der Regierung von Ober- und Mittelfranken, concerning the arrest of Pastor Söllner of Gülchsheim.

Volksgerichtshof, Criminal case 85/106/38; 24/73/38. Marianne Thekla Elisabeth Perpetua von Gustedt, November 2, 1938. Black Front, Berlin.

——, ——, 85/162/40. Michael Ernst Jouy, September 5, 1940. Student opposition in the Rhineland.

——, ——, 35, 299/44; 1L. 33/44. Father Joseph Kirchhoff, O.F.M., February 10, 1934. Catholic priest charged with opposition to the state, condemned to death.

——, ——, 85, 214/37; 1H, 31/38. Ernst August Karl Niekisch, i.a., January 10, 1939. An important source for a discussion of Niekisch's Widerstandsbewegung.

——, ——, 85, 368/38; 1H, 4/29. Karl Schäffer, April 25, 1939. Black Front, Austria.

——, ——, 85, 35/43; 1H, 47/43. Hans Fritz Scholl, i.a., February 22, 1943. The first trial of the "Munich Students."

——, ——, 105, 75/43; 1L, 147/43. Rudolf Schwarz, October 22, 1943. The trial of a man punished by death for saying in public that "Hitler chews the carpet."

——, Prosecution's brief, Alexander Schmorell, i.a., April 8, 1943. The second trial of the "Munich Students."

——, ——. Georg Schütz, August 11, 1937. Trial of a Studienrat in Rüdesheim who wrote letters denouncing the Nazis.

Wagner, Adolf. Letter, October 23, 1940, to the Bayer. Staatsminister des Innern, concerning the withdrawal of citizenship from Crown Prince Rupprecht.

Hoover Library of War and Peace. Stanford University.

Bayerisches Memorandum. Catalogue No.: Ts WW 1939, Underground Mvts., G3 B 356. A broadsheet made up in 1943 stating the case for Bavarian separatism.

Father Alois Natterer's files at the Klerusverband, Starnberg, Bavaria.

Buchwieser, Vicar General, Archdiocese of Munich. Letter, Nr. 11949, November 9, 1939, to the clergy of the Archdiocese, concerning the arrest of Father Rupert Mayer, S.J.

von Faulhaber, Michael Cardinal. Letter, January 25, 1938, to the Bavarian Minister of Education and Religion, concerning the closing of the schools conducted by order priests.

——. Letter, November 6, 1940, to the Reichsjustizminister, Dr. Gürtner, concerning euthanasia.

——. Letter, July 26, 1941, to the Bavarian Minister of Education and Religion, concerning the discontinuance of prayers in schools, as well as the removal of religious pictures and the crucifixes from the class-rooms.

Sondergericht für den Bezirk des Oberlandesgerichts, München. Trial of Father Rupert Mayer, S.J., 1b Kms — So. 32/37; 16 cfs — So. 548/37.

zu Guttenberg family, Neustadt a.d. Saale, Bavaria
zu Guttenberg, Karl Ludwig Freiherr. Zusammenfassung meiner Angaben vor

Standartenführer Huppenkothen, November 7, 1944.
——. September 5, 1937, to Kreisleiter Ingebrand, stating his reasons for refusing to join the N.S.D.A.P.

von Harnier family, Gräfelfing, Bavaria

von Harnier, Adolf Freiherr. Selections from letters to his wife, 1936-1945. Typescript, 8 p.p., n.d.
——. Reply to the Prosecution's Brief at his trial before the People's Court, March 13, 1944.
Kast, Ludwig. Sworn statement, January 19, 1940, used as testimony at Freiherr von Harnier's trial before the People's Court.
Volksgerichtshof, criminal case, 6 H 92/44; 75, 32/44. Dr. Adolf Freiherr von Harnier, i.a., June 28, 1944.

Kurt Huber family, Gräfelfing, Bavaria

Deppisch, August. Letter, April 21, 1943. to Oberreichsanwalt beim Volksgerichtshof, seeking mercy for Professor Kurt Huber.
——. Letter, April 27, 1943, to Oberreichsanwalt beim Volksgerichtshof, seeking mercy for Professor Kurt Huber.
Huber, Professor Kurt. Defense speech for his trial before the People's Court in April, 1943. Typescript, n.d.
Volksgerichtshof, criminal case, 6J 24/43; 1H, 101/43. Alexander Schmorell, i.a., April 28, 1943. The second trial of the "Munich Students."

Siegfried Huber family, Prien am Chiemsee, Bavaria

Weintz. Regierungsrat, Die Illegale Monarchistische Bewegung in Bayern. Geheime Staatspolizei, Munich, October, 1939.

Karin Klublatt family, Tegernsee, Bavaria

Probst, Christoph. Letter, February 22, 1943, to his mother.
——. Letter, July 7, 1942, to his brother, Dieter Sasse.
——. Letter, December 13, 1942, to his brother, Dieter Sasse.
——. Letter, December 18, 1942, to his brother, Dieter Sasse.

Unpublished Memoirs

von Aretin, Erwein. Die Frühjahrstage 1933; Die Bayerischen Monarchisten und Hitler's Machtergreifung. Typescript, 12 p.p., n.d. A useful description of the events in February, 1933 in Munich by one of the participants. Written after May, 1945.
Bericht über die Anti-National-Sozialistische Tätigkeit der Bayerischen Heimatbewegung. Typescript, 5 p.p., Hoover Library, Stanford University, Cat. No.: Ts WW 1939, Underground Mvts., G3, B, 355.
Bericht über die Vorgänge beim Tod des H.H. Dompredigers Dr. Johann

Maier. Typescript, 3 p.p., n.d. Probably written in May, 1945 by someone at the Chancery office in Regensburg.

Deppisch, Augst. Memoir of the trial of Professor Kurt Huber. Typescript, 18 p.p., August 27, 1945.

Fackler, Franz Xaver. Episoden aus dem 3. Reich. Typescript, 5 p.p., February, 1951.

van Gestel, Father. Jesuiten in den Banden von Dachau. Typescript, 10 p.p., February 15, 1947. Gives the names and origins of all Jesuits in Dachau and also an account of their activities in the concentration camp.

zu Guttenberg, Therese Freifrau. Lebenslauf Freiherr Karl Ludwig von und zu Guttenberg. Typescript, 2 p.p., n.d.

Klublatt, Karin. Memoirs of her son, Christoph Probst. Typescript, 3 p.p., n.d. Useful particulars on the life of Christoph Probst, one of the "Munich Students."

Martel, Johann. Die Bayerische Widerstandsbewegung und das Haus Wittelsbach. Typescript, 3 p.p., n.d. A monarchist's account of the von Harnier Kreis.

Müller, Joseph. Lebenslauf. Typescript, 5 p.p., November 7, 1945. Dr. Müller's own account of his anti-Nazi activities.

Natterer, Alois. Auswirkungen eines kirchlichen Erlasses. Typescript, 3 p.p., n.d. A description of the effect on the Bavarian fraternity, Rhätia, of the Pastoral Warning issued by the Bavarian Bishops, February, 1931.

Niederschrift über die Sitzung des Philister-Ausschusses vom 8. Juli 1932 im Lesezimmer des Hotels Union. Typescript, 6 p.p., n.d. A post-war reconstruction of a meeting of leading members of Rhätia deliberating on the question of National Socialist membership.

Sasse, Dieter. Bericht über die Münchener Studentenbewegung, 1943. Typescript, 5 p.p., n.d. A postwar report written by Christoph's brother.

Scholl, Inge. Das andere Deutschland. Typescript, 13 p.p., n.d. A report of the "Munich Student Revolt" by Hans and Sophie Scholl's sister.

Schuster, Karl. Erlebnis-Bericht eines katholischen Geistlichen aus der Zeit des Hitler-Terrors. Typescript, 18 p.p., September 18, 1946. Father Schuster's account of his opposition to National Socialism.

Übersicht: Konzentrationslager; warum hat das Deutsche Volk geschwiegen? Typescript, 20 p.p., n.d. A sympathetic account of the ever-increasing opposition to National Socialism, especially during the war.

Published Documents

Alt, Karl. *Todeskandidaten; Erlebnisse eines Seelsorgers im Gefängnis München-Stadelheim mit zahlreichen im Hitlerreich zum Tode verurteilten Männern und Frauen.* Munich, 1946.

Das aufgebrochene Tor; Predigten und Andachten gefangener Pfarrer im Konzentrationslager Dachau. Munich, 1946.

Beckmann, Joachim. *Evangelische Kirche im Dritten Reich; Kirchliches Jahr-buch für die Evangelische Kirche in Deutschland. 1933-1944. 60-71 Jhg.* Gütersloh, 1948.

Bischof Graf von Galen spricht; ein apostolischer Kampf und sein Widerhall. Edited by H. Poortmann. Freiburg im Breisgau, 1946.

Dokumente aus dem Kampf der katholischen Kirche im Bistum Berlin gegen den Nationalsozialismus. Berlin, 1946.

Dokumente zum Abwehrkampf der deutschen evangelischen Pfarrerschaft gegen Verfolgung und Bedrückung, 1933-1945. Edited by Fritz Klinger. Nürnberg, 1946.

Die Evangelische Kirche in Deutschland und die Judenfrage; Ausgewählte Dokumente aus den Jahren des Kirchenkampfes. 1933-1943. Geneva, 1945.

von Faulhaber, Michael Cardinal. *Der Bischof und sein Klerus; Predigt beim Priestergottesdienst im Dom zu München, 19. Feb. 1936, zum 25. Jahrestag der Bischofsweihe.* Munich, n.d.

——. *Die christlihe Weltanschauung; Sylvesterpredigt des Herrn Kardinals im Dom zu München, am 31. Dezember 1935.* Beilage zum Amtsblatt Nr. 1 der Erzdiözese München-Freising vom 15. Januar 1936.

——. *Christentum und Germanentum; Sylvesterpredigt in St. Michael zu München, 31. Dezember 1933.* Munich, n.d.

——. *Christentum und Heidentum; Licht und Finsternis; Predigt in Altötting, 8. Sept. 1934.* Munich, n.d.

——. *Der Eckstein zwischen Judentum und Christentum; Predigt in St. Michael zu München, Advent, 1933.* Munich, n.d.

——. *Die Freiheit der Kirche; Predigt bei der Papstfeier in München, St. Michael, am 10. Februar 1935.* Beiblatt zu Nr. 3 des Amtsblattes der Erzdiözese München-Freising vom 11. Februar 1935. Munich, n.d.

——. *Judaism, Christianity and Germany.* New York, 1934. The five sermons of Cardinal Faulhaber given at St. Michael's in December, 1933, rendered into English.

——. *Münchner Kardinalspredigten, 2. Folge:* "Leidenschaft und Tatkraft"; "Das Christentum im deutschen Volk"; "Elternrechte und Elternpflichten." Munich, 1937.

——. ——, 3. Folge: "Papstpredigt, 1937: Das Reichskonkordat, Ja oder Nein?" München, 1937.

——. *Steinwürfe gegen den Thron der Päpste; Predigt in St. Michael in München am Papstsonntag, 9. Feb. 1936.* Beilage II zum Amtsblatt Nr. 6 der Erzdiözese München-Freising vom 18. Feb. 1936. Munich, n.d.

Gerlich, Fritz and Naab, Ingebert. *Prophetien wider das Dritte Reich.* Edited by Johann Steiner. Munich, 1946. A very important source of pre-1933 opposition to Hitler.

Hermelink, Heinrich. *Kirche im Kampf; Dokumente des Widerstands und Aufbau der Evangelischen Kirche in Deutschland, 1933-1945.* Tübingen,

1950. The definitive study of the Protestant Churches' opposition to National Socialism.

Heuberger, Anton. *Offene Worte eines katholischen Geistlichen; Guter Priester und bezw. oder guter National-sozialist?* Weimar, n.d. (1936). A Catholic priests expresses opposition to the majority of the Catholic hierarchy's attitude toward National Socialism.

Hirtenbriefe für die Erzdiözese München, Fastenzeit, 1934: Die Sittenlehre der katholischen Kirche. Munich, n.d.

——. *Fastenzeit, 1936; Der Bischof und sein Bistum.* Munich, n.d.

Hirtenwort an die katholischen Arbeiter- und Arbeiterinnenverbände, über Arbeiterseelsorge in gegenwärtiger Stunde. Beilage II zum Amtsblatt Nr. 12, vom 4. Juni 1935. Munich, n.d.

Jannasch, W. *Deutsche Kirchendokumente; die Haltung der bekennenden Kirche im Dritten Reich.* Zürich, 1946.

von Moltke, Helmuth James. *Letzte Briefe aus dem Gefängnis Tegel.* Berlin, 1951. The leader of the Kreisau Kreis explains his opposition to National Socialism.

Neuhäusler, Bishop Johann. *Kreuz und Hakenkreuz; der Kampf des Nationalsozialismus gegen die katholische Kirche und der kirchliche Widerstand.* 2 volumes. Munich, 1946. The fundamental source book on the history of the opposition of the Catholic Church to National Socialism.

Pätel, Otto. *Deutsche Innere Emigration.* New York, 1946.

Pastoralblatt des Bistums Eichstätt, 84. Jhg., Nr. 4, February 4, 1937. A seven-page reprint containing the retraction by Father Heuberger of his broadsheet, listed above, as well as Bishop Michael Rachl's letter to Father Heuberger disciplining him for his pro-Nazi and anti-Catholic sentiments.

Pfluger, Wilhelm. *Gedenkrede anlässlich der Trauerfeier für Dr. Adolf Freiherr von Harnier in St. Ursula zu München, June 30, 1945.*

Rundschreiben Seiner Heiligkeit Pius XI., durch Gottes Vorsehung Pabst, an die ehrwürdigen Brüder Erzbischöfe und Bischöfe Deutschlands und die anderen Oberhirten, die in Frieden und Gemeinschaft mit dem Apostolichen Stuhle leben; über die Lage der katholischen Kirche im Deutschen Reich. Munich, n.d. The encyclical of March, 1937: "Mit brennender Sorge."

Steltzer, Theodor. *Von deutscher Politik; Dokumente, Aufsätze und Vorträge.* Frankfurt am Main, 1949. A collection of documents of the Kreisauer Kreis.

Strasser, Otto. *Revolution oder Faschistischer Krieg?* Prague, n.d. A document from Otto Strasser's radical rightist years.

Tell, Michael. *Die dritte indogermanische Lautverschiebung,* being in actuality but the outside title for: *Kampfgruppe Scholl, Attila der Letzte: Adolf Hitler vor dem Gerichtshof des Weltgewissens.* Freier Deutschland, 1944. An interesting curiosity, especially as a camouflaged document of opposition to Hitler. The book is now in the possession of Professor Karl d'Ester of the University of Munich.

Zeugnisse der bekennenden Kirche; eine Sammlung von Kundgebungen und Synodalbeschlüssen. Bad Oeynhausen, 1935.

Zeugnis und Kampf des deutschen Episkopats. Edited by K. Hofmann. Freiburg im Breisgau, 1946. A small collection of sermons and pastoral letters on National Socialism.

Published Memoirs

Ballhorn, Franz. *Die Kelter Gottes: Tagebuch eines jungen Christen, 1940-1945.* Münster, 1946.

Delp, Alfred. *Im Angesicht des Todes.* Frankfurt am Main, 1947.

von Hassel, Ulrich. *Vom anderen Deutschland, 1938-1944.* Freiburg, 1947.

Haecker, Theodor. *Tag- und Nachtbücher, 1939-1945.* Munich, 1947.

Hess, Sales. *Dachau; eine Welt ohne Gott.* Nürnberg, 1946. A Benedictine's account of life in Dachau.

Hofmann, Karl, i.a. *Sieger in Fesseln; Christuszeugnisse aus Lagern und Gefängnissen.* Freiburg im Breisgau, 1949.

Huber, Clara. *Kurt Huber; zum Gedächtnis.* Regensburg, 1947. A useful compilation of reminiscences of and tributes to Professor Kurt Huber; especially useful for the short biography presented by Frau Professor Huber.

Hüttel, Wilhelm. (Walter Hagen, pseud.). *Die Geheime Front; Organisation, Personen und Aktionen des Deutschen Geheimdienstes.* Linz, 1950. A few important revelations here, especially the history of the so-called plot on Hitler's life in the Bürgerbräukeller, November 9, 1939.

Kampe, P. Johann Gualbertus, *Meine Gefängnisse.* Würzburg, 1949. The history of a Carmelite's imprisonment by the Nazis.

Pies, Otto, S.J. *Stephanus Heute; Karl Leisner, Priester und Opfer.* Kevelaer, 1950. A moving account of a young man's life and death for his religion.

Steinwender, Leonhard. *Christus im Konzentrationslager; Wege der Gnade und des Opfers.* Salzburg, 1946.

Strasser, Otto. *History in My Time.* London, 1941.

——. *Hitler and I.* London, 1940.

SECONDARY SOURCES

Books and pamphlets

Änderl, F. X. *Bavaria: the problem of German Federalism.* London, 1943.

von Aretin, Erwein. *Das bayerische Problem.* Munich, 1924.

——. *Wittelsbacher im K.Z.* Munich, n.d. A pamphlet describing the Nazi persecution of members of the Wittelsbach family.

Bayles, William David. *Seven were hanged.* London, 1945. A confusion of the facts relating to the "Munich Student Revolt".

Bösmiller, Franziska. P. *Rupert Mayer, S.J.; Dokumente Selbstzeugnisse und Erinnerungen*. Munich, 1946.

Bowen, Ralph H. *German Theories of the Corporative State; with Special Reference to the Period 1870-1919*. New York, 1947.

Bride, A. "Tyrannicide; Tyran et Tyrannie," *Dictionnaire de Théologie Catholique*, XV, Part 2, 1988-2016, 1948-1988. Paris, 1950. Semi-official statement of Catholic opinion on tyrannicide.

Brink, Michael. *Revolutio Humana*. Heidelberg, 1946. Written in memory of Father Alfred Delp.

Buchberger, Bishop Michael. *Gibt es noch eine Rettung? Gedanken zur heutigen Zeit und Lage*. 2. Aufl. Regensburg, 1931. An attack on National Socialism by the Bishop of Regensburg.

Butler, E. Amy. *Darkness over Germany*. London, 1943. A very interesting and useful wartime book.

Dahlerus, Birgit. *Der letzte Versuch*. Munich, 1948.

Dawson, Christopher. *Religion and the Modern State*. London, 1936. Useful for Catholic opinion on corporatism in the twentieth century.

De Profundis. Munich, n.d. An anthology of anti-Nazi poetry.

Dittmar, William R. *The Government of the Free State of Bavaria*. Williamsport, Pa., 1934.

Duncan-Jones, Arthur S. *The Struggle for Religious Freedom in Germany*. London, 1938. Of particular importance for an appreciation of Protestant opposition to Hitler.

Eberle, Joseph. *Das Los der christlichen Presse im Dritten Reich*. Bregenz in Vorarlberg, 1945.

von Faulhaber, Michael Cardinal. *Deutsches Ehrgefühl und Katholisches Gewissen*. Munich, 1925.

Gengler, Ludwig. *Die deutschen Monarchisten, 1919-1925*. Kulmbach, 1932.

Grob, Rudolf, *Der Kirchenkampf in Deutschland; Kurze Geschichte der kirchlichen Wirren in Deutschland von 1933 bis Sommer 1937*. Chiefly the Protestant situation.

Gröber, Conrad. *Handbuch der religiösen Gegenwartsfragen*. Freiburg im Breisgau, 1937. A very revealing and interesting summation of Catholic opinion on a variety of topics.

Guardini, Romano. *Die Waage des Daseins*. Tübingen, 1946. Father Guardini's eulogy on the "Munich Students."

Gurian, Waldemar. *Der Kampf um die Kirche im Dritten Reich*. Luzern, 1936. An early presentation of the problem.

Hagmann, Meinrad. *Der Weg ins Verhängnis; Reichstagswahlergebnisse, 1919-1933, besonders aus Bayern*. Munich, 1946.

D'Harcourt, Robert. *Catholiques d'Allemagne*. Paris, 1938. The best critical study of the relationship of National Socialism and the Catholic Church.

Heiden, Konrad. *A History of National Socialism*. London, 1934.

Hermes, Richard. *Witz contra Nazi; Hitler und sein Tausendjähriges Reich.* Hamburg, 1946.

Hudal, Bishop Alois. *Die Grundlagen des Nationalsozialismus; eine ideengeschichtliche Untersuchung.* Leipzig, 1937.

Husarek, Paul. *Die Toten von Dachau; Deutsche und Österreicher.* Munich, n.d. A list of thirty thousand persons, with date and place of birth and the date of death.

Jung, Edgar J. *Die Herrschaft der Minderwertigen; ihr Zerfall und ihre Ablösung durch ein neues Reich.* Berlin, 1930.

Kaufmann, Walter H. *Monarchism in the Weimar Republic.* New York, 1953.

Kogon, Eugen. *Der S.S. Staat; das System der deutschen Konzentrationslager.* Munich, 1946.

Krüger, Kurt. *Kommentar zum Reichskonkordat nebst Einleitung und dem Texte der Länderkonkordate.* Berlin, 1938. A Nazi account of problems raised and solved by the concordat with the Catholic Church.

Kuble, Ph. *Die Konzentrationslager, eine Gewissensfrage.* Singen-Hohentwiel, 1945. A Jesuit theologian's consideration of German concentration camps.

von Leers, Johann, *Der Kardinal und die Germanen.* Hamburg, 1934. A Nazi reply to Cardinal Faulhaber's Advent sermons.

Manhattan, Avro. *The Catholic Church against the Twentieth Century.* London, 1950. Stridently anti-Catholic. Chapters ten and eleven discuss Nazi Germany's relations with the Vatican.

Micklem, Nathaniel. *National Socialism and the Roman Catholic Church.* London, 1939. Short account of the Nazi persecution of the Catholic Church; some documents translated.

Mohler, Armin. *Die Konservative Revolution in Deutschland, 1918-1932; Grundriss ihrer Weltanschauung.* Stuttgart, 1950.

Müller, Franz Joseph. *Der Katholische Episkopat in der Nationalen Revolution Deutschlands, 1933; Dokumente und Materialien.* Freiburg in der Schweiz, 1934.

Natterer, Alois. *Der bayerische Klerus in der Zeit dreier Revolutionen: 1918, 1933, 1945.* Munich, 1946.

Naumann, Alfred. *Es waren ihrer sechs.* Stockholm, 1944. A novel inspired by the "Munich Student Revolt."

Niekisch, Ernst. *Die dritte imperiale Figur.* Berlin, 1935.

——. *Entscheidung.* Berlin, 1930.

——. *Ost-West; unsystematische Betrachtungen.* Berlin, 1947.

——. *Das Reich der niederen Dämonen.* Hamburg, 1953. A book confiscated by the Nazis und used as evidence at Niekisch's trial in 1937.

Picard, Max. *Hitler in uns Selbst.* Zürich, 1946.

Pribilla, Max. *Deutsche Schicksalsfragen; Rückblick und Ausblick.* Frankfurt am Main, 1950.

Rauschning, Hermann. *Germany's Revolution of Destruction.* London, 1939.

Reed, Douglas. *Nemesis? The story of Otto Strasser and the Black Front.* Boston, 1940.

———. *The Prisoner of Ottawa; Otto Strasser.* London, 1953.

Ritter, Gerhard. *Carl Goerdeler und die Deutsche Widerstandsbewegung.* Stuttgart, 1954.

Rothfels, Hans. *The German Opposition to Hitler.* Hinsdale, Ilinois, 1948.

Scholl, Inge. *Die Weisse Rose.* Frankfurt am Main, 1952.

Schmid, Heinrich. *Apokalyptisches Wetterleuchten; ein Beitrag der Evangelischen Kirche zum Kampf im Dritten Reich.* Munich, 1947. An account of the Nazi persecution of the Protestant Church in Bavaria.

Schrader, Frederick Franklin. *Church-State in Germany.* New York, 1933. A pro-Nazi account of Church-State relations; contains an English translation of the Concordat.

Schütz, W. W. *Pens under the Swastika; a study of recent German writing.* London, 1946.

Schweder, Alfred. *Politische Polizei; Wesen und Begriff der politischen Polizei im Metternichschen System, in der Weimarer Republik und im nationalistischen Staate.* Berlin, 1937.

Schwend, Karl. *Bayern zwischen Monarchie und Diktatur; Beiträge zur Bayerischen Frage in der Zeit von 1918 bis 1933.* Munich, 1954.

Sendtner, Kurt. *Rupprecht von Wittelsbach, Kronprinz von Bayern.* Munich, 1954.

Strasser, Otto. *L'Aigle Prussien sur l'Allemagne.* New York, 1941.

———. *Aufbau des deutschen Sozialismus.* 2nd edition. Prag, 1938.

———. *Free Germany against Hitler.* Brooklyn, n.d.

———. *Germany Tomorrow.* London, 1940. An interesting statement showing the author's retreat from the "Conservative Revolution."

———. *Der letzte Abwehrkampf.* Munich, 1931.

———. *Wohin treibt Hitler.* Prag, 1936.

Strölin, Karl. *Verräter oder Patrioten; Der 20. Juli und das Recht auf Widerstand.* Stuttgart, 1952.

Studien zum Mythus des XX. Jahrhunderts; Amtliche Beilage zum Kirchlichen Amtsblatt für die Diözese Münster, October 15, 1934. A Catholic refutation of Alfred Rosenberg's ideas.

They Fought Hitler First. New York, 1945. Some interesting statistics on concentration camps.

Vossler, Karl. *Gedenkrede für die Studenten: 18. Februar 1943.* Munich, 1946.

Weisenborn, Günther. *Der lautlose Aufstand; Bericht über die Widerstandsbewegung des deutschen Volkes, 1933-1945.* Hamburg, 1953.

———. *Memorial.* Berlin, 1948.

Westermayer, H. E. *The Fall of the German Gods.* Mountainview, California, 1950.

Winiewicz, J. M. *Have we Allies inside Germany?* London, 1944. A very negative appreciation of the opposition of the Christian Churches to National Socialism.

Periodical literature

von Aretin, Erwein Freiherr. "Die bayerische Königsfrage," *Süddeutsche Monatshefte,* XXX (January, 193, 231-241).

——. "Königskrone oder Hakenkreuz? Dokumentarischer Tatsachenbericht," *Münchener Allgemeine Zeitung,* (1947-1948), Nr. 6-7.

——. "Der Monarchist und der Sozialist in Zelle 39," *Münchner Merkur,* Nr. 57 (March, 7, 1953).

Brink, Michael. "An den Rand geschrieben," *Der Brenner,* XVII (1948), 126-130. Useful for understanding Professor Huber's part in the "Munich Student Revolt."

Conze, Werner. "Die deutsche Opposition gegen Hitler," *Politische Literatur* (1953), 210-215.

Dörschlag, Siegfried. "Ostorientierung, nur eine Perspektive," *Die Tat,* XII (1920-1921), 41 ff.

Eltzbacker, Paul, "Die Rettung durch den Bolschewismus," *Die Tat,* XI (1919-1920), 171-175.

Fackler, Franz X. "Der Ruf des Gewissens," *Film und Leben,* Nr. 7 (1950), 42-54. An appreciation of the activities of the von Harnier Kreis.

"The German Catholics and the Twentieth of July," *Dublin Review,* July, 1946).

"Gestapo jagt den Schmied von Kochel," *Bayerische Landeszeitung,* January 13, January 21, January 28, February 4, February 11, 1949.

Held, Joseph. "Die Tragödie Bayerns und seines Königshauses," *Regensburger Tagesanzeiger,* 122, October 13, 1950; 125, October 20, 1950; 131, November 4, 1950; 134, November 10, 1950; 137, November 17, 1950; 143, November 25, 1950; 146, November 8, 1950; 149, December 16, 1950; 152, December 23, 1950; 155, December 30, 1950.

Huch, Ricarda. "Die Aktion der Münchner Studenten gegen Hitler," *Neue Schweizer Rundschau* (September, 1948).

——. "Willi Graf," *Die Wandlung* (January, 1948).

von Jan, Heinrich. "Verfassung und Verwaltung in Bayern, 1919-1926," in *Jahrbuch des Öffentlichen Rechts,* XV (1927), 1-50.

Jünger, Ernst. "Die Geburt des Nationalsozialismus aus dem Kriege," *Deutsches Volkstum* (August, 1929).

"K.Z.," "Umriss einer deutschen Widerstandsbewegung," *Die Gegenwart,* October 30, 1946.

Kogon, Eugen. "Der politische Untergang des europäischen Widerstands," *Frankfurter Hefte* (May, 1949).

Klerusblatt; Organ der Diözesan-Priestervereine Bayerns und ihres Wirtschaftlichen Verbandes, 1920-1945. A very important source of official Catholic opinion in Bavaria during the Nazi period.

Mitteilungsblatt des Bayerischen Staatsministeriums für Sonderaufgaben, Nr. 18, October 30, 1948, 71-72. Containing the record of the denazification trial of Schmidt, the porter who found Hans and Sophie Scholl in the University of Munich on February 18, 1943.

Moersdorf, Klaus. "Probleme des deutschen Konkordatsrechts," *Münchner Theologische Zeitschrift,* Vol. 6, n. 1, 1-15.

Monarchie; Zeitschrift für deutsche Tradition, 1929-1934. A very important source for an understanding of monarchists' aims in the years immediately before and after the Nazi seizure of power.

Müller, Erich. "Zur Geschichte des Nationalbolschewismus," *Deutsches Volkstum* (October, 1936), 782-90.

Niekisch, Ernst. (Friedrich Baumann, pseud.). "Fascismus und National-Bolschewismus," *Schweizer Monatshefte* (July-August, 1936), XVI, 196-204. The aims and ideals of the *Widerstandsbewegung* clearly set forth by its leader.

Pfarramtsblatt; Mitteilungen aus Amtsblättern für den kathol. Klerus Bayerns, herausgegeben vom Landesverband der Diözesan-Priestervereine. E.V., 1921-1945.

Pies, Otto. S.J., "Als Jesuit in Gefängnis und K.Z.," *Mitteilungen,* Nr. 111, 133-141. A Jesuit priest's account of his life in concentration camps in Nazi Germany.

Pötzsch, Fritz. "Vom Staatsleben unter der Weimarer Verfassung, Januar 1920 bis Dezember, 1924," in *Jahrbuch des Öffentlichen Rechts,* XII (1925), 99-101.

Rings, Werner. "Das Unglück der deutschen Intelligenz," *Neue Schweizer Rundschau,* XIII (December, 1945), 455-468.

Ritter, Gerhard. "Der deutsche Professor im Dritten Reich," *Gegenwart* (December 24, 1945).

Rübsamen, Walter. "Kurt Huber of Munich," *Musical Quarterly,* XXX (1944), 226-233.

Süddeutsche Monatshefte, XXVIII-XXXIII, 1930-1936.

Traunsteiner Nachrichten, September 9, 28, 23, 1950. Information relating to the execution of Seidel, Bruckmeier, Richl, Wehnert, and Vogel for their part in *Freiheits-Aktion Bayern.*

Weisenborn, Günther. "Bilan d'une résistance," 1933-1945. *Documents,* 1953, 597-604.

Weisse Blätter, Monatsschrift für Geschichte, Tradition und Staat, 1934-1942. An important source for conservative opinion during the Nazi period, 1934-1942.

Werner, Alfred, "Trotzky of the Nazi Party," *Journal of Central European Affairs,* XI (January, 1951), 39-46.

ERRATA

Pg.   4, 1.   14 for *that* read *than*
 „   18, 1.   9 for *quit* read *quite*
 „   20, 1.   7 for *Ceasars* read *Caesars*
 „   21, f.n. 43 for *Welcher* read *Welche*
 „   22, 1.   17 for *layman* read *laymen*
 „   25, 1.   2 for *is* read *it*
 „   29, 1.   23 for *abe* read *able*
 „   83, 1.   8 for *may* read *May*
 „   85, 1.   2 for *imposters* read *impostors*
 „   87, 1.   36 should read "you should *not* teach . . ."
 „   93, f.n. 7 for *Infromation* read *Information*
 „   98, f.n. 86, 1. 7 for *form* read *from*
 „ 139, 1.   1 for *succes* read *success*
 „ 140, 1.   13 for *meeting* read *meetings*
 „ 156, f.n. 26, 1. 4 for *territorities* read *territories*
 „ 158, 1.   3 for *Häcker* read *Haecker*
 „ 161, 1.   4 for *unthingking* read *unthinking*
 „ 161, 1.   31 for *legistation* read *legislation*
 „ 173, 1.   9 for *happness* read *happiness*
 „ 174, 1.   16 for *open* read *openly*
 „ 176, 1.   5 for *senselss* read *senseless*
 „ 176, f.n. 71, 1. 1 for *readers* read *reader's*
 „ 180, 1.   3 for *students* read *students'*
 „ 182, 1.   3 for *Grimmiger* read *Grimminger*
 „ 183, 1.   9 for *8* read *8th*
 „ 184, 1.   3 for *Bollonger* read *Bollinger*
 „ 184, f.n. 88 for *Sarrbrücken* read *Saarbrücken*
 „ 201, 1.   22 for *Students* read *Students'*
 „ 204, 1.   14 for *through* read *though*
 „ 204, 1.   17 for *invadede* read *invaded*
 „ 211, 1.   10 for *as* read *an*

INDEX